URBAN DREAMS, RURAL COMMONWEALTH

AMERICAN BEGINNINGS, 1500–1900

A Series Edited by Edward Gray, Stephen Mihm, and Mark Peterson

Also in the series

*Building a Revolutionary State: The Legal
Transformation of New York, 1776–1783*
by Howard Pashman

Sovereign of the Market: The Money Question in Early America
by Jeffrey Sklansky

National Duties: Custom Houses and the Making of the American State
by Gautham Rao

*Liberty Power: Antislavery Third Parties and the
Transformation of American Politics*
by Corey M. Brooks

*The Making of Tocqueville's America: Law and
Association in the Early United States*
by Kevin Butterfield

*Planters, Merchants, and Slaves: Plantation Societies
in British America, 1650–1820*
by Trevor Burnard

*Riotous Flesh: Women, Physiology, and the Solitary
Vice in Nineteenth-Century America*
by April R. Haynes

Holy Nation: The Transatlantic Quaker Ministry in an Age of Revolution
by Sarah Crabtree

A Hercules in the Cradle: War, Money, and the American State, 1783–1867
by Max M. Edling

Frontier Seaport: Detroit's Transformation into an Atlantic Entrepôt
by Catherine Cangany

Beyond Redemption: Race, Violence, and the American South after the Civil War
by Carole Emberton

The Republic Afloat: Law, Honor, and Citizenship in Maritime America
by Matthew Taylor Raffety

Conceived in Doubt: Religion and Politics in the New American Nation
by Amanda Porterfield

URBAN DREAMS, RURAL COMMONWEALTH

The Rise of Plantation Society
in the Chesapeake

PAUL MUSSELWHITE

THE UNIVERSITY OF CHICAGO PRESS
CHICAGO AND LONDON

The University of Chicago Press, Chicago 60637
The University of Chicago Press, Ltd., London
© 2019 by The University of Chicago
All rights reserved. No part of this book may be used or reproduced in any manner whatsoever without written permission, except in the case of brief quotations in critical articles and reviews. For more information, contact the University of Chicago Press, 1427 E. 60th St., Chicago, IL 60637.
Published 2019
Printed in the United States of America

28 27 26 25 24 23 22 21 20 19   1 2 3 4 5

ISBN-13: 978-0-226-58528-4 (cloth)
ISBN-13: 978-0-226-58531-4 (e-book)
DOI: https://doi.org/10.7208/chicago/9780226585314.001.0001

Library of Congress Cataloging-in-Publication Data

Names: Musselwhite, Paul, author.
Title: Urban dreams, rural commonwealth : the rise of plantation society in the Chesapeake / Paul Musselwhite.
Other titles: American beginnings, 1500–1900.
Description: Chicago ; London : The University of Chicago Press, 2019. | Series: American beginnings, 1500–1900
Identifiers: LCCN 2018031112 | ISBN 9780226585284 (cloth : alk. paper) | ISBN 9780226585314 (ebook)
Subjects: LCSH: Chesapeake (Va.)—History. | Urbanization—Virginia—Chesapeake Region.
Classification: LCC F232.C43 M87 2019 | DDC 975.5/523—dc23
LC record available at https://lccn.loc.gov/2018031112

♾ This paper meets the requirements of ANSI/NISO Z39.48-1992 (Permanence of Paper).

For my parents and for Meg

CONTENTS

	Acknowledgments	ix
	Introduction: "Our Folly and Ruining Singularity"	1
1.	Garrison Towns, Corporate Boroughs, and the Search for Order under the Virginia Company	23
2.	From Corporate Communities to County Courts in the Early Stuart Empire	56
3.	The Political Geography of Empire in the English Revolution	86
4.	Planters, the State, and the Restoration City	116
5.	Towns, Improvement, and the Contest for Authority in the 1680s	148
6.	The Imperial City and the Solidifying of the Plantation System	181
7.	Urban Growth and Country Thought in the Planters' Golden Age	219
	Epilogue: "This little Common wealth"	253
	List of Abbreviations	271
	Notes	273
	Index	333

ACKNOWLEDGMENTS

In a book about ideas that repeatedly lacked the support to be realized, it seems particularly important to acknowledge the contributions of the many individuals who helped me translate my thoughts into publishable form. Of course, as every author admits, it is impossible to account for every idea, labor, and act of kindness that made this book possible. However, it is a long-anticipated pleasure to be able to thank those who have given so much to this study and, by extension, to me.

My research has been supported by the financial and institutional resources of numerous organizations and archives. I received graduate scholarships from the Order of the First Families of Virginia and the National Society of the Sons and Daughters of the Pilgrims. I am grateful for archival research grants from the Huntington Library, the Folger Shakespeare Library, the Colonial Williamsburg Foundation, and the Virginia Historical Society. Beyond financial assistance, though, I am particularly grateful for the tireless support of librarians and archivists at each of these libraries, especially Doug Mayo and George Yetter at Colonial Williamsburg, who strove to assist me even as their resources were stripped away. I also owe a tremendous debt to the staff at the Maryland State Archives, the Maryland Historical Society, the Library of Virginia, the Library of Congress, the British Library, the London Guildhall Library, the Mitchell Library, and the UK National Archives. Librarians at the College of William and Mary's Swem Library, the University of Glasgow Library, and the Dartmouth College Library have also patiently handled my many requests and excuses about overdue books. Also, digital resource coordinators at the Maryland Historical Society and the Mariners' Museum in Newport News, and especially Marianne Martin at Colonial Williamsburg, have generously accommodated my tight deadlines to help corral the images for this book.

I began the research for this book as a graduate student at the College of William and Mary. My path to graduate school was shaped most powerfully by two individuals, Peter Reason and Clive Holmes, whose teaching revived my love for the past at critical moments in my college and university education. In its early stages, this project benefited immeasurably from the ideas, advice, and support that I received from members of the William and Mary community. It might seem obvious that a book about early Chesapeake towns would begin life in Williamsburg, but when I arrived, I intended to study neither the Chesapeake nor urban history. Credit for changing my direction must go to Alec Haskell, whose seminar inspired me to grapple with seventeenth-century political culture, and to James Horn, who encouraged me to hunt for the connections between English ideas and Chesapeake realities. As inspiring as these intellectual experiences were, it is important to acknowledge that for me, as for many, graduate school took a psychological toll; I am deeply grateful that the college's counseling service was there at some bleak moments. Most of all, though, it was the advice and encouragement of my adviser, James Whittenburg, and the support of Carolyn Whittenburg that got me through. Without Jim's unceasing interest in my work and his cool-headed words of wisdom in the midst of moments of crisis, I would never have completed my degree. While at William and Mary, I also profited immensely from the ideas and critiques of Gail Bossenga and Warren Billings; from the friendship of a number of the Omohundro Institute postdoctoral fellows, particularly Mark Hanna, Jonathan Eacott, Molly Warsh, and Dan Livesay; and from the solidarity of my fellow graduate students, particularly Céline Carayon, Lucie Kyrova, and Hank Lutton.

I was immensely fortunate to begin my academic career at the University of Glasgow, among scholars who offered advice and ideas as I began to reframe this study. I am extremely grateful to the members of Glasgow's early modern history group, particularly convener Thomas Munck, and also to Phil O'Brien, Liam Riordan, Lydia Plath, Julia Smith, Hamish Scott, and Frank Cogliano, who all enriched my time in Scotland. Most of all, I am deeply indebted to Marina Moskowitz and Simon Newman, whose advice and encouragement transformed me from a graduate student into a professional historian.

I have been equally lucky to be blessed with wonderful colleagues since arriving at Dartmouth College. Bob Bonner has been a great mentor, an insightful reader of my work, and a supportive department chair. Carl

Estabrook has been a wonderful interlocutor as this project has developed and has always been ready to offer insightful scrutiny and encouragement. I have learned much from many great conversations with Roberta Stewart, Rich Kramer, Colin Calloway, Pamela Voekel, Kris Ray, and Jere Daniell, and from the advice and friendship of Rashauna Johnson, Udi Greenberg, Stefan Link, and Jennie Miller. It has also been a pleasure to bounce my ideas off many great Dartmouth students over the past few years; in particular, Emily Burack and Nate Greabe helped with my research and provided another set of proofreading eyes for portions of the manuscript. Organizing the time and resources to undertake this research would have been much harder without the tireless assistance of Gail Patten. The fantastic maps of Chesapeake town locations were drawn by Jonathan Chipman; his patience was saintly.

This book, of course, is the product of a network that extends far beyond institutional boundaries. It has been shaped by conferences, workshops, and conversations in many venues. The thanks that I owe for many incisive questions and helpful references cannot begin to be counted. I was particularly lucky to participate in the Heidelberg University Spring Academy in American Studies in 2010 and the Alternate States symposium sponsored by the Center for British Studies at the University of California, Berkeley, in 2013. I would especially like to acknowledge the insights that I received, in these and other venues, from (in no particular order) Phil Stern, Emma Hart, Trevor Burnard, Phil Withington, Andrew Fitzmaurice, Julie Richter, Ron Hoffman, Frederika Teute, Holly Brewer, Jim Horn, Jamie May, Susan Kern, Lorena Walsh, Edward Papenfuse, Cary Carson, Carl Lounsbury, Julie King, Paul Halliday, Alec Haskell, Emily Rose, Steve Pincus, Natalie Zacek, Brian Carroll, Leanna McLaughlin, Alan Orr, Misha Ewen, Josh Beatty, Dave Brown, Aaron Slater, Michael LaCombe, Jessica Roney, Allison Bigelow, Jaap Jacobs, and Marianna Dantas. I am especially grateful to Jean Russo, who offered invaluable guidance on early Maryland records and searched for materials for me in the papers of the late Lois Green Carr. Mark Peterson, Jim Rice, Colin Calloway, Bob Bonner, and Henry Clark graciously invested considerable time in reading an early draft of the manuscript and provided important feedback as part of a manuscript review seminar sponsored by the Dickey Center at Dartmouth. Becky Kohn also read and commented on the first two chapters. Tim Mennel and the anonymous readers for the University of Chicago Press have been invaluable in helping me clarify the argument and prune the text.

My greatest pleasure is to be able to finally acknowledge the huge contributions of friends and family, who have (just about) kept me sane through many years of research and writing. While in Williamsburg, I was immensely lucky to be part of the wonderful community at Peace Hill, and particularly to have the friendship of Mel and Justin Moore and Kate and Nimel Theodore, whose visits and words of encouragement have extended that community to New Hampshire. Ever since she arrived in Williamsburg, Nadine Zimmerli has been as much a supportive friend as an insightful colleague. I am extremely grateful to my adopted Maryland family and particularly to my in-laws, Steve and Diane Tilley, for acting as gracious hosts for my many research trips to Annapolis, and in recent years for their seemingly inexhaustible enthusiasm for childcare. When I set off, more than a decade ago, on the path that has led to this book, I realized that it meant putting three thousand miles between me and my family in Wales, but I did not recognize how hard that would be for both me and them. I am thankful beyond words for their love that has bridged that divide. My parents, Jan and Phil Musselwhite, taught me to explore, to debate, and to show compassion, which has made me the historian and the person that I am; despite their concern that I might never get a "proper job," I have always been able to depend on their unconditional support. Most of all, I am grateful to Meg and Toby, who have had to live with this book for what must seem (and in one case is) a lifetime. Toby has brought joy and laughter to the last few years of wrangling this book into publication. Meg has seen it evolve over many more years. She has sacrificed so much to allow me to research and write. She has listened to and debated every idea in this book a million times. She has reassured me through each faltering step. She has gifted countless hours of her professional editorial skills to the many iterations of this text. For all of this and so much more, I can never begin to thank her enough.

Introduction: "Our Folly and Ruining Singularity"

> I must send them for a pattern to the whole World; yea, and to be upbraided by the Heathen Nations, who generally do Cohabit. Let the Brute Beasts Check them, who generally resort together in Droves; I'll send them to the Fishes of the Sea, who swim together in shoals; The very fouls of the Air do flock together; All these concur in upbraiding our folly and ruining singularity in our manner of living, and scattered Habitation.
>
> —Francis Makemie, *A Plain and Friendly Perswasive to the Inhabitants of Virginia and Maryland For Promoting Towns and Cohabitation* (1705)

In 1705, Presbyterian clergyman Francis Makemie excoriated the Chesapeake colonies of Virginia and Maryland as fatally flawed societies. We might expect to read such a damning indictment in the early years of the Virginia colony, with its notorious dysfunction; but the Chesapeake in the early eighteenth century, after a hundred years of development, has traditionally been portrayed as a stable oligarchy built on tobacco plantation agriculture and slavery. For Makemie, however, Virginia and Maryland still exhibited a fundamental flaw: their lack of towns. This absence of towns distinguished the Chesapeake colonies from the rest of English America, the rest of human civilization, and even the rest of God's creation. The dispersed settlement structure posed an existential threat to the "Body of the present Constitution of Virginia." Towns were essential places for "promoting and encouraging Education and Virtue" and "Checking and discountenancing Vice and Immorality." Makemie was building on an established European understanding that urban places were not merely clusters of buildings but coherent communities, political bodies, and legal spaces that gave structure to and regulated the lives of residents and nonresidents alike. Makemie concluded that a century of stunted urban development had led to class tensions, an increasing reliance on enslaved labor, and a weak economy. All of the Chesapeake's distinguishing features could ultimately be explained by its lack of urban structures, and thus any effort to address the region's problems had to begin with towns and cities.[1]

Makemie was not alone in expressing this opinion. In fact, he was contributing to a contest between planters, merchants, and imperial officials over how to urbanize the Chesapeake that had been ongoing since the foundation of Virginia in 1607. Cities had been a centerpiece of the Virginia Company's plans during the first years of settlement. Virginia's royal governor, Sir John Harvey, had sought "to reduce, and draw the people into Townes" in the 1630s. Maryland colonists in the 1670s had grumbled about their proprietor, Lord Baltimore, because he had not "marked and laieth out, lands for Townes." Practically every account of the region in the seventeenth century lamented its lack of towns. The legislatures of both colonies debated dozens of pieces of legislation designed to spur urban development. The Chesapeake was seemingly obsessed with what William Byrd II would later term "cities in the air."[2]

Despite this preoccupation, the Chesapeake region remained rural for a century. In his satirical 1708 poem *The Sotweed Factor*, Maryland poet Ebenezer Cook noted that even visitors to the Maryland capital of Annapolis would "scarcely meet, With Market-place, Exchange, or Street." Planned towns withered on the vine. Thomas Jefferson in his *Notes on the State of Virginia* famously suggested that although *"laws* have said there shall be towns" in the region, *"Nature* has said there shall not." Decades of research have broadly confirmed these conclusions. The region was dominated by plantation estates scattered along the many estuaries of the Chesapeake. Planters traded directly with London merchants and imported their manufactured goods. It is easy to see why generations of historians have dismissed the fixation on urban development as a fruitless footnote to the story of tobacco and slavery.[3]

In this book, I argue that the absence of urban places was no mere coincidental product of Chesapeake plantation agriculture. In fact, the relationship between plantations and towns was quite the opposite. A century of failed urban development was instrumental in forging the contours of Chesapeake society. For Makemie and his contemporaries, people rather than economic and environmental forces built towns, and the decisions they made in this process had profound implications not just for individual wealth but also for the structure of their society and its relationship to the English (later British) Empire and the Atlantic economy. Although settlements that modern observers might recognize as towns were largely absent from the seventeenth-century Chesapeake, the idea of urbanity was ubiquitous and deeply influential; it facilitated conceptual shifts and redefinitions in the nature of what the plantation system was and how it was justified and defended. The cities and towns that were debated in the Chesapeake were such potentially powerful institutional, commercial, and communal structures that new proposals to establish them inevitably raised critical questions about what kind of commercial and political order colonists were building on the tobacco coast. These questions were not fully answered for over a century. When they were resolved in the eighteenth century, it gave rise to a unique planter agrarian worldview that inscribed an artificial belief in the incompatibility between plantations and cities that continues to inform scholarship to this day.

By taking the voluminous debate over urban establishment seriously, this book challenges the conventional narrative that plantation capitalism was an inevitable system built pragmatically by people on the periphery of empire. Planters, we have long been told, were a uniquely aggressive, hardheaded class of individuals who scrambled after wealth until they discovered a profitable staple, at which point they oriented their entire society around this Atlantic cash crop. These supremely practical and rational people cared little for political principles and adapted a lifestyle and legal tradition from rural England to accommodate indentured servitude and eventually enslaved labor. Scholars have suggested that any efforts to restructure the system were nothing more than whistling into the wind. By obscuring the human agency behind these broad economic forces, the explanations give the impression that the Chesapeake's settlement form was determined inexorably by rational responses to its geography, climate, and crops.[4]

In fact, though, planters were deeply conscious of their political-economic system. The century-long contest over urban development acted as a catalyst that refined broad discussions about competing interests and ideas through particular concrete proposals that drew planters and merchants from across the class and wealth spectrum into dialogue with emerging theories about commerce and the state in Britain. Scholars have carefully reconstructed the ways in which generations of planters consciously adapted racial ideologies and legal structures to justify exploitation of the enslaved; but they have generally neglected to trace the similar process by which those planters shaped the political economy of their societies in order to correlate their private interests with the public good.[5]

Chesapeake planters' ideas about the political economy of the empire in the century and a half before the imperial crises of the 1760s have largely been overlooked. They have been bracketed as a unified creole interest on the periphery of empire that conflicted with, and eventually became reconciled to, imperial mercantilist principles.[6] Political-economic debates, though, were vibrant in early modern plantation societies, and the whole concept of mercantilism was a more fluid and contested set of economic philosophies than historians have previously appreciated.[7]

Planters were actively involved in constructing the commercial empire in which they could manipulate state power to exploit, enslave, and commodify labor in the production of global luxury commodities. This process required more than simply brute force and racism: the system of exploitation also needed to be structured and rationalized within contemporary understandings of commerce and imperial sovereignty. Rival plans for towns and cities—advanced by different factions of planters, merchants, and imperial officials—provide the raw materials from which it is possible to reconstruct a rich variety of subtly distinct attitudes about issues ranging from free trade to price controls and poor whites' access to economic opportunities. The battles over these plans reveal the extent of the political-economic work that elite planters had to do, over the course of a century, to construct and legitimize a protocapitalist commercial system built around slavery and staple agriculture. They also help to explain the unique political ideology planters developed in the eighteenth century in an effort to conserve the system they had built.[8]

THE CHESAPEAKE

This story of plantations and cities is a Chesapeake story. It could not be otherwise. As Makemie had pointed out, the lack of towns made the Chesapeake a notorious "singularity." The Earl of Shaftesbury, planning the Carolina colony in the 1670s, cited Virginia's lack of towns as evidence of the "Rashnesse and Folly [that] will expose the Plantation to Ruin." By the mid-eighteenth century, the Chesapeake's rurality had become a defining mark of its identity. This rurality has attracted the attention of modern scholars, but much of this attention has focused on explaining the forces hindering town growth and extrapolating a fundamental incompatibility between plantations and cities. In fact, the challenges of town building in the Chesapeake were far from inevitable or typical for plantation regions. They reflect the uniquely drawn out process of plantation development and consolidation in the Chesapeake.[9]

The seventeenth-century Chesapeake was startlingly rural. Historians have painstakingly quantified and analyzed land and probate records to reconstruct an account of life for early colonists. Their work suggests that, after the infamous tribulations of the first two decades of English settlement in Virginia, colonists built a rough-hewn society around tobacco. A concerted campaign against the region's indigenous peoples during the 1620s allowed English colonists to seize large areas of land, and the custom of headright, in which fifty acres were granted for each individual transported to the region, meant that this land was quickly parceled out. Planters turned to tobacco, which was relatively easy to grow and required little capital investment. Unregulated merchants offered a ready market for tobacco and supplied the region with a steady supply of poor indentured white laborers (overwhelmingly male). In this fluid society, planters neglected permanent homes and spread out across the region in search of the best virgin land for tobacco; practically all of the acreage opened onto one of the region's many rivers, and so planters quickly erected docks on their own land and dealt directly with ship captains. Through the seventeenth century, the planter gentry gradually consolidated their control over the best lands and the tobacco trade, and they increasingly converted to enslaved African labor, reinforcing a pattern of sprawling estates and dominating rural, county-based local institutions.[10]

Archaeological evidence reinforces this picture of a "scant urbanity." Jamestown is the archetype for the pattern of urban failure. Established by the first Virginia expedition in 1607, on a swampy peninsula jutting into the James River, Jamestown had a checkered history. The town had a longstanding status as the "metropolis" of Virginia, and planters and officials repeatedly invested in efforts to develop its public infrastructure and private homes. Examples of ambitious brick architecture marked the town, but they frequently stood cheek by jowl with abandoned and unfinished properties. Spurts of development were followed by periods of neglect and by repeated efforts to relocate the capital to an alternative site elsewhere in the colony. At its most flourishing, in the late 1630s and early 1640s, twelve substantial new houses were built in Jamestown, and the town boasted six taverns, but even after another round of development in the 1660s, contemporaries reported that the capital only had approximately twenty habitable residences; it probably never had a permanent population that exceeded five hundred. This still made it the largest urban center in the seventeenth-century Chesapeake, though, outstripping St. Mary's City in Maryland, where Lord Baltimore's plans for a capital city never generated more than a couple of hundred permanent residents.[11] Beyond these capital cities, the many urban places planned in the seventeenth century either remained empty fields or became clusters of a few wooden houses.[12] Because these places left few marks in either the archaeological or archival records, urban life has seemed irrelevant.

In the eighteenth century, the fortunes of the Chesapeake's towns turned around. The new colonial capitals of Annapolis and Williamsburg, both established in the 1690s, grew steadily; their ambitious street plans were gradually filled out with homes, taverns, shops, and artisans' workshops. By the 1770s, both cities had about two thousand inhabitants, and their populations swelled during the so-called public times when provincial assemblies and courts were in session. While this growth paled in comparison to Philadelphia or Kingston, it was a dramatic departure from the seventeenth-century pattern.[13] After midcentury, the growth of the large port cities of Baltimore and Norfolk and inland trading entrepôts such as Richmond, Fredericksburg, and Winchester transformed the Chesapeake even more radically. By the time of the Revolution, Baltimore and Norfolk both had populations of more than six thousand; they featured diverse economies and dense streets populated by poor and enslaved laborers, comparable with other Atlantic port cities.[14]

Despite this dramatic transformation, though, towns and cities have remained largely irrelevant to our picture of the colonial Chesapeake. This is partly a function of the deliberate efforts of the region's eighteenth-century planter gentry. After a century of promoting urban growth, leading planters began seeking to restrict urban institutional maturation. Although they actively speculated in property in new towns, they consciously prevented the development of new urban identity or authority. They intentionally distanced themselves from the urban world developing in their midst. The famous Virginia planter William Byrd noted that he felt so out of place in Norfolk that he may as well have been from "China or Japan." Thomas Jefferson concluded that Virginia had "no towns of any consequence," denying significance to the quickly developing urban network. The Chesapeake's remarkable rurality went from reality to rhetoric.[15]

The stereotype of the rural Chesapeake has endured, though, because historians have embraced this self-perception of the eighteenth-century Chesapeake gentry and implicitly accepted the incompatibility of cities and plantations. They have focused almost exclusively on explaining how and why the region coped without towns. Jefferson initiated this discussion, arguing that the lack of towns was a product of the Chesapeake's many navigable rivers, which made trade easy and discouraged the coalescing of commerce. This thesis has been refined, with scholars pointing to the nature of tobacco—a product that required minimal secondary processing—as the main factor hindering town growth until parts of the region converted to grain farming in the eighteenth century. Others have traced the ways urban services were fulfilled by other means in the region. This debate, though, employs modern definitions of urban functions and assumes that their absence was the defining feature of the region. It reduces plantations to merely tools for the primitive accumulation of New World resources and defines urban centers as the sophisticated apparatus of capitalism that remained, for good or ill, on the other side of the Atlantic.[16] Cultural and legal scholars, by contrast, have portrayed the Chesapeake's rural society as a product of the particular English immigrants who settled the region, suggesting that early colonists from agrarian regions of western England established a manorial culture.[17] Social historians have seen the process as more organic, tracing the way ordinary men and women made the best of their scattered lifestyle by establishing county and parish institutions for dispersed communities.[18] All of these perspectives on seventeenth-century development implicitly point toward the image of the eighteenth-century Chesapeake that existed in the minds of the planter class, defined by hierarchical and deferential county communities, in which the social mobility and dynamism of urban life seemed anathema to the pastoral world of the plantation elite.[19] The new port cities of the eighteenth-century Chesapeake have been largely dismissed as the exceptions that proved the rule of rural dominance. Norfolk, one scholar has concluded, was "a thing apart" from the rest of Virginia society.[20]

In reality, plantation agriculture was not incompatible with urban growth. Cities flourished in other plantation colonies. Bridgetown was one of the largest towns in the seventeenth-century English Atlantic, and Kingston and Charleston were two of the five largest cities in British America at the American Revolution. Other European plantation societies boasted far larger cities. Plantation cities were thriving centers for the organization of the export trade in staple commodities, and also for the trade in imported manufactured goods, provisions, and, most important, enslaved people. These cities also frequently coordinated the local economy and provided a base for lawyers, clergy, and administration. These urban spaces differed from one another and from those of other American colonies and European states, but each fit within a political and economic pattern that supported large-scale, slave-powered agriculture. The urban centers that developed in the Chesapeake during the eighteenth century, therefore, were not an anomaly within a predominant rural pattern but part of a network of political and economic hubs across the plantation world.[21]

This was hardly news to the men and women of the early Chesapeake. Planters, merchants, and officials all assumed that towns and cities would shape the way they lived and traded. By focusing on explaining the Chesapeake's supposedly inevitable rurality, we have all but ignored the contemporary discussion about the issue, assuming that the calls for urbanization came from marginal figures or unrealistic metropolitan officials hung up on abstract notions about cities as symbols of civility, while the majority happily accepted dispersed settlement.[22] In fact, the lack of towns and cities in the seventeenth century, and their subsequent growth in the eighteenth century, provoked intense contemporary concern. Many members of Chesapeake society were involved in the reams of correspondence, hours of legislative debate, and days of surveying and building that went into the effort to urbanize the Chesapeake, and, by the eighteenth century, most white people were frequent visitors to the region's small towns.

What really made the Chesapeake distinctive, then, was not an inexorable economic pattern or rural tradition, but the region's persistent self-conscious debates about cities, which continued even after urban growth took hold. No other plantation region expended so much time and energy deliberating over urban plans. This was because, far from being on an inevitable path to a preordained plantation economy that precluded urban growth, the Chesapeake experienced a uniquely protracted and contested struggle to build a full-fledged planter society. While urban centers in other plantation regions quickly developed structures of power and identity in a symbiotic relationship with a consolidating planter class, the ongoing debate about urbanization in the Chesapeake reflected continued uncertainty about the precise contours of the plantation system in which they were supposed to fit.

From the outset, the establishment of the Chesapeake plantation system was a profoundly uncertain process. Both Virginia and Maryland were established with the explicit dual purpose of generating new wealth through commercial commodities while also building new, well-governed commonwealths in the New World.[23] Contemporaries realized that this was a tricky balance to maintain. Political thinkers were acutely aware that trade encouraged individuals to pursue their own private interests at the expense of the good of the commonwealth. Although English society had commercialized over the sixteenth century, it was still bound by a system of local exchange, regulated markets, and middlemen, ostensibly designed to hold these instincts in check.[24] Establishing such systems in the new colonial context was always going to be a challenge. After the conversion to tobacco agriculture in the mid-1610s, Chesapeake planters found themselves uniquely exposed to the emerging global commodities market. Everyone was dependent upon the export of a single crop for all of their clothing, tools, and household goods. To make matters worse, tobacco was purely a luxury commodity, reliant on the controversial fashion for smoking. In early modern terms, it did not add real material worth to the realm. Far from seeing tobacco agriculture as a basis on which to build a society, commentators, including the king himself, described Virginia as a commonwealth "built upon smoke" that could "soe easie be turned into aire."[25]

These fears were well founded. In the absence of market regulations, after the dissolution of the Virginia Company, tobacco production expanded, and prices began a volatile downward spiral. This unstable and declining market discouraged long-term investment in infrastructure, and planters became dependent on credit secured against the tobacco harvest, discouraging diversification. Without formal market controls, trade was a fierce competition between personal networks of planters and merchants, resulting in nefarious dealings and exploitation of bound and enslaved laborers. To make matters worse, colonists also had to confront growing demands from imperial officials for a cut of the diminishing tobacco profits.[26]

Questions lingered throughout the seventeenth century over the region's economy. It was by no means clear how to maintain a stable and profitable economy in the Chesapeake and what role tobacco and enslaved labor would play. Planters in sugar- and rice-producing regions certainly engaged in introspection about their economy and struggled against imperial policies, but they did not do so by debating the fundamental spatial and institutional structure of their society.[27] In these regions, suitable land was more circumscribed, and the white population remained smaller, hastening the transition to an intensive, slave-driven plantation system dominated by a narrow elite who defined political and economic structures on their terms and exercised influence in the imperial metropolis.[28] Tobacco never generated sufficient profits before the eighteenth century to justify major investment in enslaved labor, and conditions on the tobacco coast were sufficiently tolerable (compared to the Caribbean) that white servants continued to migrate.[29] In these circumstances, the construction of a narrow planter elite required careful maneuvering and political manipulation over generations. As John Coombs has shown, some powerful individuals did consciously convert their labor forces to enslaved Africans by the mid-seventeenth century; equally, though, the white population of the region continued to expand, pushing the frontier of settlement westward, provoking conflict with native peoples, increasing the demand for infrastructure, and swelling the tobacco output in an already depressed market.[30] This period was hardly a halcyon time of opportunity; it was an era of uncertainty, dissatisfaction, and competing visions for the Chesapeake economy.

Even as tobacco and slavery took root, no single pattern of economic development emerged for the whole tidewater region. The Chesapeake became a patchwork of subregions with different strains of tobacco, different plantation management strategies, and different labor forces. As elite planters succeeded in consolidating their power in the prime tobacco-growing areas, settlement continued to grow, moving into areas where soil quality and climate made tobacco cultivation marginal. Some parts of the region—south of the James River, on the Eastern Shore, and in northern Maryland—shifted away from tobacco cultivation entirely in favor of grain farming.[31] The Chesapeake, therefore, effectively straddled the divide between what modern observers might describe as plantations and commercial farms. On this plantation frontier, the system of intensive, slave-based cultivation of exotic staples had to be consciously built and carefully supported and maintained with both political and economic influence.

It was these uncertain circumstances that generated a persistent debate over urban development. Towns and cities held the potential to generate new forms of local or imperial authority that could control markets, police trade, or generate revenue; they could help planters accumulate capital to trade independently; they could also offer the potential for new industries employing poor whites displaced by the consolidation of the plantation economy. By building particular kinds of towns, contemporaries recognized that they could shape the kind of plantation society that the Chesapeake might yet become. Urban development was uniquely central and persistently contentious in the Chesapeake because it was an explicit site of contestation in the piecemeal and complex emergence of a slave plantation complex in the region.

Because it provided a concrete point of conflict within the process of plantation consolidation, the Chesapeake urban debate reveals a broader array of the opinions and ideas involved in this process than we can get by just telling the teleological story of the few who wrestled and terrorized their way to its peak and the institutional structures they built. Many poor and middling planters left no written record of their political ideas or aspirations for the colonial economy, but by reading the decisions they made to reside or invest in urban spaces as conscious contributions to political-economic discussions about the shape of the region, we can recover their perspective. We can reconstruct the history of political-economic thought in early America from the bottom up.[32] The perspectives of the enslaved are much harder to recover in these ways. Enslaved people had considerable ability to shape early modern Atlantic urban spaces through their day-to-day actions and social networks.[33] In the eighteenth century, when sizable enslaved populations resided in the Chesapeake's towns, their actions and the threat they posed to colonial authority became critical to the debate. Nevertheless, for many of the seventeenth-century urban places considered in this study, plans and projects for new towns rarely developed far enough to generate these kinds of opportunities. This book argues that many more people were involved in contesting the political-economic structures than we have previously realized, but access to these particular channels of power was still ultimately restricted by race.

Exploring the persistent urban debate across the Chesapeake also provides a tangible means of tracking the way politics and economics intersected in the development of the plantation system. Because town development was fundamentally political, it was debated discreetly within the jurisdictional bounds of Virginia and Maryland. Virginia, after 1624, was a royal colony. Maryland, by contrast, was a proprietary province controlled by the Catholic Calvert family, who struggled throughout the seventeenth century to assert their authority over the province in an atmosphere of febrile confessional tensions. However, these constitutional boundaries also cut across the Chesapeake's subregions, creating subtly different constellations of economic interests. The point of exploring these two overlapping narratives throughout this study is not to argue for two clearly divergent patterns; in some situations, Marylanders were more proactive in urban development, and at other times, they resisted it more forcefully. By considering Virginia and Maryland together, though, this study demonstrates the multiple contingent responses to changing economic and political circumstances at particular moments.[34]

The Chesapeake story of urban development is clearly anomalous, but not for the reasons we have long assumed. The region was not marked so much by a lack of towns as by an intensely fraught relationship with them, which reveals the complex negotiations involved in building, justifying, and defending a plantation system. Thus, it is an anomaly well worth exploring. Understanding the decisions that turned tobacco into a plantation staple and pulled parts of the Chesapeake region into the slave plantation complex has much bigger stakes than merely a curious provincial story. It is a story grounded in particular tidewater places that intersects with larger Atlantic and imperial developments. It can help us better understand the contingent process of shaping spatial and institutional structures through which Europeans commodified different resources across the extra-European world. New England's towns, Pennsylvania's small-farmer neighborhoods, the Caribbean's intensive plantations and mercantile entrepôts, and the Chesapeake tidewater's gentry estates were not inevitably divergent products of geography and cultural traditions. There were moments in the Chesapeake when each of these other alternatives was actively pursued. Staring down the political and economic paths not taken—the dreams for an urban Chesapeake—highlights the decisions that formalized the region's particular plantation system. It reminds us that the spatial, commercial, and institutional structures of the plantation system were, just like its racial categories, not the product of an "unthinking decision" but of conscious and long-running political-economic debates on both the provincial and the imperial levels.[35] It was the winners of this particular debate in the Chesapeake who helped to shape a viciously abusive system of capitalist agriculture built on racism and exploitation, while framing it in the civic language of agrarian republicanism that has long made the tobacco coast seem like a rural backwater with "no towns of any consequence."[36]

THE CITY

The debate over the structure of Chesapeake society centered on urban development because of the central role that towns and cities played in early modern thinking about politics and society. A discourse on "cities and peopled townes," written around 1580, probably by London lawyer James Dalton, explained that "the propagation of Religion, the execution of good policie, the exercise of Charity, and the defence of the country" were "best performed by townes and Cities" where "civill life approcheth nearest to the shape of that misticall body whereof Christ is the head, and men be the members." These roles (in politics, religion, commerce, and social order), and the analogy to the metaphorical body, are often associated with the expanding vision of state and imperial institutions in the early modern period. In many respects, though, they were first conceptualized and contested in relation to the city. The emergence of European states and empires involved accommodating, co-opting, and subsuming the legitimacy and authority of cities and towns in a gradual and piecemeal fashion. Colonial polities and economies, including English plantation societies, were established alongside this process of state formation, and not after it, and were inevitably caught up in it.[37]

Medieval Europe witnessed an explosion of urban growth. In many cases, this growth occurred because of the wealth generated through commerce, and it was therefore in tension with the predominant hierarchies of the nobility and the church that were defined through landownership. For this reason, many medieval cities carefully guarded their autonomy, developing structures of consensual governance and market regulations. This pragmatic urban independence was reinforced by the Renaissance rediscovery of classical texts, particularly Aristotle's *Politics*, which offered a new coherence to ideas about the city as a political community. Reading in this rich vein of city-based thought, humanists came to believe that it was in belonging to an urban community that individuals could be encouraged to put aside their private commercial interests, pursue the common good, and abide by the rule of law. As a result, those who wrestled with questions about how to reform politics and society and manage the rising tide of commercialization—even in predominantly rural regions such as the British Isles—did so primarily in terms of cities.[38]

Classical precedent, though, also taught other, very different, lessons about the importance of cities. Imperial Rome provided a vivid example of the way in which cities could amass wealth, support expansion, and foster empire. While medieval monarchs had been happy merely to extract tribute from autonomous cities, the sovereign monarchs of the sixteenth century aspired to a supreme unitary authority and saw urban centers more as seats of power.[39] The Italian scholar Giovanni Botero particularly emphasized this message in his 1588 treatise on the "Greatness and Magnificence of Cities." Botero outlined the advantages that "great" cities could offer to monarchs and explored the means by which they might encourage urban growth. He suggested encouraging nobles to relocate into cities to centralize governance, spur the consumer economy, and generate state revenue.[40] By the time Botero articulated these ideas, they had already been put into practice. Italian city-states had been integrated into territorial monarchies, and in Spain, the powerful monarchy encouraged aristocrats to dominate urban communities and suppress civic autonomy. The result was a new form of courtly cities, saturated with baroque displays of royal power and an elite consumer culture.[41]

In an extension of these ideas, cities became the foundation of Spanish imperial plans in the Americas. Cities had been the basis for Roman imperial expansion, and so they were an obvious model for Spanish monarchs who saw themselves as heirs of Rome. They quickly set about establishing cities in the Americas, either co-opting the urban spaces of indigenous communities or laying new foundations with orderly grids and baroque architecture. Urban autonomy, though, was not part of the design; the Spanish crown established direct control through the appointment of officials to *cabildos* (town councils) and used cities as nodes for imperial oversight and control. These wealthy and tightly controlled Spanish American cities became an object of jealous fascination among other Europeans by the second half of the sixteenth century.[42]

The construction and organization of urban space both within and beyond Europe was thus critical to early modern state building. Urban institutions defined citizenship in an increasingly commercial society; they provided local frameworks for the active civic participation that helped to mobilize armies, regulate trade, and undertake public projects. Equally, though, they became centers for the exercise of more expansive monarchical authority, as tools and symbols of monarchical power that stretched out from their confines to tap the resources of surrounding hinterlands. The city was at once the antecedent, the adversary, and the agent of the nation-state.

In England, these contradictory impulses of civic autonomy and monarchical authority both played a crucial role in the kingdom's transformation during the early modern era. In the sixteenth century, England entered a period of consistent urban growth, spurred by population increases, the rise of Atlantic commerce, and new industries, which would take it from one of Europe's least urbanized societies to one of its most flourishing urban cultures. Between 1550 and 1700, London's population went from 75,000 to 575,000, and steady growth also characterized many smaller towns.[43] This period, though, also witnessed ambitious new claims to sovereignty on the part of the Tudor and Stuart monarchs. The growing size and self-confidence of the kingdom's towns, and the growing aspirations of its monarchs, came together in an unprecedented program of urban incorporations. Incorporation involved the granting of a royal charter to a discrete and limited group of urban freemen who represented the civic community; it made them a single legal entity with the right to own common property, and it gave them jurisdiction over petty crimes and market regulation, the authority to levy fines on members of the community, and (in most cases) the right to representation in Parliament. There were thirty-eight such corporate boroughs in England before 1500, but by the 1640s, that number had rocketed to 181.[44] Charters combined an acknowledgment of urban civic autonomy with an assertion of royal sovereignty, ideally helping to hold these ideas in stable tension. The multiple, overlapping meanings of incorporation thus offer an ideal window into the range of ideas about urbanization in England.

In one sense an urban charter was a recognition, on the part of the Crown, of the legitimacy of a long-standing urban civic community. The Elizabethan political philosopher Sir Thomas Smith, in his study of England's constitutional structure, *De Republica Anglorum*, had identified urban citizens as a discrete part of the social order with a firmly established identity. Contemporary pamphlets, such as Edmund Boulton's *The Cities Advocate* (1629), lauded the age-old traditions of the urban craftguilds and the exclusive status of citizens, as members of "the politicall bodie or state of a Citie immortall." John Stowe's *Survey of London* (1598) also captured this sense of immortal civic identity. At over five hundred pages, it was an exhaustive history of the city's neighborhoods and its civic leadership stretching back centuries. Corporate leaders sought to bolster this distinct identity by investing in new town halls, renovated marketplaces, and schools.[45]

This was more than merely local pride; it reflected the broader European association of autonomous urban communities with civic virtue. Those who achieved the status of citizens saw themselves as members of consensual participatory communities, bound together through networks of officeholders and communal conventions, to pursue the common good. Phil Withington has argued that many English townspeople saw their incorporated communities as "city commonwealths" that "resembled nothing less than Aristotle's *Polis*."[46] These attitudes were part of a broader discussion of "commonwealth" in early modern England, which emphasized that the realm as a whole was a community made up of active participants and officeholders working for the good of the whole; this ideal, though, had a particular salience in compact and delineated urban communities.[47] Formal membership in an incorporated city commonwealth involved specific rights and responsibilities. William Scott's *An Essay of Drapery, or The Compleate Citizen* (1635), while offering an unrealistic exhortation to virtue that few urban dwellers probably lived up to, provides a window into what these rights and duties were; Scott urged citizens to be honest and industrious in their work, guarded in their public discourse, and prudent with their riches in order to contribute to local philanthropy. The expression of civic virtue could also take a more militaristic form through membership in urban militias (known as trained bands).[48] These virtues flowed from, and also justified, citizens' particular privileges to trade within their towns, and their right to self-government and representation. While corporate towns were far from democratic, they had an ethos of participatory governance that embraced all citizens, stretching from those who served as neighborhood constables all the way to the senior offices of the aldermen and the mayor. Pageants and festivities rehearsed these shared bonds and reminded leaders of their civic duty.[49]

For many citizens these secular civic structures also overlapped with their sense of the Protestant church as a limited corporate community bound by a covenant among members who actively pursued sanctification. Puritanism, like citizenship, emphasized a culture of conversation, communalism, and virtue in pursuit of the common good. The radical puritan divine John Goodwin argued that the right of congregations to govern themselves was akin to "grants of Government and rule within themselves unto Towns and Corporations." Unsurprisingly, many urban corporations came under the influence of puritans and became vehicles for this Christian brand of humanism, laying the basis for the model of puritan town governance that later shaped New England.[50]

Royal charters validated and helped to institutionalize these civic ideas. Incorporated towns had a distinctive legal status, new sources of reliable communal income, and new authority to regulate their own internal social and commercial order. Formal incorporation gave them the capacity to control their membership, allowing them to limit competition, stabilize prices, and inculcate communal standards of conduct. It also allowed them to hold communal property, which could be rented out to generate revenues to fund new civic building projects, schools, poor houses, and puritan lectureships.[51]

At the same time, though, the incorporation of English towns and cities was also a tangible sign of their dependence upon royal support and their integration within the monarchical state. Before the era of incorporations, many of the kingdom's smaller towns had come under the direct authority of neighboring nobles. Royal charters created new unmediated bonds between town leaders and the Crown, allowing monarchs to arbitrate contests between aristocrats and urban citizens and thereby strengthening their claims to sovereignty. James Dalton, in his discourse on cities and towns, explained that "in respect of the whole Realme, London is but a Citizen, and no Citie, a subject and no free estate, an obedienciarie, and no place indowed with any distinct or absolute power." Whatever local jurisdiction the corporate borough might exercise, Dalton noted, its judgments could always be appealed to royal courts; its militias were also ultimately at the beck and call of the Crown. When he described the development of London's corporate offices, he was careful to note that they were "given by the Prince, and not chosen by the Citizens," until Richard I had granted the city the right to elect its own officers in return for a hefty payment. This picture of urban charters as symbols of benevolent royal patronage fit well with the patriarchal vision of kingship advanced by James I and Charles I during the early seventeenth century.[52]

Beyond merely securing loyalty, charters also served the interests of the Crown by making towns and cities more effective tools for the management of commerce and resources. Many charters overrode long-standing informal traditions of popular participation; corporate constitutions typically granted authority to aldermen who served for life and who filled vacancies by co-option, not election. Most towns still had an elected council, but the trend was toward oligarchies. Rituals that had previously celebrated communal bonds were gradually replaced by spectacles, such as London's Lord Mayor's Show, that emphasized the authority of the civic leadership derived from their associations with the royal court. Contemporary playwrights even picked up on the rise of oligarchy, using a new genre of city comedies to satirize pretentious civic leaders.[53] The Crown relied upon these urban elites, particularly in London, to fund the growing expenses of the state, either through loans or through the purchase of rights to collect customs duties (known as "farms").[54] By the second half of the seventeenth century, towns and cities also became permanent bases for directly appointed Crown officials, such as customs and excise inspectors. Edmund Boulton, who heaped praise on London's citizens in *The Cities Advocate*, still argued that the capital was a place where "the sinews of warre, and peace, abundance of treasure, are stored up, as in the Chamber of the King." This was a sentiment redolent of continental thinkers, such as Botero, with his emphasis upon great cities bringing glory, prestige, and power to the sovereign.[55]

Urban charters were therefore multivalent documents that held together distinct strands of thinking. They elided the seeming contradiction between towns as autonomous civic communities ideally suited to the cultivation of virtue in a commercial context and towns as dependent bodies who existed to offer loyalty, funding, and logistical support to the sovereign and the state.[56] The wax-sealed vellum scrolls on which these documents were written, though, could not always bind these conflicting forces, especially as the demands of the state became greater and the complexity of the urban economy grew. Many of England's urban corporations drew upon their autonomous civic identity as they played a leading role in the resistance to Charles I during the English Civil Wars. Royalist supporters of the king were convinced that the corporate towns had been leading instigators of the conflict, and they acted to restrict their freedom after the restoration of Charles II in 1660. Charles II and James II undertook a concerted campaign to rescind and reissue urban charters in order to replace civic leaders who resisted their policies. Many corporations actively resisted these efforts, but royalists, such as Robert Brady, mocked claims that towns and cities were "small Commonwealths, lifted out of the chaos, and fixed upon the surface of the earth," and derided their claims to "extravagant, uncontroulable, and absolute Powers, and absurd Rights." Only in the eighteenth century did Britain's urban corporations become integrated within the infrastructure of the state, then manifested in Parliament. Urban charters, then, were ground zero in the contest of state building in seventeenth-century England. There was more at stake in these conflicts than simply local privileges; they addressed the fundamental question of how the common good was defined and whose interests mattered in its formulation; they determined how and under whose control the resources of England's rapidly commercializing and urbanizing society would be managed and deployed.[57]

It was precisely the ambiguity of urban governance, though, that made towns and cities such a potent tool for English colonization. Establishing urban spaces in colonial settings seemed key to cultivating local civic communities, which would encourage individuals to fight in defense of a new colony, to contribute labor to public projects, and to accede to rules governing commerce and exchange. This civic virtue would also help to justify, in the minds of Europeans, the occupation of foreign lands and the subjugation of indigenous peoples, under the pretext of spreading this form of civil commonwealth across the globe.[58] Equally, though, towns provided a tangible symbol of imperial sovereignty, they facilitated trade and the exploitation of colonial resources, and they strengthened the state's capacity to generate colonial revenue. They were simultaneously tools of commonwealth building and state building.

The English framed their efforts to colonize Ireland in the late sixteenth century around just such a vision. One of the leading advocates for Irish plantations, Edmund Spenser, wrote in his *View of the Present State of Ireland* (1596) that towns should be established there as "free boroughs and incorporate under bailiffs," with "the privilege of a market," because this would "strengthen and enable them to their defence."[59] Officials concurred and established many new corporate towns during colonizing efforts in Munster and Ulster. Although these towns were heavily fortified, for contemporaries, such as Spenser, the walls were only the most visible manifestation of the civic order emerging from the corporate structure. Planners consistently compared these towns to Roman colonies or the militaristic city-state of Sparta rather than to the castles of feudal lords. They also intended urban civic communities to facilitate public investment in commercial and agricultural development. For example, the Crown established the corporate city of Londonderry, under the control of London's livery companies, in order to strengthen trade ties between Ulster and London. It was, at once, an independent community empowered to regulate trade and, at the same time, a tool for expanding the commerce of the realm.[60] The preference for an urban corporate structure also influenced the earliest plans for English America. In 1587, when Sir Walter Raleigh sent his ill-fated second expedition to Roanoke, he instructed that they establish themselves as the "Corporation for the City of Ralegh."[61] Wherever early English colonists went, they planned towns and cities to balance their pursuit of civic and imperial goals.

It is hardly surprising, therefore, that urban development was central to plans for the Virginia colony. The Virginia Company instructed their first group of colonists to establish a town, and Captain John Smith soon reported that the site they had selected and named Jamestown was "a verie fit place for the erecting of a great cittie."[62] Smith's comments likely alluded to Giovanni Botero's recently translated study of "great" cities and the power and prestige that they offered to their sovereigns. Equally, though, Virginia Company officials were soon also planning autonomous urban corporations in an effort to promote civic virtue. The competing impulses of urban development, toward civic autonomy and imperial authority, quickly manifested themselves in the Chesapeake.

Throughout the seventeenth century, as the Chesapeake became an overtly commercial society driven by tobacco, efforts to build towns were always plagued by questions about the political identity and economic purpose of urban spaces. In other parts of the Atlantic world, urban structures were established, informed by the experiences and ideas of the founding generations, and they gradually evolved in the face of internal and external pressures.[63] Along the tobacco coast, no single unified vision for an urban political and economic structure managed to take hold. This was not because the region's colonists came from a closeted English rural culture hostile to urban development. On the contrary, they were fully aware of the potential power of towns and cities and engaged with contemporary contests over the nature of urban governance. For example, a group of Maryland planters in 1676 addressed a petition to the "Lord Mayor and Aldermen with all the good cittizens and merchants in London and elswhere in England, whoes off spring wee are."[64] Planters, merchants, and officials all repeatedly turned to the establishment of towns and cities in an effort to organize and control what they saw as a dysfunctional political and economic structure. In doing so, though, they wrestled with the multivalent meanings of urbanity. At various times they planned incorporated and unincorporated urban places, under the auspices of either the Crown, the colonial proprietor, the legislative assembly, or the leading planters. The range of powers and privileges granted to proposed towns coalesced in a seemingly endless number of variations. The entangling of different urban forms was amply evinced by the overlapping terminology of cities, towns, boroughs, villages, and ports, all of which took on subtly different valences for different people. The terminology that contemporaries chose when discussing urban spaces was significant and has therefore been preserved as far as possible throughout this study, even though this comes at the expense of a clearly defined taxonomy that might appeal to modern social scientists.

The repeated deadlock, failure, and adjustment of urban plans in the Chesapeake offer a unique opportunity to refine our understanding of the evolution of city-state relations in British political thought. Throughout this study, it is clear that ideas about urban organization and identity in the Chesapeake were constantly in dialogue with the domestic process of state building in the British Isles.[65] Because of the many urban false starts, the debate in the Chesapeake was largely over "cities in the air," which lacked their own internal dynamics and traditional privileges, and so it always drew upon the latest trends from English/British politics.[66] Chesapeake towns were nearly always new models, not running repairs. They therefore offer a way to excavate, in the absence of some of the other complicating factors, the shifts in attitude toward the relationship between city, state, and empire.

Most importantly, though, the range of plans reveals the way in which all those involved in the colonization of the Chesapeake negotiated the construction of the plantation empire through engagement with the question of urban civic authority. The jumble of potential urban authorities was part of an English/British imperial state that was developing gradually from a patchwork of overlapping and competing sovereignties, including towns and cities, but also chartered trading companies, proprietorships, feudal manors, county courts, imperial customs offices, and private plantation estates. As Lauren Benton has argued, "patterns of jurisdictional conflicts" between these different forms of sovereignty can reveal the "structural shifts" that shaped particular parts of the empire. When seeking to understand developments in political economy and mercantilism, urban sovereignty is a particularly critical element, through and against which commercial empire was constructed. In the Chesapeake, conflicts over urban jurisdiction, and between urban plans and alternative forms of authority, gave form to competing ideas about political autonomy, market regulation, and civic legitimacy, and ultimately helped the planter elite to assert and legitimize their power.[67]

∴ ∴ ∴

This book is organized chronologically to trace the evolution of urban debate and its effects on the Chesapeake. Each chapter focuses on a period when the need for urbanization became the subject of discussion. It considers the motives that drove these urbanizing efforts and the ways in which they drew upon changing English ideas about urban institutions, commerce, and the state. Each chapter then analyzes the reasons why the resulting initiatives largely failed to bear fruit and explores how the debate cemented the building blocks of the plantation system.

Ultimately, this study demonstrates how, through the urban debate, Chesapeake planters came to formulate their understanding of their own plantation estates and their county communities as civic spaces endowed with the legitimacy and authority to control the market. Each effort to develop urban spaces encouraged the people who became the planter elite to refine their own governing institutions and strategies. These refinements eventually gave rise to the world of the eighteenth-century planter gentry, who were innovative businessmen and slave drivers closely aligned with English commercial interests as well as a self-consciously civic republican and patriarchal elite. Ironically, this carefully crafted identity within the British commercial empire meant that as urban growth quickened in the mid-eighteenth century, Chesapeake planters happily invested in urban real estate but worked to restrict urban institutions, which now represented a threat to the gentry's aspirations to civic and commercial hegemony. They embraced their rurality. They did so, though, not because they all shared an innate cultural predilection to recreate a paternalistic world of feudal manors, but because bitter experience had taught them that it was the safest way of securing their political and commercial position within the British Empire and the Atlantic world.

This agrarian civic identity created the fertile ground on which Chesapeake planters would cultivate ideas about imperial political economy during the 1760s and 1770s. Scholars have previously explained the appeal of "country" thought and agrarian republicanism in the revolutionary

Chesapeake with reference to the immediate economic and political circumstances in the aftermath of the Seven Years' War, and the influence of imported eighteenth-century English radical thought. However, these interpretations neglect the region's long history of urban civic debate.[68] The political-economic ideas of the Chesapeake's revolutionary generation, briefly explored in the epilogue, cannot be fully understood without reference to the long negotiation between imperial structures, civic principles, and the realities of plantation economics that had been manifested in the region's urban debate ever since the establishment of Jamestown.

CHAPTER ONE

Garrison Towns, Corporate Boroughs, and the Search for Order under the Virginia Company

Everyone involved in the foundation of Virginia assumed that the process of planting a colony was synonymous with establishing a city. When the Virginia Company of London dispatched its first fleet in 1607, company leaders gave directions to lay out streets for an orderly urban settlement that would be a center for trade with local native peoples.[1] Even during the colony's infamously desperate first years, the company's commitment to an urban structure only increased. In his 1609 pamphlet *Nova Britannia*, Virginia Company leader Robert Johnson promised to revive the colony's fortunes by abandoning the fruitless search for precious metals and focusing on permanent settlement instead: the company would "settle out of hand, sixe or seven plantations more, al upon, or neare our main River [the James River], as capitall townes." Johnson's vision for Virginia's future assumed that new "plantations" would tap the agricultural resources of the Chesapeake and that these "plantations" would simultaneously be "capitall townes."[2]

This was hardly surprising. The entire plan for English plantation in the Americas in the late sixteenth and early seventeenth centuries was driven by a Renaissance humanist ambition to build new orderly commonwealths in the New World. At the same time, this humanist thought taught that urban spaces were essential to instill civic virtue and maintain order within a commercializing commonwealth. Commerce, which was predicated on the pursuit of private profit, was traditionally seen as a threat to an orderly commonwealth in which everyone labored for the common good, but carefully structured urban communities were seen as the means to diffuse its negative effects. These ideas had sparked a dramatic flourishing of urban political culture in Elizabethan England, which has been described as an "urban renaissance." The English experiment with colonialism, though, was the ultimate testing ground for new commonwealth creation; new colonies directly confronted questions about how to enforce authority, organize labor, and manage markets. Unsurprisingly, then, the answers to all these questions were framed in urban terms. Urban plans had guided English colonial projects in Ireland and at Roanoke, and they were foundational for the Virginia Company. As the colony evolved over the next fifteen years, every official who developed plans to establish, maintain, and expand settlement assumed that the process of plantation was an exercise in urban development.[3]

These ideas may appear barely relevant to reality in the colony, because the first Virginia colonists did not have anything that we would recognize as a town. For nearly a decade, the beachhead settlement at Jamestown barely staggered along; resupplies were unreliable, the colony faced persistent war with the Powhatan Empire, and the population mostly huddled behind the fortification's palisade. Eventually, in the early 1610s, settlement expanded to a number of other sites, both up- and downriver from Jamestown. High mortality left their makeshift houses sparsely occupied and poorly maintained, and, aside from a church, the settlements lacked recognizable urban public buildings. Harsh discipline and military infrastructure made the settlements appear more like desperate beleaguered garrisons rather than bustling towns.[4]

Yet because, like Johnson, everyone remained convinced that these places were the foundation of towns, their subtly distinct ideas about what towns and cities were, and how they should function, were at the heart of the debate about the nature, purpose, and organization of the new Virginia commonwealth. The absence of the long-standing traditions and infrastructure that undergirded the relationship between English towns and their hinterlands forced colonists and colonial promoters to grapple with the question of how to mandate urban settlement and the development of urban markets in order to make them effective regulators of commercial life. Although they shared a common humanist outlook, many of those involved in the Virginia colony had different views about how to create a union of wills in the colony, an equitable distribution of the spoils of colonization, and an orderly, defensible royal dominion. Were military authority and commercial monopolies necessary to make people settle in towns where they could be overseen? Could individual leaders use tenancy to construct towns that would maintain order? Or were incorporation and common land the most effective means to unite self-consciously urban communities in pursuit of the common good?

Divergent answers to these questions about urban development were central to the bitter divisions that came to plague the Virginia Company's leadership, and as a result they help capture the far-reaching significance of these divisions, which have long been dismissed as petty personal rivalries.[5] Conflicting ideas about urban development formed a consistent strain through the rivalries that beset the company's leadership, reflecting different ideas about how to balance commerce and order in the new colonial commonwealth. These philosophical positions, and the ways they intersected with James I's hardening opinions about the constitution of his realm, played an underappreciated role in the conflicts that eventually led to the company's dissolution.

However, their significance was greater than the fate of these few investors. The urban development debate gave shape to the emergence in the Chesapeake of distinct political-economic positions. It helped Virginia's planters and leaders grope toward a formula for making the colony both a profitable enterprise and a stable commonwealth. The often contradictory efforts to structure urban societies in Virginia drove the company's major reforms, including the allocation of private estates, free access to the tobacco market for small-scale Atlantic merchants, and the structuring of indentured servitude, all of which laid the foundations for the development of the plantation economy. Understanding these reforms within the context of distinct urban plans makes clear that they were not merely pragmatic responses to the necessity of short-term profits, but the result of broader political-economic debates that had unintended consequences for the construction of a nakedly commercial society. Eventually, the evolution of civic and political-economic ideas that this debate sparked began to break down Johnson's neat symmetry between plantations and towns.

"CAPITALL TOWNES"

The revival of interest in American plantations in England at the start of the seventeenth century spurred new discussion about the civic foundations of colonization. English colonial projects had always had two distinct objectives: they aimed to establish a new commonwealth in America capable of bringing order to the New World and earning glory for the English Crown, but they also sought profits for themselves and wealth for the English state. These goals were in tension—not necessarily incompatible, but also not obviously complementary. The leading Elizabethan proponents of colonization, such as Sir Humphrey Gilbert and Sir Walter Raleigh, had pursued their plantation schemes with the objective of earning honor and wealth for themselves and the Crown, but they had been regularly accused of acting purely out of private interest and a lust for gold. Proponents of the new scheme for Virginia colonization in 1606 sought to address these problems by structuring the venture as a joint-stock company, in which merchants would pool their capital and share responsibility for governance.[6] As Henry Turner has argued, the balancing of private and public interests was the "raison d'être" of the joint-stock corporation.[7] The joint-stock form, though, did not straightforwardly resolve all the complex questions about the colony's priorities and structures. The colony's first two years were marked by high-profile failures in the company's search for gold and a passage to Asia and its trade with native peoples. The size and length of the investment required made a joint-stock made up purely of merchants difficult to justify. In 1609, the Crown reorganized the company under a new charter, with a broader base of shareholders and a wider array of powers to govern a nascent colonial commonwealth, sparking a flurry of new writing in England about the ambitious civic goals of colonization.

Ongoing reframing and reorganization of the company in London during these years had a profound effect on the colony's commercial, legal, and physical order. At the core of this transformation was a subtle shift in expectations for towns and cities in the new colony. The company's first efforts to address the conflict of commerce and virtue were built around the pursuit of a great trading metropolis with a regulated marketplace, but after 1609, the company shifted toward a martial ideal of multiple garrison towns as an urban backbone for their commonwealth. Careful attention to the different valences of urban planning reveals the intersection between realities on the ground in Virginia and evolving humanist ideas in London, which laid the foundation for the debate over commerce and order in the Chesapeake.

When it first began planning in 1606, the merchant leadership of the newly established Virginia Company harbored a variety of dreams for future profits, but they were all predicated on the establishment of a major commercial city in America. Many colonial promoters believed that Virginia's indigenous people might already have a great city, ready to be conquered or merely integrated within the English commercial orbit. This was a model the English were utilizing elsewhere, setting up trading factories in Asian cities, and one the Spanish had employed successfully in Mexico and Peru. Early accounts and illustrations from the failed Roanoke venture and from the early years in Virginia noted that America was "very wel peopled and towned." Investors hoped that the presence of towns suggested that the native people already possessed structures for civil discourse and trade that could foster a network of commercial enclaves. But the first Virginia colonists struggled to establish this kind of relationship with the Powhatan Empire that dominated the lower Chesapeake Bay. Though the idea of conquering and occupying Powhatan towns persisted, it soon became clear that the English would also need to build their own urban space.[8]

While they searched for an indigenous metropolis to co-opt, the Virginia Company leadership also instructed the first colonists to lay the foundations for their own urban trading hub that could become a great commercial city. The company's plans revolved around trade with native peoples and extraction of precious metals, and for this it was essential to create an urban space to facilitate open and orderly commerce. They directed the expedition leaders to structure their initial settlement as an orderly city with "houses Even and by a line that Your Streets may have a Good breadth & be carried Square about your market place."[9] It was significant that the first adventurers were told to organize their new town around a marketplace. The company's first charter had not contained a grant of monopoly trading privileges and had laid out specific provisions for noncompany shipping, suggesting that they intended to welcome any merchants and establish a bustling entrepôt. By designating a marketplace as the core of their city, the company's investors intended to harness and regulate this open market in ways that would attract merchants, concentrating and channeling commercial wealth through their city. The insistence on orderly streets also reflected the Renaissance conviction that a well-structured urban plan would attract residents and capital and tangibly manifest imperial authority. All of this fit with the model of urban development recently articulated in Giovanni Botero's *A Treatise, Concerning the Causes of the Magnificencie and Greatnes of Cities*, which first appeared in English translation the same year the company was chartered. Captain John Smith played up to these aspirations when he pronounced Jamestown "a verie fit place for the erecting of a great cittie."[10] In reality, though, any trade the colonists did develop with the Powhatan took place on Powhatan terms and in Powhatan communities. Furthermore, planters desperately seeking to survive on precious few rations were hardly in a position to set up market stalls for exchange among themselves. Jamestown by 1609 was certainly not a trading metropolis; it had just a few dwellings and a small church.[11] Yet this fact should not obscure the company's initial preference for following Botero's model for a "great" city, focused on commerce, the accumulation of capital, and the projection of an orderly built environment.

John Smith may have played to the company's aspirations, but he was also the first to voice concerns with this vision, and he did so specifically by critiquing the structure of Jamestown as an urban community. Smith shared the humanist assumption that the colony would be built around cities, but he saw these places as critical not simply to commercial order, but also to defense and discipline. His account of Virginia's early struggles repeatedly emphasized that Jamestown was riven by private interests and that men refused to labor for the common good, hampering efforts to defend themselves against the Powhatan. His advocacy of harsh discipline is well known, but it is often overlooked that his proposed solutions began with a radical reorganization of Virginia's nascent urban space, in order to make it capable of inculcating virtue in the way he considered most effective. As he noted, his first task was "the building of James Towne." For Smith, Jamestown's initial model had been too grand. The colony had no need of the "Parliaments, plaies, petitions, admirals, recorders, interpreters, chronologers, courts of plea, nor Justices of peace"—the urban offices most prized by Botero's vision. He favored a martial definition of civic virtue akin to that which had developed in the late sixteenth-century Irish plantations. Smith believed that the company needed a compact and orderly town primarily in order to pursue military discipline under an individual leader with a single-minded commitment to the common good.[12] Although Smith left Virginia in the autumn of 1609, accounts of the horrors of the "Starving Time" during the following winter, when a Powhatan siege led to famine and cannibalism, reinforced his message.[13]

A martial civic vision also fit with the changing outlook of the Virginia Company back in London. After its initial high-profile failure to generate quick profits, the Virginia Company was reorganized in 1609 under a new charter with expanded powers and a broader base of shareholders drawn from the gentry across England. These individuals, who knew little of Atlantic commerce, were attracted by a new message that de-emphasized immediate profit in favor of a national civic project to establish a new English commonwealth in America. Company leaders argued that colonists needed to abandon the search for quick riches in favor of collective labor on defenses and food supplies.[14] As Johnson's *Nova Britannia*, published amid this reorganization, attests, they believed that this would require a new commitment to establishing "capitall townes," but they also recognized that these places would have a different structure and character than they had initially envisioned for Jamestown. A flood of new promotional literature, which the company targeted at potential new shareholders across England, drew new classical humanist connections between urban space and martial virtue. Robert Gray, in *A Good*

Speed to Virginia (1609), compared the colony to the famously militaristic, anticommercial city-state of Sparta. In a 1609 sermon preached at the departure of the colony's new governor, Lord De La Warr, William Crashaw likened Virginia to the establishment of Rome, emphasizing not the city's long republican heritage, but the efficacy of imperial Rome's "strict forme of government, and severe discipline." In the Virginia Company's 1610 promotional tract, *A True Declaration of the Estate of the Colonie in Virginia*, company leaders reminded readers that "Tacitus hath observed, that when Nero sent his old trained souldiers to Tarantum and Autium (but without their Captains and Centurians) that they rather made a number, then a Colony: euery souldier secretly glided into some neighbour Province, and forsook their appointed places: which hatched this consequent mischeife; the Cities were uninhabited." For the company leadership, classical history demonstrated that there was a symbiotic relationship among civic order, martial law, and populous cities.[15]

Emulating Rome and Sparta in Virginia would require restructuring the colony's settlement pattern. Acting governor Sir Thomas Gates was instructed to divide the surviving colonists and the first batch of new planters, who were dispatched in 1609, into three fortified towns—Jamestown, Henricus, and Kecoughtan—"over every one of wch," the company insisted, "you must appointe a discreete Comaunder that shall sett yor men to severall workes" on common land belonging to the whole community. The colony's new leaders were also instructed to draft a new code of martial law, which became known as the *Lawes Divine, Moral, and Martial*, that compelled colonists to labor and discipline by threatening execution for even minor infractions.[16] Crucially, however, this legal structure was predicated upon the new garrison towns, with instructions being directed to the "governor" of each settlement and a requirement that "the Governor never lie out of [his] Towne or Fort whereby hee may the better keepe good espial upon all officers." The emphasis on a military governor in each place demonstrated that these were not to be open commercial centers, but the instructions still made clear that they were to be towns. Gates's instructions also reiterated the requirement that "every streete may answere one another," implying an orderly town plan, but now the centerpiece of the plan could be a "Storehowse" instead of a marketplace, implying a more centralized and less commercially oriented vision.[17]

When Gates and Lord De La Warr, the colony's new governor, reached Virginia almost simultaneously in 1610 (Gates having been shipwrecked on Bermuda for six months), they immediately began to focus on restructuring Jamestown. Most buildings inside the fortifications were razed and new structures were erected. The following year, an influx of new colonists arrived and helped to establish the "City of Henricus" just below the falls of the James River; others were sent to reinforce Kecoughtan, at the tip of the James-York peninsula. Though these new foundations were aggressive moves in the struggle against the Powhatan, the settlements were still consistently described in urban terms. Ralph Hamor described Henricus as an orderly town with "3 streets of well framed howses, a hansom Church, and the foundation of a more stately one laid . . . beside Store houses, watch houses, and such like." This report suggested that the new town, and the martial civic vision that underpinned it, provided precisely the kind of structure that Virginia had been lacking.[18]

Dividing Virginia's population into fortified towns had advantages in the face of persistent food shortages and ongoing war with the Powhatan, and so it is tempting to see the company's persistent focus on compact settlement as pure pragmatism.[19] However, the decisions on the ground in Virginia during these years cannot be disentangled from the rhetoric of the classical military city-states that underpinned the company's 1609 reorganization. Urban space provides the key connection between the realm of evolving humanist ideas in London and practical realities in Virginia. The form, structure, and function of urban spaces were a barometer of ideas about the balance between commercial opportunity and the common good. With nothing to show for the company's earliest commercial hopes for trade, precious metals, or a route to the East, and in the midst of war with the Powhatan, that balance had shifted toward a martial civic model. Virginia's urban spaces were no longer the "great cities" initially envisioned by the company but rather garrison cities where virtue was manifest in military service. The city, though, remained the critical framework through which these different valences of civic humanism were negotiated and implemented.

BERMUDA CITY AND ARGALL TOWN

The garrison city model of the early 1610s successfully stabilized the Virginia enterprise. However, military discipline did little to encourage experimentation with new crops or industries, and so profit from the colony remained elusive; it also gave Virginia a grim reputation in England. The early 1610s were years of order but also of stagnation. New reports published in London felt compelled to plead with company shareholders to "persist with alacritie and cherrefulnesse" in their investment.[20] Nevertheless, by 1614, leaders on both sides of the Atlantic increasingly concluded that the colonial commonwealth needed to be redesigned once again. Instead of the unanimous change of direction that occurred in 1609, though, this reassessment led to starkly divergent visions of the colony's future, organized around either a commercial monopoly, a system of large manorial land grants, or a local corporate structure. All of these plans, though, remained thoroughly predicated upon an urban structure for the colony. Thus, towns and cities form the basis of a common discourse that helps demonstrate the coherence of these divergent plans and the true stakes over which Virginia's planners and planters battled in the second half of the 1610s.

The first efforts to address Virginia's lingering economic stagnation arose in the Chesapeake itself. Governor Thomas Dale, who had enforced martial law since his arrival in the colony in 1610, had begun to doubt its effectiveness. In June 1613, he wrote to company leaders complaining that despite his strictness he still struggled to make men work for the common good: "My heart bleeds," he exclaimed, "when I think what men we have here." Dale's solution was to found a new kind of urban community. He selected a group of the most experienced colonists and relocated them to a site at the mouth of the Appomattox River, just downriver from Henricus, which he formally incorporated as Bermuda City. The exact terms of the new city's charter have not survived, but it contained a clearly defined cohort of corporate citizens (numbering seventeen by 1616) and a hierarchy of offices. In 1615, Ralph Hamor described Bermuda City's corporate patent as a dramatic political innovation and "a businesse of greatest hope, ever begunne in our Territories there."[21]

Dale's corporate plan was part of an effort to encourage new commerce and industry without imperiling the colony's orderly structure. Beginning in 1613, Dale had experimented with granting certain colonists individual small plots of land to cultivate, freeing them from communal labor in the company's fields and encouraging individual industry. By the following year, the few surviving colonists who had arrived on the first voyages in 1607 were reaching the end of their seven-year contractual service to the Virginia Company, and Dale was under increasing pressure to expand the privatization of land for these individuals. Following a peace treaty with the Powhatan in 1614, the colonists also had greater freedom to occupy land. Rather than issuing a wave of private land grants that would disperse the colony's planters across the region, though, Dale pursued a corporate model as the most appropriate way of binding free, landholding individuals within the bonds of the colony's commonwealth. The corporate structure tied all new grants of private land to a continued collective commitment to public property and shared agriculture; the corporation received a grant of "many miles of Champion [open level ground], and woodland," much of which was to remain in common ownership, and each citizen was expected to hire two newly arrived company servants to support the larger civic objective of peopling and cultivating these public lands. Dale likely saw the grant of a large common acreage to the citizens at Bermuda City as an important part of fostering civic bonds within their new community of private landowners. These civic bonds were also manifest in the new city's system of self-government, with its hierarchy of corporate officers. John Rolfe, in his survey of the colony's organization in 1616, confirmed the significance of Bermuda City's structure. He described each of the town's in the colony, noting who "hath the commaund" in each place and emphasizing that martial civic order still held in much of Virginia, but after explaining the details of the Bermuda City charter, he pointedly wrote that Deputy Governor George Yeardley "for the most part liveth" in Bermuda City and did not mention anyone in "command" at the corporation.[22]

Although Dale himself left no account of his precise rationale for establishing Bermuda City, a proposal for a similar scheme developed practically simultaneously for the English plantation in Ulster illuminates the logic and vision behind Dale's actions. Thomas Blenerhasset, in *A Direction for the Plantation in Ulster* (1610), sought to address the same problems of high costs and sluggish profits that plagued the Virginia enterprise. His solution was to unleash private interests, because "this word Myne is a strong warrior, every man for his owne will adventure farre." However, Blenerhasset cautioned against simply granting free land to English planters, because private landowners would lack the capacity for their own defense and therefore needed public works; instead he proposed gathering the "scattered plantation" into corporate towns that could muster "at any time at an houres warning with five hundred men well armed." Holding this community together required a governor "of wisdom, wealth, and authoritie, such as wil be obeyed," but also a corporate community where "all the undertakers have recourse unto the consultations [because] the meanest may sometimes bring foorth a necessary knowledge." As Phil Withington has demonstrated, Blenerhasset was drawing upon the example of English city commonwealths as a model for the pursuit of the common good in the plantation context, allowing regulation of private enterprise and collective defense. Blenerhasset's pamphlet was published after Dale's departure for Virginia, and there is little reason to suppose that he read it, but the similarities to Bermuda City suggest that both men were drawing from English corporate civic culture and applying these political and economic ideals to the difficult realities of establishing new colonial communities that were both stable and profitable.[23]

While Dale was developing his plan for Bermuda City in the mid-1610s, company officials in London were also reevaluating Virginia's commercial potential. The cultivation of tobacco had begun turning a profit in Bermuda, and John Rolfe had cultivated similar strains in Virginia, so with the onset of peace between the planters and the Powhatan, company stockholders finally began to see the potential for a return on their decadelong investments through tobacco production and Indian trade. To ensure that these long-awaited profits would be shared in an orderly fashion between all investors, instead of being spirited away by private merchants, the company leadership established, for the first time, a formal monopoly over Virginia's trade. This monopoly would be exercised through a subsidiary company, known as the Magazine, with agents in each of Virginia's cities. In theory everyone would receive a fair price for their crops, the supply of necessary manufactured goods from England would be guaranteed, and investors would receive modest profits, all managed through the colony's urban hubs.[24] Like Dale's Bermuda plan, the Magazine scheme located authority within a corporate structure, but the Magazine differed from Bermuda City in that its corporate structure embraced the whole colony and was located in London rather than in the colony itself. Monopolies were controversial in early Stuart England, and some contemporaries saw them as naked state-sponsored corruption.[25] However, the Crown envisioned the monopoly trading privileges of a joint-stock company as a reward for the civic and governmental functions that the company fulfilled on behalf of the state. Similarly, we should not assume that all contemporaries viewed the Magazine as purely an effort at commercial exploitation. For some, it represented a corporate conceptualization of how Virginia's trade could be managed to ensure an equitable distribution of resources, a stable social order, and continued funding for the colony's public projects.[26]

The Bermuda City corporation and the Magazine monopoly were not necessarily mutually incompatible, but their ability to coexist was never fully tested because by early 1617 both plans were being challenged by Samuel Argall, who had replaced Dale as the colony's leader. Argall was a ship captain with extensive experience in Virginia—he had been instrumental in perfecting a faster sailing route to the colony and also in forcing the Powhatan to negotiate the peace treaty of 1614. When he returned to England in 1616, though, he was distinctly unhappy with the reforms that Dale had implemented. He successfully lobbied the company to transform

Dale's system by establishing large landed estates and granting their owners extensive power to organize settlement, enforce law, and control trade. Argall and one of his close allies, the veteran planter John Martin, were unsurprisingly the first to receive these generous land grants that came with a form of land tenure equal to that of "any lord of any manours in England."[27] Argall's success in pitching this plan was likely a reflection of the growing influence of his patron, the militant-Protestant privateer the Earl of Warwick, within the company. The company leaders may also have agreed to the proposals because of their dire financial situation; they were in no position to pay seven-year dividends that had been promised in 1609, and so granting estates was an easy way to discharge debts. Furthermore, they had recently developed a similar system of large landed estates for Virginia's sister colony, Bermuda, where tobacco agriculture had firmly taken hold and the plantation project seemed to be advancing with far greater speed and success.[28] Regardless of the motive, though, it was clear that Argall's vision for large manorial estates and settlement arranged around personal patronage was a direct challenge to Dale's urban corporate plan.

When Argall returned to Virginia in 1617 as both acting governor and new manorial landlord, he immediately implemented his plan by undermining Dale's corporate model. He singled out Bermuda City when he wrote that Virginia was in a "ruinous condicon" because of the "carelessness of ye people & lawless living"; within three weeks of his arrival, he had relocated most of the Bermuda residents who were still company servants back to Jamestown. Those who remained on Bermuda City's lands were transferred to the command of one of Argall's deputies. In response, nine of the citizens, led by the "Recorder" (the title of the senior legal officer of an English corporate borough), penned a complaint against the governor for expropriating land "belonging to them." Their protest reflected how seriously they took their status as an urban corporate community, but it did them little good. Four months later, Argall decided to dismantle Bermuda City's corporate structure entirely and return it to its status under the *Lawes Divine, Moral, and Martial* by commissioning a military provost marshal to govern the city in the same way as Virginia's other settlements. Despite the fact that the colony was now at peace with the Powhatan, he argued that "in all places of Warrs and Garrison Towns it [martial law] is most Expedient and necessary."[29]

Over the next year, Argall replaced the corporate model with his own vision for the colony, structured around towns and hinterlands governed by personal patronage. He quickly began developing his large personal estate around Argall Town, on the site of the former Paspahegh village near Jamestown. He quickly relocated company assets to his new town, including cattle, servants, and free colonists whom he bound through extensive debt obligations. He erected housing in a compact community that would lay the basis for a private town peopled by tenants and surrounded by land under his personal control. Furthermore, having already undermined the Bermuda corporation, Argall also lobbied against the Magazine monopoly, in order to channel the agricultural output of Argall Town and the supply of English goods for his tenants through his private network of ship captains and merchants.[30]

Just as with Dale's corporate plan for Bermuda City, we can understand Argall's objectives for Argall Town by looking at contemporary experiences in Ulster, where the corporate model had also been challenged by an individual patronage system. By 1611, the Privy Council was concerned about the slow progress in implementing an urban corporate plan in Ulster, and they changed the process of incorporation; instead of relying upon the coalescing of communities of English settlers, the responsibility for urbanizing Ulster was given to servitors (the holders of large new landed estates). These rural landholders, who had already taken up grants across Ulster, were to site and build the urban infrastructure in place of corporate communities themselves. Servitors were given wide-ranging powers as superintendents over the towns and were expected to attract sufficient population to justify incorporation within four years. Even among those towns that did transition to corporate governance, though, many of the appointed officers of the new corporations retained personal ties to the previous superintendent. Moreover, the servitors retained the vast majority of the common land allocated to the communities, making the new towns dependent upon rural gentry who controlled the agriculture that generated wealth, rather than being landlords in their own right. This Ulster experience demonstrated that there was a credible alternative to the corporate city commonwealth model for the establishment of towns—a model that made a gentry patron the overseer of infrastructure and development and the guarantor of the public good.[31]

It is easy to dismiss Argall as a tyrannical military commander selfishly lining his own pockets at the dawn of Virginia's tobacco boom, but reducing his governorship in this way obscures the genuine debate ongoing within the colony and the company about the best way to structure commerce and maintain political order. Argall used new land grants from the company to build not simply a private estate but also a new urban community under his patronage that would transform the colony's spatial and political order. Archaeological evidence and scant documentary records suggest that Argall Town was a well-organized and well-built town. That Argall faced a vicious backlash was a product of the fact that his model attracted principled opposition. Some of his opponents, when considering the situation at Argall Town, may have been reminded of the argument by the famous English humanist writer Sir Thomas Smith that if a landlord had "five thousande or ten thousande bondmen whom he ruled well, though they dwelled all in one citie, or were distributed into diverse villages, yet that were no common wealth: for the bondman hath no communion with his master, the wealth of the Lord is onely sought for, and not the profit of the slave or bondman." Sir Edwin Sandys made this precise point about the dangers of dependence and the erosion of common interests when he decried Argall for despoiling the colony's "publique." Although evidence about the character of Argall Town is thin, in the context of the governor's confrontation with Bermuda and his rejection of the Magazine, it appears that he was using the town to construct an alternate vision of Virginia's balance between commerce and order.[32]

Bermuda City, Argall Town, and the Magazine represented distinct ways to structure a new commercial agricultural commonwealth. These competing urban plans reveal that developments in Virginia during the 1610s were directly informed by transatlantic political debates and that actors on the ground in Virginia framed their actions to contribute to this discourse. Proponents of the three rival ideals drew from contemporary English debates about commerce and corporate order, they clashed on the ground in the James River valley in 1617, and they ultimately laid the groundwork for a radical reorganization of the company over the next few years.

THE "GREATE CHARTER" AND THE CORPORATE BOROUGHS

By late 1617, complaints about Argall's conduct in Virginia had drawn a new group of investors into active involvement with Virginia Company business. This new group, led by the prominent parliamentarian Sir Edwin Sandys, fundamentally reimagined the Virginia venture over the next three years by building upon Dale's corporate plan for Bermuda City and establishing corporate city commonwealths across the colony. They articulated this new vision as a basis for "a flourishing State" with "a laudable form of Government by Majestracy and just Laws" in the instructions drafted for Sir George Yeardley, who was dispatched to replace Argall in

November 1618. Contemporaries, grasping the import of the reforms, christened the instructions as the "greate Charter" for Virginia. Ever since, the instructions have been famous for ordering the gathering of the first Virginia General Assembly and for facilitating the first major wave of private land grants. Fundamentally, though, Yeardley's instructions were about the organization of Virginia's urban spaces. They were a direct response to the debate about Dale's and Argall's rival urban plans. Their vision for political and commercial order cannot be understood apart from the specifically urban foundations upon which it was built. The company's new leadership committed to the idea that a series of self-governing city commonwealths would provide the basis for land distribution and political authority. Understanding the "great charter" in this way reveals both the radicalism of Sandys's plan and its inherent weaknesses, both of which ultimately laid the foundation for private plantation agriculture.[33]

Sir Edwin Sandys was steeped in the corporate civic humanist tradition, and this informed the way he perceived the company's troubles in the mid-1610s. Sandys was a prominent MP who defended the rights of Parliament, and the boroughs that constituted it, against James I during the first two decades of the seventeenth century. During his leadership of the Virginia Company, he was active in representing the Kent port town of Sandwich in Parliament, defending the particular rights of its citizens; Sandwich had a particularly rich civic heritage as part of the league of "cinque ports" along the coast of the English Channel that had long had a distinct identity and special privileges.[34] Given Sandys's experience and outlook, it is hardly surprising that, even before he became the company's treasurer (chief officer), he had been inspired by the accounts of Bermuda City. John Rolfe, during his visit to England in 1616, had provided company leaders with details about the incorporation of Bermuda City, and before he returned to the colony, Sandys prevailed upon him to pen the only surviving account of Bermuda City's corporate structure. Furthermore, it was upon receiving Rolfe's account in 1616 that the company first advertised their intention to distribute shares of land to investors "all about the new Townes now erected," and Sandys was among the leading investors in one of these new ventures. Sandys's frustration with the way Argall subverted these plans and frustrated his own aspirations to establish a corporate borough in Virginia played a critical role in encouraging him to take a more active role in the governance of the company. The experience of Bermuda City was clearly foundational to the way he thought about the colony; his close ally Nicholas Ferrar recalled many years later that Argall's governorship had been marked with "intolerable oppression and injustices" that had driven the planters to "adopted to themselves each *Burrough* their severall Patrons as in way of protection against this Government." It was these boroughs, acting as self-conscious political communities, that resonated with Sandys and his allies, and it was the rights of these communities that they felt compelled to protect.35

The struggle between Argall and Bermuda City was the clear subtext behind the company's dramatic 1618 reforms. In the autumn of 1618, before he became treasurer, Sandys led the effort to have Sir George Yeardley replace Samuel Argall as governor, and he was primary author of the famous instructions issued to Yeardley. As the instructions make clear, Sandys's first priority was to protect what remained of the urban corporate structures that Dale had put in place. Yeardley was strictly cautioned to guard against those (almost certainly meaning Argall) who "for gain and Worse respects [aimed] to draw many of the ancient Planters of the said four Cities or Burroughs" away from their communities or infringed their corporate rights. The selection of Yeardley, the most senior official to have resided at Bermuda, as the new governor also represented Sandys's conscious effort to find a leader well versed in and sympathetic to the corporate urban model.36

Yeardley's instructions were primarily about extending the Bermuda City model to the whole colony. The number of incorporated "Cities or Burroughs" was quadrupled as Bermuda City (now called Charles City) was joined by corporations for Jamestown, Henrico, and Kiccowtan (later renamed Elizabeth City). Drawing upon the experience at Bermuda City, these newly incorporated towns were to control the shift toward privatized landholding. Individual planters who had completed their service to the company were each granted one hundred acres of land, but these grants were tied to one of the company's incorporated boroughs, and grantees would be required to be members of that corporate community. The first individual grantees, William Fairefax and his wife, Margery, were described as "of James Cittie" and were granted two hundred acres on the condition that twelve acres would be held around his "Mansion house" in Jamestown.37

The corporations were to guard against the conflict and competition that might arise with private landownership by balancing these private estates with large grants of public land. Yeardley was instructed to lay out 4,500 acres of public land in each corporation. This land would be rented to new colonists who would be transported to Virginia, generating an income for the corporation that would pay local officials and the costs of building new infrastructure, and also support other projects such as a college for educating Indians; in the process, new arrivals would have access to land ready for cultivation and preexisting communities to integrate within. This public land was entrusted to the management of the new corporate bodies, whose officers would be supported by the income they generated. Using rental profits to fund the expenses of governance also liberated offices from dependence on taxes that risked making them beholden to particular planter interests. Steady accumulation of common property in Elizabethan corporate boroughs had underpinned the flourishing of urban political culture in England, encouraging corporate leaders to erect new infrastructure and assert their independent political identity. Corporate common land in theory also helped to provide each corporation's citizens with a shared stake in community resources, incentivizing a commitment to the common good even among planters now farming their own estates and providing resources to test new crops and industries that they could not afford to sponsor alone. Sandys made the balance of public and private explicit, explaining that "the maintaining of the publiq in all estates" was "of noe lesse importance, even for the benefit of the Private, then the roote and body of a Tree are to the perticuler branches." Common land would secure corporate communities and foster civic virtue freed from "all occasion of oppression and corruption," even as the colony shifted to commercial tobacco agriculture.[38]

The new vision of urban common land was not limited to the company's four corporate boroughs. Another key part of the company's reform plans was to invite groups of Virginia investors to pool their resources to patent large new grants termed "particular plantations." These particular plantations could be wholly owned by groups of private investors, but they were also intended to become new boroughs with independent political identities rather than merely vast agricultural estates. Each particular plantation was required to send colonists (both free planters and servants) to settle as a compact community that would eventually receive its own corporate charter; thus, while capital and coordination would be provided by a group of private investors, and profits would flow directly back to them, the particular plantations were to eventually become independent corporate boroughs of Virginia on a par with the four company corporate boroughs. To this end, each new particular plantation was also promised an additional free endowment of "fifteen hundred Acres of Borough Land for the public use," just as the existing company boroughs received. No new landowners in the redesigned Virginia venture were to be free from commitment to their local commonwealth and the "public use" of the land on which it was built.[39]

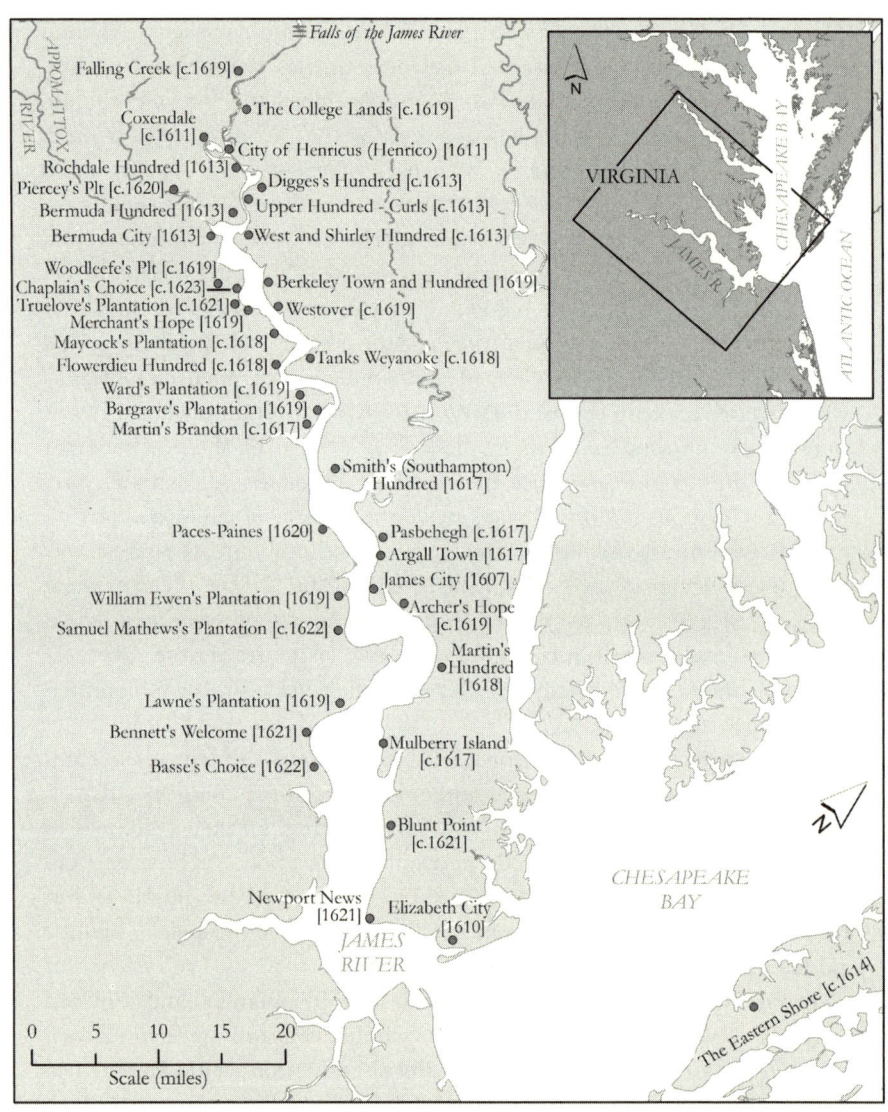

1.1 Map of plantations in Virginia under the Virginia Company
This map shows the locations of all the plantations established during the period of Virginia Company governance, including those established by the company and by private groups of investors. Many of these settlements were destroyed or abandoned after the Powhatan assault in March 1622. (Adapted from J. Frederick Fausz, "Patterns of Settlement in the James River Basin, 1607–1642" [MA thesis, College of William and Mary, 1971], and Martha McCartney, *Virginia Immigrants and Adventurers, 1607–1635: A Biographical Dictionary* [Baltimore: Genealogical Publishing Company, 2007], 30–31, and in consultation with James Horn.)

This urban corporate structure for landownership was clearly articulated in the new wave of promotional literature intended to attract new planters and investors after 1618. Pamphlets emphasized the potential for landownership but always paired it with the stability of corporate life. One account, penned in autumn 1618, proclaimed that the company's revised plans for Virginia addressed the prior misgivings of potential investors because they "infranchise the fower townes allready in being, & all other plantations begun, or heereafter to bee erected, into corporations, under the name of burroughs or citties. Then they allotte the same corporations into publique landes, not only for the use of the company heere in Englande, but also for the maintenance as well of the magistrates & officers, as of the ministers belonging to the said corporations. Lastly they sett downe what landes or im[m]unities every p[er]son is presently to enioye, according to there merritt and quality, & what duties they are tyed to."[40] Provision for private land was portrayed as an outgrowth of the corporate system, and not the other way around. Corporate order also preceded land distribution in the company's 1620 promotional tract, *A Declaration of the State of the Colonie and Affaires in Virginia*, which explained that "the people are all diuided into seuerall Burroughs; each man hauing the shares of Land due to him." The company's new pitch was not about attracting investors in search of cheap land; it was intended to appeal to those familiar with the rights and representative structures of early modern England. The distribution of private land, so critical to the development of tobacco agriculture over the next generation in Virginia, was thus predicated upon this civic vision.[41]

The corporations' responsibility for cultivating participatory citizenship and civic virtue was most firmly underscored by Yeardley's instructions to establish an assembly in the colony. The new representative body for the whole colony was to consist of delegates chosen from each of the corporate communities (called "burgesses," a term specifically associated with urban citizens). It was intended to be an accretion of the deliberative and participatory process that occurred in each individual borough, just as the corporate towns and cities of England were represented in Parliament; Phil Withington has described the parliamentary enfranchisement of English boroughs as "an expression of the freemen's fictional personality," rather than an individual right belonging to residents of the particular towns that elected MPs. Just as in the majority of these English cases, there is no record of the corporate communities holding ballots to select their representatives for the first General Assembly in 1619; rather the selections were likely made by the corporate leadership in each borough.

Ultimately, it was the corporate community, rather than individual colonists, that was being represented. The famous gathering of the first Virginia General Assembly in Jamestown in 1619 can therefore not be fully understood without an appreciation for the corporate urban communities upon which it was built.[42]

The new corporate urban communities also served as the basis for the colony's new legal structure. Yeardley's instructions explained that incorporation would provide for "just Laws for the happy guiding and governing of the people." All plantations would henceforth be constrained to enforce "equall and like law and orders with the rest of the colony," providing the basis for adoption of English common law in Virginia. Incorporated boroughs would facilitate the practice of common law by creating communities capable of mustering juries of local peers, but also establish local by-laws. A later articulation of the corporations' legal powers explained that they had liberty "to frame and make orders ordinances and constitucons" and that this authority belonged not just to the original investors in private plantations but also to the corporate body, including "the people there inhabiting under them." The creation of an urban corporate structure for Virginia was intended, therefore, to secure a uniform legal system in the colony and to anchor this legal code in a participatory model of corporate citizenship.[43]

In spring 1620, Sandys and his allies in the company's new leadership demonstrated even greater faith in the legal capacity of Virginia's new corporate commonwealths when they abolished the Magazine's trading monopoly. The new company leadership were eager to undermine the Magazine. It had been criticized for supplying poor-quality goods at inflated prices. Sandys was also one of the leading opponents of Crown monopolies in Parliament, arguing that they placed individual private interests and Crown patronage above the common good. The decision, though, was not a vote of confidence in unregulated free trade and protoliberalism. In removing the monopoly, Sandys was trusting instead in the regulatory capacity of the local corporate system in Virginia to guard against the threat posed by an equally feared source of corruption, free trade. As civic societies with common economic interests, corporations were now expected to monitor and administer their marketplaces just as English boroughs did through their marketplace courts, known as "courts of piepowder." The immediate context for the removal of the Magazine's monopoly demonstrates the connection to the corporate structure. At the February 1620 Virginia Company meeting in which the Magazine monopoly was ended, investors also agreed to allow citizens of particular plantations to draft ordinances for "the better orderinge and dyrectinge of their Servants and buisines" to fill the regulatory void. A few months later, company leaders pushed to further empower the corporations by establishing a committee headed by the London corporation's recorder, Sir Robert Heath, to "frame out" the "pticularr Governmt by way of Incorporacon for every Cittie and Burrough." While they awaited the committee's report, company leaders wrote to the Virginia Council to insist that "the Markett be open for all men" but warned them not to take advantage of this freedom, noting that the "oppression and grinding of the poore wee in or hearts abhor, and require youe severely to punishe."[44]

Company leaders quickly recognized, though, that in order to make this new system of local urban regulation work, Virginia's economy would need to become more diversified. The process of corporate regulation common to English boroughs was predicated upon the balancing of interests among merchants, craftsmen, and local farmers. This system was less effective in Virginia, where everyone turned to tobacco production in the late 1610s and was therefore in direct competition. Planters were not in a position to control prices or the terms of labor contracts in the face of cutthroat competition for what might be the last few clothes or tools from the season's merchant convoy. This culture of competition in the planters' economy would become a consistent civic concern for a century. It created incentives for well-placed individuals to make private deals with merchants; it also encouraged these established colonists to exploit new immigrants.[45] Sandys and his allies were well aware of these problems, and they acted to address them by working to diversify the colony's economy beyond tobacco, in order to make local urban market regulation more effective by peopling each corporate community with diverse interest groups. The company's leaders endorsed ambitious schemes for iron, silk, and wine production, and this has been characterized as a desperate effort to supplement the company's revenue, but they also made a particular point of sending out quotidian craftsmen, such as blacksmiths, carpenters, and potters, who would provide a domestic market to balance transatlantic trading interests. Investors in the private plantation boroughs also sent large numbers of craftsmen and artisans to their settlements. Deputy Governor Yeardley's instructions specifically provided urban land grants to artisans (not to large-scale manufactories for the production of new exports), and the company insisted that they be kept to their trade and not lured away to plant tobacco. The point of this diversification was not primarily to fill the company's coffers, but to drive people away from the booming tobacco trade, because, as Robert Gray had earlier explained in *A Good*

Speed to Virginia, "without Artificers and tradesmen a common-wealth cannot flourish nor endure."[46]

The clearest evidence of the Virginia Company's practical faith in the new borough corporations came through elaborate plans for erecting "guesthouses" in each borough. In an effort to populate the new city commonwealths, Sandys and his allies embarked on an ambitious plan to transport thousands of new planters (including a large contingent of women for the first time) to serve as tenants on corporate land and make it productive. Guesthouses, first envisioned in 1620, were a response to the lack of facilities that had greeted the initial wave of these migrants. They were the ultimate symbol of how new laborers were supposed to be employed under the corporate system. The new houses were to be the colony's most significant public works projects, each accommodating fifty tenants until the new arrivals could build their own housing. From the company's perspective, their construction provided the perfect opportunity for corporate city commonwealths to sacrifice for the common good. In a printed broadside in May 1620, company leaders proposed that the "ancient generall Burroughs" should each erect a guesthouse "at their common charge, labour, and industry." To emphasize the project as a test of the boroughs' nascent civic virtue and a break from martial law, they explicitly refrained from forcing colonists to contribute to the construction because they preferred to "try the love of the Colony, [rather] than their obedience by command." The dispatch of waves of new migrants who would lay the basis for the tobacco plantation labor system over the next two years was therefore actually predicated upon the assumption of urban civic corporate oversight.[47]

Counter to their image as greedy opportunists, most of the people who took up the company's new offer also believed in the corporate vision. Officers in the company's four main boroughs took their duties seriously. Homes and palisades were erected, and some progress was made on public projects; one of the planned guesthouses had been erected in Henrico by 1621.[48] New investors in particular plantations also seized the opportunity of the corporate plan. A group of Gloucestershire investors, whose plans for a particular plantation are uniquely well documented, bear this out. They agreed with the company "to transport at their owne cost and charges divers psons into Virginia, And there to erect and build a Towne" and within seven years to give it "letters and grants of incorporacon." The investors instructed the first contingent of planters to "erect and build a towne to be called Barkley" and to establish rituals and local offices to strengthen the corporate bonds of the town. The instructions carefully distinguished

1.2 Richard Schlecht, Wolstenholme Towne as it may have looked prior to March 22, 1622
Wolstenholme Town was intended to serve as the urban core of the particular plantation of Martin's Hundred. The layout and character of the site have been revealed through extensive archaeological excavations. (Courtesy of the Colonial Williamsburg Foundation and Richard Schlecht/National Geographic Creative.)

between the borough of Berkeley and the surrounding hinterland that the investors named Berkeley Hundred, suggesting that these spaces would have distinct political identities; they also told the first planters to enclose four hundred acres of land, as part of the common borough allocation of fifteen hundred acres. The Berkeley records make clear that the founders modeled their plantation on an English city commonwealth.[49]

The chance to construct corporate civic societies also appealed strongly to radical religious elements in England (who did not yet have an outlet in New England). The Virginia project had always been partly informed by a providential dream of building a perfected Protestant society in the New World, but the corporate plan was ideally suited to attract colonists who shared this radical vision. Puritans were disproportionately represented in English corporate boroughs during this era, and they embraced the independence and authority that urban charters afforded them, so it made sense that they would be attracted by the corporate provisions of Sandys's plan. A number of puritan leaders saw the company's corporate plan as an opportunity to create new religious and civic communities; one, Christopher Lawne, was a leader of the English separatist church in the Netherlands, who brought 110 colonists to establish a particular plantation named Lawnes Creek, at a site just downriver from Jamestown. Sandys's plan was even responsible for attracting the most famous group of radical religious exiles in early America, the *Mayflower* pilgrims, who initially intended to establish a community within the bounds of the Virginia colony.[50]

All of this radical political experimentation was tightly intertwined with the economic transformation that tobacco agriculture was bringing to Virginia during these same years. By 1620, tobacco production had exploded, new waves of immigrants were disembarking each year (often to face privation, hard labor, and an early grave), and planters were finally beginning to make money. The private land, free trade, and bound labor on which this system was built, though, were all products of the carefully crafted program of civic reforms. Tobacco was not pioneered on isolated rural estates. The Virginia of the tobacco boom was structured around four self-governing city commonwealths and a few dozen new communities that were envisioned as future corporate boroughs. This urban vision emerged from the same culture, appealed to the same people, and wrestled with the same challenge of maintaining civic virtue and communal bonds in a commercial commonwealth that we normally associate with the New England town. It was this urban structure that rationalized the distribution of land, legitimized the liberalization of trade, and facilitated the influx of bound labor. These changes did end up laying the foundations for an exploitative system of plantation agriculture, but they were initially part of a coherent vision for the future of the colony that was wrestling with, rather than bowing to, the potential of commercial development. New immigrants and industries were intended to support the re-creation of Virginia as a network of city commonwealths that would help to balance order with economic opportunity and provide a civic structure for a commercial colonial venture. That Sandys and his allies did not succeed in fully implementing their plan was the result of a series of military, political, and ideological shocks that rocked Virginia and England in the early 1620s.

BACKLASH AGAINST THE CORPORATE BOROUGHS

The failure of Sandys's corporate vision was not a foregone conclusion. The colony certainly struggled, as it would for a century, to find alternative export commodities to diversify its economy, and colonists suffered from startlingly high mortality rates. Far more devastating was the March 1622 Powhatan attack that killed nearly 350 colonists and wiped out many of the colony's nascent boroughs. It is undeniable that these disasters in Virginia were severe blows to Sandys's vision, but his commitment did not waver, and the company planned to rebuild on the urban corporate foundations after 1622. That they did not get this chance was primarily because the urban corporate vision came in for sharp critique in the colony and in England during the early 1620s, which undermined their leadership and ultimately encouraged the Crown to rescind the company's charter in 1624. The Virginia Company's dysfunction during these years has long been viewed as a product of bitter personal rivalries. The personal acrimony, however, was rooted in this broader battle over the appropriateness of the urban corporate plan for securing order, defense, and profit in Virginia.[51]

Within the colony, some of the fundamental features of the urban corporate plan were quickly challenged and adapted. The extensive acreages available in early Virginia meant that the limited supply of laborers, rather than land, constrained tobacco production; labor was the true measure of wealth. With so many opportunities to acquire land, tenancy was an unattractive option for free colonists. As a result, the vision of common land farmed by tenants providing an endowment for each city commonwealth could not succeed without a persistent supply of new men and women compelled to serve as tenants.[52] The delegates reviewing the "great Charter" in 1619 understood these problems, and they implored the company to "sende men hither to occupie their landes belonging to the fower Incorporations, as well for their owne behoofe and proffitt as for the maintenance of the Counsel of Estate." Only once they had seen this influx of manpower, they implied, would they go to the effort of formalizing the corporate constitutions that it would support. Sandys readily complied with these entreaties, but the result was a glut of ill-prepared immigrants who quickly succumbed to disease. The vision of tenants bound to the public land of particular urban corporations gradually shifted to a model of servitude on the estate of an established planter, followed by freedom (for those who survived) to settle wherever they could patent ground. This shift was partly driven by colonial leaders' self-serving improvisation, but it was still framed as a conscious engagement with the corporate plan. Virginia leaders were very explicit about the fact that servitude was designed to address the shortcomings of the corporate model and thus shore up its foundations. Late in 1621, Captain Christopher Newce, who led the corporation of Elizabeth City, proposed converting the company's tenants to servants who would be sold to cover their transportation costs and (supposedly) improve their survival rates, before being transferred back to the company's lands as established tenants. Newce claimed that his plan would "restore the fier in the hartes of the Adventurers." Company officials in London rejected the proposal, but planters on the ground continued to strengthen the system of servitude and pull it further from the structures that Sandys had envisioned.[53]

The most serious blow to Virginia's corporate boroughs, though, was struck by the Powhatan chief Opechancanough and his men on March 22, 1622. The Powhatan launched a coordinated attack, killing 347 planters in a single morning. Seven of the eighteen boroughs, particularly those in the upper James region, were totally destroyed, including Henrico and Bermuda City. The assault obviously completely stalled the development of many of the colony's corporate boroughs, and it neutered the optimistic development even in the places that survived.[54]

At the same time, the assault raised philosophical questions on both sides of the Atlantic about the appropriateness of Sandys's urban corporate model. Faced with the difficult task of defending his remaining colonists against further Powhatan attacks, Francis Wyatt, who had succeeded George Yeardley as governor, quickly concluded that the colony's future lay in a return to a military model. He concentrated the survivors in Jamestown under military discipline. This plan, though, brought him into conflict with company leaders in London, who vociferously rejected a return to military-style governance. The company instead insisted that the colonists repopulate the corporate boroughs. This was, they argued, the method "most effectuall for the engageing of this State, and securing of Virginia." They certainly did not favor dispersed settlement—explicitly warning against the dangers of "inordinate straggling"—but they believed that concentration under military, rather than corporate, rule would undermine their first priority, which was to reestablish the civic virtue that would encourage planters to defend their communities.[55] The response of Wyatt and his council in Virginia showed how close, and yet how far apart, their conceptions of urban community were. The council wrote that they had "Carefully repayred the decays of James Cyttie, and invited men to builde theire," and colonists were "Cheerfully" doing so until "your Letters of Dispersinge men againe" that "made every man looke to his privatt [interests]." Before the company's orders were received, they had all agreed "to seate together in two or three great bodyes . . . And noe doupt would have drawne on the building of fortified Townes" had the leaders in London not intervened. Like the officials back in London, the colonial leadership believed urban communities were essential to cultivating civic virtue and bolstering defense, but they had divergent ideas about how exactly their political and social structure achieved these ends. Sandys and his colleagues remained convinced that consensual city commonwealths were key. They even resurrected the plan for building guesthouses. In their view, the selfishness of straggling planters who ignored borough development had led to the colony's weakness to Powhatan attack in the first place. By contrast, Wyatt and his fellow councillors were convinced that fortified towns with rigid military hierarchies were the only way to enforce order and service to the commonwealth in the midst of the new Powhatan war.[56]

While officials argued over the best way to proceed, surviving planters gravitated to the homes of a new class of military leaders who provided defense and a steady supply of food in the midst of war and the subsequent famine. One such figure was William Harwood, who became known as the "Governor" at Martin's Hundred, one of the corporate settlements devastated by the 1622 Powhatan attack. After the attack, Harwood converted the nascent borough into a palisaded home that became the core of his larger agricultural estate. Archaeological evidence suggests that Harwood was not alone—this period saw a significant increase in the number of private palisaded homes. These estates did not emerge fully formed out of the tidewater mud though. They were conscious adaptations of the original corporate structure.[57]

This shift away from the corporate plan and toward individual estates was not an inevitable development though; it would not have gained traction had it not been for challenges to the civic corporate vision back in England. Faced with growing opposition in Parliament, James I and his courtiers were increasingly skeptical of the commonwealth view of the English constitution, and they were particularly concerned about the governing pretensions of corporate boroughs. Commentators, including Lord Chancellor Francis Bacon, argued that corporate citizens were merely private subjects who might be beneficial to the state's commerce, but who had "no aptitude for or claim on the public business of running an empire."[58] Royal skepticism about English corporate authority was dramatically heightened in the early 1620s, when the king perceived that increasing opposition to his policies in Parliament was being driven by MPs, including Sandys, who represented corporate boroughs. When James elected to dissolve Parliament in January 1622, in the face of MPs' harassment of royal courtiers and opposition to his foreign policy, reports began to circulate at court blaming the kingdom's "pettie corporancons" and describing them as lawless "Receptacles for Theeves." Urban civic corporations were becoming the main obstacle to the king's aspirations for increased authority over the realm.[59]

The Crown's budget deficit and the prospect of an expensive European war also pushed the king toward another vision of colonial commercial regulation—through a direct royal monopoly. The granting of monopolies on the production of certain goods, in exchange for hefty payments from the prospective monopolist, was a long-standing and controversial practice. It was, though, a means of bringing commerce more directly under royal control and generating a more guaranteed revenue for the Crown. With the onset of the tobacco boom, reorienting the tobacco trade around an importing monopoly seemed like an obvious way to generate revenue and have the colony serve the needs of the realm, as defined by the king. The Virginia Company's exemption from duties, which had been granted for seven years in 1612, expired in 1619 and opened the possibility for more profitable state regulation and taxation. This was seized upon by Lionel Cranfield, the surveyor general of customs who would soon be appointed Lord High Treasurer. In 1620, the king granted a monopoly to Sir Thomas Roe and his associates, allowing them to control all tobacco imports and collect the mandated duties in exchange for £16,000. The limits this placed upon the Virginia tobacco trade proved very burdensome. By 1622, the company felt compelled to purchase the right to act as the tobacco monopolist, paying the Crown the revenue on one-third of all the tobacco they imported. Sandys and his allies, who had been determined to revoke the Magazine monopoly, were forced to accede to a new retail monopoly under Crown control. The company's desperate efforts to meet this cost, and claims of corruption in the collection of tobacco taxes, provoked Sandys's opponents and helped to further poison relations within the company. Crucially, though, the king's decision to grant the monopoly on tobacco provided further evidence that he was disillusioned with the local civic corporate approach to commercial organization and regulation that the Virginia Company had taken and that he sought to bring more control and profit back to the Crown.[60]

Increasing hostility to urban corporate communities also played a central role in the case that rival factions of Virginia Company investors began to make against Sandys and his allies. The opposition to Sandys and his allies came from two different groups: firstly, the elite London merchants, led by Sir Thomas Smith, who had controlled the company before 1618 and who sought a return to the focus on quick profits for the company's English investors; secondly, the faction built around the puritan adventurer and pirate, the Earl of Warwick, who was keen to redirect the company to focus on attacking the Spanish.[61] Both groups saw the civic corporate plan as an extravagant experiment that undermined their goals, and both recognized that it was a liability in light of shifting royal opinion. They provided a damning drumbeat of evidence against the corporate plan. Barely a year after the corporate plan had been put into practice, one of Warwick's allies in the colony, Secretary John Pory, began to point to its problems; he wrote fatalistically that relying on corporate participatory institutions would fail because whenever planters were asked to contribute to public works, they "repyned as much as yf all their goods had bene taken from them."[62] The inability of most boroughs to defend themselves against the 1622 attack underscored this message about the weakness of the corporate structure. The former governor of Bermuda (and another close ally of Warwick), Nathaniel Butler, made this point in a vitriolic screed titled "The Unmasked Face of our Colony in Virginia." His description of the colony in the aftermath of the attacks painted a vivid picture of the failure of urban civic community: according to Butler, external markers of order, such as well-maintained streets, wharves, and houses, were completely absent. Sandys's opponents in London built upon these vivid images and explained that the company's faith in incorporated boroughs had led them to completely abandon order and defense and caused the colony to degenerate into chaos. This picture played directly to the growing royal perception that corporate communities of merchants and artisans were incapable of truly governing a commonwealth.[63]

Other critics argued that the colony's corporate boroughs were not only ineffectual, but also a threat to Crown authority over the colony. Merchant John Bargrave suggested that the "great Charter" was intended to establish a "free state in Virginia" and pointed out the "mischiefe they [the Sandys faction] have done by their profuse throwinge out libertie." Bargrave's statements were more than wild accusations; he was a humanist scholar who backed up his critique with an alternative model for colonial governance. His proposal included an urban element and even offered cities a degree of self-government, but instead of making them the sole foundation of the commonwealth, he proposed to place the corporate boroughs under the supervision of a landed gentry. Colonists were to be divided into five classes, with the highest-ranking patricians owning land both in England and Virginia, having powers akin to "leiuetenauntes of sheires in England," and also acting as urban patrons; the cities themselves were to be overseen by a hereditary class of mayors and aldermen, who made up the third tier of the social hierarchy. In contrast to Sandys's plan, Bargrave's balance of urban and rural power structures was deliberately intended as a closer approximation of England's own complex political geography—an amalgam of classical and feudal traditions where urban corporations and rural gentry could coexist in salutary tension that would keep them both loyal to the English Crown.[64]

The need to balance, or even replace, the corporate system with a rural gentry became a focus of many critiques of the company in the early 1620s. Not long after Sandys's corporate plan had been launched, the deposed governor Samuel Argall, the former governor Sir Thomas Gates, and other allies of the Earl of Warwick drafted a joint petition claiming that they were "willing & ready" to return to Virginia and invest in the colony, but only if there was a radical change in the colony's organization. They demanded that the colony be placed under the government of men recognized for their "Eminence, or Nobillitye," who would garner the respect necessary to temper the colonists' "vulgar and servile Spiritts." Other proposals from the same period, by Richard Caswell and Sir John Danvers, also suggested establishing a land-owning nobility in the colony.[65] John Martin, the well-connected veteran planter who had received a large manorial estate at the same time as Argall back in 1616, developed his own plan for a rural gentry. Martin had repeatedly resisted efforts to integrate his earlier land grant, an estate known as Martin's Brandon, within the corporate system laid out in Yeardley's instructions. After the Powhatan attack of 1622, Martin felt vindicated, and he began to articulate his own vision for the colony that would involve subjugating the Powhatan and bringing them under the control of a rural gentry. He claimed that the native chiefdom contained thirty-two towns, which was roughly equal to the number of English shires. Given this symmetry, he proposed that each English shire should "send over 100 men a peece to posesse theise 32 sheires . . . undr the Comaund of some Noble Generall." Every English shire would nominate "Justices of peace . . . and other Officers under them as here in England," so the colony's order would be rooted in an established local identity and gentry hierarchy. Martin's plan completely rejected the urban corporate form. The only towns were to be the county seats stolen from the Powhatan ready-made—Martin made no mention of a distinct class of artisans or citizens.[66]

The critiques of Butler, Bargrave, and Martin were not simply the product of petty factionalism; they played into the emerging critique of urban corporate authority that the Crown had inaugurated. The role of corporate governance in Ulster was also under attack in the early 1620s. Ulster investor and landholder Sir Thomas Phillips launched a campaign to expose the failings of London's corporate leadership who had been charged with funding and managing the development of Londonderry and Coleraine and to convince the Crown to revoke London's colonial grant. Phillips's core message was that the corporate model for Londonderry had failed and that it needed to be replaced by direct royal supervision of a system of gentry landownership and urban patronage.[67] During these years, the king also moved away from the corporate model for new colonial projects. James I, and later Charles I, began issuing individual proprietary charters to courtiers, including Sir Ferdinando Gorges (New England), Lord Baltimore (Newfoundland), and the Earl of Carlisle (the Caribbean). These charters not only signaled a shift away from the joint-stock corporate form for colonial management, but they also dictated changes in how authority was structured within the new colonies. When George Calvert, 1st Lord Baltimore, received a charter for his Avalon plantation in Newfoundland in April 1623, the Crown granted him authority to organize the institutions of local government, but the role of urbanization was heavily circumscribed. Functions previously fulfilled by corporate boroughs, such as defense, justice, and economic regulation, were granted specifically to Baltimore. He received "absolute power and authority" to designate "Seaportes, Harboures, Creekes . . . with such rightes, Jurisdictions & freedomes & Privileges" as he saw fit. A distinct section gave him the right to confer "Titles and dignityes" and also "likewise to erect and incorporate Townes into Burroughes, and Burroughes into Cityes, with convenient privileges and Immunityes according to the meritt of the Inhabitants," in order "that the way to honors and dignityes may not seem to be altogether precluded." Under this new vision of the plantation project, the corporate borough was stripped of its independence, and the charter was portrayed as purely a means of securing loyalty and maintaining order through patronage. The critique of the Virginia Company unmistakably fit within this broader pattern of a shift away from corporate self-government and toward a system of royal and noble patronage.[68]

In October 1623, after proceedings to dissolve the Virginia Company had begun, the king issued a blueprint of the new form of government he hoped to impose on Virginia. It made no reference to the corporate structure. Instead, James dispatched commissioners to Virginia with instructions to report "how many severall Plantations there be, and which of them be publique, and which private and particular." Events in the palisaded compounds of the Chesapeake and the corridors of power in London over the previous two years had helped to fundamentally shake the deep-rooted assumption that urbanization and plantation were intimately linked, as they had been for Robert Johnson in *Nova Britannia* fifteen years before.[69]

: : :

For the generation of ambitious colonial projectors who led the Virginia Company, urban development was essential to the establishment of a colonial commonwealth. Humanist principles, classical history, and English and Irish precedent all agreed that urban communities were the building blocks of any new commonwealth. This conclusion was not simply the product of abstract cultural chauvinism or military necessity; it was because towns and cities brought otherwise self-serving individuals together into society, cultivating the virtue that was essential to the orderly regulation of commerce and organization of defense.

The question, however, was how to establish these towns and cities to best mediate between colonists and the new markets in land, labor, and commodities that they were creating in Virginia. This question was central to the colony's purpose and identity. Garrison towns under the patronage of leading officials represented one pole within this debate, and independent corporate communities represented the other. Ultimately, Argall Town, Bermuda City, and many of the private boroughs succumbed to the devastation of the 1622 Powhatan attack, and the model for English colonization in the Chesapeake was still fluid at the time the company was dissolved. However, the fact that these urban plans miscarried does not make their foundations irrelevant. The political-economic assumptions that lay behind the competing urban plans in early Virginia were crucial to facilitating the distribution of private land and the inauguration of a large-scale system of servant labor. These building blocks for the plantation system, laid while tobacco agriculture was just beginning to flourish, were deliberate first steps in the piecemeal formulation of a political-economic order designed to reconcile commercial tobacco agriculture with contemporary ideas about civic virtue.

But they were only first steps. The anxieties about commerce and order in a colonial commonwealth were hardly resolved. Sandys's plan may have been abandoned in Virginia and lambasted in England, but the alternatives proposed in the early 1620s, for establishing a stable gentry and a dependent network of towns, were hardly easier to achieve. For this reason, even as they retreated into fortified private homesteads, the planters of Virginia continued to value the official labels of corporations and towns, which Sandys had left them. The pursuit of the chimerical city and the debate about commerce and order in the Chesapeake was only just beginning.

CHAPTER TWO

From Corporate Communities to County Courts in the Early Stuart Empire

On May 24, 1624, James I rescinded the Virginia Company charter, leaving the colony in an uncertain position. Over the next few years, tobacco made the region prosperous, merchants multiplied, and shiploads of laborers arrived (many against their will), but this boom only reinforced questions about how the region was going to be governed. James I, who had decided to rescind the company's charter, died early in 1625 without settling on a new form of government for the colony, leaving it unclear what legal, political, or commercial structures bound planters to each other or to England. Charles I added to the confusion a few years later when he granted the northern portion of the Chesapeake Bay to the Calvert family to establish the proprietary colony of Maryland.

Most accounts of the Chesapeake after the fall of the Virginia Company suggest that this constitutional confusion gave the region a "wild west" character—making it a lawless frontier where English officials were either incapable of or uninterested in exerting their authority and everyone simply established ad hoc legal and commercial systems with an eye to the main chance.[1] In fact, though, the disorderly and confused nature of Chesapeake commerce and society was universally condemned, and the humanist pursuit of a settled colonial commonwealth remained a central objective for everyone involved in colonization. In the absence of the Virginia Company's overarching authority, questions about the organization of settlement, labor, and commerce actually became more fraught, because they had greater potential to quickly influence the unsettled balance of power within the colonial commonwealth and also to shape its uncertain relationship with the English Crown and realm. The renewed struggle over urban development in both Virginia and Maryland in the 1630s brought into focus the very real commercial and constitutional stakes involved in the seemingly practical efforts to build agricultural estates, pioneer new industries, and establish mercantile connections. Behind these activities lay increasingly divergent ideas about the purpose of planting and the structure of authority between the Crown and the planters.

Ambitious plans for development at Jamestown, and at the new Maryland capital St. Mary's, concretized and catalyzed these growing divergences. Urban development remained one of the clearest ways to establish claims to civic authority over the Chesapeake's booming tobacco trade. This new struggle, though, was now more than simply a debate over how best to cultivate civic order in the Chesapeake, as it had been under the Virginia Company; it reflected growing divisions back in England between the Crown and Parliament over the power of the monarch and the legitimacy of autonomous urban civic communities. The conflicting impulses of civic autonomy and royal authority within English urban communities, which had long been held together through the multivalent nature of urban corporate charters, were beginning to pull apart as the Stuart kings articulated a more personal form of direct authority over their realm. The growing tension between court and country in England was a crucial context for the debate over local political and economic institutions in the Chesapeake.[2]

Many of the planter leaders who rose to prominence in Virginia during the 1620s increasingly envisioned their personal estates and private trading networks as civic structures that took on the responsibilities of the Virginia Company's former corporate communities. By the mid-1620s, the Chesapeake came under the influence of a group of dominant planters. These individuals continued to invest in development at Jamestown and maintained many of the titles and offices associated with the old corporate system. However, they increasingly defined their identity as rural planters and reframed civic rhetoric to celebrate the independence of their plantation estates as the foundational building blocks of English commonwealth in America.[3] Meanwhile, Charles I and his new proprietor in Maryland, Cecil Calvert, 2nd Lord Baltimore, advanced a starkly different vision for local authority grounded upon personal patronage and centralized regulation of trade. The Crown's skepticism about urban corporations had, as we have already seen, played a central role in the downfall of the Virginia Company. Through the late 1620s, in the face of criticism and opposition from Parliament, Charles I built upon this skepticism and began to articulate a growing confidence in his personal authority.[4] Royal and proprietary officials in the Chesapeake translated these ideas into a new vision for Jamestown and St. Mary's as centrally controlled commercial hubs that would stabilize and stimulate the Chesapeake economy.[5]

The decisions of the Crown, Lord Baltimore, and those who opposed them reflected distinct strains of political-economic thought that contended over what commodities should be produced, how they should be traded, and the forms of imperial civic structure that would follow. Their competing political and commercial interests were articulated through different ways of organizing plantation space around urban centers. Jamestown and St. Mary's became critical to the contest over the shape of the Stuart empire.

The city's themselves failed to live up to the aspirations of either side, but it was in the context of this debate over the civic legitimacy and authority of urban spaces that the Chesapeake planter elite adopted the county as a jurisdictional framework to reinforce their claims to commercial and political order. In both Virginia and Maryland, claims to county authority were a direct response to the articulation of royal and proprietary plans for centralized urban hubs. The Chesapeake's county structure, which would come to define planter political culture for two centuries, was a product of a political-economic debate catalyzed by conflicting ideas about urban development. Far from being simply the instinctive response of a planter class neglected by the English Crown and predisposed to rural gentility, counties were, from their inception, consciously designed to dialogue with the system of Atlantic commerce and the Stuart state. They were a particular choice from among the patchwork of jurisdictions that made up English local governance, designed to legitimize the de facto economic and social authority that leading planters exercised over their communities by veiling it in the civic authority of England's ancient rural institution of local governance.[6]

DIVERGING CIVIC VISIONS FOR THE CHESAPEAKE

When Virginia's leading planters addressed the king in 1624, shortly after news of the Virginia Company's demise, they frankly acknowledged the problems with their commonwealth. "Povertye," they explained, meant that they had not "the meanes to fortifie, nor to sett up those staple comodities wch require a longe expectation of proffitt." Although tobacco prices were high, they noted that unregulated merchants and wartime instability hindered the pursuit of the common good. They were committed, though, to rectifying the problems. They highlighted for the king the progress they had made in building a colonial commonwealth since the 1618 reforms and sought to convince him to maintain his support for their efforts by limiting taxes and relaxing rules on land grants. These, they maintained, were the only means to secure the "publique utilitie." Crown officials were not entirely out of sympathy with these pleas. Although James I and Charles I were increasingly desperate to generate revenue from their American domains, they too continued to see the ultimate objective of colonization as the cultivation of new English commonwealths and expressed concern about signs of disorder in the Chesapeake. Charles instructed Governor Sir George Yeardley to look to the health of the commonwealth above all, ordering him to pursue the "extirpating of Vice & the incouragement of virtue and goodness." He maintained that his aim was ultimately "the settling of a *firme* Plantation."[7] For everyone involved in charting the future of Chesapeake planting at this stage, then, colonial development was still bound up with civic concerns; everyone recognized the trouble with the unstable tobacco economy and sought a means to balance private gain with the public good of the colonial commonwealth. Over the next fifteen years, however, the opinions of leading planters and the king about how to achieve these civic goals increasingly diverged, and so, therefore, did the role they envisioned for urban development.

During the 1620s, authority in Virginia was increasingly consolidated in the hands of an established planter leadership who dominated the governing council, but the power that these men exercised was anything but ad hoc and opportunistic. The men and women who came to dominate the Chesapeake in these years were well connected to powerful statesmen in England, and they consciously set about to remodel Virginia society, claiming authority as "planters" whose civic and spiritual duty was to oversee and nurture English colonization.[8] They adapted the company's corporate civic structure to create a system that they claimed was better able to deliver stability and order, but which also happened to bolster their personal authority. The urban corporate offices and traditions that the company had established did not vanish overnight with the dissolution of the company.[9] Colonial leaders were particularly anxious to retain the colony's General Assembly, through which "all the fremen" in each plantation had their voices heard.[10] However, with the colony returning to a wartime footing after the outbreak of the Second Anglo-Powhatan War in 1622, colonists became increasingly dependent upon local military leaders, who provided protection and badly needed food supplies. These men converted the company-era particular plantations into fortified compounds, and they began to modify the corporate jurisdictions, creating a system of so-called monthly courts, where they exercised considerable judicial discretion in the application of English law.[11]

The leading planters claims to civic authority also extended into the commercial realm in the midst of the ongoing tobacco boom. Since the elimination of the company Magazine in 1620, the Chesapeake's booming tobacco trade had been open to all; anyone with a ship and the capital to stock it with supplies could try their hand in the tobacco trade. The result was an influx of small-time traders—English shopkeepers and ship captains with little experience in long-distance trade. These individuals did not arrive in the colony on a regular schedule, and their dealings were increasingly difficult to police. Prices for tobacco remained high in England in the early 1620s, but the supply of shipping was highly unpredictable, and the quality of tobacco being produced was extremely variable (due to planters' lack of experience and high mortality), so the potential to make a fortune or suffer a devastating loss was ever present; in these circumstances, the temptation to engage in nefarious dealings in order to secure desperately needed supplies was irresistible.[12] The colony's council continued to promulgate company-era rules against corrupt trading practices, such as engrossing and forestalling the market, and in some places they retained the offices of cape merchants (public storekeepers).[13] These regulations, though, ultimately assisted the council members and other leading planters in cultivating personal ties with particular merchants. Many of these individuals fostered close connections with one of the informal networks of small merchants, either through kinship, shared ties to particular towns or regions of England, or mutual affinity for strains of radical Protestantism. This gave them the most reliable supplies of English goods and indentured laborers, allowing them to dictate terms of trade to their neighbors and to consolidate their estates as large agricultural enterprises.[14] In the unregulated, undersupplied, and war-torn region, though, these planter-merchants consistently portrayed their commercial leadership as vital to the safety and security of the colony. They anxiously fought against any Crown efforts to centralize the tobacco trade through a new monopoly in England or to increase duties on tobacco, arguing that only they—as planters—were best placed to regulate trade for the common good. At "so farre a distance," the General Assembly claimed, the Crown did not have "perfect knowledge of the Country," and so they argued that it was not "fit that any mayne project be sett a foot," without their "approbation."[15]

Planters made the same case in relation to future economic development and diversification of the colony's economy. They were acutely aware of the shortcomings of tobacco as a commercial crop and took active steps to sustain the company's search for alternative commodities. The General Assembly in 1624 passed legislation requiring each planter to cultivate twenty vines and four mulberry trees (for silk production).[16] Samuel Matthews, one of the leading planter-merchants who likely helped to draft these new rules, took the requirements seriously. He embarked upon numerous diversification projects on his private plantation estate with considerable success. Matthews's English associate John Ferrar noted that he had a "fine house" and a workforce of "forty Negroe servants" trained in various crafts, which allowed him to "cause Leather to be dressed," flax spun, grain milled, and pots molded from the abundant natural resources of his private estate without any labor on his own part. The critical aim of achieving a balanced and diversified economy that could support an orderly civic society seemed to be realized on Matthews's private estate. This vision of the Virginia landscape owed much to the contemporary idealization of the "Country House" as a miniature private commonwealth in the literature and poetry of the upwardly mobile English gentry who were busily enclosing and improving their estates in the early seventeenth century. Ferrar, like the poets valorizing English gentry estates, emphasized the bountiful natural landscape of the Matthews plantation and his personal ingenuity in organizing its exploitation, while downplaying the exploitation of unfree labor. According to this picture, it was Matthews's independence as a planter gentleman operating an extensive private estate that provided the impetus for him to invest in new commodities and industries for the good of the whole society. This was the logic that lay behind the leading planters repeated calls for the Crown to confirm and guarantee the land grants they had received from the company and to allow them to patent even larger acreages.[17]

Planters also recognized that agriculture was not the only route to riches in the Chesapeake; some pursued the fur trade in the region in a similar fashion. One of Virginia's provincial councillors, merchant William Claiborne, was at the forefront of these efforts. He formed a trading alliance with the Susquehannocks in the northern Chesapeake, which then lay within the Virginia patent. To support this venture, he had established a new trading center on an island in the middle of the northern Chesapeake Bay, which he christened Kent. Kent Island quickly became a bustling trading post with a few dozen homes and warehouses, but most of the individuals who resided there were all employees of Claiborne's venture. The settlement was both a town and a private plantation, just as the Virginia Company had envisioned for particular plantations in the late 1610s. However, it did not lie within the territorial bounds of any of the original corporations established by the Virginia Company, and although it did send a burgess to the Virginia General Assembly in the spring of

1632, its precise status within the political structure of the colony was never established. Kent Island represented the apotheosis of the planters' vision of private civic development—an orderly, compact commercial community, pursuing the economic and social maturation of Virginia society, under the direction of a hard-nosed and practically minded planter.[18]

Idealization of the private plantation estate as a crucial civic institution did not mean that leading planters completely abandoned urban development. In the aftermath of the 1622 Powhatan attack, local officials had made efforts to revitalize and develop Jamestown in particular. They surveyed and sold lots in the area just to the east of the existing settlement site and christened it "New Towne." The new urban space consisted of two main streets extending east from the old fort compound, with a few dozen houses and a number of wharves and docks along the quayside. Recent archaeological excavations have suggested that numerous artisans operated in New Towne in the late 1620s. The planter leadership invested because they still viewed urban development as a mark of civic pride. The 1624 General Assembly even hyperbolically claimed that "many Cities of great Rumour" in Spanish America, "after threescore Years Progress, are not to be compared in their Buildings to ours."[19] As a critical civic space, though, they intended Jamestown to come under their personal control. A number of the colony's leading planters invested heavily in the redevelopment of Jamestown, including George Menefie, Abraham Piersey, and Richard Stephens, intending to use the city and the corporate structure that they retained from the company's reforms as a base for their growing commercial networks. Menefie owned prime waterfront property in New Towne and began operating a forge on the eastern fringes of the town. He built a position of influence in Jamestown on the basis of his investment: in 1626, he became the official merchant for Jamestown, and in 1629, he represented the city in the General Assembly. For these men, investment in Jamestown was obviously about personal commercial interests, but it was also about playing a central role in an autonomous urban hub that provided a civic heart of their planter-controlled commonwealth.[20]

However, this vision of the planter's vital civic role in establishing an English commercial commonwealth was increasingly diverging from the English Crown's growing faith in paternalistic royal absolutism. In the domestic sphere, Charles I became increasingly disillusioned with Parliament because of its resistance to new taxes, which he desperately needed to fund ongoing European wars. He developed a new philosophy of royal power, arguing that he should govern the realm directly and personally in the interests of stability and order. In 1629, he embarked on eleven years of "personal rule," during which he governed without Parliament. The primary source of Charles's anger at Parliament, and his main preoccupation during the personal rule, was the Crown's fiscal crisis and the need to generate extra revenue to meet the dramatically expanding costs of European warfare. However, as Kevin Sharpe has argued, Charles understood his personal rule as not "simply a fiscal device, but a means of stabilizing and regulating, of guaranteeing rights and investments, of promoting efficiency, perhaps most of all in Caroline England of ordering through royal control." After their resistance to additional taxes, the king increasingly saw the commercial community and the improving landlords of the realm as a source of disorder and instability and sought to restrict their independence and the workings of the free market. He established new corporations to regulate artisan communities, such as glaziers, brick and tile makers, and silk producers, and issued new instructions to clamp down on price gouging. The king also supported numerous schemes, or "projects," proposed by developers who promised to revolutionize trades such as soap making with new techniques; he granted them monopoly trading privileges in exchange for sizable payments into the royal treasury. The Crown stood to generate revenue, but the larger objective was the improvement of the realm through direct royal oversight of innovation, rather than the chaotic influence of the market. These actions were all part of an effort to return to "a world in which the economic preoccupations with profit, interest and competition were to be subordinated for the order of the commonweal." They brought revenue to the Crown, but, more importantly, Charles believed that he was bringing order to the realm through direct dependence upon royal patronage.[21]

Given his interests in measures that both promoted order and promised revenue at home, it was logical for Charles I to interest himself in the civic problems associated with tobacco cultivation in the Chesapeake. Royal officials were alert to reports of corruption and commercial disorder in the Chesapeake. Accounts from the colony, some of which have been used by historians to paint a picture of chaos and exploitation in the early Chesapeake, survive precisely because they were of interest to the Crown and were preserved in official records. The case of planter-merchant Abraham Piersey was of particular concern to the Privy Council, because it demonstrated the potential for corruption within the informal system of commercial-political alliances that developed during these years. Piersey had been the Virginia Company's merchant at Jamestown and was appointed the military commander there in the aftermath of the Powhatan attack. He quickly turned his position to private profit by ensuring that his English trading partners controlled the market for desperately needed supplies in Jamestown. Angry planters who accused him of extortion were indicted for their troubles. Finally, in 1626, former Virginia Company official George Sandys presented the Crown with evidence that Piersey had also been embezzling funds from the colony's public supplies that had been left over from the company era. The new court of Charles I was already conscious of the need to conserve the colony's resources in light of domestic financial pressures and the cost of sending supplies to the colony, so the Privy Council took the accusations seriously, writing immediately to Governor Wyatt to suggest that, "knowing himself to be out their reach," Piersey "kepeth possession of their goods."[22] The Crown was also receiving complaints that commercial disorder was leading to imbalances in social and labor relations that were corrupting the legal system. For example, during the summer of 1626, the Privy Council was approached by Thomas Powell with a tale of seventeenth-century identity theft. When Powell's brother Captain Nathaniel Powell had died in the colony, "one William Powell, being onely of name but noe way of Kine, to the said Capt. Powell" had been granted the right to administer the late captain's estate by corrupt or inept officials and had pocketed a sizable sum in outstanding debts. All of this evidence flowing back to London suggested that unrestrained commerce was corroding the social and legal structures of Virginia society. From the Crown's perspective, men such as Piersey, far from being the sole protectors of the English planter commonwealth, were a threat to its very survival. They exploited the commercial and political disorder and the vacuum of royal authority to turn public funds into private wealth.[23]

Of particular concern to royal officials was Virginia's total dependence upon tobacco production. Because it imposed taxes on every barrel of tobacco imported, the Crown seemingly had an incentive to encourage the expansion of tobacco production, but concerns about tobacco as a commodity incapable of supporting a permanent commonwealth were ubiquitous in royal proposals for the region. The nature of tobacco as a luxury commodity without a guaranteed market seemed to lend itself to short-term trading arrangements and wild price fluctuations. Tobacco offered quick profits for merchants but discouraged long-term investment in land and housing in the colony, which undermined social stability and the establishment of civic communities. During the 1620s, the Crown became increasingly convinced that the planter elite themselves were the primary reason that the region's economy was failing to diversify. Charles excoriated the planters' short-term focus on profits and lamented that Virginia was "wholly builte uppon Smoake, Tobaccoe being the only meanes it hath produced," and that it could "soe easie . . . bee turned into aire."[24] Another royal official opined that "there was very litle hope of such a plantation as must be supported by no more solide a commoditie then smoke."[25] As early as 1626, the king's investigations into the tobacco trade had led him "to Command" that planters diversify their production. This strict order was very much in keeping with the Crown's support for new projects in England, in that it emphasized profits but also a return to a balanced commercial order through innovations in the production of mundane manufactured necessities. While the Privy Council retained hope for alternative luxury goods such as wine and silk, they also pushed more prosaic commodities and trades such as pitch, tar, potash, and salt. They hoped to establish precisely the same kinds of artisans and craftsmen that the Virginia Company had unsuccessfully dispatched to Virginia in the late 1610s.[26] In September 1630, they even allowed ship captain John Preen to escape a legal claim over the ownership of his vessel because the delay would have resulted in "staying the Artificers" bound for the colony. Later that same month, they drafted a recommendation for Thomas Grendon, who was migrating to Virginia to set up an array of new crafts; they believed his project demonstrated commitment to "bend all his indevors for the imployment of his Majesties Subjects, and the good of the Common Weale." These moves were not driven solely by the desire for revenue. They reflected a royal conviction that diversification would stabilize the colony's economy, reducing its vulnerability to market shortages and gluts and in the process limiting the opportunities for ruthless merchants to manipulate these extremes.[27]

The civic assumptions that lay behind these royal concerns were not fundamentally different from those of the planters. No one was yet thinking in terms of global commodity markets or the pure economic interest of the state; they shared a conviction that the tobacco economy was disordered and that public investment and regulation were key to establishing a stable commonwealth. But the Crown was developing a distinct plan for achieving these goals. When James I died not long after rescinding the charter of the Virginia Company, Charles decided to abandon his father's plan to issue a new charter to a select group of merchants. Instead he retained personal rule over the colony.[28] He remained interested, as his father had been, in generating revenue from the colony, but his motives were far from straightforwardly pecuniary. Soon after the decision to retain Virginia as a royal colony, the Privy Council developed new proposals to address commercial injustice and to demonstrate the king's personal concern for ordinary planters by sending ships laden with supplies to be sold at "indifferent prises." The following year, in instructions to Sir George Yeardley, who was returning to the governorship of the colony, the Crown's primary orders regarding the tobacco trade were not focused on raising additional royal revenue, but upon strictly enforcing laws against market manipulation and redirecting the entire colony's energy toward producing a more diverse range of commodities. The Privy Council explained that the king's objective was to encourage colonists with the knowledge of his personal concern and princely care, in order that they be prompted to pursue "diligent endevors for the publique benefit." The logic here precisely matched Charles's domestic thinking—direct Crown intervention would hearten his subjects and inspire them to civic virtue under his watchful protection. This was an objective that fit perfectly with the king's larger goal of imposing royal order on his unstable commercial commonwealth.[29]

The challenge for Charles was to go beyond these stern instructions and actually develop new institutional structures for the Chesapeake. Despite his intentions, the king's tools for shaping commercial policy were limited by the capacity of his small state apparatus; furthermore, the revenue generated by the disorderly but booming tobacco trade always appealed to the cash-strapped monarch and tested his resolve to impose greater commercial regulation. Nonetheless, Crown officials repeatedly experimented with schemes to generate revenue and virtue in Virginia simultaneously. A royal revenue commission in the late 1620s toyed with a scheme proposed by projector William Anys that would have made Charles I the sole importer and retailer of tobacco. This project was built upon the king's fiscal desperation, and it would have made Anys a personal fortune, but it was still framed explicitly to address the intersection of commercial and social disorder in Virginia. Anys promised to purchase tobacco with necessities such as "shoes, stockinge and such other commodities" that the Crown believed private merchants were neglecting in favor of alcohol and luxury consumer goods. He noted that providing these essential commodities "at easy rates," which current mercantile arrangements denied to the majority of planters, would free ordinary planters from the influence of powerful planter-merchant networks and place them directly "in the power of the State."[30]

Anys's scheme provoked vocal opposition from established merchant-planter networks and was abandoned, but it spurred fresh political-economic debate in the early 1630s. The representatives of the leading planters and independent merchants pushed the king to reestablish the

Virginia Company under their control. As a renewed joint-stock venture, the reestablished company would have returned the Crown to the pattern of using corporate charters to balance private interests and civic regulation. However, Charles was still concerned to retain greater control than his father had held over the former Virginia Company. The Privy Council concluded in May 1633 that a new company "tends to [the colony's] great loss, and hinderance, besides [the new company] shall bee forced to abandon a great number of poor people there, wch for want of Supplies will not be able to subsist."[31] The Crown framed its rejection of the joint-stock plan in distinctly Caroline terms, as a gracious royal pursuit of civic order that put the needs of all colonists ahead of private profit. The Crown's fiscal problems were, of course, an ever-present reality beneath these negotiations, but royal efforts at reform were predicated upon the belief that Virginia was perpetually unsettled and that its civic problems would only be resolved by imposing greater royal control over the colony's commercial and political systems.[32]

This new vision of civic order and stability, built upon direct royal authority, reshaped Crown expectations for urban space in the Chesapeake. Domestically, Charles worked to limit the independence of English corporate towns. He replaced corporate marketplace regulation with royal rules on weights, measures, and prices that were dictated to urban communities across England; he established building commissions manned by royal officers that reshaped the urban built environment; and he invested heavily in redeveloping the port town of Dover to centralize trade and customs collection and replace the independent boroughs who had resisted his efforts to increase and streamline taxation.[33] When Charles contemplated the need for urban development in Virginia, it was clear that it should be on similar terms to these English reforms: offering a way to diversify and urbanize the region that would seize power back from the merchant-planter community and regrant it only on strict conditions of civic action and loyalty. In the late 1620s, the Privy Council discussed a new plan that lamented how "covetousness onely . . . thrust men upon their desseins" in Virginia and that offered to address this problem by establishing a new English plantation built around a town of artisans under direct Crown supervision. Although this project never got off the ground, the ideal of building a new political order with urban institutions persisted.[34] At the dawn of the 1630s, Charles found two men prepared to pursue a bold restructuring of English planting in the Chesapeake: his new governor for Virginia, Sir John Harvey, and the courtier-turned-proprietor Cecil Calvert, Lord Baltimore.

"THOSE WAYES WHICH ARE MOST PROPER TO MAKE IT A COUNTREY"

A matter of months after Anys's proposed tobacco monopoly was shelved in 1628, the Privy Council began planning to dispatch a new governor to Virginia. Their choice was naval captain Sir John Harvey. He was already familiar with Virginia's problems, having headed the commission that had inspected the colony in 1623, and he spent the next year in England preparing for his posting.[35] During this period, he witnessed the influence of the planter-merchant network as it lobbied for the reestablishment of the Virginia Company. At the same time, though, as he lingered in London, he also had a front-row seat for the emerging crisis in the Crown's relationship with the city's corporation. Similarly, he would have struggled to ignore the tense showdown with Parliament in 1629 when the realm's commercial community united to oppose the king's new customs duties.[36] As a result, when Harvey finally set out for Virginia in 1630, he did so with a clear sense that the balance of power between the Crown and urban commercial interests needed to be adjusted. He was determined to follow the instructions he had received from the Privy Council and institute the kind of civic change that the Stuart court had been pursuing in Virginia for nearly a decade. The keystone of this transformation would be the dramatic reorientation of local governance and settlement structure in Virginia, with urban redevelopment and centralization of trade at Jamestown as a centerpiece. These were, as Harvey explained, "those wayes which are most proper to make it [Virginia] a countrey." It was this ambitious agenda that brought him into violent confrontation with leading planters, and which eventually led to his forcible ejection from office. The showdown, however, proved to be crucial in forging the foundations of Virginia's political and commercial order.[37]

When he arrived in Virginia in 1630, Harvey quickly grasped the nature of the challenges he faced. He concluded that the reports reaching England about misgovernment and corruption were well founded. There was a large middling rank of planters whose access to trade and justice was being restricted by the planter-merchant leadership who controlled law and commerce. After less than a year in Virginia, Harvey had amassed a wealth of lurid details about what he called the "Publique Cabbell" among the colony's councillors; he recounted to English officials one especially troubling example in which the colony's council heard the case of a planter who was engaged in a commercial dispute with one of their fellow councillors, only to dismiss the case and convict the man of perjury without recourse to a trial. Yet Harvey realized that stripping the leaders of their political power would be a pointless exercise without commercial reforms undercutting their dominant position in the tobacco trade.[38]

Harvey immediately set out to diversify the colony's economy and redevelop Jamestown. He set to work restoring the Virginia Company ironworks that had been destroyed by the Powhatan attack. He also encouraged the production of a range of new products such as potash, saltpeter, and wine, and he sent samples in order to encourage royal officials to make good on their promise to dispatch more skilled craftsmen. New Virginia legislation in 1633, likely inspired by the governor's agenda, required craftsmen to pursue their trades as "gunsmiths and naylers, brickmakers, carpenters, joyners, sawyers, and turners" instead of planting tobacco.[39] While no official rules stipulated that these new commercial pursuits needed to be limited to Jamestown, in practice Harvey himself invested substantially in the establishment of new diversification schemes in the capital. He converted his property in New Towne into a manufacturing "enclave" with costly new facilities, including a furnace, a brew house, and an apothecary's laboratory. Harvey could have chosen to site these nascent industries elsewhere in the colony, but he clustered them around his gubernatorial residence in order to stimulate the development of Jamestown under his direct supervision.[40]

Once this construction was under way, Harvey also pursued plans to make Jamestown the centerpiece of a new system of commercial regulation. The Crown had already advocated a plan to make Jamestown the sole port of entry to regulate trade, and Harvey pushed this proposal through, requiring that all incoming ships dock first at Jamestown to "break bulk" before moving on to trade elsewhere.[41] He also sought to bring the fur trade, currently dominated by Claiborne's Kent Island venture, under his control at Jamestown. In 1632, he reached an agreement with one of Claiborne's rivals, Henry Fleet, who had promising contacts with the native people of the Potomac valley. Harvey became a major investor in Fleet's venture and dispatched him to trade along the Potomac, likely hoping to ensure that furs flowed out through official channels at Jamestown rather than directly from Kent Island. He also advocated opening the market to greater competition by welcoming Dutch merchants, demonstrating that he was not yet thinking in imperial mercantilist terms, but rather focusing on the imposition of Stuart royal authority over a vibrant commercial hub.[42] In order to build this new royal hub, Harvey and the Crown placed their faith in a new commercial community at Jamestown. He created a committee composed of selected Jamestown merchants who agreed to act under his oversight, to begin adjudicating local commercial disputes. Significantly, he did not make any efforts to revive the city's independent corporation, preferring, like his royal employer, to keep the new urban commercial community in his own hands. Instead, he hoped to erect a new royal customhouse in the town to keep accurate accounts, a move that complemented the Crown's simultaneous domestic efforts to tighten customs enforcement. This move would have generated much-needed royal revenue, but it cannot be separated from the larger civic project of remodeling Jamestown as a royal hub. Restrictions on trade and the establishment of new merchants and artisans worked together to reinforce the king's control and the health of the commonwealth.[43]

Harvey later articulated the vision behind these moves in a report to the Crown. He explained that the king had required him to "reduce, and draw the people into Townes wch as yet is by noe other meanes, and ways to be effected then by confining the Trade to one place, wch will draw merchants and Tradesmen to build and inhabit together." He shifted quickly and easily between the economic argument that a central trading port would bring prosperity and the political argument that it offered a means to reduce the disorder of isolated rural life. For Harvey, these two factors were tightly bound together—royal economic controls would ensure uniform prosperity and a responsible civic community. He summed up this perspective when he claimed that unless commerce was centralized at Jamestown, "there must be rather a scrambling then [sic] a Trade." Only through his efforts to strengthen royal urban authority in Jamestown could the disorderly and dishonest "scrambling" of private merchant networks be organized into a genuine "Trade" that would create a prosperous colonial commonwealth for the Crown.[44]

Harvey was careful to position himself at the center of this effort to revitalize Jamestown. He invested his money, rather than that of the Crown or the colony, in the redevelopment of the capital. He also made his substantial town residence the central gathering place for government functions—he wrote to London that he "may be as well called the hoste as governor of Virginia."[45] When Captain Thomas Yong visited Jamestown in 1634, he noted that "I meet dayly with severall of the best and most understanding sort of the Inhabitants of this place and [thereby] I find really that the present Governor hath carried himselfe here with very great prudence." By 1634, as we shall see, Harvey had bitter enemies among the colony's planter-merchants, but the men Yong met in Jamestown were clearly allies of the governor who circled around his urban hub. Yong's experience suggests that there was a deeper political-economic purpose to Harvey's efforts at Jamestown—he was manufacturing new political relationships as well as new commodities.⁴⁶

Harvey's restructuring of Virginia's political economy around Jamestown was not limited to the city itself. He also reimagined the Virginia countryside as an orderly hinterland behind a new wooden palisade stretching across the James-York peninsula from Archer's Hope Creek just east of Jamestown to Queen's Creek, which flowed into the York River. The idea of a palisade had originally been floated by Governor Wyatt in the aftermath of the 1622 Powhatan attack, but Harvey seized upon it. One key purpose of the palisade was to permanently reconfigure Virginia's relationship with the Powhatan by erecting a physical boundary to exclude them and bring an end to the decade of Anglo-Powhatan warfare. In this respect, the palisade and peace settlement with the Powhatan were already part of Harvey's effort to undermine the position of the leading planter-merchants, who had used their wartime leadership to bolster their authority. However, the palisade also reshaped the colony's internal conceptual geography to bring it into line with Harvey's efforts at Jamestown. In European thought, open spaces were linked with fair trading and the public good, and dark, concealed, and private locales—such as the Chesapeake's forest-bound plantation enclaves—were associated with the kind of underhanded profiteering that most troubled royal officials. Bounding and clearing the area behind the palisade to create, in Harvey's words, "a safe range for cattle near as big as Kent," would make it a comprehensible and controllable patchwork of pastures and fields rather than isolated estates dominated by powerful individuals. He intended to fill the space behind the palisade with small planters by offering a fifty-acre lot to anyone who would settle the newly cleared land, while simultaneously blocking land grants to the leading planter-merchants. Building the palisade therefore fit neatly with Harvey's royally sanctioned endeavors to adjust the social and commercial structure of the colony. Instead of large plantations dotted along the riverbanks, Harvey envisioned small farmers scattered across a pastoral landscape behind the palisade, with the commercial and political oversight for this rural hinterland firmly anchored in Jamestown as a provincial royal city.⁴⁷

In practically all of these new projects, Harvey overrode the established interests of the planter-merchants and engendered resentment among them. It was not that the well-connected planter-merchants completely opposed diversification or urban development; as we have seen, they had promoted certain such measures themselves. In fact, Harvey was initially impressed by Matthews's efforts and commended him to the Crown, but as their diverging political-economic visions became clear, their relationship quickly soured. Matthews made clear to the governor that he thought the only appropriate way for the Crown to support diversification in Virginia was to give tax incentives to entrepreneurs such as himself to allow them to reap greater profits on tobacco that could be plowed back into development. Harvey quickly dismissed this proposal. The same division was apparent over the issue of the palisade. In the late 1620s, Matthews and William Claiborne had initially proposed building the palisade across the peninsula in exchange for large private land grants, but when Harvey arrived, he converted their plans into a direct royal operation designed to create a landscape of small planters.[48] Harvey's plans threatened the leading planters' ability to undertake civic projects on their own schedule, with their own labor force of indentured servants and slaves, and according to their own regulations. When Matthews's ally John Ferrar assessed the state of diversification in the colony, he specifically blamed Harvey for the failure to develop new commodities, confirming that the governor's efforts had soured elite enthusiasm for the shift from tobacco. The planters who dominated Virginia society, having already invested in private estates and committed to control over bound labor, preferred to find ways to tap into the potential profits of new commodities and crafts without sacrificing their private mastery.[49]

It was Harvey's intense interest in developments in Jamestown, though, that most clearly exemplified his divisions with the planter-merchants. The New Towne area had been developed before Harvey's arrival, and much of the investment had come from leading planter-merchants. But when Harvey embarked on his development in the capital, many of these men, such as George Menefie, went elsewhere. Over the next four years, while Harvey expanded his Jamestown enclave, Menefie directed much of his effort toward the development of a new private estate at Rich Neck, which, in a distinctly unsubtle move, he named "Little Towne." Menefie clearly had no intention of continuing to develop his property at Jamestown with Harvey now asserting his control over the urban space, and he elected to join the likes of Samuel Matthews in privatizing his commercial projects. With Harvey firmly in control of development in Jamestown, the planter-merchants also began a campaign to block his efforts to restrict trade to the capital. As members of the council, they stalled efforts to enforce the rules restricting trade to Jamestown. It was during this period, too, that William Claiborne ramped up his efforts to develop Kent Island as an alternative commercial center for the Chesapeake Bay: Claiborne went even further than his fellow provincial councillors by seeking a royal commission (eventually granted under the Crown's Scottish, rather than English, seal) that would allow him to trade freely through Kent Island and disregard Harvey's regulations at Jamestown or the royal charter for Maryland recently issued to Baltimore. The governor's efforts to expand and empower the colony's capital city were clearly at the center of the contest over commercial and political order in the Chesapeake.[50]

Tensions between Harvey and Virginia's leading planters simmered through the early 1630s. Overt confrontation between the governor and the most powerful planters, many of whom were members of the provincial council, was delayed because the planter-merchant leaders were actively pursuing a lobbying effort to get the Virginia Company reestablished in London. If they had succeeded in this effort, the planter elite and their allies in London would have had wide-ranging authority over the colony, monopoly control of the tobacco trade, and access to unlimited land grants, which would have undermined Harvey's efforts. In 1632, leading merchants briefly succeeded in convincing the Crown to overturn the rules restricting trade to Jamestown, but the letter containing this instruction was never sent.[51] The planters' aspirations were gradually undermined by royal policies. First, in 1632, Charles issued a proprietary charter to the Calvert family to establish the colony of Maryland in the northern half of the Chesapeake Bay. Not only did Baltimore's Catholicism seem to undermine the Protestant mission that many of Virginia's leading planters still understood themselves to be a part of, but, as we shall see, Baltimore's vision of manorial land ownership and centralized commercial regulation in Maryland had far more in common with Charles and Harvey's vision for the region than with the planters' decentralized civic vision of private estates.[52] The Maryland charter was a particular threat to William Claiborne, whose Kent Island trading post lay within the bounds of Baltimore's new grant. Harvey's assistance to the first fleet of Maryland colonists in 1634 further soured his relationship with the leading planters.[53] Also in 1634, news arrived from London that the Crown had abandoned plans to reestablish the company and had revived plans to centralize the tobacco trade under royal control.[54] Now it seemed clear that the Crown was throwing support behind Harvey's plans for centralized and carefully regulated trade through Jamestown and for limited land grants.

The leading planters resolved to take more drastic steps, crafting new political institutions in the colony that could garner the legitimacy to challenge the governor. In response to Harvey's efforts to centralize authority through the early 1630s, the planter leadership had been gradually seeking to strengthen the local authority that they exercised through monthly courts within the colony's outlying plantations and communities. The first proposal to enlarge the jurisdiction of the monthly courts came in February 1632, during the same session of the General Assembly when Harvey pushed his agenda for centralizing trade through Jamestown, diversifying the economy, and making peace with the Powhatan. The leading planters likely saw the empowering of local courts as a means to counter the threat of the governor's reforms. The following year it appeared that Harvey and the planters may have reached a compromise, as the General Assembly once again reiterated the Jamestown trade rules and added incentives to encourage craftsmen in the town, but they also made provisions for five (later increased to seven) dispersed tobacco export warehouses; this network of warehouses, if they had actually been established, would inevitably have fallen under the control of the powerful planters in each part of the colony, neutralizing the impact of bringing all incoming trade through the city by allowing them to oversee the gathering of tobacco for export, and thus controlling the supply and price of the colony's only trade in their regions.[55] This compromise did not hold, though. By 1634, divisions reopened between Harvey and the leading planters, because of the arrival of the Maryland colonists and news of the king's opposition to reestablishment of the company. It was in the immediate context of this news that the General Assembly pushed to reconfigure the monthly courts as shires and establish a network of county officials, granting increased legitimacy to the planter leadership in their respective regions.[56] Although the counties are noted in the statutes for 1634, there is no evidence that this decision was sanctioned by the Crown or even approved by Governor Harvey. Notably, Harvey's numerous letters back to London through the early 1630s made no mention of court reform or the final highly significant decision to establish shires. This silence about the contentious three-year process of negotiation over local authority that ended with the establishment of county courts—the paramount institution of English local governance—strongly suggests that it arose from something other than his own animus. The disputes over commercial regulation and the status of Jamestown had provoked the planter leadership to claim a more expansive legitimacy for their local authority across the colony.[57]

The connection between the establishment of counties and the resistance to the governor was reinforced by the crucial role that these new claims to county legitimacy played in the 1635 coup that ousted Harvey from power. During the spring of 1635, Harvey's leading opponents gathered planters together across the colony under the authority of the new county courts in order to convince them to support petitions against Harvey. When confronted by one of Harvey's allies, one man claimed that the gathering at a nearby house was "a Court kept there of the inhabitants thereabout." Although these men likely saw their actions as legitimate manifestations of a county community, Harvey's ally who later narrated the interaction refused to acknowledge the communities' status as shires, claiming that the meeting, in what was ostensibly now York County, just took place in the "lower parts" of the colony.[58] Harvey attempted to quell the opposition by imprisoning those he identified as troublemakers in Jamestown; however, this action was also interpreted in terms of a binary between Jamestown and the shires. According to Samuel Matthews, the councillor who led the opposition, Harvey had appointed a new sheriff of James City County, a "defamed fellow" who brought the governor's critics to the capital and held them as prisoners. It was clear that Matthews saw Harvey as illegitimately hijacking the new shire system to appoint officers who would reinforce his authority in Jamestown.[59] The rebellious councillors ultimately resolved the conflict by marching a contingent of armed colonists into Jamestown to bolster their case during a confrontation with Harvey. After a showdown with the governor during a meeting of the council, they arrested him and dispatched him back to England with a lengthy indictment of his government. Their dramatic actions were specifically intended to undermine the governor's control over the capital city. The whole rebellion was saturated with spatial understandings of how English state power could be asserted and utilized through towns and counties. The planter-merchant faction, conscious of the profound political and social implications represented by Harvey's efforts to reconfigure Jamestown as the center of a new diversified Virginia economy, had used the establishment of the colony's shires as a conscious effort to reclaim control over the plantation's political economy—and for the moment, they had succeeded.[60]

Harvey's expulsion was not the end of his urban vision for Virginia. Upon returning to England, he quickly won royal support for his policies. As part of this effort, his ally, Virginia's secretary Richard Kemp, wrote to London to underscore what he saw as the colony's biggest problem—the planters' resistance to centralizing trade through Jamestown. The urban hub, Kemp claimed, could aid customs collection, but it would also "tye the loose sort from runing into debt, when his whole stock were in his next neighbouring Store readily knowen"; and it would reduce the price of imports by removing merchants' "pretence" of surcharges connected to "gathering in theire debts" from "dispersed and farr distant dwellings." In essence, Kemp was encapsulating Harvey's vision that centralizing

Virginia's trade at Jamestown would create a transparent market under direct royal oversight where supplies of imported goods and stocks of tobacco could be regulated and fair prices agreed upon. Unsurprisingly, this had much in common with Charles I's own claim to be restoring order and stability to the market economy through benign royal supervision. Moreover, Kemp added, "it would likewise be an undoubted consequence that building of 'Townes' would follow, when Artificers would be there incouraged by neare and ready pay."[61]

One of Harvey's other allies, George Donne, reached a similar conclusion in his manifesto for reform titled "Virginia Reviewed." Virginia's problems arose, Donne argued, from the overmighty planter-merchants. The only solution was to rescue ordinary planters from their barbarous self-interest. Returning to the classical models so beloved of the Virginia Company's civic thinkers, he compared Virginia's situation to Europe before the advent of the Roman Empire and explained that the city of Rome had lifted the continent out of barbarity. How was Virginia to cultivate a Rome for itself? Donne's answer was to attract "Sober Well-disposed and Religious persons: Artificers of all trades able and ready, willing and endeavoring for the glory of God, the honor of their Nation, the service of their Prince and their owne comodity to rectify to perfect A common wealth considerately begun." The pamphlet was a summary of the political justification for the governor's efforts at Jamestown and an explicit articulation of the connections between diversification, commercial regulation, and urbanization under royal control.[62]

The efforts of Harvey and his allies bore fruit. The king was again inspired to turn his attention to the "irregular government" of Virginia and the "coveteous and gryping disposition" of planters who "for some pticular gaine ... hazard the common good of the whole plantacon." In an effort to address these problems "wherein the honor or dishonour of our Nation is much interested," he sent Harvey back to Virginia in 1637 armed with royal approval for a new statehouse and customhouse at Jamestown and instructions to again limit trade to the city.[63]

Harvey's first action upon his return to Virginia was to assert his authority over the county system by gathering the council for a ceremony at which he appointed new commissioners and sheriffs. He then redoubled his efforts to foster development at Jamestown. Anyone prepared to build in the town was offered free land, and current landowners who left their plots vacant were threatened with seizure. Harvey also wasted no time in drafting plans for the new statehouse the king had approved. He later claimed that twelve new houses were built within two years of his return and that there was not "a foote of [undeveloped] ground for half a mile together by the Rivers syde" by 1639. Archaeologists have largely corroborated this depiction and have also revealed that Harvey's ally Richard Kemp began an ambitious array of building projects in the capital.[64]

Once again, however, the plan to force merchants to trade through Jamestown encountered opposition. When he convened the General Assembly in the spring of 1638, Harvey immediately presented the measure as a royal order. Burgesses responded that the plan "would bee very chargeable and burthesome to the whole Colony," citing the costs of building warehouses to store tobacco awaiting shipment in the capital and the vicissitudes of transporting tobacco to Jamestown in bad weather. Noting "the remoatenes of our Plantacons one from another," they pointedly suggested that the shires, centered around their private plantation estates, were the best centers for trade, requesting that ships be allowed to "come into every County" because their homes were "a store convenient enough." They claimed that new efforts to restrict trade to Jamestown would make them "repent theire severall disbursemts" spent on long-term investments, effectively suggesting that nothing but independent authority over commerce and plantations would enable them to pursue the common good. This, of course, was precisely the logic that Harvey (and Charles I) found so troubling; he incredulously shot back that "by pretendinge disability to build stores yu intimate howe sick and languishinge a comon wealth yu have."[65]

The governor won this argument, and the restrictions remained in place, but in the end the Crown and Privy Council's pressing need to satiate the Virginia merchant community and maintain the revenue they provided undermined their commitment to his urban vision. Harvey's planter-merchant opponents had the contacts and connections necessary to bend the ears of Crown officials in England, who by the late 1630s were so desperate for revenue that they would soon recall Parliament and precipitate the events that led to civil war. They bombarded royal officials with evidence that Jamestown was inconvenient and unhealthy and that restricting trade would limit tobacco duty revenue. Harvey quickly found himself justifying his actions to the same Privy Council that had sternly instructed him to reform the colony.[66] In 1639, Harvey was recalled from Virginia and replaced as governor by the Virginia Company–era veteran Sir Francis Wyatt. The planter leadership even persuaded the Privy Council to instruct Wyatt to abandon Jamestown and relocate the capital. The elderly Wyatt failed to follow through on this ambitious suggestion of moving the colony's capital, and, as we shall see, many of Harvey's ideas for Jamestown were revived and adapted by his successor, Sir William Berkeley, in the 1640s. However, Berkeley would combine this renewed interest in Jamestown with an embrace of the county system and the established planter oligarchy.[67]

In the final reckoning, Harvey's legacy was not the urban transformation he'd hoped for, but his determination to reorganize commerce and governance had played a crucial role framing the debate over planter political economy. Harvey had adapted Charles's increasingly absolutist vision for his realm and sought to remodel the Chesapeake around a commercially vibrant but strictly loyal urban hub and a hinterland of dependent farmers. This urban project played a previously unappreciated role in Harvey's own political tribulations. It also provoked the institutionalization of the planters' rural civic vision. Virginia's nascent system of county jurisdiction and its dispersed tobacco-trading network were a direct response to the threat posed by Harvey's plans.

"HIS TOWN OF ST MARIES"

Although he might frequently have felt like it, Harvey was not alone in trying to impose new urban order on Chesapeake planter society in the 1630s. Similar tensions over urban space and political authority over commerce were played out in Maryland. The colony of Maryland was carved out of Virginia's former bounds in 1632 as a proprietary grant to George Calvert, 1st Lord Baltimore. George Calvert had been secretary of state to James I until he was forced to withdraw from court because of his Catholicism, and he and his son (who soon inherited the colony upon his father's death just a few months later) famously envisioned American colonization as a means to establish a refuge for English Catholics. However, George Calvert, as a courtier to James I during the early 1620s, was also heavily influenced by royal critiques of the Virginia Company, which shaped his plans for a more hierarchical structure for his short-lived Newfoundland colony in the early 1620s, and a decade later for his new colony of Maryland. When Cecil Calvert inherited the Maryland grant when his father died just a few months after receiving the charter, he sought to use the full extent of the wide-ranging charter powers to craft not just a new religious order, but also a new stable political structure, closely aligned with Charles I's vision for his realm. The patent provided for the creation of large semiautonomous rural manors, but also a limited number of corporate boroughs. In this vision for Maryland, land would provide the basis for a hierarchical order in agricultural regions, but corporate authority under the Calverts' direct supervision would regulate commerce. This plan corresponded closely with Harvey's ambitions for Virginia, which made him the Calverts' natural ally against the established planter-merchant networks in the Chesapeake region. Just like Harvey, though, Baltimore and his brother, Leonard Calvert (who served as Maryland's governor), encountered stiff resistance and were forced to reframe the balance of local authority and legitimize the power of the planter class through the establishment of counties.[68]

When planning for the first Maryland expedition began, Baltimore quickly demonstrated his intention to use the full extent of his charter powers to establish both manorial and corporate authority in his new province. Leading investors in the Maryland venture who qualified for a grant of one thousand acres would have their land designated as a manor, giving them the right to hold courts for the tenants. Planters with smaller acreages were organized into traditional English units of rural government known as hundreds. The plan promised to cement a conservative order under the guidance of established investors who would remain loyal to the proprietor in order to retain their quasi-feudal form of local authority.[69] However, before any manors were to be laid out, Baltimore instructed the first group of colonists to identify one location "that is probable to be healthfull and fruitfull" for a capital city "convenient for trade." Inspired by the success of William Claiborne's fur-trading venture, Baltimore embraced a commercial vision for Maryland: from the outset, he was anxious to take advantage of the flourishing fur trade to generate quick profits. The choice of location for the colony's urban center, christened St. Mary's, was heavily influenced by local native people, with whom Governor Leonard Calvert hoped to build trade ties. Early investors were not only promised the chance to become manorial lords; they were also tempted with ten-acre grants within the bounds of the new city and a joint-stock fur-trading operation to be centered there. All planters were to "build their houses in as decent and uniforme a manner as their abilities and the place will afford, and neere adjoyning one to an other." Only after construction was complete at St. Mary's would work begin on parceling out the surrounding manors.[70]

The Calvert family's commitment to this vision was sustained through the first few years of settlement in Maryland. By 1637, when Governor Calvert called Maryland's first General Assembly, planters had spread out onto agricultural estates in the surrounding region, and he called their representatives together to report to "his town of St maries," using a phrase that pointedly evoked Charles I's description of London as "our royal city."

Once they arrived, they proceeded to pass a series of legislative acts "for building of the towne," and they approved a plan to construct a building for public business that was described as "a Towne house." This legislation made clear that the town was to remain the core focus of the colony's development and that it was to constitute the central civic space in which planters and manorial lords would be united under the Calvert family's personal oversight. The relationship between town and manor was central to the way the Calverts viewed their jurisdictional landscape.[71]

Just like Harvey, however, Baltimore found this neat order difficult to firmly establish. The Calverts could offer few incentives to encourage manorial lords to surrender their commercial independence in the tobacco and fur trades to the nascent town; transatlantic trading partnerships could be negotiated on private estates without directing trade through St. Mary's. For example, one of Maryland's manorial lords, Thomas Cornwaleys, established a thriving trade network. He rejected the idea that his manor should be limited to agricultural production and that commerce should be organized through the proprietor's town, telling Baltimore that he would abandon the colony if he was limited to "what I must fetch out of the Grounde by Planting this Stincking weede [tobacco]." He particularly resented Baltimore's efforts to monopolize the fur trade through St. Mary's, explaining that he could easily evade proprietary commercial regulations by trading "from and toe Virginia without bayting at St. Maryes," and that he had resolved "toe have noe more Interest in Comon Stocks" organized in the city.[72] Cornwaleys was not alone. Very few manorial lords invested in town houses, and during its first decade, St. Mary's probably boasted no more than half a dozen houses.[73]

The misgivings of manorial lords, though, were the least of Baltimore's problems. The Calverts' dreams of using St. Mary's as a base to regulate trade were in direct conflict with William Claiborne's Kent Island settlement. Claiborne posed a particular threat because Kent Island was a preexisting alternative source of authority that lay within the bounds of the proprietary patent, and Claiborne consistently refused to acknowledge the validity of the Maryland charter. Merchants plying the bay could easily call at the island whenever they chose without ever entering the Potomac River and reporting at St. Mary's. A showdown with the Kent Island community was inevitable, and it finally came in February 1638 when Leonard Calvert led an expedition that caught Claiborne's men off guard and occupied the island. This victory eliminated the immediate competition, but the status of Kent Island and its relationship to St. Mary's remained unclear. By the late 1630s, Maryland had a notional capital city with scarcely any urban features, but its status as "town land" nevertheless remained crucial to the proprietor's model of civic commercial order.[74]

Resistance to Baltimore's spatial organization of authority around St. Mary's only worsened in the early 1640s. The Virginia planters who opposed Baltimore's colony drew increased strength and motivation from their connections with the confessional political division of the civil war in the English Atlantic. The planter-merchant network in the Chesapeake and London, including Claiborne and Matthews, had long associations with radical Protestantism, and they quickly aligned with the cause of Parliament in its struggle with the king. The planter-merchants had always been suspicious of the Calverts because of their Catholicism, but now the conflict between Parliament and the king meant that the proprietary family's religion combined with their royalism further weakened their claims to legitimate authority in the eyes of Parliamentary supporters. In this context, any effort to maintain proprietary authority over trade through St. Mary's was bound to be met with hostility.[75]

The Calverts knew to tread carefully in this volatile context, but when Governor Leonard Calvert returned from England in 1644, he brought an order from the beleaguered Stuart court that enflamed the region. Because he was no longer able to collect customs duties through the port of London, which was under parliamentary control, Charles I had granted Governor Calvert authority to establish a customs collection system for the whole Chesapeake at St. Mary's, with authority to seize the ships of London merchants. Since the granting of the charter, Baltimore had always asserted his right to designate ports and grant commercial privileges in an attempt to centralize trade at St. Mary's. Now, backed by royal authority, the Catholic proprietor's claims to urban commercial jurisdiction at St. Mary's were even stronger.[76]

The Calverts' attempt to strengthen the authority of St. Mary's was a lightning rod for colonists' discontent. When Leonard Calvert began exercising his new royal power in 1644, he quickly attracted the ire of William Claiborne and his new ally, London ship captain and merchant Richard Ingle. Claiborne was anxious for a pretext to regain control of Kent Island, and Ingle was smarting from a confrontation the previous year in which proprietary authorities had tried to convict him for making antimonarchical statements, but it was news of the new authority of St. Mary's that sparked violence. When Ingle returned to the Chesapeake in 1644, he was initially intending to trade peacefully, but he discovered that the year's tobacco harvest was already being loaded at St. Mary's by a Dutch vessel, the *Looking Glass*, and also that Governor Calvert had issued a proclamation requiring all ships to report to Maryland's urban hub. Enraged, Ingle mustered troops in Virginia for an assault on the proprietary province and particularly upon the Calverts' pretensions to commercial authority in St. Mary's. In February 1645, he sailed to St. Mary's, seized the *Looking Glass*, and began looting the homes of all the Catholic planters in the vicinity.[77]

For nearly two years, the colony was out of the Calverts' control, ripped apart by confessional divisions and class tensions, and one of the rebels' main objectives was overturning the civil and commercial authority of the explicitly defined "town land" of St. Mary's. One of Ingle's leading supporters, Nathaniel Pope, had previously purchased the "Towne house" where the colony's assemblies gathered at St. Mary's, and in the early months of the rebellion he fortified the property with earthworks to create a space referred to as "Mr Pope's fort," which served as "the center of the rebellion." In a move that paralleled the overthrow of Harvey in Virginia ten years before, the rebels clearly intended to seize and co-opt the notional urban space that was intended to anchor the proprietor's authority.[78] Testimony from those who witnessed or participated in Ingle's Rebellion corroborates the existence of a general belief that proprietary power in Maryland was embodied by the geographic space of St. Mary's. Ingle himself returned to London in 1645, and parliamentary authorities questioned him about the events in the colony. He hastened to point out that "the Countrey of Maryland and the severall ports and havens therein and especially St Georges River" were in a state of armed resistance to Parliament.[79] The sailors from both Ingle's ship and the *Looking Glass*, who were quizzed by parliamentary officials back in London, all described the events as occurring "att a place or bay called Maryland," suggesting that, despite the Calverts' claims to control over the northern Chesapeake Bay, their authority was really concentrated in St. Mary's. The sailors disagreed about whether Maryland's Catholic planters were intent on violent resistance to Parliament, but they all agreed that the proprietor's power had a precise epicenter.[80] The whole objective of Ingle and his allies was to undermine that epicenter.

Ingle's Rebellion dramatically changed life in Maryland. Leonard Calvert fled to Virginia, some of the Catholic leaders were shipped back to England by Ingle, and the English population fell dramatically. Settlement along the Potomac and at Kent Island continued (as did the confessional tensions), but those who farmed and traded in the region no longer observed the Calverts' structure of manors and city in the mid-1640s. The requirement that ships report to St. Mary's and the policies that forced Protestant freemen to answer to Catholic lords were swept away. No other structure of local government officially replaced the manors and cities. Unlike their Virginia neighbors, who had sought to neuter Harvey's authority at Jamestown through the creation of shires, Maryland's Protestant rebels did not already have a replacement structure of local government in mind to replace the order they overturned.[81]

In fact, in Maryland it was the Calverts themselves who turned to a county structure in an effort to reestablish their authority in the colony after Ingle's depredations. Counties had been part of the constitutional thinking for Maryland from the start. The proprietor's charter had described the whole province as constitutionally akin to the county palatinate of Durham in England, but it had not specifically granted permission to erect new counties. St. Mary's and its surrounding manors notionally constituted a single county, with rural subdivisions that used the traditional English designation of hundreds. However, in response to the existential challenge posed to their authority in the 1640s, the Calverts reached for the language of the county to comprehend St. Mary's relationship with the rest of its hinterland.[82]

The strategy of establishing new counties was first tested by the Calverts in relation to Kent Island in the years before Ingle's Rebellion. In 1639, after Leonard Calvert had captured the island from Claiborne, it was initially legislated into the colony's political structure as a hundred within St. Mary's County. However, this status, and by extension the authority of the officers that Leonard Calvert had left in charge on Kent Island, remained either too weak or insufficiently appealing to the community that continued to live and trade on the island; at some point in 1642, Kent Island was formally recognized as Kent County.[83] This was not an organic development reflecting the needs of a growing population; the island still boasted only seventy taxable men. However, Leonard Calvert was struggling to retain the loyalty of the island's colonists, and this loyalty was particularly crucial in 1642 as the Kent Islanders' old trading partners and allies, the Susquehannocks, were threatening the colony. As a result, before Calvert gathered the assembly in 1642 to gain support for defensive measures against the Susquehannocks, he created a new governmental structure of two coequal counties—St. Mary's and Kent—seeking to invest Kent Islanders in his colony. This gamble paid off, at least in the short term; despite repeated efforts, the island settlement's founder, William Claiborne, found it difficult to persuade the Kent Islanders, now officially part of Maryland, to rise up against the proprietor; they rebuffed his approaches specifically because he failed to offer any official alternative jurisdiction. The county had provided an alternative form of spatial authority that allowed Kent Island to be co-opted within the proprietor's structure of authority.[84]

In the aftermath of Ingle's depredations, the Calverts extended the system of county establishment. Beginning in the late 1640s, Baltimore sought to repopulate Maryland and reassure parliamentary authorities in England of his loyalty to their authority and his tolerance for religious dissenters by attracting new Protestant immigrants. Rather than returning to the manorial system, he chose to establish these new communities of men and women as distinct counties. One group, led by English immigrant Robert Brooke, settled along the Patuxent River and was designated by Baltimore as Charles County;[85] the other, made up of puritans fleeing Governor Berkeley's politics in Virginia, agreed to settle farther north on the Severn River as Anne Arundel County (named after Baltimore's wife).[86] Crucially, neither of these groups was especially large—Brooke initially brought just a few families—and thus their status was not a matter of practical necessity. Rather, their standing as counties represented an effort on the part of the proprietor to regain control over the civic structure of his province.

Ingle's uprising was a dramatic attack on both the urban and manorial structure that Baltimore had sought to build in Maryland.[87] But Baltimore, in his efforts to reestablish control, countered the Maryland rebels' overthrowing of the existing structure by consciously reshaping the political topography. Rather than simply surrendering to the rebels' desire to fill the colony with small private tobacco plantations operating independently within an unregulated Atlantic commercial network, the Calverts imagined a new county-based system of local government. Baltimore's conscious attempt to replicate the county model proliferating in Virginia suggests that he jealously eyed the stability that William Berkeley had begun to cultivate through the maturing shire system in the 1640s. In the struggle to establish civic community and commercial regulation in the tobacco planters' world, Lord Baltimore had ultimately replicated the county model that Virginia had stumbled toward over the previous decade. His next struggle, as we shall see, would be to convince his new subjects that his shires were a legitimate and effective safeguard of their commercial and political rights.

: : :

The collapse of the Virginia Company had inaugurated a quarter century of struggle to define what an English plantation should look like and how it should be governed. These tobacco boom years placed English planters in a new world of staple agricultural production within an emerging transnational commodity market, and the short-lived boom in the fur trade only confused matters further. In this context, the civic potential of urban institutions, as guardians of the common good within a commercial society, meant that urban development remained foremost in the minds of officials on both sides of the Atlantic. The inherent tensions between civic autonomy and royal patronage, which marked early modern European cities, though, was now more starkly apparent in the divisions between Crown and proprietary officials and those who styled themselves as planters. Royal and proprietary urban hubs were the first tentative steps toward one means of bringing the commerce of empire within what William Anys described as "the power of the state." In the midst of fiscal and confessional disputes, urban political authority of this kind in the hands of Harvey and Baltimore, even if ostensibly framed in terms of the common good, appeared threatening to established planter-merchant interests. The system of county courts, which emerged to anchor the rights of the Chesapeake planters over their private fiefdoms and their exploited servant laborers, represented a conscious alternative to the model of royal and proprietary urban hubs.[88]

As we shall see, though, the county system forged in the 1630s and 1640s was not necessarily a permanent solution to the planters' civic quandary. It remained stable only as long as the authority flowing from England was weakened by domestic civil strife. When state interest in commerce and the civic structure of the Chesapeake intensified again under England's Commonwealth regime and its allies in the Chesapeake, questions of urban development and authority would once again test and refine the emerging planter political economy. But the forging of the early county system meant that any future efforts to impose an urban structure would have to be reconciled with the established power and legitimacy of the county court.

CHAPTER THREE

The Political Geography of Empire in the English Revolution

By the late 1640s, amid revolutionary upheaval around the British Isles and the English Atlantic, the Chesapeake seemed to have achieved a measure of stability. Both Sir William Berkeley and Lord Baltimore had established county systems that organized local elites through ties of personal loyalty. However, this pragmatic statecraft had weaknesses. It was predicated upon the devolution of authority over commerce, social order, and religion to the rural fiefdoms of the planter community, and upon tobacco profits maintained by an influx of Dutch merchants. It was a political economy designed for local stability that would soon confront a rapidly developing commercial empire. The leaders of the new English Commonwealth, created after the execution of King Charles I in 1649, were not content merely with the submission of colonial governments that had supported the king, such as those in Virginia and Maryland. They sought to integrate the English Atlantic into a single imperial trading system that would unite and strengthen the new Commonwealth state against its European rivals through economic growth.[1] The Chesapeake region, though, still seemed woefully incapable of balancing private commercial interests with an expanded view of the common good of the entire English realm. It remained a monocultural economy reliant on foreign merchants. This was what one contemporary commentator called the "Disease" of the Chesapeake, which set it apart from the other royalist colonies that they sought to subdue. Commonwealth officials spent a disproportionate amount of energy seeking a cure for the Chesapeake's civic and political-economic ailment. This inevitably led to a renewed discussion about the need for urban development, which was now understood as a means to establish the region's place within the English commercial empire.[2]

The urban plan that Commonwealth reformers developed for the Chesapeake diverged from that previously envisioned by royal and proprietary officials. As puritans, the Commonwealth's leaders came from a tradition of political and economic thought that valued corporate urban institutions as the best means to cultivate civic order and promote industry. The experience of the 1640s, when England's boroughs—particularly London—had been in the vanguard of resisting the king, reinforced their centrality to the idea of stable and successful commonwealth. This represented a swing back toward understanding urban incorporation as the recognition of an existing civic community, not as a symbol of royal patronage. Furthermore, Commonwealth policy was informed by the ideas of a community of thinkers, gathered around German printer and scientist Samuel Hartlib, who sought to facilitate a "universal reformation" of society based on scientific approaches to economic and social problems; for them, urban centers were critical for coordinating commerce and knowledge that would facilitate new economic projects, transform individuals, and perfect society. These ideas about corporate urban governance and scientific urban growth came together during the late 1640s as Commonwealth leaders sought to solve perceived problems in the Chesapeake and unlock its potential as an integral part of a larger English commercial empire through the establishment of new independent corporate towns.

This new Commonwealth effort to support corporate towns, which was influenced by discussions of the Chesapeake's unique problems, was critical to the emergence of a broader ideal of commercial empire during the English Revolution. The most famous part of the Commonwealth's new vision of empire in the early 1650s is the Navigation Act of 1651, which limited colonial trade to English shipping. The new restrictions seem to be a concrete manifestation of a new centralized state that saw colonies as sources of raw materials that could be subjugated for its benefit. Historians have long debated why England's revolutionary government was at the vanguard of strengthening state power over the empire; contemporaries also struggled with the question of how to reconcile republican ideals with the growth of imperialism. However, understanding the debate over corporate towns in the Chesapeake helps to clarify what kind of empire Commonwealth leaders thought they were building. The architect of the Navigation Act, Benjamin Worsley, was also at the center of the effort to remodel the Chesapeake's political economy through diversification and town development—a project that had much broader aims than merely colonial subjugation. Worsley's elaborate plans for reforming the Chesapeake reveal that the origins of the new vision of English commercial empire were rooted in urban corporate institutions on both sides of the Atlantic.

Commonwealth political economists no longer viewed municipal corporations as entirely autonomous, but neither did they simply seek to make them tools of the central state. They were nodes within the larger English Atlantic puritan commonwealth, sharing a common civic culture, and connected by commercial interests that formed the ligaments of the new republican commercial empire.³

In the Chesapeake, however, reactions to these ideas were decidedly mixed. After the imposition of Commonwealth authority in the Chesapeake in 1652, the aspiration for urban development was embraced by radical puritan communities, most of whom had migrated to Maryland during the late 1640s, and they played a crucial role in once again destabilizing Lord Baltimore's authority. However, the new plans for urban development were never popular among the existing planter elite. In fact, the articulation of the Commonwealth's urban vision for the Chesapeake prompted established planters to reinforce the county system in Virginia and to take the first steps toward extolling their rural structure as a superior form of civic community. They increasingly claimed civic authority as planters, predicated upon the virtue of a rural system built on servitude and slavery.

THE CULTURE OF THE COUNTY SYSTEM

After more than three decades of upheaval, Virginia finally appeared to be enjoying a measure of stability by the mid-1640s. Governor Sir William Berkeley succeeded in using the county system to establish a stable and decentralized patronage system to reinforce his authority. Such was Berkeley's success that, as we have seen, the Calvert family also elected to encourage county courts in their effort to regain control of their colony of Maryland after Ingle's Rebellion. But this devolution of authority, long viewed by historians as part of a pragmatic tradition of local governance, was part of a particular state-building strategy that offered considerable commercial freedom to planters in exchange for their loyalty to the Stuart state. The shortcomings of this strategy were only too evident to contemporaries caught up in England's own constitutional crisis.⁴

Leading planter-merchants in the late 1630s had convinced the Crown to instruct Governor Francis Wyatt to abandon Jamestown, but when Berkeley arrived in Virginia in 1641, he reversed that decision and continued Harvey's investment in the colony's capital. He owned property in Jamestown and cultivated a community of merchants who traded through the port, and he also convinced the General Assembly to retain legislation offering incentives to craftsmen who established workshops there. By all accounts, Jamestown was a thriving place in the 1640s, boasting a busy waterfront, with accounts of up to thirty ships docked at once.[5]

Unlike Harvey, though, Berkeley saw Jamestown as an urban hub that united a powerful rural gentry. Alongside his efforts to develop Jamestown, Berkeley also increasingly devolved power to the county courts. He relaxed the rules channeling all trade through Jamestown, and while he oversaw the development of new laws against market manipulation in 1643, he left it to the county courts to enforce them, greatly expanding the power of county justices over local markets.[6] With the outbreak of the Third Anglo-Powhatan War in 1644, the counties also became loci for the organization and funding of the war effort that succeeded in defeating the colonists' long-standing native rivals and seizing control of much of the tidewater region. In stark contrast to previous governors' efforts to use compact urban settlement as a defense against Indian attacks, Berkeley encouraged independent county communities to form militia units and contribute to the construction of forts under the private control of leading planters.[7] Furthermore, the county system became an incubator for Virginia's ecclesiastical structure. Berkeley oversaw the construction of new Anglican parishes, intended not only "for the advancement of God's glorie" but also for "the weale publique." General Assembly legislation gave local vestries, made up of elite laymen, authority over church affairs, and it left the oversight of these parish vestries to the county courts. As religious and political upheaval in Britain progressed through the 1640s, Berkeley became increasingly hostile to those with puritan leanings within the colony, but on the local level, he relied upon Anglican allies within the vestry structure to enforce restrictions on dissent, giving those allies the power to oust any clergymen whose teachings seemed too radical. All of these developments in local governance helped to place increasing power into the hands of local planter leaders, who were reliant upon Berkeley for the offices on which their authority rested.[8]

Making this system work, however, required compromises that Berkeley was only able to make because of the domestic upheaval in England, with authority divided between the Crown and Parliament and neither able to impose their will on the empire. Foremost was the welcome he offered to Dutch merchants. Dutch merchant networks constituted the primary competition to the established planter-merchant networks that had dominated the Chesapeake since the 1620s. The delegation of commercial regulation into the counties ensured that the governor retained the loyalty of local elites, but in the 1620s, decentralization had bred local cliques and complaints of corruption and exploitation. Harvey's efforts to address this problem with the planter-merchant networks had focused on centralizing trade through Jamestown. Berkeley's solution was to encourage competition to liberate middling planters from the grip of the dominant London merchant networks; he cultivated alliances with planters outside this faction, some of whom had developed commercial ties with the Dutch. For Berkeley, who remained staunchly loyal to Charles I, this strategy of increasing competition also had the advantage of undermining the dominance of the planter-merchant networks linked to London's puritan community and the Parliamentary cause. He approved General Assembly legislation specifically designed to facilitate Dutch trade. In 1643, Dutch merchant David De Vries reported that Berkeley offered to host him and his men at Jamestown through the winter, where he promised "he should use me well, and would have my society." Such gubernatorial hospitality was effective: within five years, the number of Dutch ships visiting the colony tripled. Neither royal nor parliamentary authorities in England were entirely comfortable with Dutch traders carrying Virginia tobacco to Amsterdam, but as they were preoccupied with domestic war, neither side could enforce their will in the Chesapeake, and Berkeley used Dutch trade to stabilize the market and strengthen his authority.[9]

Retaining the loyalty of the county leaders also required Berkeley to safeguard the short-term economic interests of planters. He relaxed regulation intended to restrict tobacco production and force economic diversification. During these years, planters began to perfect the techniques of tobacco agriculture, making productivity improvements at the expense of their servant and enslaved laborers, who were forced to work harder. This led to further increases in tobacco production rather than economic diversification. Inevitably, increased production drove tobacco prices lower, but efficiency savings combined with the demand generated by Dutch traders helped to cushion the impact for wealthy planters and facilitated the increasing concentration of wealth.[10] Berkeley also assisted these individuals with the exploitation of labor by overseeing the imposition of new rules that granted masters increased control over their laborers. Established planters benefited from greater leeway in disciplining servants and particularly in extending their terms of service. One scholar has noted that during these years, Berkeley presided over the legal process of establishing "servitude in Virginia as a rigorous condition of subordination to a master."[11] Berkeley also agreed to exclude the trade in bound labor from all mercantile regulations, effectively giving well-connected planters—those with commercial ties to merchants who spirited unwilling servants from England or dealt in African slaves—the ability to expand their labor forces at below-market prices. In particular, the Dutch commercial nexus that Berkeley cultivated was crucial to channeling more enslaved laborers into the Chesapeake, to be purchased by well-connected political leaders.[12] The result of Berkeley's county-based political economy, as one contemporary observer noted, was a colony where intensive tobacco production choked all efforts for the "publique good" and where "the People for the Most parte" were "the worst thing that growes there."[13]

Ultimately, the glue holding this system together was patronage. Berkeley adapted the county system to increase his control over the appointment of county officials, and county residents took oaths of allegiance binding them specifically to Berkeley's regime. He used appointments to county offices to cultivate alliances with individuals such as Richard Lee, Argoll Yeardley, and provincial secretary Richard Kemp, who traded primarily with Bristol or Dutch merchants, rather than the London puritan network. These alliances reinforced his authority in the vacuum created by Britain's civil wars, and they simultaneously facilitated the growth of a plantation system supported by bound labor and Dutch trade. Summing up Virginia's colonial commonwealth in 1649, former planter William Bullock astutely compared it to a building whose beams were "but pin'd together with their interest under a common title, and slightly fastned with personall ties."[14]

It was precisely this kind of personal patronage that Lord Baltimore sought to replicate by establishing new shires in Maryland at the end of the 1640s. The Calverts spelled out precisely what loyalty the leaders of the newly created Charles and Anne Arundel Counties owed to the proprietor and what their local powers over commerce, militia, and religion would be in return. For example, the grant of Charles County to English investor Robert Brooke was specifically predicated upon "his faithfulness to us" and his support for Baltimore against those within the puritan planter-merchant network who continued to question the validity of the Catholic proprietor's charter. Furthermore, the presence of Dutch merchants in St. Mary's in the 1640s, which had provoked Richard Ingle's attack on the town, was proof that the Calverts were also keen to develop Dutch ties to circumvent the influence of puritan merchant networks.[15]

Viewed from the vantage point of 1640s England, however, Chesapeake statecraft's dependence on patronage seemed decidedly threatening. Parliamentary leaders in England were opposed to the authority that Charles I had exercised through personal patronage, and while they were struggling to check these royal impositions at home, Berkeley and Baltimore had used the county system to anchor their authority in the Chesapeake. As the decade passed and Parliament's victory became more certain, Berkeley used his position to launch verbal barbs against the Parliamentary faction—some of which were printed and circulated in England—and to enforce conformity with the Anglican Church in Virginia. Anxieties among parliamentarians in England about the corrupting influence of colonial patronage were even more pronounced in relation to Maryland, where the patron in question was Catholic. Richard Ingle was still prosecuting his suits against Lord Baltimore, and complaints from the Calverts' new Protestant tenants in Charles and Anne Arundel Counties about the oaths they were required to swear were not far behind.[16]

For the leading Parliamentary thinkers, though, the problem went beyond the religious and political loyalties of officials in the Chesapeake; the county system also seemed to hinder England's divine mission of economic and social improvement. In the 1640s, a group of radical thinkers had formed in London around the German printer Samuel Hartlib, interested in using Baconian scientific methods to generate practical knowledge about resources and manufacturing techniques that could facilitate a millenarian project to perfect society. These thinkers were particularly interested in remodeling the English economy and emulating the perceived success of Dutch commerce over the past half century.[17] For them, the problem with the Chesapeake's governance and society was that it perpetuated an addiction to tobacco agriculture that limited innovation and rendered the region incapable of contributing to the broader productivity of the English Empire. Benjamin Worsley, one of the Hartlib circle members most actively concerned with developments in Virginia and also soon to be the architect of the Commonwealth's trade policy, concluded that "at the present the Virginia Plantation doth yeeld no more benefit to the nation, but that some from hence haue a liuelihood there; and some quantities of tobacco are sent hither." He was convinced it could produce a wealth of new commodities. Evidence from elsewhere in the Atlantic world seemed to bear this out; Barbados had recently diversified away from tobacco production and was in the midst of a staggering sugar boom fueled by new agricultural and industrial techniques (at huge human cost). When he compared Barbados's success to the stagnation of Virginia, Worsley concluded that the "obstruction of all these advantages doth proceed from the present gouvernour." Berkeley, he argued, had designed the entire structure of the colony "to tye them [the planters] with the lesse Trouble to his Intrest." In doing so, he had promoted Dutch trade and "persecuted all those that have beene well affected . . . to the Religious and Industrious Settlement & Reformation" of the colony. Worsley was convinced that

Berkeley's policy of patronage was designed to serve his private interest at the expense of encouraging lazy, unproductive, and disorganized commerce that hurt the wider English Protestant empire.[18]

William Bullock, a former Virginia colonist who was also developing schemes for improvement in the Chesapeake during these years, seconded Worsley's opinion. He noted that Virginia had "no setled Government and wholesome Lawes to preserve mens lives and estates, and to maintain honest commerce" because the system was too dependent upon the governor's influence. He agreed that Virginia's political structure encouraged planters to make short-term inefficient economic choices, and so "the Disease growes by the Commoditie they have and doe make their Staple." Commenting on Bullock's pamphlet, longtime Virginia investor John Ferrar noted that weak and decentralized organization under Berkeley had also led planters to "seate downe [in widely scattered estates] more for commodiousness than health," putting their short-term capacity to produce the largest tobacco harvest above even their long-term survival, "wch is most absurde."[19]

The system that Berkeley and Baltimore had built was designed to stabilize their local authority, but it was a direct challenge to these new civic and scientific ideas. Not only did it base political power on patronage, rather than participatory institutions, and threaten the religious freedom of puritan colonists, but it also sacrificed the economic improvement of the broader English Empire. That this powerful edifice of unproductive personal rule was built upon increasing commercial ties with the Dutch, who were the main rivals to London's puritan and Parliamentary-supporting merchants, was just more damning evidence that it threatened the flourishing of an English commercial empire. Once they completely seized control of the English state after the execution of Charles I in 1649, Commonwealth officials had numerous incentives for seeking to reform the Chesapeake's political and commercial structures.

THE SEARCH FOR A COMMONWEALTH SOLUTION

In seeking to solve the perceived ills of Chesapeake society, leading thinkers of the English Commonwealth realized they would need a radical plan to deconstruct the system that Berkeley and Baltimore had built. Their political-economic vision emphasized the importance of innovation and commercial growth within a broader imperial context, but even so, they returned to a familiar institutional structure to implement this plan: they proposed radically reorganizing the region around corporate towns.

An urban solution for the Chesapeake came naturally to England's commonwealth leaders because of their puritanism. Radical strains of Protestantism in the early seventeenth century had become closely tied to corporate town-based civic structures. It is a commonplace of early American history that puritan New England was built around towns, but many scholars have seen these towns as vestiges of English village culture, rather than the assertive political-economic institutions that they were. In fact, radical Protestants largely came from the corporate towns and cities that were growing in prosperous areas of southern England, and their politico-religious thought emerged from the same Renaissance humanist assumptions about active citizenship and the pursuit of the common good that animated that urban growth. Corporate urban institutions thus fostered, and were in turn fostered by, radical Protestants, and this relationship only grew stronger during the 1640s when Parliamentary-supporting cities and towns asserted their civic autonomy from the monarch.[20]

Over time, puritan communities also adapted corporate structures and the civic pursuit of the common good by introducing a Calvinist focus on personal piety and industry. This distinctive Christian humanism pushed beyond urban corporations' previous goals of simply regulating social and economic life, toward a larger project of transforming community members to make them internally more pious and externally more productive. For example, local magistrates in places such as Salisbury and Dorchester sought to establish town workhouses to address poverty and moral laxity with a combination of poor relief, public discipline, and the inculcation of industry. These reforms placed a greater emphasis on personal industriousness, helping to nudge forward ideas about economic growth and productivity. The overall goal for each corporation, however, remained the common good of the local town.[21] As Barry Levy has shown, it was this model that puritans brought to New England, establishing towns that were not just consensual corporate units of the godly but also political institutions through which community leaders disciplined laborers and made them both pious and productive. Thus, by the late 1640s, as puritan officials in England turned their attention to problems in the Chesapeake, they could point to examples of the effectiveness of their corporate model in encouraging productivity and promoting a commitment to the common good. This seemed a sharp contrast with the privatized patronage networks that held Chesapeake society together without enforcing any standards of conduct or industry.[22]

Commonwealth leaders, though, were also attuned to intellectual currents in London that were beginning to understand towns as more than merely little commonwealths that promoted civic virtue; properly governed urban spaces were increasingly understood as also drivers of economic growth and innovation for the benefit of the state. The members of the Hartlib circle, who actively pursued scientific innovation and economic development in an effort to perfect society, were particular advocates of this new vision of urban spaces as hubs where knowledge and resources could be gathered and harnessed for their projects. One of the best windows on this worldview is provided by Hartlib circle member Gabriel Plattes in his utopian description of the fictional kingdom of Macaria, which was intended as a model for England. Plattes imagined a fictional kingdom with a representative government supported by a series of technocratic councils who applied scientific knowledge to maximize state efficiency. The result would be agricultural and industrial improvements that would make it easier to feed a growing urban population. This urban development was critical to the vision of Macaria, as it provided a hub where knowledge could be gathered and innovation fostered through easy access to resources and shared pools of information. The end result was an upward spiral of growth and a happy and productive citizenry. Plattes emphasized that "great cities, which formerly devoured the fatnesse of the Kingdome, may yearely make a considerable retribution" to the state.[23]

Plattes's ideas were mirrored in a number of more practical suggestions by other Parliamentary thinkers during the 1640s. Samuel Hartlib himself took a leading role in efforts to reform the physical environs of London because he thought the city could facilitate the larger reformation of society. This vision for urban development was not simply limited to the capital though. Merchant and political economist Henry Robinson took the ideas further, arguing in a series of pamphlets on English trade through the 1640s that "it is necessary to reduce . . . all stragling Tenements, Villages and Townes, together into so many Cities" to facilitate trade. Robinson, like many of his fellow Parliamentary thinkers, was drawn to the example of the Netherland's recent economic success, and he noted that the "first great preheminance which . . . the United Provinces have of us, is, In that their Inhabitants live together in Towns and Cities of indifferent magnitudes . . . whereby they are able to accommodate and help themselves to the best advantage." England, he asserted, needed to abandon its singular focus on London and establish a network of urban centers on navigable rivers across the world to tap the diverse outputs of various climates. He suggested that these centers be open as free ports where merchants from any nation would be welcome, but he also cautioned that trade would be "quite ruined" by completely open commerce, proposing that privileges and regulatory powers be granted broadly to whole urban corporations and large companies.[24] Even further afield, Hartlibian ideas influenced the colonial plans of John Winthrop Jr., the future governor of Connecticut. Winthrop centered the new colony on the town of New London and hoped to attract some of England's leading scientific thinkers and alchemists to relocate there and work with the Connecticut valley's resources, establishing in the process an urban center that would function as a hub for knowledge and innovation. This model of urban development combined the puritan reforming zeal to transform individuals with a scientific faith in the ability to transform commodities, all as part of a larger effort to expand English commerce and perfect English society. The corporate town was no longer an isolated and particular jurisdiction within the realm, but a critical civic node within an English network that pursued both spiritual and economic improvement.[25]

No one was better positioned to appreciate the conjunction of these ideas than the intellectual and bureaucrat Benjamin Worsley. Worsley spent his youth in London, exposed to the city's corporate structures and its radical political and religious ideas in the late 1630s, and he established connections within the city's puritan merchant community. He was also active in Hartlib's intellectual circle and thus familiar with the writings of Plattes and Robinson. Worsley spent the late 1640s in Amsterdam, where he experienced firsthand the strength of Dutch urban civic culture and simultaneously recognized the increasing Dutch encroachment on English commerce with its colonies. He became increasingly convinced that the new republican state being built in England would need to assert much stronger unified authority over the trade of its colonial possessions.[26]

As Worsley began to think about ways to perfect the commercial system of the new English Commonwealth, he became preoccupied with the problems of the Chesapeake. His puritan merchant allies were increasingly anxious to cut out Dutch competition from the tobacco trade, but his intellectual background and connections to Hartlib's circle meant that he took a broader view on the problems and the political solutions to the civic and economic shortcomings of the tobacco coast. The news that Worsley received from the Chesapeake convinced him that broader reform was not only necessary but also achievable. One practical source of information about the Chesapeake colonies that circulated among the Hartlib thinkers was former Virginia planter William Bullock's 1649 pamphlet, *Virginia Impartially Examined*, which offered a biting critique of Berkeley's patronage system. Bullock's prescription for addressing Virginia's dysfunction was very much in line with the Hartlib circle's interest in ambitious private economic projects that could also transform the civic and social order.[27] He offered a morass of practical suggestions, primarily focused on converting the colony's economy from tobacco to wheat production, but these innovations were intended to do more than increase profits. For Bullock, shifting away from tobacco, which required careful cultivation through the hot summer months, would improve living standards for the laboring class; this would facilitate the dismantling of the system of servitude that Berkeley had reinforced and transform colonial labor so that workers would find themselves "at the very first in the condition of Journeymen" (with short-term contracts and freedom to change employers) and ultimately "absolute Freemen." These agricultural freemen would be more productive when given the opportunity to pursue their own projects. Their efforts would also generate a bustling market that would spur urban craftspeople, because "where a great Merchant-like Trade is driven, as will suddenly be in this place; all Artificer and handicraft labour is dear."[28] Bullock believed this community of journeymen and craftsmen could simultaneously rebuild Virginia's civic structure and enrich the state. To achieve this, he proposed abandoning the county structure, arguing that planters could be gathered into collective "divisions" until the community was truly ready for "Shires, Hundreds, and Parishes." In the meantime, he outlined a new plan for Virginia's governance that brought the "divisions" together under a system that closely resembled an urban corporation, consisting of a council that annually selected a new governor from within its ranks. Bullock's vision provided Worsley with a model for replacing Berkeley's county oligarchs with a new civic leadership whose authority would be built upon a diverse economic base and a new class of laborers.[29]

Bullock's scheme may have been a pipe dream in 1649, but news was also reaching Worsley about a genuine effort from the Chesapeake's existing puritan communities to reject Berkeley's county system and adopt their own town-based structure. Worsley's merchant contacts reported "that not only Civill, & Industrious men, but good men" had settled in Virginia during the previous decade, "and a church 2 or 3 of the Independent, & presbyterian way, were gathered." The merchants were referring to the compact communities of puritans, many of whom were migrants from New England, who had settled along the south side of the James River over the previous twenty years.[30] These communities had pursued economic diversification, and they had fostered commercial and religious ties with New England, becoming enmeshed in a puritan Atlantic. Their desire for local control over church and society in their new home had not combined well with Berkeley's county system; the Virginia General

Assembly was forced to devote considerable time to organizing and reorganizing the counties and parishes on the south side of the James, suggesting that the new arrivals in the region were uncomfortable with the local political structures they were expected to adopt. New Englanders, though, had no doubts about the nature of the communities. They reported in 1643 that they maintained correspondence with "three several Towns in Virginia." Nor was this simply an effort to shoehorn town forms into the Chesapeake's existing rural settlement pattern. A fleeting project to relocate some of Virginia's puritans to land on the colony's Northern Neck peninsula, north of the Rappahannock River, vividly attests to the active pursuit of a puritan vision of compact community that clashed with Berkeley's county system. In the midst of the Third Anglo-Powhatan War, many colonists moved to seize large acreages of prime tobacco land on this newly opening northern frontier. Leading members of Virginia's puritan community were part of this rush into Powhatan territory, but rather than claiming sprawling estates, they planned to organize their patents as a compact contiguous acreage, implying a persistent aspiration to establish new town-based communities. These men and women, with intimate ties to Atlantic puritan networks, were already well versed in the corporate ethos of the puritan town model.[31]

The divergence in political-economic visions between Virginia's puritans and the countycentric planter system was thrown into sharp relief in 1649 when the majority of the puritans, increasingly unhappy with Berkeley's clampdown on nonconformity, abandoned their plans for the Northern Neck and agreed to migrate to Maryland. Virginia's puritans were the beneficiaries of Lord Baltimore's efforts to reassert his authority after Ingle's Rebellion. As part of his plan to implement a new county system, Baltimore granted the Virginia refugees a large area of land on the western side of the Chesapeake that he christened Anne Arundel County in honor of his wife.[32] Baltimore intended the new county to resemble the ones in which the refugees had previously lived in Virginia, directly tied to him through patronage, but the men and women who fled Virginia had a different vision. In a series of letters to John Ferrar, former Virginia Company leader, Maryland planters reported that the puritans—about seven hundred in all—intended to establish themselves in towns. Initial reports from 1650 suggested that they had "but newly settled" and "have not tyme as [yet] to bild townes," but by the following year, another correspondent noted that "at their first coming ther they seat in maner of a towne both at severn & patuxon." Archaeological evidence confirms this influx of settlers into Anne Arundel County, with a significant number of home sites around the area of Whitehall Bay north of the Severn River that all date from the 1650s. The puritan towns would come to be known as Providence and Patuxent respectively, and they would provide a model for much of the Commonwealth-era thinking about Chesapeake political economy.[33]

For English Commonwealth observers who received reports about the puritan migration, the critical point was that the Chesapeake region contained a community of "civill & industrious" people who were suffering both religious persecution and economic hardship under Governor Berkeley. Worsley's reports on the Chesapeake emphasized the "iniuries that have beene offred & practiced [by Berkeley], toward those that were willing to be forward examples, of Piety, or goodnesse or countenancers of Industry & Civility" in the colony. Worsley's observations demonstrate the way in which puritanism was part of a broader political-economic vision that emphasized the industrious pursuit of new commodities to stimulate growth within civic communities. He perceived Berkeley's efforts to enforce Anglican conformity as not simply theological housekeeping, but as an attack on the social and economic norms of the puritan community. The Chesapeake, then, seemed to be divided between a pious, industrious, and civil society of men and women working for the common good of the new English Protestant empire through an orderly town-based structure and a group of self-serving planters whose only loyalty was to a network of personal patronage ties that ultimately led back to the recently executed monarch.[34]

Inspired by this perceived dichotomy, Worsley sketched out reforms that he believed would lead to a fundamental transformation of England's oldest American colony. The key problem, as Worsley saw it, was Virginia's dependence upon tobacco. This dependence, which he believed was maintained by Berkeley's policies, imperiled citizens' capacity to pursue the public good of the wider English commercial empire. To address these problems, Worsley explored the potential for new commodities, including rice, flax, and the manufacturing of leather, linen, and distilled spirits. He proposed schemes through which his merchant allies could receive trading privileges in the colony, provided that "such a part of [their] stocke be layd out, & imployd in the introduction of such or such a new Comodity, or erecting & setting up of such or such a profitable & necessary a Manufacture." Diversification was obviously not a new goal for the region, but whereas for Sandys and Harvey it had been about creating balance to facilitate local order, Worsley was now more interested in the encouragement it would give to the puritan values of industriousness and civic virtue and the benefits those values would bring to the wider English economy.

"The increase of trading & Manufactures" in the Chesapeake, Worsley explained, would make England the key "staple and mart" for new commodities, and also "many other conveniencyes will redound to the subiects of this state . . . for then the Parliaments friends, good men, free preaching of the Gospel, Industry & Civility will bee Countenanced." Here Worsley used the same language he previously employed to describe the already established efforts of Virginia's puritan community, indicating that he saw his plan as a natural extension of the work already under way. Economic reform would reinforce these efforts, turning Virginians into civic-minded citizens who could share a common bond of commerce, industry, and faith with their brethren across the Atlantic world. It was this union of economic and religious interests that would strengthen the Commonwealth state.[35]

In 1650, Worsley was appointed secretary to the newly formed Council of Trade, which gave him the opportunity to implement his ideas for Virginia as part of a broader vision for the future of the English commercial empire. One of the Commonwealth's first priorities was to develop plans to bring the remaining royalist colonies, including Virginia, under Commonwealth control. The new government dispatched a formidable naval fleet to impose the authority of the Commonwealth state with military force. However, in the case of Virginia, Worsley seized the opportunity to push his broader reforming agenda. Although he had many friends among London's merchant community who were eager to reclaim their stranglehold over the Chesapeake tobacco trade, he was careful to emphasize that "good to mankind & to the Comon wealth," not short-term commercial advantage, was the ultimate objective of the Commonwealth takeover in Virginia. The council's 1651 commission to replace Berkeley and bring Virginia's government under parliamentary authority was granted to Robert Dennis, Thomas Stegge, Richard Bennett, and William Claiborne (the merchant who was a longtime opponent of Baltimore's charter rights in Maryland). All of these men had connections to London's merchant network, but their commission did not give them any special trading privileges, and it also required them to call a new assembly to gain the colony's support for broader reforms. Although the details of their instructions have not survived, we know from their subsequent actions that they were ordered to promote the development of new corporate towns to enforce commercial regulations and encourage economic development. Worsley insisted that the plan was not intended to undermine Virginians' "just Libertyes," but merely to undercut the patronage system and offer them "a more perfect liberty." He was sure that this would encourage the "Richer, soberer, & perhap the greater part of the Plantation," who would be "glad of the friendshyp & Government of Parlaiment."[36]

Worsley was clearly building his plans on the basis of the information he had received about development in the Chesapeake. Significantly, one of the commissioners, Richard Bennett, was the leader of the puritan community that had migrated to Maryland. He had returned to England in the intervening years to complain about Baltimore's proprietary governance, likely bringing a glowing report of the progress of the new towns of Providence and Patuxent that he and the puritan transplants from Virginia were establishing in Maryland, and of the potential for further development using this urban model. Bennett (along with William Claiborne, who had a particular ax to grind against Lord Baltimore) probably played a crucial role in persuading officials to expand the commission to encompass the whole Chesapeake, thereby also bringing Maryland's puritans under its protection. The towns that Bennett described were precisely the model that Worsley and the Council of Trade had in mind for the cultivation of "Industry and Civility."[37]

The plan for the Chesapeake, though, was just one part of an emerging Commonwealth vision for commercial empire that Worsley developed during these years. The Council of Trade was established by the Commonwealth regime with the broader goal of regaining control of England's commerce from the Dutch and also ensuring that "ye poore people of this Land may be set on work . . . and that the Commonwealth might be enriched thereby."[38] The council's plans for achieving this broader goal centered on promoting new urban development. Directly echoing the ideas of Henry Robinson, they first proposed transforming a number of English towns into free ports, where merchants of any nation could trade. The objective was to make England a general clearinghouse capable of competing with the Netherlands as the hub for the world of rapidly globalizing commerce and in the process revitalizing the Commonwealth's provincial towns and generating employment for the poor. As England's relations with the Dutch soured during 1651, the free port scheme was replaced with the Navigation Act, which sought to stimulate English trade in precisely the opposite way; it prevented foreign merchants from importing goods (other than their own domestic products) into England or its colonies, thereby requiring colonial trade to be carried by English ships to English ports, channeling commodities through the realm's urban centers by force.[39]

Although this was a radical reversal of policy, it nevertheless reflected one critical continuity in the thinking of Worsley and others at the Council of Trade. Both proposals focused on stimulating urban growth through state policy, and both would rely upon local urban institutions for enforcement. Crucially, the Navigation Act did nothing to hinder the growth of colonial crafts, manufactures, or local merchandising; the goal was not merely to subjugate colonial planters to English mercantile interests, but to build upon Worsley's plan for Virginia by encouraging urban and commercial growth around the English Atlantic. The Navigation Act was unquestionably an unprecedented expansion of state power, predicated on an increasingly unified vision of the state, but one built upon an interlocking network of new urban hubs that would naturally align with the greater cause of improvement for the new English Commonwealth. This was a vision shaped in no small part through Worsley's meditation on the Chesapeake's unique political-economic problems.[40]

The Commonwealth commissioners, who left England for the Chesapeake just as the Navigation Act was being finalized, were not simply the shock troops of mercantilism imposing the commercial hegemony of the newly centralized English state. Their mission was to once again remodel the Chesapeake's economic and political structure, establishing and strengthening urban communities that would fit within a new Atlantic network of civil, industrious, and godly corporate towns stretching from Bristol to Boston and Bridgetown. These urban communities would be bound together by a new commitment to expanding commerce. They would share "an inclination" rather than a compulsion, "to depend upon this State." In Worsley's words, the commissioners sought to "settle a gouvernment sutable to the interest of this Common-wealth in the advancement of Religion ciuility Industry & trade by the meanes of such adventurers as will owne the Parliaments Authority there and act vnder it."[41]

"REDUCING, SETTLING, AND GOVERNING"

That the first Navigation Act did not lead to broader imperial economic reform reflected the fact that implementing the more ambitious elements of the scheme in the Chesapeake proved to be far more complex than simply asserting the authority of the Commonwealth regime. When the commissioners Richard Bennett and William Claiborne made it to Virginia in the early spring of 1652 (Stegge and Dennis died en route), they momentarily squared off with Governor Berkeley, but after some posturing, the governor agreed to surrender. Given the commissioners' naval strength and the colonists' reliance on trade, Berkeley could never realistically have resisted the Commonwealth's authority. Bennett and Claiborne immediately asserted the power of Parliament and promulgated the Navigation Act. The bigger challenge for the commissioners, though, was establishing new commercial communities to displace the planter oligarchy. Only in Maryland would they enjoy a measure of success by empowering the existing urban communities, with destabilizing and deadly consequences for Baltimore's appointed leaders.[42]

The commissioners certainly took their instructions for the "Reducing, Settling, and Governing" of the Chesapeake seriously. Richard Bennett assumed the governorship of Virginia and immediately called a new assembly in March 1652. About one-third of the elected burgesses had never served in the assembly before, and Edward Major, a known Parliamentary sympathizer, puritan, and neighbor of Bennett, was selected as Speaker. Another third of the burgesses, however, were allies of Berkeley and veterans of recent assemblies. This tense balance led to compromises as the burgesses set about completely revising Virginia's statutes to reconcile them with Commonwealth rule. In some cases, they preserved the status quo; the county structure was maintained minus its explicit references to the monarch, and regulations governing servitude and native diplomacy were copied into the new statutes. Crucially, though, the commissioners simultaneously pushed for reform in the colony's political-economic structures. Central to this effort was the passage of "An Act Concerninge townes and corporations," empowering local communities to establish autonomous municipal corporations. "Nothinge," the act's preamble explained, "will more Conduce to the good subsistance and welfare of this Countery of Virginia in the peaceable government thereof, and the Increase and maintenance, of trade, and Commerce, then the gatheringe, and settling the people, and Inhabitants into townes, And Corporations." This language closely echoed the thinking of Parliamentary political economists and members of the Hartlib circle, and it signaled the arrival of the Commonwealth's ambitious agenda in the Chesapeake.[43]

This plan, had it been embraced by significant numbers of Virginia planters, would have completely reoriented the colony's political and commercial geography. The act made no mention of Jamestown, where Berkeley had established an urban hub, and instead made it legal for the people "of any, or Everye Countye, to agree, and Joyne amongst themselves in a societye, and Incorporated bodye, or bodyes in one, or more places." The provisions of the new act empowered individuals to construct new urban political units with exclusive and exclusionary commercial privileges. New corporate towns were allowed to admit "as many Burgesses to be made free of the said Corporation, as they shall thinke ffitt and Conveniente"; they were also empowered to annually elect a mayor, a sheriff, and twelve aldermen, and they were promised "such priviledges and freedoms as any the Incorporated townes of England," including the right to make bylaws and control the market by restricting access to only formal members of the urban corporation. This was no token effort at encouraging diversification and countering Dutch influence. It was a not-so-subtle challenge to the power of the county courts under Berkeley's governance. It extended a free invitation to individuals who may have wanted to break away from the county system and establish communities with their own political and economic identities, legitimacy, and authority. Though it would likely have placed commercial regulation into the hands of men allied to the Commonwealth and amenable to the interests of the puritan London merchant network, it was hardly the most straightforward means of achieving that end. Rather, the act was intended to bolster urban commercial interest groups as independent civic communities and to establish a thick web of economic and cultural connections that would bind them to the larger English commercial empire rather than to a local patron such as Berkeley. These corporate towns would have fulfilled Worsley's ambition for a network of communities that shared a commitment to "Industry and Civility." And in doing so, they would have reoriented Virginia's culture and political economy around a system highly reminiscent of the puritan town communities of New England.[44]

Ultimately, though, the Commonwealth's radical corporate plan ran up against the entrenched interests of Virginia's leading planters. It is not entirely clear how the commissioners envisioned the new corporate towns being populated, but they were likely counting upon their allies within the puritan community; Worsley had argued that a reformed Virginia would immediately attract a fresh influx of England's poor, as well as a returning flood of religious radicals who had fled during Berkeley's rule.[45] Many of Berkeley's allies in the General Assembly probably assented to the legislation because they were confident that few men and women would actually take up the offer to establish corporate towns. They were proved correct. Many members of Virginia's puritan faction had left for Maryland or elsewhere in the English Atlantic during the late 1640s and were not lured back to establish new towns. With the outbreak of the Anglo-Dutch War just a couple of months after the General Assembly, any hopes of encouraging state-sponsored immigration by "honest privat men" also disappeared because of the uncertainty and danger of wartime Atlantic travel and trade.[46] For those already in Virginia, new corporate towns held little appeal when the colony's recent victory over the Powhatan had opened large new acreages for extensive tobacco agriculture. The slow uptake of the corporate scheme also meant that, in the absence of new town officers, the commissioners lacked an effective means of enforcing the Navigation Act around the dispersed colony; Dutch and royalist trade continued, sustaining tobacco demand and profits and creating a self-fulfilling cycle that disincentivized poorer planters from shifting to urban trades. Even Parliamentary supporters, such as Samuel Matthews, likely stood to lose more than they would gain by establishing new urban corporations in their neighborhoods. Ultimately, despite Worsley's grand ambitions, the urban corporate plan proved incapable of disrupting the tobacco plantation system.[47]

In Maryland, however, the plan to reorganize the Chesapeake's spatial geography achieved dramatic results. In March 1652, while the General Assembly was gathering in Virginia, the commissioners journeyed to Maryland to assert their authority over the colony, despite the fact that in England Baltimore was scrambling to safeguard his charter under the new regime. William Claiborne's long-standing grievances against Maryland over Kent Island obviously played a crucial role in encouraging the commissioners' actions. Notably, however, Bennett and Claiborne rose above personal vendettas. Instead of seeking retribution against the proprietor's allies, they focused on bolstering the political identity and authority of the puritan towns of Providence and Patuxent that Bennett had helped to found, and whose existence had helped frame Chesapeake policy back in London.[48]

By the time the commissioners arrived in Maryland, the colony's puritan towns seemed to be increasingly in need of their protection. Following the death of Governor Leonard Calvert in 1647, Baltimore had bestowed the governorship on William Stone, a Protestant Virginian merchant, as a symbol of his commitment to protect his new puritan colonists. Stone, however, had begun to alienate the puritan towns, particularly by seeking to bolster loyalty to Baltimore by requiring all colonists to swear oaths of allegiance to the proprietor. Oaths had been one of the main issues of contention between Berkeley and the Virginia puritans, and they were even more threatening when imposed by a Catholic proprietor. As a result, residents of the new puritan towns felt that their political independence was under threat when the commissioners reached St. Mary's City with the authority of the Commonwealth behind them. In exchange for allowing Stone to remain governor, the commissioners made him agree to stop acting in Baltimore's name and tinkered with the colony's governing council to ensure that the puritan towns were well represented.[49]

These changes laid the foundation for an urban structure in Maryland. For the first couple of years, Stone nominally governed the puritan towns without really interfering in their trade and internal affairs, effectively allowing them to function as autonomous urban corporations. Archaeological evidence suggests that the largely independent towns thrived in the mid-1650s. Providence, on the Severn River, was a loosely compact settlement with a nascent new craft economy and distinctive urban architecture. Written records from the 1650s are extremely sparse, but they also suggest that the settlers in Charles County, which had been established by Robert Brooke, formed a nucleated settlement on the Patuxent River that was referred to as Patuxent.[50]

However, the delicate compromise between the town communities and Stone's government floundered early in 1654. The governor received word that Lord Baltimore had succeeded in getting his proprietary authority reconfirmed by Oliver Cromwell's new Protectorate government in England. Baltimore instructed Stone to reimpose the oaths that bound colonists through the county structure to his personal authority. He also ordered Stone to strip all authority from Robert Brooke of Charles County because of Brooke's submission to the Commonwealth commissioners. Stone's response illustrated the close correlation the proprietor expected between county government and loyalty: Brooke's Charles County was wiped from the proprietor's map of Maryland, to be replaced with a new shire named Calvert County. Baltimore clearly understood that the construction and naming of spaces was crucial to the patronage relationship on which his power rested.[51]

Baltimore was wrong to think, though, that he could create loyalties as easily as he could change names on a map. Patuxent and Providence would not surrender their political identities and authority without a fight. Just as Stone was preparing to fully reestablish Baltimore's county system in the summer of 1654, Bennett and Claiborne returned to Maryland and met "with Some of the people of Putuxent & Severne" to plan the overthrow of proprietary authority. Their case against Stone and Baltimore was built upon the legitimacy of their urban communities independent of the authority emanating from St. Mary's.[52] Instead of bringing their complaints to Stone at St. Mary's, the puritan leaders gathered at Patuxent and then sent word to the governor to meet with them at a neutral site in the woodland equidistant between Patuxent and St. Mary's. They deliberately ignored the status of St. Mary's as Baltimore's capital and instead treated the towns of the colony as distinct political spheres with a jurisdictional no-man's-land in between.[53]

This distinct constitutional understanding was articulated in a sudden profusion of printed pamphlets about the confrontation. In their 1655 tract, *Virginia and Maryland; or, The Lord Baltimore's printed case, uncased and answered*, the leaders of the puritan towns rejected Baltimore's county structure in terms reminiscent of Worsley's critique of Berkeley's patronage-based authority, arguing that he "appoints all Officers, even to the meanest degree; and who flatter him most, are sure to have it." This system, they opined, was not only "ill Managed" but also "ill Founded." Their language was steeped in anti-Catholic tropes intended to delegitimize Baltimore's rule, but they also made a particular point of contrasting the corruption of the proprietary system with the legitimacy of the puritan towns that contributed to the empire in precisely the way Worsley had envisioned.[54] They appended to their tract petitions to English authorities from the puritan colonists that recast their political units as the "Inhabitants of the North-side of the Patuxent River" and "Inhabitants of Severne, *alias* Ann Arundel County." They portrayed their towns as coherent communities of "House-keepers and Freemen" threatened by Baltimore's renewed efforts "to set over us the old form of Government formerly exercised by him" and with "none to flie to."[55]

Throughout the pamphlet war sparked by the events in Maryland, place names were central to the effort to contest Baltimore's authority. The authors defending the puritan coup repeatedly emphasized that the impetus came from the "people at Providence." For example, Leonard Strong, in his narrative titled *Babylon's Fall*, described Providence as "the chief place of residents" and persistently implied that it was a compact settlement. Baltimore's defenders found Strong's claims in this respect troubling enough to warrant a direct rebuttal; John Langford's *Refutation of Babylon's Fall* specifically addressed the issue of Providence's identity and explained to readers that the place was "by them called Providence, but by an Act of a Generall Assembly there called Anne-Arundell in Mariland." John Hammond went further, challenging even the name the puritans gave to the Severn River and insisting that they had done little apart from establishing a "fort at Ann Arundell."[56]

Stone ultimately surrendered his authority to the commissioners and their puritan allies, giving them the power to design a new government that reflected their understanding of the colony's political geography.

Under the authority of William Fuller, one of the town leaders of Providence, the colony's capital was relocated from St. Mary's to Patuxent. They also gathered a new assembly, made up of "the Burgesse of every respective County and Limit." It is unclear precisely what they meant by "Limit," but the alternative term suggests a partial rejection of the county designations that Baltimore had imposed. When the time came to appoint new county sheriffs, they only named one man, Captain John Smith, who would serve in St. Mary's, implying that Maryland once again had but one county around St. Mary's and that the rest of the colony was defined by new urban corporate institutions.[57]

The final humiliation for Baltimore came in 1655, when the eruption of violence revealed that the puritan towns had tangible military power. In the spring of that year, Stone rallied support to reassert the proprietor's authority. He recommissioned officers in Baltimore's name and marched to the new de facto capital at Patuxent to seize the provincial records. He then led his force north to face down the town of Providence. As Stone's men approached Providence, they were confronted by the town's militia. They charged into battle with the cry of "Hey for Saint Maries," reinforcing the idea that they were fighting in defense of their preferred version of the province's political geography. The cry proved ineffectual, though: Stone was embarrassingly defeated in what became known as the Battle of the Severn. He was captured, and a number of his men were executed for treason. The defeat proved that the county system in Maryland had failed. The puritan towns of Providence and Patuxent, bolstered by the support of the English puritan state, viewed themselves as legitimate, distinct, and consensual political communities, with their own names and identities that residents were willing to defend with their lives.[58]

In a broader sense, the definition of the town in the Chesapeake had evolved by incorporating elements from the changing ideas of political economy in England and the town culture in New England, all of which were circulating around the puritan Atlantic. The ideal of the urban civic community that had informed colonization in the region from the outset was now intertwined with the English commercial empire's goals of "Industry and Civility." In Worsley's vision of ever-expanding commerce and industry, urban corporate structures—the symbol and the embodiment of common ideas and interests—would unite an exclusively English network of colonists and merchants.

Yet despite the efforts of the Commonwealth's commissioners to impose this system on the whole Chesapeake region during the early 1650s, the political structures in Virginia and Maryland looked dramatically different from each other by the middle of the decade. Both colonies ostensibly had governments loyal to England's successive Commonwealth and Protectorate regimes. The crucial difference lay in the colonies' local government and political geography, and it grew out of different reactions to the Commonwealth's political-economic vision. Despite Baltimore's dreams of county-based political stability, Maryland was now a collection of autonomous entities, including towns that closely guarded their status as cohesive communities embedded in an English Atlantic network of puritan urban communities. Virginia's planters had been presented with precisely the same option of establishing corporate towns that promised to transform their social order and unite them with the political economy of the English Empire, but their established interests in the tobacco economy and their lack of affinity with the puritan civic vision meant that they had few incentives to throw off the decentralized plantation system that they were coming to dominate. These differences vividly represented alternative political-economic paths and alternative roles for the Chesapeake within the framework of the emerging English commercial empire.

"EXTRAORDINARY GOOD NEIGHBOURHOOD"

To those whose status and fortunes were tied up with the Chesapeake's system of extensive plantations and county patronage, the Commonwealth's vision of corporate towns within a puritan commercial empire represented a profound threat, not only to their short-term fortunes but also to their political-economic vision. In their efforts to resist the Commonwealth's urban model, Virginia planters and Baltimore's supporters in Maryland began to refine the justification for their private and rural plantation system.

After initially accommodating the commissioners' agenda, Virginia's burgesses soon returned to strengthening their powers over a rural hierarchy. The act for establishing corporations was quickly allowed to lapse, and in March 1655, when Richard Bennett vacated the governorship, the burgesses made a bold move to support county authority by drafting a new act that established local markets in each county. The legislation empowered county courts to regulate commerce and specifically rejected the creation of new commercial jurisdictions distinct from the counties or the establishment of preferential trading privileges for particular groups. To ensure that this system would work even with the recent dramatic increase in settled land seized from the Powhatan in the 1640s, the General Assembly also created six new counties in as many years in the prime tobacco regions of the Middle Peninsula and the Northern Neck.[59]

In the counties themselves, aspiring elites also consolidated their position. John Pagan has documented the way in which leading planters on the county bench in Northampton County gradually adapted English common law to give them more control over their servant labor force. The officeholding elite in Chesapeake society were not only able to exploit their servants more effectively; they were also able to expand their pool of labor as warfare around the Atlantic—spurred by England's conflicts with the Irish, Scots, Dutch, and Spanish—generated increasing numbers of forced laborers, both European and African, to sweat over the tobacco crop. As John Coombs has carefully documented, the officeholding elite of Virginia's counties increasingly marked themselves off from their neighbors with early and large investments in enslaved African laborers. All of these developments helped to foster new social networks between well-established planters based around kinship, neighborhood, and office holding. Social historians analyzing local records have pointed to these years of war and disruption as the moment when Chesapeake communities began to coalesce around an established local hierarchy.[60]

Ironically, as the planter elite strengthened their county communities through the 1650s, the position of Jamestown, the only urban space in Virginia before the Commonwealth's intervention, was actually diminished. After Berkeley surrendered the governorship to Richard Bennett, he remained in the colony as a private citizen, but he sold his property in Jamestown and removed to his plantation, Green Spring. Berkeley retained his status within the planter community, but he abandoned—either of his own volition or at the behest of the commissioners—his prominent position in the capital city. For other planters and merchants, there was probably less incentive to have ships call at Jamestown. Many planters flouted the Navigation Act by continuing to trade with the Dutch, and so they had every reason to avoid Jamestown, as the only place in the colony where the limited apparatus of the state held any sway; small ships operating out of New Amsterdam were able to surreptitiously navigate the Chesapeake's small creeks. Archaeological evidence suggests that Jamestown declined dramatically during the 1650s, losing much of the status it had mustered as a commercial hub since the 1630s.[61]

In support of these local developments, Berkeley and Baltimore's allies reinforced an alternative vision of civic harmony that was not reliant on a diverse economy and a corporate urban community. Berkeley laid out this position in 1651 in a speech to the General Assembly as he sought to rally planter support against the anticipated Commonwealth commissioners. He appealed to the burgesses by describing them as an independent gentry class threatened by the impositions of the English state and its merchant allies, who denied even the assurance that they might "eat the bread for which our owne Oxen plow, and with our owne sweat we reape." This was more than simply an abstract defense of English liberties grounded in landownership; it was also a positive case for the colony's existing rural civic structure. Berkeley argued that Commonwealth rule offered no more wealth, liberty, security, or peace than the current arrangements provided. In a striking parallel to Worsley's invocation of "Industry and Civility" for the good of the empire, he argued that the colony's structure was already able to support "Industry & Thrift." For Berkeley, though, the key to achieving these virtues was not a corporate urban structure but the mutual bond between himself and the leading planters that created stable gentry rule. Ten years later, when describing Virginia to the newly restored Charles II, he would laud the rich gentry lineage of Virginia's leading families. Berkeley's point was that Virginia's planters were a stable gentry class who were more than capable of extracting the natural bounty from the land and supporting the common good of their community without the need for corporate institutions and state-sponsored mercantile projects.[62]

The clearest surviving articulation of the ideas of rural virtue in the Chesapeake during this period comes from Maryland, where Baltimore's allies vigorously resisted the imposition of the puritan urban vision. After Governor Stone's defeat in 1655, one of Baltimore's allies in Maryland, John Hammond, penned a damning indictment of the puritan community's urban pretensions to civility and industry. Providence and Patuxent's rejection of Baltimore's proprietary commercial order, Hammond claimed, had loosed the "licentiousnesse of those parts"; merchants would now "sell commodities to whome they list, and lighting on greater prices, would of their own accords (after delivery made) repossesse themselves again, scoffing at any pretence of Law or Justice." He saw the puritan towns as incapable of effective economic regulation. The following year, in *Leah and Rachel* (a lengthy pamphlet about the best ways to cure the ills of Maryland society), Hammond contrasted the upheaval in the colony with the peaceful order now pervasive in Virginia. He explained that in recent years "civil, honourable, and men of great estates flocked in [to Virginia]: famous buildings went forward. Orchards innumerable were planted and preserved; Tradesmen set on work and encouraged," and "staple Commodities, as Silk, Flax, Pot-ashes" were being developed. Hammond emphasized that, contrary to Worsley's indictments, this was no "Lubberland" where sloth reigned supreme. He praised Virginia's rural community based around "great estates" and social order in which planters were "generally affable, courteous and very assistant to strangers," and where county courts met regularly and "hardly can any travaile two miles together, but they will finde a Justice." Crucially, Hammond unfavorably compared England's towns and cities to the "pleasant and profitable" life available in Virginia. All of the essential civic attributes, such as "extraordinary good neighborhood and loving conversation," could be realized in the dispersed community of large estates and did not require the radical transformation that Worsley and the Providence citizens had sought.[63]

These ideas evoked the contemporary evolution of a strain of agrarian civic thought in England. In his idealistic vision for the English republic, *The Commonwealth of Oceana* (1656), political theorist James Harrington adapted republican ideas to address the crises of the Cromwellian Protectorate, which, as David Armitage has demonstrated, emerged from the same challenges of reconciling republicanism with England's expanding imperial ambitions. Harrington argued that the only way to abate the dangerous influence of private interests in the republican state was to structure society around a permanently fixed balance of landownership. He proposed an agrarian law that would prevent landed estates from growing or diminishing and thereby stabilize the commonwealth by securing the political legitimacy of a fixed community of landholders. "The country way of life," he concluded, was more amenable to the cultivation of virtue than the factious world of urban politics. Although Berkeley and Baltimore would never have agreed with Harrington's republican premise, the imposition of the Commonwealth's imperial commercial vision had begun to lead planters toward similar conclusions about the landed foundations of civic virtue.[64]

The Commonwealth's effort to impose corporate towns upon the Chesapeake had thus given rise to this first articulation of planters' agrarian civic claims, which would gradually strengthen over the next half century. Leading planters had taken steps to strengthen their position within their county communities, allowing them to pursue the accumulation of larger estates and the intensification of commercial agriculture under the protection of the apparatus of the colonial state. They also began to defend this private development by combining claims to individual property rights with assertions about the virtue of their rural agrarian hierarchy. These innovations were not simply driven by the pragmatic imperatives of tobacco production; they were responses (both conscious and unconscious) to the debate, which the Commonwealth regime and its puritan allies had revived, about towns and commercial regulation on the tobacco coast.

:::

The commencement of Commonwealth rule in 1649 triggered intense scrutiny of the political economy and civic order of Chesapeake society, and the question of urban development again provided a touchstone for alternative institutional and civic structures. Civic assumptions about the weakness of the tobacco economy had not changed, but Commonwealth thinkers now placed this problem within a new imperial framework that saw commercial interests as potentially beneficial if they could be harnessed to unify the English Empire under a banner of Protestant mission. In this context, the county system in the Chesapeake posed a problem, because it was grounded on patronage, privileged stability, and seemed to discourage economic improvements that could serve the interests of the larger commercial empire. It provoked the articulation of a new Commonwealth vision for commercial empire.

Most scholars have tended to explain the Council of Trade's interest in Virginia as a product of the self-serving and short-term goals of London's merchant community, who were allowed to dictate Commonwealth commercial policy. In their analysis, the merchants helped to establish a new imperial model in which the needs of the periphery were subjugated to the interests of those who controlled the newly empowered metropolitan state.[65] It is true that long-standing commercial rivalries informed the struggle for control within the Chesapeake. However, viewing the framing of the Navigation Act as a straightforward "mercantilist" measure that attempted to use state power to impose metropolitan interests upon a periphery misses the genuine debate about what the goals of expanding English Atlantic commerce should be and what kind of institutional structures would facilitate those goals. This was a debate that grew out of new providential, scientific, and political-economic ideas. The repeated failure to generate both prosperity and civic order in the Chesapeake meant that the region had remained central to this debate.

Understanding the Navigation Act as intimately and consciously bound up with another ambitious and unsuccessful effort to reform the Chesapeake colonies helps to place new imperial commercial policies in the broader context of political-economic visions for the future of the empire. Worsley's plans for the Chesapeake, out of which his ideas about port cities and the state regulation of commerce emerged, were not driven simply by the financial interests of his merchant friends but by a fundamental disagreement with the state-building strategies of Berkeley and Baltimore. Commonwealth thinkers completely rejected the system of county patronage and the conception of civic and commercial order that underpinned it, and sought to transform the political and economic structure of the region through a new variant on the puritan corporate town model. The Navigation Act initially reflected a vision of a union of English corporate communities all focused on industry, growth, and innovation within a puritan providential framework. This was clearly a step toward the unification of the English state and empire, but it was not the beginning of efforts to erect a state apparatus to suppress colonial manufacturing and turn plantations into monocultural suppliers of raw materials. Over the next few decades, English officials would go on to articulate a more comprehensive theory of colonial economic dependence, but the meaning of mercantilism had yet to be fully worked out. It was, though, the conceptualization of the corporate borough as an autonomous civic community, rather than the royal patronage model followed by Harvey and Berkeley, that actually laid the intellectual foundation for binding urban communities within a more powerful imperial state. The evolving conception of urban identity and jurisdiction was critical to the framing of England's expanding dreams of commercial empire.

The central importance of municipal corporate forms and ideas to the Commonwealth's vision of commercial empire also helps us to better understand the particular civic vision that the Chesapeake's established planter class developed to push back against the threat of imperial encroachment. Viewing the Commonwealth's policy as just the naked imposition of state power tends to make the planters' resistance look like a protoliberal defense of free trade and land rights. In reality, the Commonwealth commissioners offered a coherent alternative political economy built around distinct town-based communities, which succeeded in winning some adherents in Maryland. In this context, established planters actually embraced a civic defense of the societies they were building, reinforcing local regulation rather than stripping it away in favor of a free market and justifying their authority by asserting the virtuous credentials of their "extraordinary good neighbourhood."[66] As a practical manifestation of these claims to authority, many of Berkeley's erstwhile allies and supporters in Virginia reinforced the shire structure and used it to strengthen their control of land distribution and the policing of bound labor. These were the key ingredients for the intensification of plantation monoculture and the exploitation of forced labor, and they emerged not as stopgap tools in a pragmatic headlong rush for profit maximization, but as a conscious effort to justify planters' capacity to manage commercial development.

Events in England during the Cromwellian Protectorate weakened the corporate vision behind the puritan reforms for the Chesapeake. But even as the Commonwealth's corporate vision was swept away, the dream of a new centralized commercial empire remained. For officials and planters in the Chesapeake, the question of how their vision of political economy and civic order fit within this new empire would be the defining challenge for the second half of the century. All agreed that urban spaces, in some form or another, still had a role to play.

CHAPTER FOUR

Planters, the State, and the Restoration City

After nearly two decades of upheaval, restoration came to the Chesapeake in 1660. The Stuart monarchy in England returned to the throne, Sir William Berkeley was restored to Virginia's governorship, and Lord Baltimore reasserted his authority in Maryland. These momentous changes seemed to validate the planter elite's emerging rural civic vision. Yet, if these planters thought that the Stuart Restoration would allow them to sweep away the Commonwealth's mercantilist plans and reinforce their local authority, they were to be disappointed. The revenue potential of Atlantic trade was simply too tempting for the cash-strapped new monarch, Charles II. He eagerly retained the services of those who had built the mercantilist architecture of the Interregnum and replaced the Commonwealth's nullified Navigation Act with a new act that strengthened its provisions. Leaders of the planter class in the Chesapeake soon realized that protesting and petitioning metropolitan officials to change their policies would not suffice to maintain their local hegemony. They needed to make concessions to accommodate new royal imperial authority while keeping their carefully crafted local control over commerce, labor, and land. Yet again, the key to crafting this compromise seemed to lie in the establishment of the right kinds of urban spaces. Over the next decade, Berkeley and Baltimore embarked on the Chesapeake's most ambitious urban development projects to date.[1]

New urban development was an obvious but also highly fraught way for Baltimore and Berkeley to address the challenges of this new era because the reconceptualization of urban spaces and institutions was at the heart of the new Stuart vision of empire. Even though the broad outlines of Interregnum commercial policies remained in place when the monarchy returned, the particular role of urban institutions in facilitating it radically changed. The Commonwealth leaders who originally conceived of the Navigation Act had anchored its enforcement in corporate towns, but this proved to be the last gasp for truly independent urban institutions in the English Atlantic. Even before the Restoration, Oliver Cromwell had begun meddling in the makeup of England's corporate boroughs to ensure their loyalty.[2] The new Stuart leadership was even more suspicious of independent city governance. Their perception, partly justified, was that England's corporate boroughs had been the vanguard of the English Revolution, and, as Thomas Hobbes evocatively put it, their distinct identities made them "many lesser commonwealths in the bowels of a greater, like worms in the entrails of a natural man."[3] No one in the newly restored Stuart court would deny that towns and cities, as drivers of commercial and economic growth, were vital to the realm, but they were convinced that their identity and authority needed to be severely circumscribed. Around the English Atlantic, the new Restoration leadership reenvisioned cities and towns. They decisively shifted away from the understanding of municipal charters as a balance between civic autonomy and direct royal patronage that had dominated early colonial urban development, and toward a view of cities and towns as nodes of imperial commercial and military power.

Having observed this consolidation of imperial urban authority firsthand in London, Berkeley and Baltimore both concluded that they could harness and repurpose this new Stuart vision. They set out to build and refurbish urban spaces and institutions that reflected the new ideas and aesthetics at the heart of the Stuart vision of empire, in an effort to project and channel state power. This effort to reconcile planter society with the commercial empire resulted in considerable investment in new urban space, but ultimately it once again proved better at framing political-economic challenges than framing actual urban homes and warehouses. The group of increasingly well-established planters to whom Berkeley and Baltimore hoped to appeal soon discovered that the Restoration city did not augment their influence over imperial commercial policy. The costs were too great and the benefits were too few. In divergent ways, the elite planters of Virginia and Maryland used their leaders' new urban plans as a foil that helped determine what kinds of political power and economic connections they needed to reinforce their own decentralized leadership.[4]

Yet by coming to terms with the Restoration empire in this way, the leading planters provoked the resentment of their poorer neighbors, who were angered at the narrowly focused and half-hearted urbanization effort. The controversial city plans symbolized a political economy that was increasingly dominated by relations between wealthy planters and the state. The expanding group of disadvantaged men and women articulated an alternative urban vision that helped galvanize their political and economic outlook. For them, urban development was still about local consensual social and economic authority designed to safeguard their interests within the intensifying commercial empire. Conflicts over the control of urban space played a significant role in sparking the social unrest of Nathaniel Bacon's famous 1676 Virginia rebellion and parallel upheaval in Maryland. Practical debate about the construction of urban spaces thus offers an unrivalled window on the political-economic debate around the intensification of empire that stretched from the halls of Whitehall all the way to the poor planter's smoke-filled parlor.[5]

"CREATURES OF MONARCHY"

The fiscal and political imperatives of the Restoration laid the foundations for a transformation in urban authority and identity. Given that financial problems had continually plagued Charles I and helped spark his war with Parliament, it was clear that the new monarch would need a more secure revenue stream. Maintaining and expanding the Interregnum policy of generating revenue from colonial trade offered a solution. The Convention Parliament that laid the groundwork for the king's restoration offered him a guaranteed annual revenue, but fully one-third of this money was now to come from customs duties. To secure his money, Charles II had little choice but to adopt the expansive vision of commercial and economic growth developed by members of the Hartlib circle. Many of the merchants who had funded English imperial expansion during the Interregnum were welcomed into new royal Councils for Trade and Foreign Plantations, and Parliament approved the passage of a new Navigation Act that reinstated the provisions of the annulled Commonwealth act, with the explicit objective of generating new state revenue. The new king's enthusiasm for commerce also meant accepting the virtue of limitless urban growth, which created conduits through which mercantile prosperity could flow and be tapped.[6]

However, for the Crown to benefit from commercial growth, it had to more effectively control urban spaces. Prosperous towns and cities had helped to propagate puritan and revolutionary leadership in the early seventeenth century, and they were still centers of potential opposition to royal authority. The Restoration, though, offered a way to reimpose royal control, because it threw the corporate structure of English urban life into chaos. New corporate charters issued during the Interregnum had led to purges and counterpurges of borough officials, undermining urban political legitimacy. In advising the king on how to settle the local disputes that this confusion generated, his trusted adviser the Marquess of Newcastle warned that "Every Corporation, is a petty free state, Againest monarkey"; he urged that to "uphold your Majesty in peace and wealth, your Majesty's care and labor must be to reduce and keep them in their due subjection," suggesting that "itt were good to have some Considerable Townes, that are Built much uppon trade, but nott so many."[7] Newcastle's advice was, at least partially, acted upon. In 1661, Parliament developed a plan to reorganize England's boroughs. The "Act for the well-governing and regulating of corporations" removed many suspected radicals from urban leadership and began the process of reconceptualizing urban corporations as "extensions of crown government . . . created by the monarch to maintain the public welfare and the King's peace."[8]

The effect of this reconceptualization was most immediately visible in changes to the institutional and physical structure of London. The corporation of London abolished popular election and reinforced the power of its oligarchic leadership, made up of royal allies drawn from London's merchant elite who invested in new monopoly companies and farmed customs duties for the state.[9] Efforts to reinforce state authority in London also led to a new focus on royal rituals and monumental architecture. Charles revived the tradition of triumphal entries into the capital. When he arrived in the city for his coronation in 1661, he passed through a series of specially constructed triumphal arches with allegorical allusions to his Augustine ambitions to rebuild the city as a royal imperial metropolis. And over the next few years, he made good on this commitment, sponsoring plans to purify the city's air to reduce both physical and figurative pollution and pushing for the passage of a highway act that would reorder the London streets. When much of London was destroyed by the Great Fire of 1666, Charles seized the opportunity to further impose royal order. The fire's devastation provided the illusion of a blank canvas on which the king could impose new street plans that would project royal order. The plans were never fully implemented, but nonetheless the rapid influx of wealthy nobles around the fashionable royal court in the 1660s still helped to spur the development of the city's new West End with orderly architecture and refined entertainments. London's physical and institutional space was becoming a model for the refashioning of urban life around a new political culture that tied urban residents and elite sojourners to the state.[10]

London was critical to the new royal vision not simply because it was a political center, but also because it was the nation's leading port. Because of the growing importance of trade, the desire to reinforce royal authority was felt most strongly in port cities. Sir Matthew Hale, the king's new chief baron of the exchequer, penned a treatise emphasizing royal authority over England's port towns. Hale explained that "a port is of concernment to the whole trade of the kingdom, and also to the defense of the kingdom, the increase of shipping and mariners, and the increase of the king's revenue, which is of a common good to the kingdom." Control over port towns was now central to both the mercantile and martial strength, and, in the imperial framework of the Restoration era, those were the terms in which the common good of the realm was now calculated.[11]

If the king were to realize these imperial ambitions, however, he would need to extend authority over towns and trade beyond England's shores. During the 1660s, the Duke of Ormond, Charles II's new Lord Lieutenant of Ireland, began to refashion Dublin to create what Robin Usher has called "a conduit through which Ireland could be ruled." Dublin Castle was renovated, and Ormond also encouraged local merchant Humphrey Jervis to construct a fashionable suburb for elite Irish urbanites. Farther afield, Charles also imposed direct authority over the newly acquired North African port of Tangier; he pumped two million pounds of infrastructure investment into the port city, established a new oligarchic corporate leadership, and dispatched a garrison of troops to enforce his authority, all in an effort to create a new hub for English Mediterranean trade. These imperial cities replicated the urban vision of London, with military and commercial infrastructure, overt symbols of royal authority, and a class of urban oligarchs loyal to the new royal state.[12]

In the plantation regions, too, new ideas about urban governance took hold. Port Royal, the boom town of the recently conquered island of Jamaica, was a notorious haven for privateers and smugglers, who proved to be a constant irritant to imperial authorities; however, official efforts to reform it focused on bringing it under the direction of a coterie of loyal merchants (especially the royal monopoly company of African merchants). Between the 1660s and the 1680s, Port Royal was organized around military companies and never received a corporate charter.[13] Likewise, the Fundamental Constitution for the new proprietary colony of Carolina insisted that towns were crucial but required that they be designed by proprietary officials and that "it shall not be lawful for any one to build in any town" if they did not follow the models dictated from London. They also insisted that private interests should be "overruled" so that urban buildings could "grow more beautyfull," for the "Reputation, Security, and Advantage" of the colony. Everything about these new urban spaces was designed to remind citizens of imperial power.[14]

The Chesapeake was now part of a royal commercial empire in which towns and cities were taking on new power and identity. The king needed revitalized port cities to anchor his expanded mercantile reach, but he also feared the potential for these cities to become, as Newcastle had put it, "petty free state[s], Againest monarkey." In the words of a royal official, Sir Ellis Leighton, who lectured Dublin's municipal officers on this subject in 1672, Charles needed cities to be "creatures of monarchy" that "ought nimbly and readily to obey all the motions of [the king's] hand." Retaining control over these spaces against both foreign enemies and domestic corporate autonomy would require an overt military and bureaucratic presence and the tightening of alliances with elite merchants. Unsurprisingly, then, when the king's new Council of Plantations first wrote to Virginia introducing the new royal regime, it demanded that the colony supply a list of "the Rivers, Ports and Publick Strengths and Defenses." These new royal expectations would frame how Berkeley and Baltimore thought about reshaping their place within the new Restoration empire.[15]

VIRGINIA'S CURE

Early in 1660, while Charles II was still preparing to return to England, the Virginia General Assembly beseeched former governor Sir William Berkeley to resume his post. Berkeley agreed, but he recognized that new challenges awaited him. The county structure he had helped to build had maintained order on the local level, but weak provincial leadership, economic uncertainty, and political disorder over the past decade meant that the persistent structural problems of the tobacco economy had only worsened. By 1660, tobacco prices seemed on the brink of collapse. Berkeley believed the dilemma remained the "unstaplenes of the Commoditey"—in essence tobacco's inability to provide reliable profits upon which a stable society could be built. He lamented the lack of a "publick Stock" that hindered the development of infrastructure; "our liberty to doe good onely to ourselves," he opined, "is the main obstacle of our progresse." This diagnosis still faintly echoed Sir Edwin Sandys's concerns from half a century before, but Berkeley quickly came to realize that he would need a bold new approach that linked his pursuit of the common good of Virginia with the new commercial empire. He reenvisioned Jamestown as a hub where local elites could entrench their authority over the colony's political economy and address the ills of the tobacco economy by establishing stronger bonds with the larger royal imperial culture.[16]

Immediately after his return to office in 1660, Berkeley began efforts to revive Jamestown, but he initially did so along the same lines he had first pursued before the Interregnum. He loosely followed the pattern of a loyal but independent urban hub that had first been pioneered by Sir John Harvey. Jamestown had declined through the 1650s; a number of buildings, including the statehouse, had been lost to fires, and there were likely no more than a handful of habitable dwellings remaining in the town. Berkeley immediately set to work to revive the capital. With the Commonwealth-era Navigation Act annulled by the Restoration, he felt free to negotiate a new commercial treaty with the Dutch. Crucially, he sought to restrict all of this commerce to Jamestown, and he planned new roads to funnel overland as well as shipborne trade through the capital. He also reestablished the lapsed practice of allowing the city its own burgess in the General Assembly. At this stage, Berkeley still saw the capital as a vibrant independent commercial hub for Virginia's rural planters.[17]

However, when Berkeley returned to England in 1661 for the first time in fifteen years, he encountered the transformed political and physical landscape in London. He probably noticed the ceremonial arches that still stood from Charles's coronation earlier that year, he likely heard from old friends at court about the radical shake-up of the kingdom's boroughs, and he could not have missed the pace of new construction in the capital. For Berkeley, however, the most pertinent change was in the Crown's political-economic outlook. The new Councils for Trade and Foreign Plantations had already begun planning a replacement for the Commonwealth's Navigation Act.[18] Of even more immediate concern to Berkeley, a leading merchant imperialist, Martin Noell, had also drafted a proposal specifically for the reorganization of Virginia's trade. Noell shared Berkeley's concern that Virginia's economy had fallen behind those of Barbados and New England, and he also agreed that a crucial part of this deficiency was the lack of towns. However, Noell's solution rejected the model of Jamestown as a commercial hub, arguing instead that cities should facilitate "the Increase and Regulation of Trade and the Benefitt of the Crowne, and the avoyding fraud in the paiements of his Majesties Customs." Noell proposed that the king mandate all trade be confined to one or two locations in each of the Chesapeake's major rivers. Only those who could invest substantial sums in property and infrastructure at these sites (likely transatlantic merchants such as Noell) should gain "Privileges and immunities" to trade in the new port towns. The towns Noell had in mind fit precisely with the model that the Crown was pursuing around the English Atlantic. They were to be nodes of royal control over trade and revenue, rooted in a close alliance between the Crown and an Atlantic merchant oligarchy.[19]

By the time Berkeley formally presented his *Discourse and View of Virginia* to the royal court the following year, he had already absorbed some of these new realities. He maintained his opposition to the renewed Navigation Act, but he also employed the developing agrarian planter vision that he had first enlisted to resist the Commonwealth's authority in order to portray Virginia as an organized rural community that already contributed to the empire. At one point Berkeley rehearsed the family names of colonists, making connections to English gentry lines to prove that they were "as good families as any Subjects in England." He advocated the pursuit of a diversified range of commodities as a rural endeavor that would allow this orderly planter elite to add "to the Wealth, and Glory" of "our Nation." Notably, he barely mentioned the work that he had already begun to revive Jamestown, which now lay in contravention of the Crown's policies. Berkeley was at pains to demonstrate that Virginia's dynamic rural society was stable and loyal to the Crown, capable of contributing to the mercantile empire, and not in need of the kind of radical restructuring that Noell had planned.[20]

Berkeley had not completely abandoned his plans for urban development. Rather, he had subtly extracted the quest for urban development from the discussion of provincial political economy, thereby removing it from Noell's sphere of influence, and repackaged it to fit with the new vision of urban spaces as centers for orderly royalist culture. Berkeley, as a strident supporter of the monarchy, court culture, and the established church, could easily get behind this element of the royal plan. Roger Green, a Virginia clergyman who traveled to London with Berkeley, was the natural spokesman for a reformulated urban plan that emphasized religion and royalist culture more than economics. He articulated this vision in a pamphlet, *Virginia's Cure*, which was published in London at the same time as Berkeley's *Discourse and View of Virginia*. Green identified "our People's scatter'd Habitations" as Virginia's greatest problem. He lamented the lack of "Christian Neighbourhood," which deprived the people of "the Benefit of Christian and Civil Conference and Commerce." This perspective obviously contradicted Berkeley's rosy picture of Virginia's counties as thriving civic communities, but Green did not advocate replacing those counties with alternative corporate communities. Rather, he proposed new rules for "reducing" planters into one town in each county.[21] Elite planters would be "enjoyned" to build a house in their local town and visit weekly to attend church services and state ceremonies, ensuring that they fostered close connection with the wider empire through the rituals of the state and the established church. Green's plan offered a means to sacralize and spatially demarcate Virginia's growing social and economic distinctions, and embed them within a broader imperial culture of royalist architecture and ceremonies. Instead of channeling commerce to spur this urbanization, Green suggested a collection throughout England to fund the construction of homes and public buildings. This vision of county towns marked by grand new public buildings and serving primarily as social and political centers for the neighboring gentry was strikingly similar to that which was beginning to develop in England. Green concluded his pamphlet by comparing Virginians to "plants [that] now grow wilde" and proposing that his plan would make the colony "like a garden enclosed." This metaphor corresponded with the language that English gardener John Evelyn was using at precisely this moment to promote his plan for a horticultural perimeter around London that would suppress urban disorder. Green and Evelyn shared a vision of urban space as a cultural and political tool that would strengthen the bonds between local elites and the state.[22]

When Green spoke of "well governed" and "well ordered" towns, he was rehearsing sentiments very much after the king's own heart. Berkeley and Green had proved quick studies. They may not have been completely convinced by the new court's vision of empire, but they tailored their plans to dovetail with the Crown's larger objectives, replacing a commercial city with hubs for royalist and Anglican culture. It worked. In September 1662, when Berkeley received his new instructions before returning to Virginia, town building was the first detailed item on the list. The order combined Noell's and Green's plans: it called for one town on each of Virginia's rivers, where all legitimate trade under the Navigation Act should be conducted, but it also ordered that the planter elite who sat on the provincial council should contribute by each building a new house at Jamestown. A few years later, likely inspired by Green's plea for urban centralization of ecclesiastical authority, the king and the archbishop of Canterbury drafted a plan to establish a cathedral at Jamestown for a new diocese encompassing England's Atlantic empire, which would have further strengthened the city's position within the network of imperial governance.[23]

Berkeley's instructions offered new kinds of incentives for the colony's aspiring elites to contribute to urban development. Notably absent was any commitment to offer commercial privileges to particular towns or to limit the enforcement of the Navigation Act. The alternative incentive was the leverage that wealthy planters might gain from investing in warehouses at the crossroads of imperial trade and becoming part of the imperial commercial system. This leverage would, Berkeley hoped, allow Virginians to pursue policies to lessen their debilitating dependence upon tobacco within a framework that would appeal to royal authorities. When Berkeley returned to the colony, he quickly developed legislation to restrict tobacco production and support new industries. Berkeley argued that diversification away from tobacco would now be both appealing to the planter elite and profitable for the imperial treasury because elite investment in urban hubs would streamline customs collection and commercial bonds between planters and merchants. However, realizing this vision would require Virginia's elites to invest heavily and commit to a new style of urban political culture. Berkeley would need to persuade the planters to take this risk.[24]

The governor honed his new urban plan during the return trip across the Atlantic. Scarcely a month after reaching Virginia, he gathered the General Assembly and presented them with a new vision for Jamestown. No record of the burgesses' reactions has survived, but Berkeley professed himself happy with the act they passed in response to his ideas. It began by claiming inspiration from "his majesties royall commands" and went on to lay out town-building provisions unlike any seen before in the Chesapeake. Instead of focusing on commercial regulations, the act outlined an architectural vision for Jamestown, including details of the construction schedule and the labor requirements. Despite the fact that the capital's existing homes were overwhelmingly made of wood, the act specified that the area henceforth designated as the "towne" would consist only of thirty-two new brick houses, each "forty foot long, twenty foot wide," and arranged around a four-acre square. Building in brick around a square was a bold and expensive move, reminiscent of new developments in London's West End, and would distinguish the space from Virginia's existing built environment. The act's insistence that only brick houses would henceforth be considered as part of the official town created a further separation, effectively creating a distinct institutional space—an elite town within the town. Berkeley also retained direct personal oversight of the project, suggesting that his experience in London had left him with a clear idea of what he wanted Jamestown's new construction to look like. It was clear that Berkeley's objective was to create an urban space reflecting the latest imperial vision, one dominated by large, expensive buildings and their wealthy owners.[25]

The act, though, was not what royal officials had envisioned. Although it promised future development of similar towns along the colony's other rivers, which had been critical to Noell's plan for the colony, the provision was an afterthought, relegated to a final paragraph of the act.[26] Berkeley's focus was on Jamestown. The aim of the act was to bring Virginia's elite together in a political orbit around the capital city in order to legitimate their authority as a ruling class within the empire. Construction in Jamestown was to be funded through a general levy on tobacco, but building was to be managed by the justices of each county. Relying upon county courts created a concrete link between local community leaders and a new civic space. The plan also offered elite planters concrete incentives to establish urban ties. Only planters who contributed to the construction would be allowed to also erect warehouses necessary to establish a mercantile presence in the new capital. If Virginians were to be prevented from trading with the Dutch, then Berkeley hoped to make Jamestown a space through which the planter elite would control the flow of English political and economic power. Berkeley was constructing a political center for Virginia similar to, but not truly dependent upon, Restoration London. It was to be, in his own words, "the Hart and Centre of the Country."[27]

Berkeley's revitalization plan met with early success. At least four counties and five individuals agreed to construct houses at Jamestown, and Berkeley himself proposed to build eight more. Within a year, four houses had been erected. Excavations at Jamestown have confirmed that at least three major brick buildings, constructed in a distinctive row-house style with multiple units in a single structure, were undertaken during these years. The plan to construct a grand square was quickly jettisoned, but nevertheless, the scale, style, and brick construction of the buildings still implied the creation of a new kind of urban space in which Virginia's commercial and political elites could conduct their business.[28] Berkeley also succeeded in attracting investment from some of the wealthiest planters and merchants in the colony. Influential London merchant Micajah Perry had been persuaded to invest in Jamestown property, as had Thomas Ludwell, one of the wealthiest planters in Virginia. Ludwell later wrote to officials in London in 1665 to report that the colony had "allreaddy built enough to accommodate both the publique affairs of ye country and to begin a factory for merchants." By "factory," Ludwell likely meant a commercial consortium through which wealthy planters and Atlantic merchants might begin to control the provincial market in tobacco and other commodities—an alternative to a civic corporate structure. These early signs suggested that the governor had found some allies for his new vision of Jamestown.[29]

But the early enthusiasm did not endure. After the initial rush of indi-

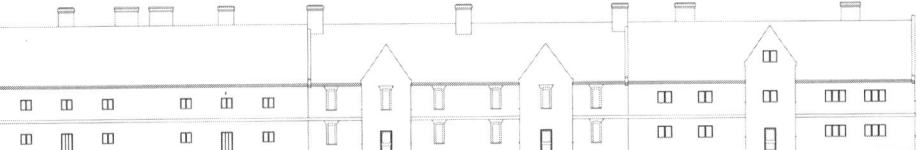

4.1 Reconstructed south elevation of the Ludwell-Statehouse row house at Jamestown, delineated by William J. Graham Jr. The largest of the brick row-house structures built in Jamestown during the 1660s contained four separate dwellings. The colony's new statehouse was added to the eastern end of the row by 1665. (Courtesy of the Colonial Williamsburg Foundation.)

viduals and counties committing to construct houses, it became harder to find investors. Berkeley wrote to London lamenting the parsimonious elites who refused to contribute to the project. In the face of this reluctance, the General Assembly revised the legislation to bring the building process completely under the governor's control, but this change failed to address the fundamental lack of funds. Archaeological evidence suggests that some of the row houses were left unfinished. In the early 1670s, a law against repairing Jamestown's old wooden housing stock, intended to promote building in brick, was lifted, and the capital's makeshift quality had definitively returned.[30]

The explanation for the failure of Berkeley's plan lies in the geopolitical and commercial realities of the mid-1660s. First, the Second Anglo-Dutch War (1665–1667), which disrupted shipping and trade, discouraged investment in commercial infrastructure and diverted public funds toward defense. Second, despite Ludwell's upbeat assessment, the city never succeeded in developing a "factory for merchants" that could exercise authority over the colony's political economy and arrest the prevailing downward trend in tobacco prices. While construction was pressing ahead at Jamestown, Berkeley invited representatives from Maryland and Carolina to the town to negotiate limits on the region's tobacco crop, hoping to raise its price by limiting supply. This plan relied upon the theory that urban development would make the management of the tobacco trade and the collection of taxes more efficient and thereby make the proposal revenue neutral for merchants and the Crown. But the representatives struggled to find a compromise that worked for all sides and could also gain royal approval. The nascent commercial community at Jamestown had failed to help in addressing the colony's biggest political-economic problem. Finally, Jamestown redevelopment also did little to address the increasing shortage of cheap, exploitable labor in Virginia. Supplies of white indentured servants were not keeping pace with the expansion of tobacco production, and by the 1670s, they began to contract. The wealthiest planters were already purchasing enslaved laborers, but the Crown's monopoly slave-trading company, the Company of Royal Adventurers Trading to Africa, could not be persuaded to dispatch slave cargoes to the region. Despite the new commercial and political infrastructure at Jamestown, greater profits were available shipping enslaved people to the Caribbean. This meant that wealthy planters needed to find surreptitious ways to acquire enslaved people from merchants who operated outside the royal monopoly, but this trade was obviously not facilitated by an imperial political and commercial center at Jamestown. All of these factors meant that urban development offered few concrete incentives for elite planters.[31]

During the 1670s, the wealthiest planters turned away from Jamestown to further refine the plantation system. They dealt with low tobacco prices by growing ever larger quantities. To do this they invested in ever larger tracts of fertile land, developed trading connections across the southeastern interior to channel enslaved indigenous people to the colony, and expanded connections with the Caribbean to import enslaved Africans outside the nominal royal monopoly.[32] These same planters also began to perfect the consignment system, in which cargoes of tobacco were shipped to London at their own risk and sold there on their behalf; this system offered elite planters the best prices and allowed them to draw their poorer neighbors into their orbit by overseeing the export of their crop as well. This gave elite planters more control over their trade than they had enjoyed through previous planter-merchant networks and at least as much influence as a local merchant-factory would have offered. In 1665, leading planters in the General Assembly took steps to cement their local control by reestablishing the system of county marketplaces, which had been initially proposed during the late 1650s. These locations were pointedly not labeled as towns, and they came under the jurisdiction of county courts, further facilitating the consolidation of power among local elites. With the consignment system and local marketplaces, the planter elite achieved many of the objectives that Berkeley had set out for Jamestown by other means.[33]

Even Berkeley himself scaled back investment in Jamestown and redirected his energy toward renovations at his Green Spring Plantation home, which he turned into a new space for elite socializing. Cary Carson has identified Green Spring as the first of Virginia's fashionable banqueting halls that stood in for an urban cultural sphere by providing the leading planters a space to cultivate their elite culture. Although Berkeley's allies, such as Ludwell, continued to own property in Jamestown, by the 1670s, Green Spring, lying only four miles from the city, had become a rural retreat for the colonial elite from the official business of the capital. By 1666, Berkeley had returned to championing the agrarian civic vision, claiming that the planters "live here after the simplicity of the first age" and could practically "forget al sounds that did not concerne the businesse and necessities of our farms."[34]

In many respects, then, the consolidation of the gentry, which was a key step in the development of Virginia's plantation system, was tied to efforts to rebuild Jamestown and reposition the colony within the English Empire. Berkeley's plan for Jamestown pointed toward the ways in which Virginia's aspiring planter class would need to come to terms with the empire, even if the grandiose urban vision itself failed to achieve this reconciliation. Proposals for urban development once again had the counterintuitive effect of reinforcing planters' faith in their own rural civic authority within the empire. The expensive failed experiment at Jamestown, though, was galling for poorer sections of Virginia society because its failure reinforced the growing distance between the wealthiest planters and the rest of Virginia's white population, breeding resentment against the governor's pretentious vision of a Restoration city and laying the groundwork for future conflicts in the colony.[35]

BALTIMORE'S BOROUGHS

Maryland's struggles with Commonwealth-era urban plans had been far more intense than Virginia's. For a significant portion of the 1650s, the Calverts' authority had been usurped by the corporate towns of Providence and Patuxent. It might seem surprising, then, that after they regained control of their colony, they turned to urban development as the solution to its political and economic woes. The difference was that the towns the Calverts dreamed of building reflected the new Restoration vision; they envisioned them as spaces that would mediate between the proprietor, his planter subjects, and the Stuart court.

Baltimore definitely needed a new plan for his colony. Despite having reestablished authority over Maryland in the late 1650s, the proprietary government faced fundamental challenges that combined long-standing religious tensions with new political and economic pressures. Many colonists remained highly suspicious of the proprietor's Catholicism, and in an era of falling tobacco prices, these fears increasingly led them to see ulterior and private motives behind proprietary efforts to restructure the economy. Meanwhile, the centralizing Stuart court was increasingly uneasy over the independence that colonial proprietors enjoyed, especially when they were perceived to hinder commercial regulation. The proprietor and his family were thus stuck between the anxieties of colonists and the demands of the Crown. All the while the price of tobacco was falling at an even faster rate than in many regions of Virginia. It was clear to the Calverts that politics and economics were increasingly intertwined and that to reinforce their authority they would need a new system that balanced their interests with those of colonists and imperial officials.[36]

From the moment they regained authority over Maryland in the late 1650s, the Calverts began searching for ways to fundamentally refashion the political and economic order of their colony. In September 1659, Baltimore's brother Philip Calvert, who had recently become secretary of the colony, was entertaining New Netherland emissary Augustine Herrman in St. Mary's. He confessed to his guest that "he wished Maryland may be so fortunate as to have cities and villages like the Manhattans." The fact that Calvert was hosting a Dutch emissary attests to his interest in cultivating Dutch trade to help transform the colony. His carefully worded urban aspirations, though, reflected a precise idea about how the political-economic potential of such trade would be organized. Earlier in their conversation, Herrman had reported news from New Netherland, probably including new trading restrictions introduced in the 1650s that had increased the influence of the city of New Amsterdam over its rural hinterland. When Calvert stated his desire for a system of "cities and villages like the Manhattans," therefore, he was envisioning a hierarchy of settlements that linked rural production with urban development. In other words, he was rejecting the model of quasi-autonomous corporate towns, such as Providence and Patuxent, in favor of an urban hierarchy that could be more easily brought under proprietary control. Philip Calvert and his nephew Charles (later the 3rd Lord Baltimore), who became Maryland's governor in 1661, would spend the next fifteen years trying to realize this ambition.[37]

The first step in this plan was the revitalization of St. Mary's City. The cultural and political credentials of Baltimore's capital city had been undermined by the puritan regime, and so reestablishing its authority was a priority. Soon after the arrival of Governor Charles Calvert in 1661, he and his uncle Philip embarked on a project to redevelop St. Mary's City. They intended to restore St. Mary's City as a central urban space designed under their guidance and for the purpose of inscribing their authority.[38] Their plan began with the construction of a new statehouse, which they described as "the Cuntry's worck at St Mary's." The new architectural centerpiece of the capital was to be an impressive edifice with a hipped roof and a cupola, marking the leadership's cosmopolitan taste. In addition, though, their plans for the statehouse also sought to lay the foundations for an elite community at St. Mary's; the legislation that authorized the construction also promised free three-acre lots in the capital to colonists wealthy enough to build substantial 1,200-square-foot homes on them. The first phase of redevelopment at St. Mary's City clearly focused on inscribing the aesthetic and the elite culture of the Restoration city under direct proprietary patronage.[39]

Over the next decade, the Calverts expanded upon this vision for the city. In the late 1660s, as the statehouse was nearing completion, work began on other public buildings in the city, including a new Catholic chapel, which reinforced the city within an ecclesiastical hierarchy akin to the proposed cathedral at Jamestown. Furthermore, archaeologist Henry Miller has argued that Philip and Charles Calvert organized the city's new construction around a formal symmetrical plan, anchored by the placement of four public structures (the statehouse, the prison, the chapel, and a mill) at the termini of equidistant straight lines, converging at a crossroads formed by the town's private residences. The lines stretching out toward these public buildings were intended to show viewers in the town center—potential new urban residents and planters who visited the proprietor's new capital—the city's close relationship to the proprietor's state infrastructure. There were obvious parallels with the contemporary plans to remodel London after the Great Fire, which also sought to reinforce the connection between the power of the state and the organization of the city. St. Mary's City was intended to manifest and reinforce the Calverts' control over the institutions that ordered life in the colony.[40]

The Calverts' ambitious plans were not limited to the physical landscape though. In 1668, Charles Calvert granted the city a proprietary charter. At first glance, this appears an odd choice, given the suspicions with which many Restoration royalists viewed urban corporations. However, many Crown officials were reconceptualizing urban corporations as branches of the state, and the St. Mary's City charter fit squarely within this framework. It made the people of St. Mary's and "ye Circuits & prcints and priviledged places" within one square mile into "an Incorporated Citty" led by a mayor, a recorder, six aldermen, and ten councillors—each appointed for life with no provision for popular election. The charter named the senior officers, including Philip Calvert as mayor, and charged them with selecting the councillors. This provision was intended to bind a select group of influential men directly to the proprietor. These men had sole jurisdiction over the city and power to appoint constables and make bylaws. This bold constitutional move provides a vital context for understanding the city's formal urban plan, suggesting that politics and planning combined in a proprietary effort to forge a loyal corporate center to support the provincial institutions erected there and help the Calverts to maintain and justify their control over the colony's political and economic order.[41]

One corporate city, though, was just the starting point for Philip Calvert's vision of "cities and villages." The St. Mary's City corporation had extensive authority over markets and fairs that would allow it to control trade in its region, but the Calverts intended to use this model to establish a new loyal class of officials for the whole colony. To achieve this goal, they would obviously need more than just one urban center. St. Mary's City was never intended to be alone. Through the early 1660s, the Calverts seem to have been involved in efforts to encourage trusted individual colonists to establish new towns. One individual recruited to fulfill such a role was the New York merchant Augustine Herrman, who had initially discussed urbanization with Philip Calvert back in 1659. Herrman was granted a manorial estate in Maryland on the condition that he also erect a port town, to be called Cecilton. Other new urban places, including Herrington and Battletown, also appear to have been established in these years.[42] During the late 1660s, while work was still continuing on the capital, Charles Calvert initiated a broader plan to integrate these nascent towns into a provincial proprietary economic network. In June 1668, five months before St. Mary's was incorporated, the governor—without consulting the colony's assembly—issued a proclamation designating eleven other port towns across the colony, where all trade was to be concentrated. Although the sites were not immediately granted charters akin to the one given to St. Mary's, they were promised "Jurisdiccons libtys & privildges," implying that they were expected to be new spaces that would develop outside the current county structures of local governance and that certain individuals would receive particular authority to oversee the new commercial spaces under the patronage of the proprietor. In this plan, the Calverts went beyond Berkeley's ambitions, trying to replicate their vision of urbanity from St. Mary's City across the colony in order to have full control over politics and commerce.[43]

The Calverts' motives for wanting this new power were partly defensive. During the 1660s, they were increasingly trapped between the competing mercantile interests of their subjects and the English state. Many

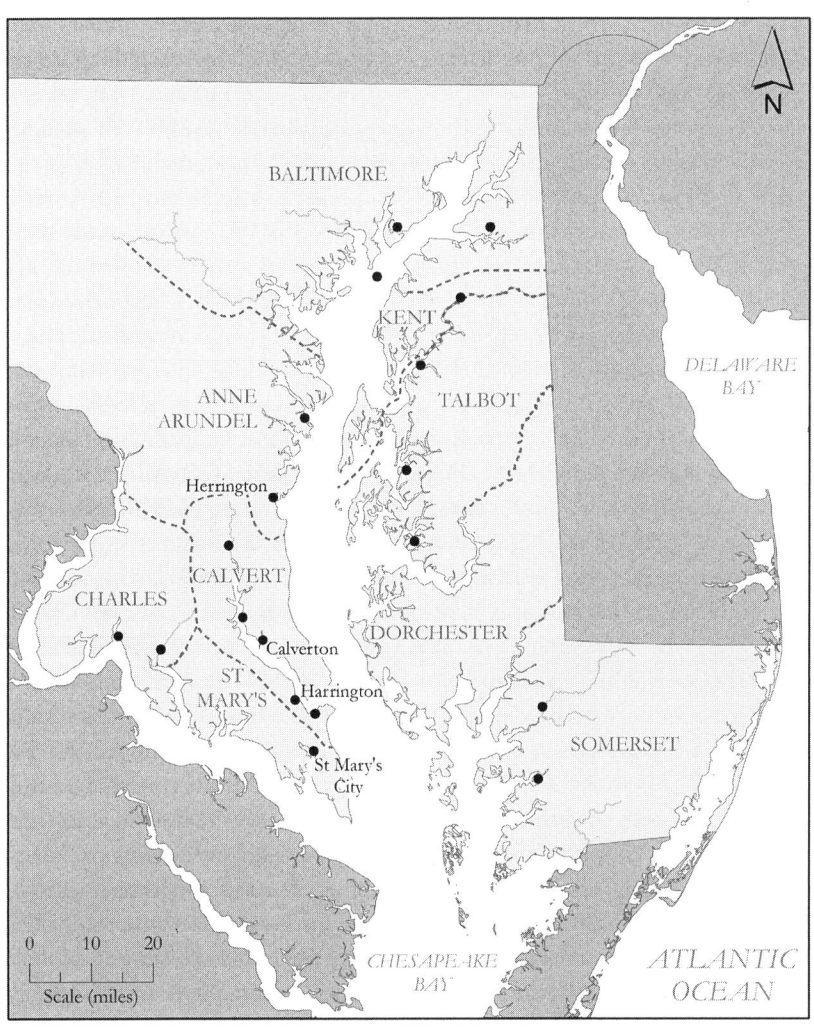

4.2 Map of Maryland town locations, 1667–1671
This map shows all of the identifiable locations of the port towns designated in proclamations by Lord Baltimore in 1668, 1669, and 1671. Names are only given for sites where clear contemporary evidence of naming exists, even if the town site later developed a recognized name. (Some information adapted from Shomette, *Lost Towns of Tidewater Maryland* [Centreville, MD: Tidewater, 2000], appendix.)

colonists were evading the tobacco duties that generated proprietary revenue and even contesting his right to tax them. Equally, however, the Calverts also had to deal with the new mercantile zeal in Whitehall. Protestant opponents still seeking to discredit Baltimore in London increasingly accused him of lax enforcement of the Navigation Acts. Significantly, just a few months after the proclamation establishing port towns in 1668, Baltimore received fresh warnings from Whitehall about the proper enforcement of the Navigation Acts. It seems likely that the establishment of port towns was partly intended to help him fulfill (or at least appear to fulfill) these requirements while also retaining personal control over the colony's commerce.[44]

But the new port towns also constituted a more proactive effort to reshape Maryland's political economy. Charles Calvert explained that the plan was "necessary for the good of Trade." What he had in mind was candidly revealed by his uncle Philip Calvert, in a letter to the governor of New York, Richard Nicholls. Calvert explained that the towns were intended to counter the influence of New England merchants (whose trading connections had been established during the Interregnum), who he believed brought the wrong kinds of commodities to the colony. Merchants who brought rum and other unnecessary goods and demanded nothing but tobacco were perpetuating the dependence upon the weed, thereby furthering the colony's economic malaise and reducing potential proprietary revenue. The Calverts intended the new port towns to be part of a broader effort to reform the economy by limiting tobacco production and encouraging diversification. New ports controlled by proprietary allies were intended to give the Calverts greater control over commerce, regulating what commodities were exchanged and encouraging new trades. Baltimore also attempted to negotiate with the Company of Royal Adventurers Trading to Africa to establish regular slave imports, which would have been disembarked in one of the Calverts' new port towns, giving them control over this potentially transformative shift in the labor system. When Governor Calvert reissued the port proclamation in 1671, he also designated a new port town on the land of Jonathan Sybery, a merchant from Talbot County who had begun importing slaves through the intercolonial trade. By handpicking commercial allies and rooting their interests in towns, with the potential for future incorporation along the lines of St. Mary's City, the Calverts hoped to directly shape the economy, controlling the supply of labor, incentivizing the production of commodities for particular markets, and taxing the resulting exports.[45]

The scale of the Calverts' ambitions was evident in the publications they sponsored in these years. In order to make the new towns a reality for merchants and officials in London, the Calverts realized they would need to be inscribed on maps. They approached Augustine Herrman, who had cartographic skills and a wealth of experience in Chesapeake trade, and commissioned him to produce a new map of Maryland that would include the new port towns. The map noted every town named in Baltimore's proclamations and also included Herrman's Cecilton, even though evidence suggests that few had yet seen any actual construction. The map was astonishingly accurate in many respects, but the inclusion of the towns, which thus far only existed in the Calverts' imagination, suggests that the accuracy was a carefully calculated ploy. Making the map the new gold standard in Chesapeake commercial navigation would thereby make the new towns appear a fait accompli and direct visiting ship captains toward the new proprietary urban infrastructure.[46]

Baltimore also found another means of promoting Maryland's towns through the *America* volume of John Ogilby's new world atlas. When Ogilby published his *America* volume in 1671, he included a new account of Maryland written with Baltimore's assistance. Amid the predictably glowing description of the colony's climate, he included a very specific account of the port towns. He explained that there were "Foundations Laid of Towns ... according to his Lordships Proclamation," with "Houses already built in them, all uniform, and pleasant with Streets, and Keys [sic]."

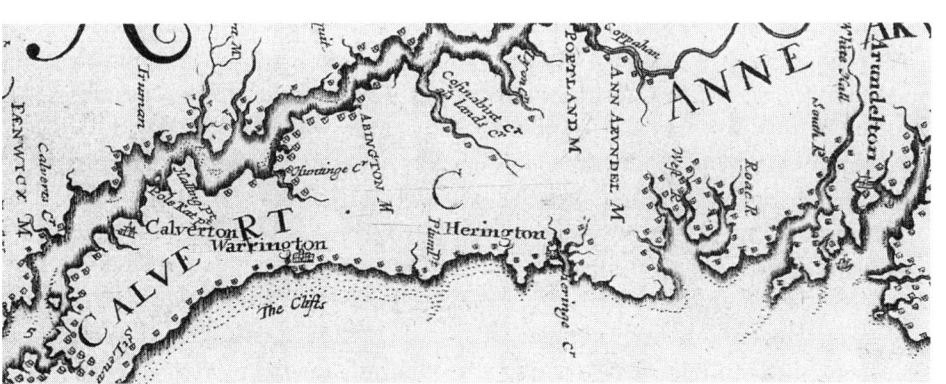

4.3 Augustine Herrman, *Virginia and Maryland as it is Planted*... (1673), detail Augustine Herrman's detailed map of the Chesapeake, published in 1673, represented a new level of cartographic precision in charting the region. However, at the particular request of Lord Baltimore, Herrman included distinct symbols and names for the new towns that the proprietor had recently established, particularly in the area of Calvert and Anne Arundel Counties, shown here. (Courtesy of the John Carter Brown Library at Brown University.)

There is little evidence to bear out this degree of physical construction, but this was obviously how Baltimore wanted the organization of his colony to be perceived in England. In addition, Ogilby explained that St. Mary's had been "erected into a City" and that it now included the Calvert family's residences, a provincial records office, and municipal defenses. Architectural details and the focus on planning and public buildings were unmistakably intended to alert readers that Baltimore had firm control over his urban spaces and partook of new royalist aesthetic strictures.[47]

Back in Maryland itself, though, the Calverts' plans immediately became a point of contention with the provincial assembly. The new authority of the St. Mary's City corporation was particularly irksome. When the General Assembly gathered in 1669, two of the new corporate officers, Recorder John Morecroft and Alderman Thomas Notley, who were elected to represent St. Mary's County, immediately became embroiled in a dispute with fellow delegates. Both men were accused of channeling information to the governor about the proceedings of the lower house of the General Assembly, and Morecroft was impeached on accusations of illegally prosecuting offenses under the jurisdiction of the city corporation.[48] Tensions peaked when the delegates drafted a list of grievances against the proprietor. These grievances focused on proprietary efforts to bypass their jurisdiction through measures such as establishing the provincial licensing of attorneys and creating new offices that charged "Fees exceeding & contrary to [those allowed by] Acts of Assembly," and also the increasing presence of "vexatious Informers" in their midst. None of these concerns explicitly referenced St. Mary's City's charter, but it was a clear subtext. First, the assembly's anger at attorney licensing reflected a fear that Baltimore was limiting the legal profession to a narrow group operating in the city. Second, the complaint about new officers almost certainly related to the creation of a mayor, recorder, and aldermen at St. Mary's—no other new offices had been created recently. Finally, the vague reference to "vexatious informers" was likely an oblique allusion to Morecroft and Notley's tattling to the governor about lower house business at the start of the session. The lower house was convinced that new corporation officers were a coterie of Baltimore loyalists who were usurping their authority.[49]

Philip Calvert's response to the grievances confirmed that the urban plan represented precisely such a threat. Calvert lectured the lower chamber that "they are not to Conceive that their privileges run paralell to the Commons in the Parliament of England," and a better model would be "the common Council of the City of London which if they act Contrary or to the overthrow of the Charter of the City run into Sedition."⁵⁰ Calvert was negating comparisons between the Maryland Assembly and the English Parliament, but the alternative framework he suggested demonstrated that he was familiar with new royal attitudes toward urban governance. His argument emphasized that the common council of an urban borough was dependent upon Crown authority and required to work within the bounds of their charter, and that if they did not, then it lay within royal prerogative to check corporate "sedition" by revoking the charter.⁵¹ The primary objective of his argument was to limit what assembly delegates could object to within the bounds of Baltimore's charter. However, in the context of St. Mary's City's incorporation, the comparison that relegated the Maryland General Assembly to the status of a corporate entity also implicitly warned delegates that they were no longer constitutionally unique. Maryland now had two common councils—the assembly and St. Mary's own corporate common council. Both were dependent upon the proprietor, just as English urban corporations were now considered dependent upon the Stuart state. Philip Calvert was hinting at a future in which a network of proprietary corporate entities might act as legitimate sources of rights and privileges alongside, or even in place of, the recalcitrant delegates who refused to pursue policies that the proprietor believed served the common good of the community.⁵²

Ultimately, though, such threats were hollow because the Calverts could not encourage urban investment by individuals capable of staking a claim to the new political and economic powers that new towns offered. There is no evidence to suggest that development beyond St. Mary's City matched Ogilby's hopeful descriptions. The initial costs of building, as well as the difficult proposition of enforcing commercial restrictions once the towns were established, made taking up the proprietor's offer very risky. Meanwhile, confessional and constitutional tensions in Maryland made overt involvement in the Calverts' project unappealing for the majority of planters. The fact that development at St. Mary's was overtly Catholic, with the erection of the chapel being central to the urban plan, made many Protestants increasingly suspicious of the legitimacy of the proprietary family's commercial regulation as a whole.⁵³

Instead of investing in the Calverts' port towns, local Protestant elites worked to strengthen the county system. In 1671, the lower house of the assembly forced Governor Calvert to agree to devolve new powers to county courts. Many of the critical administrative functions of the county court were established or reinforced during two 1671 assembly sessions. Counties gained control over taxation, land conveyances, weights and measures, road construction, and orphans' estates. The delegates also crafted acts to attract specie by setting inflated exchange rates, to encourage the importation of slaves, and to promote the production of linen and flax by granting county courts the authority to pay bounties.[54] The Calverts probably accepted much of this legislation as a pragmatic necessity, because there were legitimate needs for local justice and administration that the still-notional port towns could not meet; the governor's assent was also an important quid pro quo to win assembly acceptance for the raising of tobacco duties that provided their income. The slew of legislation, though, combined to form a coherent alternative planter vision of Maryland's political economy that looked strikingly similar to what was being pursued by the rising class of Virginia grandees. It was anchored in decentralized authority, the pursuit of new large-scale agricultural staples, and conversion to an enslaved labor force that would offer the maximum control over production. It represented a clear and comprehensive alternative to the Calverts' port towns. Governor Calvert attempted to hit back by reducing county representation in the lower house of the General Assembly and simultaneously granting representation to the St. Mary's City corporation, but this did little to reverse the consolidation of independent county elites, who became ever more hostile to the proprietor.[55]

The ultimate failure of the port town scheme should not, however, obscure the extent of the Calverts' ambitions. They had returned to power at the Restoration with the idea of using urban development to promote a new political-economic order in their colony, which would cultivate commercial allies, establish new political loyalties, and ward off the Crown's direct interference. Although the Calverts' plans may now appear to have been impossible dreams, leading Protestant planters in Maryland most definitely considered them a plausible cause for alarm. They resisted the proprietor's plans for St. Mary's because they perceived that behind them lay the specter of the extensive direct authority the Calverts hoped to assert over politics and commerce. Maryland's elite Protestant planters responded with the outlines of a decentralized vision of provincial political economy. The consolidation of power among the county elites, which scholars have seen as an organic emergence of local institutions, was actually driven by an incipient Protestant elite who rejected the opportunity to tie their status to the proprietor through incorporation in port towns. Without the support of at least a significant minority of the leading planters, the Calverts could not hope to enforce their port town structure, and their authoritarian vision of urban spaces withered on the vine. However, for the Calverts' poorer subjects, this urban failure in the midst of an economic crisis represented a fundamental betrayal.

"THE COUNTRY'S GOOD WELFARE IS THEREBY UTTERLY INTERRUPTED"

Although they frequently implied it, Berkeley's and Baltimore's struggles to attract investment in their new urban plans was not a sign that planters were archpragmatists, myopically focused on the next tobacco crop. These years were actually marked by considerable long-term investment by the Chesapeake elite. The wealthiest planters converted to slave labor, experimented with new forms of merchandising, and invested in diversification projects. The critical point, though, was that these were investments that redounded purely to the private benefit of the elite. This was clearly a political-economic decision, and it was one that would soon come in for intense criticism. Increasing numbers of marginalized individuals in both Chesapeake colonies did not have the luxury to make these investments. Freed from their indentures but lacking the capital to invest in the large-scale production that was increasingly necessary to turn a profit from tobacco, they bore the brunt of falling prices. Although they had not been the focus of Berkeley's and Baltimore's town-building campaigns, they did feel the need for transformation that an urban economy would bring, with opportunities for new industries, provincial trade, and local regulation. Writing to the Lord Chancellor Clarendon, just after implementing his plan for Jamestown, Berkeley noted that "the poorer sort see that want and misery will sooner Come upon them for want of a Town then on the rich men." During the 1660s and 1670s, some of these "poorer sort" began to articulate an alternative vision for urban development that became a tangible manifestation of their divergent political-economic outlook, which eventually helped to foster anger, resentment, and open rebellion.[56]

Hints of an alternative urban vision were evident from the earliest days of the Restoration. While royal officials considered Berkeley and Green's plans for Virginia in 1662, they also received a proposal from an impoverished former servant, Anthony Langston, who had returned to London looking to parlay his knowledge of the Chesapeake to gain employment. Langston developed plans for a new iron industry in Virginia, but he also argued that it would require new incorporated urban communities populated with poor English artisans to complement the existing rural population and satisfy expanding colonial demand for manufactured goods. Without "trade between Town and Country," Langston explained, grand plans for new staple commodities, which both he and Berkeley were advocating, would fail for lack of a balanced market.[57] In an even more ambitious urban plan for the neighboring Albemarle region of Carolina, Virginian George Milner proposed establishing semiannual shooting competitions to attract planters to regional markets that might provide the commercial foundation for corporate towns. The chief benefit, Milner explained, would be that "Moneys once stirring here, Labourers may be payed [and] indigent, weake, aged people & children may be imployed." Milner believed that poor tradesmen from Barbados, whose labor was being displaced by enslaved workers, could also be shipped to the Chesapeake. Drawing people together in this way would "whet, polish & improve ye manners & wits of men"—work that he claimed had been overlooked in Virginia and Maryland.[58]

Both Langston and Milner bore witness to the persistence of a local civic vision of political economy. For them, towns were crucial because they were communities of traders and craftsmen with a symbiotic relationship to the surrounding planter community, regulating the local economy in the interests of the common good by supplying their rural neighbors with manufactured necessities at a fair price and offering opportunities for those without the capacity or the capital to plant. These proposals harkened back to the corporate towns that had promised to transform the Chesapeake in the 1650s, but they also went beyond Commonwealth-era thinking and expanded upon Hartlibian ideas about labor and productivity. They reflected a growing awareness that middling and poor white laborers no longer needed to be lured away from tobacco to maintain a stable market; these individuals were increasingly being excluded from staple agriculture by falling prices, enslaved laborers, and elite consolidation. They now needed to be offered new opportunities for productivity that would help maintain their civic virtue while contributing to the broader growth of the commercial empire.[59] For the men and women who shared this perspective, the urban plans of Berkeley and the Calverts, with their emphasis on elite architecture and narrow merchant oligarchies, were a clear betrayal. As provincial councillor Francis Moryson explained, Berkeley's building project at Jamestown disillusioned many poorer planters and even caused "hundreds of people" to desert the colony because of the heavy tax burden imposed to pay for elite buildings. Without the context of Langston's and Milner's proposals, these complaints might seem symptomatic only of general dissatisfaction at urban development. In fact, though, they were indicative of principled opposition specifically to the governor's model of urbanity.[60]

The epicenter of this opposition in Virginia lay in Jamestown itself. Scholars of the era have paid careful (and warranted) attention to the region's frontier, where a shortage of land for newly freed servants and a shifting nexus of native geopolitics generated resentment against the planter elite that eventually burst forth during Bacon's Rebellion in 1676. However, contemporary commentators were convinced that the main source of opposition to the colony's leadership lay in the taverns of Jamestown. They identified two men—Richard Lawrence and William Drummond—who spent a decade struggling with Berkeley over the right to control the capital.[61]

Drummond, a Scottish migrant, had briefly served as governor of the Albermarle settlement in northern Carolina in the early 1660s—and so was likely aware of Milner's urban plan for that region—but he lost his position and returned to Virginia after falling out with Berkeley, who was one of the Carolina proprietors. From that point onward, Drummond sulked around Jamestown. He and his wife, Sarah, owned property in the town and a plantation just off Jamestown Island, where he established a workshop manufacturing tobacco pipes. He likely used his Jamestown property to maintain clandestine connections to the growing web of Scottish traders operating illegally in the English Atlantic. These craft and commercial ventures challenged Berkeley's authority and vision for the city and led to growing animosity between the two men.[62]

Drummond's friend and neighbor in Jamestown, Richard Lawrence, was an Oxford-educated immigrant who arrived in Virginia after the Restoration, quickly married a widowed Jamestown tavern keeper, and established a legal practice. The tavern he and his wife operated was one of the town's largest wooden structures—in direct contravention of Berkeley's aspirations to convert the capital to brick. He used the watering hole as a base for trading with visiting ship captains and helped arbitrate commercial disputes. Lawrence was also likely behind proposals to establish a new town common as an exclusive privilege for the capital's resident population, but he was not part of Berkeley's hoped-for urban establishment. He also sought to make Jamestown a more egalitarian space and a hotbed for resistance to the emerging plantation labor hierarchy. During the winter of 1673/4, Lawrence opened his tavern to servants who had fled Berkeley's plantation, and he railed against "the forwardness advarice and French despotick methods of the govern'r." Lawrence's Jamestown establishment may even have challenged the hardening racial divisions in Chesapeake society. One report noted that he openly engaged in a sexual relationship with one of his slaves, "in so fond a Maner, as though Venus was cheifely to be worshipped in the Image of a Negro." It is impossible to know if the unnamed enslaved woman engaged in the relationship consensually, or whether this was sexual exploitation akin to that which took place more clandestinely on many plantations. The critical point, though, was that Lawrence's actions worked to mark off Jamestown as an urban space where emerging norms about race and sex could be more openly transgressed.[63]

Lawrence was clearly promoting a very different urban culture in Jamestown, but he was also seeking to challenge the governor's authority in the capital more directly. He railed against the governor to anyone who passed through the tavern. In the spring of 1672, he also launched legal suits against Berkeley's allies, including a bitter dispute with Richard Awborne, clerk of the general court and one of the few provincial officials to reside in the city. Far from being a center of gubernatorial and state authority, Jamestown was becoming the center of a biting critique of Berkeley's administration.[64]

By the mid-1670s, Lawrence's and Drummond's opposition became part of a much broader crisis through their alliance with Nathaniel Bacon Jr. In 1676, Bacon, a hotheaded young English gentleman, directly challenged Berkeley's authority because of the governor's perceived failure to address native attacks on frontier settlers. Bacon raised an army of poor planters, servants, and slaves that temporarily seized control of the colony. The resentment of the ragtag rebel force, though, was mixed with the concrete grievances of men such as Lawrence and Drummond. Despite having no connections to the frontier or the Indian trade, Lawrence and Drummond became early allies of Bacon, and they integrated their critique of Berkeley's economic policies and urban plans with the other objectives of the rebels. In fact, some contemporaries believed that Richard Lawrence was the true ideological mastermind behind the uprising.[65]

When, in the early stages of the rebellion, Berkeley called a new assembly in an effort to calm tensions, it was Lawrence—who was elected to represent Jamestown—and not Bacon, who led the opposition in the new House of Burgesses. The legislative program of this June 1676 session represented the first articulation of Virginia's poor and middling planters' full range of grievances. The burgesses enacted a more aggressive Indian policy to placate Bacon's frontier followers, as well as a limit on taxes and a measure that would reduce the influence of Berkeley's elite allies over county courts. The new legislation also included, almost certainly at Lawrence's instigation, "An Act Limmitting the Bounds of James Cittie," which rolled back Berkeley's vision of the capital. The act restricted the city's electoral district to Jamestown Island itself and prevented anyone but the "house-keepers, freeholders and freemen" of the town from casting ballots there, thus excluding elite planters who happened to be visiting the capital or those who owned land nearby. It also gave townspeople the right to formulate their own bylaws, freeing them from the oversight of James City County and raising the possibility that a new urban corporation might be created to administer them. The reforms to Jamestown have been long overlooked in the familiar narrative of the events of Bacon's Rebellion, but they represented the first step in reasserting the independence of the capital's community and its influence over provincial political economy.[66]

Once negotiations between Bacon and Berkeley gave way to open conflict, Bacon himself began to channel the anger of ordinary planters regarding the governor's urban plans. Although his primary focus was on attacking native peoples, his "Declaration of the People" also pointedly criticized the failure of Berkeley's urban plans, claiming that the governor had done nothing to advance the colony "by Fortifications, Townes, or Trade." At the same time, he expressed suspicion about the political machinations conducted in Jamestown's official spaces, arguing that Berkeley had used "Arts, Artificers, promises and Arguments . . . to sway and bring over the minds of men in Townes." These seemingly contradictory statements, claiming that urban development had failed while also suggesting that its success had undermined good government, actually reflected the precise critique that had been building over the past decade. Berkeley's development at Jamestown had cultivated all of the worst corrupting tendencies of the Restoration city without any of the civic benefits of urban society and economic improvement.[67]

The distinction between the urban growth that was actually necessary and Berkeley's elaborate Jamestown plans resonated beyond the rebel leadership. In 1677, in the aftermath of the rebellion, the Crown solicited lists of grievances from each county as part of an effort to diagnose the rebellion's causes. The grievances suggested that many planters had frustrations over urbanization. Grievances from Isle of Wight, Surry, and Stafford Counties complained about Jamestown, but they took issue with the style and manner of the development there, not town building in general. Surry, which lay immediately across the river from Jamestown, offered the most pointed critique, noting that "great quantityes of tobacco" had been levied for Berkeley's project, which was particularly egregious because the town houses "were not habitable by reason ye were not finished." They characterized Jamestown as a "place of vast expense & extortion." These were not the complaints of people who saw no reason for towns; they were a critique of Berkeley's overambitious design. Other grievances gathered in

1677 actually called for new towns, including a plea from Rappahannock County for "the erecting townes in every County in this Collony wthall Convenient Speed." In the context of the anger that was expressed toward the corrupt county elites and the continued low price of tobacco, the prospect of new urban communities with distinct social and political hierarchies offered a means to neuter elite influence and generate new economic opportunities.[68]

These critiques of urban development also struck a chord with poor planters in Maryland. Although not directly involved in Bacon's uprising, a growing faction of middling Protestant planters in Maryland who were actively hostile to Baltimore's authority expressed solidarity with the Virginia rebels. Late in 1676, they penned a polemic tract titled *A Complaint from Heaven with a Huy and crye and a petition out of Virginia and Maryland*, laying out a case against corrupt authorities in both colonies. The Marylanders made clear that they shared Bacon's grievance over town development. The *Complaint* was filled with anti-Catholic conspiracy theories, but it also lambasted Baltimore's urban policy. "Why," the *Complaint*'s authors asked, "did Hee [Baltimore] not primitivo tempore cause his Surveyor Generall to have marked and laieth out, lands for Townes for his Lordship's and the publicq use?" In an oblique reference back to the Providence and Patuxent puritan towns, they suggested that New England towns were the ideal model. Crucially, they made a distinction between the "publicq use" and the proprietor's interest. Towns founded in recent years reflected only the latter, as the Calverts had made "Merchandize of the lands and will make Townes on 50 or 100 acres without comons or possibility for poore people to live in." The authors of the *Complaint* clearly saw errant urban policy as a commonality between both Chesapeake colonies: in both places, it was hindering opportunities for ordinary planters in favor of local elites.[69] And these authors were not alone in Maryland. Another outspoken critic of proprietary authority, Robert Carvile, became an alderman of the St. Mary's City corporation, infiltrating the corporation previously dominated by proprietary allies. Just like Richard Lawrence in Jamestown, Carvile fought against the Calverts' pretensions to direct authority over St. Mary's City. Even in the intended bastion of proprietary authority, colonists were expressing frustration at elite control over urban space.[70]

The conflict over urban development also explains the central role that Jamestown played in the events of Bacon's Rebellion. Both Bacon and Berkeley expended time, resources, and blood during the summer of 1676 to control Jamestown. Although Bacon was primarily interested in fighting native peoples, he was repeatedly lured back from his western depredations by a fixation over control of the few swampy acres of Jamestown Island. Only after Bacon first captured Jamestown in July 1676 did he issue his formal declaration overthrowing Berkeley's authority. Likewise, when Berkeley attempted to reclaim Virginia in September, he began by reconquering the capital city. Berkeley's success encouraged Bacon to return to lay siege to the capital once again. The governor held out for five days, worried about the "reputation we should lose" by abandoning Jamestown. Eventually, however, he retreated back to the Eastern Shore, and instead of occupying the capital, Bacon, Drummond, and Lawrence decided to burn the town, starting with their own residences. Some accounts suggest this was a tactical decision to avoid another siege, but contemporary observers were not convinced that this entirely explained the destruction; Ann Cotton, in her account of the revolt, noted that Bacon "burns it downe to the ground to prevent a futer seege, *as hee saide,*" implying that she had doubts about the rebel's claim. In fact, Jamestown posed little threat to the rebels. There were not enough houses there to station an army, and even though Berkeley's men had been able to rely on food stores left by town residents, the siege had lasted only five days—and the stores, of course, were now used up. The rebels were likely more concerned with eliminating the threat Jamestown posed as a symbol of authority. After all, the city that Berkeley had sought to construct had played a prominent role in their grievances. It was safer to destroy completely this rough-hewn copy of Restoration urbanity than risk it falling back into the governor's hands.[71]

Jamestown was more than simply a backdrop for the events of Bacon's Rebellion. The rebellion was shaped by a range of grievances intertwined with native geopolitics and local rivalries. Furthermore, as Peter Thompson has shown, some of Bacon's supporters consciously crafted rural identities as yeoman householders. For others, though, such as Richard Lawrence and the Maryland authors of the *Complaint,* the betrayal implicit in Berkeley's and Baltimore's urban ambitions was central.[72] Overlooking the importance of this grievance sells short the rebels' conscious engagement with the Atlantic debate about the future political economy of the colony and the empire. Describing them as merely rural regulators or restless servants in the process of being replaced by slaves artificially narrows the range of possibilities that remained open at that moment for the Chesapeake's development. Richard Lawrence and William Drummond were not merely frustrated aspirants to Virginia's planter elite; instead, they wanted to change how that entire hierarchy worked. They sought to adapt older civic models of urban development to undermine the local planter oligarchy and generate new opportunities for productive labor within the commercializing empire.

::::

In June 1676, Charles Calvert left St. Mary's City for London. The colony he left looked little like the map he had commissioned from Augustine Herrman a decade before; it had few of the "cities and villages" that his uncle Philip Calvert had wished for, and its plantation estates were multiplying under the control of an emerging Protestant gentry. When Charles reached London, he was asked to report to the Crown on the situation in Maryland. He explained that, besides St. Mary's City,

> other places wee have none that are called or cann be called Townes. The people there not affecting to build nere each other but soe as to have their houses nere the Watters for conveniencye of trade . . . And for this Reason it is that they have beene hitherto only able to divide This Province into Countyes without being able to make any subdivision Into Parishes or Precincts which is a Worke not to be effected until it shall please God to increase the number of the People and soe to alter their Trade as to make it necessary to build more close and to Lyve in Townes.[73]

This was an admission of defeat for the Calverts' ambitious urban plans that had been designed to reassert their authority over Maryland and placate royal officials.

In the context of what was generally a defensively worded report to English officials who had the power to revoke his charter, it made sense for Calvert to suggest that only God could achieve what he personally had failed to engineer. But just as he was writing this report, restless Marylanders were preparing the *Complaint from Heaven* as an indictment of his failure to encourage true urban development. Calvert was obscuring the fact that there was still considerable support for town building but that it was grounded upon a vision for the colony's future that was antithetical to his interests. Yet most historians have accepted Calvert's judgment that pragmatic planters had no interest in urban development. They portray Baltimore's and Berkeley's unsuccessful urban plans as vanity projects of little interest to ruthlessly rational planters, who recognized that tobacco offered the only path to wealth. As a result, they have overlooked the fact that urban development encapsulated distinct political-economic visions of empire in the Chesapeake during these years.[74]

In reality, the attitudes of planters across the economic spectrum were more complex than Calvert suggested. The urban development Berkeley and Baltimore proposed was of a particular kind, informed by concurrent royal ideas about state authority and commercial integration and calculated to secure the positions of their allies in this new imperial reality. But for those with the capital to establish alliances with English merchants and with the resources and connections to import enslaved Africans and Indians, the cost of building in Jamestown and St. Mary's City was not worth the return of a seat in Virginia's "Merchants Hall" or on St. Mary's Aldermen's Bench. These individuals found ways, both legal and illegal, to trim their sails to the new mercantilist system without expensive urban patronage. But they were doing so by increasingly restricting opportunities for their poorer white neighbors. For these marginalized whites, urban civic community still represented a path to employment and influence. Towns would provide opportunities beyond tobacco production in crafts, local provisioning, and small-scale marketing. To these men and women, the lackluster progress of urban development, in the face of stagnating tobacco prices, and the expensive elite plans from which they were necessarily excluded were a clear sign that the leadership in both colonies had abandoned civic ideals. This division of opinion holds the key to understanding why town development was both a grievance and a demand for those who rose up during Bacon's Rebellion.

It is easy to dismiss Berkeley's and Baltimore's urban plans as elaborate boondoggles, but they were much more than that. They were a colonial derivative of the Stuart court's new vision for urban space, and their deployment crystallized the tensions involved in reinforcing the planter elite within the new imperial structure. Recognizing this reveals that Bacon's rebels were not simply reacting against their growing marginalization within the Chesapeake's plantation system; they were articulating an alternative political-economic vision for the region. Because of the significance of these divergent urban visions, the question of towns would become even more critical in the aftermath of the revolt. With the power and the priorities of the Chesapeake's growing lower order of white residents now laid bare, the crisis of the late 1670s would spark a decade of confrontation as the planter elite, Maryland's proprietary family, and the Stuart state competed over a new round of urban plans in an effort to win their loyalty.

CHAPTER FIVE

Towns, Improvement, and the Contest for Authority in the 1680s

In the autumn of 1676, William Sherwood became one of the first Virginians to arrive in England with an eyewitness account of Bacon's Rebellion, which he published as *Virginia's Deplored Condition*. His pamphlet's subtitle promised "Murders" and "Rebellious outrages," but Sherwood actually began with a detailed explanation of Virginia's county system. This was not mere scene setting. The decentralized structure, Sherwood argued, was at the heart of the colony's "deplored condition." Virginia's elite had ignored urban development and "turne[d] Land lopers," buying up vast tracts and thereby exacerbating class divisions. The solution, he suggested, was a radical new policy to encourage "Warehouses to be built, and soe in p[ro]cess of times Townes" that would stimulate the economy for all planters.[1] As the dust settled on the rebellion, almost everyone came to agree with Sherwood's assessment. Both the planter elite and imperial officials made urban development a core objective for the Chesapeake over the next decade. Practically every legislative session in both colonies debated urban plans, and most counties actually saw those plans partially implemented.

Troubles with tobacco, including overproduction, falling prices, and scattered settlement, were all decades old, but Bacon's Rebellion changed the conversation about how to address them. The tobacco trade was rapidly being consolidated into the hands of a few large merchant houses, the best land had been patented by the planter elite, and the increasing exploitation of enslaved laborers restricted opportunities for poor whites. New Virginia governor Thomas Culpeper explained to the Lords of Trade in 1681 that the tax structure was "unequal," poverty was endemic, and "our Buying of Blackes hath extremely contributed" to the falling tobacco prices that undergirded the entire mess. Even within the established planter class, distinctions and rivalries were growing as aspiring planters jockeyed for position. However, the growing sophistication of Atlantic trade and the ambitions of the imperial state meant that the kinds of local regulation contemplated in the early seventeenth century were no longer practical. Urban spaces, which were now overwhelmingly described as towns, were no longer envisioned as independent civic corporations, but as pieces of commercial infrastructure that would foster economic opportunities for the region's poor planters. These ideas drew upon a new rhetoric of "improvement" gripping England. But crucially, towns were now improvements rather than improvers. They were now constructed under the direct patronage of the state or with the support of wealthy private individuals. The unresolved question was whether it should be the empire, the planter elite, or (in Maryland) the proprietor who brought this new fillip to the Chesapeake and won the loyalty of desperate poor whites in the process.[2]

Having "growne sensible," as one provincial councillor noted, of their "Wild & Rambleing way of Living," the Virginia elite, who had declined to invest in Berkeley's Jamestown, experienced a sudden conversion to the virtues of urban development because it offered a way to reestablish the legitimacy of their local leadership. Supporting new urban projects in their communities offered a means to highlight their sensitivity to local concerns and their civic credentials as a genuine ruling class.[3] Bacon's Rebellion has long been recognized as a turning point for class relations in Virginia. In the aftermath of the revolt, elite planters began to use the politics of racial and gender difference to reinforce their hegemony. Yet these subtle appeals took a generation to develop. The planter elites' urban development agenda in the 1680s reveals that these cultural strategies were predicated upon a more immediate, self-conscious effort to reestablish legitimacy by providing solutions to the region's political-economic challenges.[4]

Just as the Chesapeake elite began to deploy urban plans, however, the Stuart court also began pursuing Chesapeake urbanization as a way to respond to Bacon's Rebellion. At the moment of the rebellion in the late 1670s, the Crown was already beginning to strengthen the institutional bonds of the imperial state beyond those that had been erected at the Restoration, and the diagnosis of the problems in Virginia directed this new imperial energy in the direction of urban development. Discussion of the Chesapeake in London throughout the 1680s became synonymous with debate over town development. Royal officials embraced the idea of establishing new towns as a means of demonstrating the efficacy of absolute royal rule for poorer planters. The Crown hoped that by winning the loyalty of ordinary planters through new economic opportunities, they could bypass the provincial elite and achieve tighter control over commerce.

Town plans were the tangible manifestation of assertive new Stuart imperialism in the 1680s. As a result, they drew colonists into England's political crises, as people on both sides of the Atlantic debated the legitimate limits of royal authority. In Virginia, royal officials' determination to direct town development provoked battles about the authority of the House of Burgesses. In Maryland, however, urban development catalyzed a bigger crisis. There the growing fear of the Stuart Crown's drift toward Catholicism and arbitrary government resonated with fears about the proprietor's Catholic faith. This meant that the policies and decisions of Charles Calvert, now 3rd Lord Baltimore, were subject to even closer scrutiny. When imperial pressures and popular demand brought the new craze for urban development to Maryland, it quickly became a critical divisive issue. Baltimore's efforts to keep control of new towns and satisfy royal expectations led suspicious planters to see urban places as symbols of arbitrary proprietary power. Towns became a key battleground in the struggle over proprietary authority that finally provoked revolution in Maryland in 1689.[5]

Urban development plans provided a direct link between the local contests involved in the forging of the planter elite and the constitutional issues that were rocking English society. They made the recovery from Bacon's Rebellion an intelligible part of the partisan political divisions of the wider empire in the 1680s. Elaborate town plans were repeatedly redrafted because they allowed all those involved to appeal to visions of the public good that would undergird their control over this system. Ultimately, in both colonies, the contest over towns reshaped provincial administration and class relations within the context of a new imperial political economy.

"UNITY, INDUSTRY, AND OBEDIENCE"

Charles II immediately recognized that Bacon's Rebellion presented both the need and the opportunity for radical reform on the tobacco coast. The king quickly dispatched both a military force to help suppress the uprising and a royal commission to help diagnose its causes. Upon their arrival, the military force found Bacon dead and the rebellion fizzling out, but the commissioners' work was just beginning. They wrote to each county requesting that colonists compile lists of grievances. The responses they received confirmed Sherwood's diagnosis of the colony's ills, zeroing in on the low price of tobacco, the corruption of local leadership, and the need for towns. Concurring with these popular demands, the royal commissioners reported that unless towns were established, poor planters would either "Abandon their Plantations" or "make Corne instead of Tobacco and soe sullenly sit down carelesse of what becomes of their own Estates, or the Kings Customes." These comments encapsulated a new imperial attitude: Crown officials were primarily concerned with maintaining customs revenue and the flow of profitable commodities, and they now had more sophisticated ideas about how to achieve this. They were concerned that new economic opportunities be developed for poor planters in order to ensure the Chesapeake was a loyal and stable part of the empire. The Crown's new urban policy in the Chesapeake would be about generating economic growth that would both feed imperial coffers and also win loyalty and obedience from planters across the economic spectrum.[6]

In light of the commissioners' postmortem, Stuart officials firmly committed to a new urban plan. The Committee for Trade and Plantations wrote to Virginia's provincial council in December 1677 to enquire about potential sites for towns. Before they received a reply, the newly appointed governor, Lord Culpeper, drafted his own proposal that "there bee Towns built there one on each great River" and that "noe ships whatsoever bee permitted to load or unload but at ye said places." Crucially, he added that "in case different Interests hinder ye Assembly there from agreeing the places, His Majesty . . . to direct them and to grant them all necessary privileges." This plan was intended to funnel all trade through a limited number of locations endowed with commercial privileges that came directly from the Crown. Although Virginia's burgesses could weigh in on selecting the locations, the ultimate authority to set them was to remain with the king. Culpeper combined this proposal with others for securing a permanent tobacco duty to pay provincial officers and maintaining a garrison in the colony. In short, it was a key plank of a wholesale imperial reordering of Virginia. The Committee for Trade and Plantations approved Culpeper's town-building proposal the following year and instructed him to reestablish Jamestown as "the Metropolis of Our said Colony and Dominion," adding that he should "from time to time, give us an account" of his progress. These instructions, which imperial bureaucrat William Blathwayt described as "strict orders," suggested that the Stuart court intended to radically restructure the economic and political framework of Virginia.[7]

But why would the king settle upon this specific prescription for Virginia? In order to understand the logic behind the imperial response to Bacon's Rebellion, it is crucial to view it in the context of the Crown's ideas about urban governance more generally. Imperial plans for Virginia built upon several years of growing Crown ambitions for centralized commercial regulation. In the 1670s, primarily because of the financial burden of renewed war with the Dutch, royal officials increased their efforts to assert state authority over commerce and local government around the English Atlantic, with the objective of expanding production and generating new revenue.

The first part of this new Stuart drive for commercial control involved reforming the customs system. In 1671, Crown officials ended the practice of farming out customs collection at English port towns, bringing it directly under the authority of a reorganized network of imperial bureaucrats in a smaller number of designated ports. That same year, customs officials first floated a plan to require all tobacco to be traded at specific locations in the Chesapeake to prevent customs evasion. Although this proposal was not enacted, it did help inspire the passage of Parliament's 1673 Plantation Duty Act, which required all ship captains to post bonds guaranteeing to transport enumerated commodities, such as sugar and tobacco, directly to England (as opposed to sending them into the intracolonial trade). The act made revenue collection more efficient and directed the flow of commodities back to England in ways now perceived to serve the best interests of the larger imperial economy. This level of imperial commercial control required a network of official nodes where that control could be enforced, and the 1673 act confirmed royal plans to station customs officers around the Atlantic to administer the new bond system. Even before Bacon's Rebellion, then, the Crown was focused on constructing an imperial bureaucratic infrastructure for commercial regulation.[8]

Political turmoil in the late 1670s also reinforced the Crown's belief that boroughs should be treated as nodes of the state rather than independent communities. In 1678, spurious rumors of a so-called popish plot to assassinate Charles II and pave the way for the ascension of the Catholic James, Duke of York, sparked furious attempts to remove James from the succession. This dramatic upheaval, known as the Exclusion Crisis, involved popular protests concentrated in the kingdom's larger boroughs, and particularly in London. In response to this urban disorder, Charles increasingly articulated a more expansive view of royal authority over boroughs. The early 1680s witnessed a concerted royal effort to revoke borough charters using the legal writ of *Quo Warranto* and reissue them to men who were seen as more loyal. Most famously, the king engaged in a long struggle to rescind London's charter. Behind these legal maneuvers lay a fundamental rejection of urban corporate identity and self-government;

the Tory legal scholar and historian Robert Brady encapsulated this position, arguing that "Burghs were not distinct Commonwealths, or Governments, nor the Burgesses Statesmen," and openly mocking the "Absurd Rights, they have of late Years pretended to."[9]

This concerted attack on English urban self-government explains the style of town development the Crown pursued in the Chesapeake in two ways. First, it inclined the Crown against incorporated towns in Virginia. When they first discussed Culpeper's Virginia town proposals in 1678, officials debated whether the new towns ought to be incorporated, but when they drafted Culpeper's official instructions the following year, in the midst of the Exclusion Crisis, they had dropped all reference to the prospect of incorporating the towns. Second, following the revocation of London's corporate charter, the metropolis's leading tobacco merchants became the king's key allies in governing the capital city, and in return for their loyalty, they began to exercise influence over imperial policies regarding the Chesapeake, which they would eventually use to neuter elements of Chesapeake town plans that did not suit their interests.[10]

The state's increasing interest in urban spaces, though, was about more than ham-fisted efforts to assert political and mercantile authority; it also represented an extension of new ideas about the state's role in economic growth. With his influential essay *Political Arithmetick*, political economist Sir William Petty began to transform the way that officials thought about England's growing population, arguing that, if effectively utilized to generate economic growth, it could benefit rather than hurt the state. Facilitating this efficient employment, though, necessitated urban development.[11] These ideas were developed further by the speculative builder and political economist Nicholas Barbon, who argued that urban growth stimulated consumerism, which encouraged industry and innovation that would employ the ever-growing populations. This cycle, Barbon argued, would strengthen the nation militarily and fiscally and reinforced national prestige. Furthermore, both Petty and Barbon emphasized that the new urban consumer economy could be heavily taxed, generating new sources of revenue that would reduce the Crown's dependence on Parliament. Under this system, Petty argued, political opposition would give way to "Unity, Industry, and Obedience." Thus urban growth would mutually reinforce the Stuart's authoritarian vision of urban governance, reframing the economic relationship between the individual and the state. "There is nothing," Barbon argued, "that is more in the interest of the Prince" than urban development. He was quick to emphasize, though, that achieving such a goal would necessitate royal collaboration with entrepreneurs and merchants, such as himself, who could provide the needed capital to spark development.[12]

During the 1680s, these abstract ideas were converted into concrete projects on both sides of the Atlantic, which paralleled imperial plans for the Chesapeake. Following the overthrow of London's charter, Sir William Petty drafted an elaborate proposal to transform the city, controlling the flow of people, establishing banks and societies for merchants, and promoting refined entertainments.[13] The governor of New York, Sir Edmund Andros, was also active in promoting improvements to urban infrastructure in New York City with the support of a carefully cultivated Anglo-Dutch merchant elite. Andros took a conquered port town that had been a hotbed of resistance to the mercantile system and began to convert it into an English imperial entrepôt. In 1684, Barbados governor Sir Richard Dutton also identified seaport towns as "the very doors to the islands," and he sought to develop the colony's urban infrastructure as part of the empire's efforts to control commerce in slaves and sugar. A few years later, James II considered a plan to establish a central "factory" on each of the sugar islands in order to bring commerce more directly under royal control. Behind all of these projects lay a new perception that towns and cities were no longer civic communities but imperial hubs that facilitated growth and economic improvement, efficiently channeling capital and labor for the benefit of the imperial state, and using the resulting prosperity to pacify political opposition.[14]

The new focus on urban development in the Chesapeake was part of a coherent new political-economic vision for empire. Barbon's vision of urban development generating full employment and thus cutting the taproot of disorder seemed ideally suited to the troubles in Virginia, and it helps to explain why towns were suddenly so high on the Crown's agenda for the region. Beginning in 1678, the Crown displayed a persistent commitment to a new urban future for the Chesapeake not only to assist customs enforcement but also to provide new economic opportunities for poor whites and thus smooth the way toward imperial integration of the tobacco economy. Although they became increasingly beholden to the short-term interests of London's own merchant community, and increasingly saw towns as merely a means to rationalize colonial revenue collection, neither Charles nor James ever completely abandoned the broader objectives of the plan. However, as Charles Calvert reported to the Committee for Trade and Plantation from bitter experience, town development was far from easy. A competing vision of plantation political economy would be articulated by the county elites across the tidewater, who were scrambling to reestablish their own threatened authority.

"THE COUNTRY IN GENERALL IS NOW MOST DESIROUS OF IT"

It is easy to underestimate the uncertainty that hung over Virginia in 1677 following the collapse of Bacon's Rebellion. Sir William Berkeley was trying to reestablish his authority, but in the process, he was exacting vengeance on opponents, which bred continued distrust. Many of the leading planters were seeking to reassert their authority in their counties, but the grievances gathered by the royal commissioners attested to continued frustration with the county oligarchs. Signs of the dislocation of authority in Virginia were everywhere. When Berkeley gathered the General Assembly in late February 1677, a majority of the burgesses favored abandoning Jamestown and building a new capital city. They also approved plans to redraw county boundaries across parts of the colony, suggesting that they recognized the breakdown in effective government within some of the existing shires. At another session of the General Assembly the following year, the burgesses passed an act allowing planters on the colony's western frontier to establish self-governing military districts under their personal command, a move later characterized as "Catonizing" the province. During this same session, the General Assembly also broadened authority for county justices to draft their own bylaws, giving them greater scope to exercise local authority. In short, the county institutions that had organized life in Virginia were suddenly in flux.[15]

Virginia's economy was as unsettled as its spatial politics. A temporary rise in tobacco prices after the rebellion encouraged overproduction and a predictable price slump in the late 1670s. When Culpeper arrived in 1680, he wrote that "the low price of Tobacco staggers me" and that "the continuance of it, will be the Totall and speedy ruine of this noble Colony." As elite planters reestablished their estates, even they, with the benefit of their economies of scale and new supplies of enslaved laborers sent by the Royal African Company after the rebellion, could no longer count on the weed to return a healthy profit. The coastal trade to the Caribbean and the northern colonies, which had previously helped to sustain the region, was under pressure as a result of the Plantation Duty Act, which required all tobacco to be shipped to England. For elite planters, particularly in the regions of Virginia that produced the highest quality sweet-scented tobacco, the situation heightened the importance of securing consignment arrangements with consolidating English merchant houses. But as tobacco prices fell and supply increased, such relationships intensified rivalries between planters, who competed to establish the best merchant connections; such relationships would allow them to offer the best prices when purchasing their neighbors' tobacco for consignment and thereby enable them to dominate the tobacco trade in their communities.[16]

It was into this troubled situation that Culpeper brought his royal instructions to impose urbanity. When he arrived in 1680, he greeted the General Assembly with the news that the king had "concluded on ye Necessity of haveing one or more Townes in yt Country" and that, to this end, he would establish three or four port towns for all loading and unloading of goods. He predicted that "sevll difficulties will occur," but he lectured the burgesses that without towns "no othr nacon evr begun a plantacon, or any yet thrived as it ought." The emphasis was very clear: urban development was a royal plan, and he was merely seeking advice on implementation.[17]

To many in Culpeper's audience, however, towns held a different appeal, one grounded in the same assumptions about economic plight but framed as a way of reestablishing their own local authority. Despite his commitment to imperial town development, which he had expressed repeatedly in London before his departure, Culpeper proved amenable to the planter elites' ideas. He was keen to secure a permanent arrangement for funding his gubernatorial salary, and in return for assenting to this measure, the new governor allowed the burgesses to reshape the Crown's urban plans. Given this freedom, the burgesses immediately adjusted the rationale for urban development, claiming that towns were "Soe much desired and of soe great advantage to this poore Colonie." Provincial Secretary Nicholas Spencer later asserted that widespread poverty had induced "inhabitants of the Country to thinke of Cohabitation [in towns]." The burgesses here mirrored the Crown's claims that urban development would benefit the poor, but they inserted themselves as the architects of this economic development. The burgesses replaced Culpeper's suggested three or four towns with twenty—one in each county—and declared that the locations would be "appointed by ye Burgesses" rather than by gubernatorial fiat. The finalized 1680 Act for Cohabitation and Encouragement of Trade and Manufacture, by its very existence, contradicted the king's intention that Culpeper rely upon royal prerogative to develop towns. The act outlined the price to be paid for the land on which the towns would be built, how it would be sold, and how the tobacco trade would be restricted

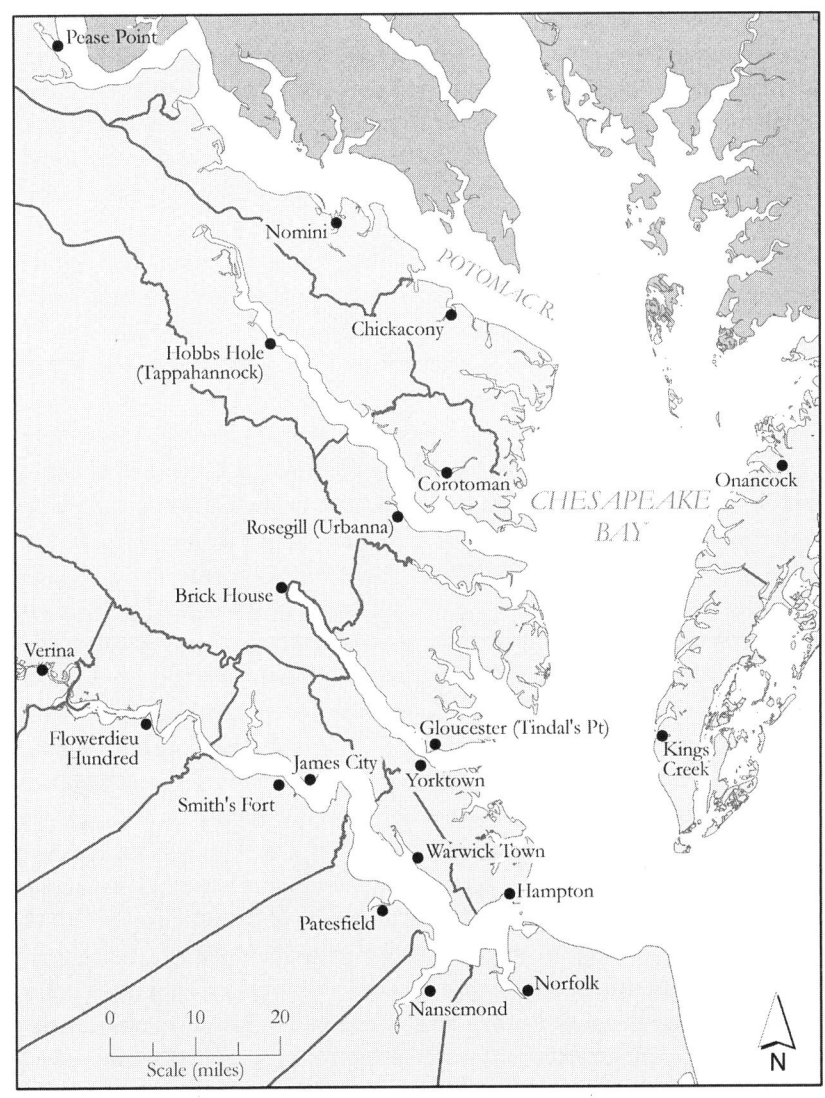

5.1 Map of Virginia town locations in the 1680s
This map shows the locations of the towns established by the Virginia General Assembly's 1680 "Act for Cohabitation and Encouragement of Trade and Manufacture." Names are spelled as they appeared in the original legislation, even if later spelling and usage varied.

to the towns. It never mentioned tax collection, focusing instead on support for marginal planters. Half-acre lots were to be sold for only one hundred pounds of tobacco each, provided that the purchaser made the lot a permanent residence. Town residents could also enjoy five years' exemption from county taxes and protection from creditors.[18] In addition, the act reflected the burgesses' intention that new urban populations fit within existing power structures. The towns were appointed "for" the counties rather than alongside them, and county justices were to oversee the land sales and the trading restrictions. The existing planter elite in each county intended to dominate the new spaces, which would be centers for agricultural marketing and local improvement projects that would earn the appreciation of their poorer neighbors.[19]

This vision of urban improvement was clearly at odds with the Crown's objectives, but it did fit with other trends in England. During this period, English provincial towns were becoming increasingly potent symbols of county identity; members of the local county gentry invested in improving their built environment and made them regional social hubs. Outside these ceremonial centers, local landholders also oversaw the development of new towns built around specific economic innovations; in the seventeen years from 1673 to 1690, sixty-two new towns were planned in England. The most dramatic development occurred when the Lowther family of Cumbria transformed the coastal village of Whitehaven into a mining town and Atlantic port. The Lowthers retained authority over the new town, but they presented the development as a service to their county community. A similar pattern was developing in Scotland, as local gentry there worked to stimulate development and catch up with their neighbors to the south.[20]

The vision underpinning these investments was apparent in the work of English projector Andrew Yarranton. In Yarranton's lengthy volume, *England's Improvement by Sea and Land* (1677), he advanced a head-spinning array of schemes to help "those poor Cities and Towns that depend upon Trade." Where Yarranton departed from contemporaries such as Petty and Barbon was in his focus on provincial improvement that would support the populations of small towns and ward off the influence of powerful state-backed merchants. Yarranton's most ambitious proposal was for a new town in the English Midlands built around granaries that would protect the wheat crops of "the poor Countrey people" from "Rats and Mice with Four Legs" but also from "Rats with Two Legs"— the London merchants who bought up their stock at below-market value. Although Yarranton's treatise likely did not make it across the Atlantic, it can help interpret the intentions of the planter elite as they simultaneously drafted their urbanization plans. Many Virginia planters could have readily identified with concerns about rats with two legs who bought and sold their livelihoods. This vision of improvement did not conform to the Stuarts' statecentric ideal, but neither did it reflect earlier visions of civic independence. Rather, it represented a gentry impulse toward speculation in improvements that reinforced their local status.[21]

Evidence from the surviving county records suggests that local elites across Virginia quickly grasped the opportunity offered by the 1680 act. In more than three-quarters of Virginia's counties, representing a broad cross section of the colony's economic subregions, the towns were laid out within two years. This represented a considerable financial commitment. In addition to the 500 pounds of tobacco paid to the surveyor, the act stipulated that each county had to purchase the fifty-acre town site for 10,000 pounds of tobacco. All of these outlays would need to be paid by county taxes and would not be repaid until all of the town lots were sold. This was potentially quite burdensome: for example, Lower Norfolk County's 1682 levy included 10,800 pounds of tobacco to purchase the town land, which represented nearly 10 percent of the total annual county costs for the year and added an extra 13 pounds of tobacco to the levy from every tithable. Furthermore, in at least three cases, the county justices proposed relocating their courthouse to the new town, reinforcing the ties between the site and the county elite, but also adding to the public expense. The 1680 act was thus not merely a pipe dream; it was taken up by county leaders at considerable cost because it provided a clear and tangible way for them to take back practical control over their communities.[22]

However, the potential power of new towns for local elites also meant that they crystalized local rivalries. Where elites were relatively unified, the town-building process was straightforward. In Accomack County, for example, two justices served as the trustees and purchased the appointed land from fellow county leader Edmund Scarborough, naming the site Scarburgh Town in his honor.[23] In other counties, though, leading planters tussled over town building because of the potential commercial and political advantages it might offer. Middlesex County—home to Robert Beverley, one of the architects of the act—witnessed the most contentious implementation. Middlesex justices approved the land purchase for their new town immediately after the act's passage. However, they made no progress because the site lay on Rosegill Creek, on land owned by the powerful provincial councillor Ralph Wormeley, who persistently refused to sell. The county justices, including Beverley and Christopher Robinson (who hosted

"Severall meetings at his house about ye Towne"), were locally influential, but their status could not match Wormeley's, either in provincial politics or in commerce. (Wormeley was a consigning partner of leading English tobacco merchants.) However, because they had ensured that the 1680 act specifically located the town directly across the creek from Wormeley's imposing Rosegill Plantation, the ambitious justices were empowered to compulsorily purchase the land at the heart of Wormeley's trading network. The town would take advantage of Wormeley's prime commercial site and allow Beverley, Robinson, and their allies to claim control over it by grounding their authority upon their commitment to the well-being of the community. It was hardly surprising that Wormeley stubbornly resisted.[24]

The powerful potential of the authority that the act offered was clearly revealed when, in 1682, the Middlesex justices sought to deploy the town's jurisdiction even though Wormeley still refused to sell and the site remained an empty field. Thomas Wharton, a friend of Beverley and Robinson, filed two suits against ship captains for not abiding by the town act's trading restrictions. Technically, all ships were supposed to load and unload their cargoes at towns after September 29, 1681. The two captains who were targeted were likely trading with Wormeley, who made a rare visit to the county court to hear the cases. The whole episode demonstrated the way that new towns might create alternative patterns of legitimate authority, reshuffling the hierarchy of commercial and political power.[25]

The Middlesex case also revealed that urban authority had broader implications for the planters' power within the English Empire. Wharton's case allowed Beverley to frame the town-building project as a crusade to bring English merchant networks under greater scrutiny, thereby winning allies among his poorer neighbors. Just as Wharton was bringing his suit, poor planters in the area began rioting. The rioters were suffering from the ongoing tobacco depression in general, but Beverley connected the unrest to the failure of town development. Lord Baltimore, observing from Maryland, described the riots as "some discontents and dissatisfaction ... abt the buisnes of Cohabitacon."[26] Beverley capitalized on the discontent by circulating a petition calling for a meeting of the General Assembly to address the delays in town development, the flouting of the town act, and the continued economic crisis. Acting governor Sir Henry Chicheley (Culpeper had returned to England) was in a tricky position because within days of Beverley's demands, he received news that the Crown had suspended the town act. He called the assembly but then quickly prorogued them again once he realized that they might take radical action. Beverley circulated the news of this truncated session as evidence of indifference to the plight of ordinary Virginians, helping further stir local rioting and claiming personal political authority. Chicheley framed the situation very differently, claiming that Beverley was engaged in demagoguery "to the great dissatisfaction of the most and best part of ye colony." Whichever assessment was closer to the truth, the critical point was that Beverley's orchestration of these disturbances, known as the Plant-Cutter Riots, was an outgrowth of the urban development plan and the ultimate example of the way it allowed county elites to legitimize their leadership and seek to shape imperial policy by claiming to represent the desperate circumstances of their neighbors.[27]

For the most well-connected members of the elite (such as Ralph Wormeley), their merchant allies, and the imperial officials with whom they enjoyed an increasingly close relationship, this potential power was too much of a risk. When they first received the act, royal officials expressed shock that the House of Burgesses would even contemplate the establishment of towns through provincial legislation when "setting out of Wharfes and keys is never done in England but by his Ma[jes]ties Comission[ers of Customs]." This statement reflected the Crown's vision for the towns as nodes within an administrative network. Imperial officials lamented what Culpeper termed the "ill use made of" the town proposals.[28] London merchants, with vested interests in avoiding troublesome suits such as the one brought by Wharton, were quick to suggest that Virginia's elite planters had been manipulating Culpeper's original plan without actually investing in facilities for the good of the community. Customs officials concurred that the Virginia plan was merely designed to restrict tobacco production and raise prices; the original royal proposals, they countered, had promised to "be of Gen[era]ll Good to the Planters as well Rich as Poore." Imperial officials remained convinced that, if properly executed, urbanization could build bonds between struggling planters and imperial power, making enforcement of mercantile restrictions easier and reducing merchants' costs while also ensuring the productive employment of the colony's full labor force.[29]

In line with this reasoning, officials dismissed the General Assembly's plans to restrict tobacco production, but rather than rejecting the act entirely they merely suspended it pending a major redesign, leading to tensions that would last through the 1680s. Culpeper proved unwilling to remain in Virginia to implement imperial plans, and so the task fell to the king's new governor, Lord Effingham.[30] As an outsider with no Virginia connections and rigid loyalty to Stuart policies, Effingham immediately aroused the suspicions of the Virginia elite, but it was his determination to implement the imperial vision of urban development that provoked the most consistent and bitter tensions. The battle between the burgesses' vision of towns and Effingham's instructions on the issue crystalized competing visions of empire and cultivated the planter elites' self-conscious political identity.[31]

Effingham made clear that he intended to hold to the royal vision on town development; he signaled his intentions clearly through efforts to reestablish Jamestown, building an imperial capital on the ruins left from Bacon's firing of the city. Soon after his arrival in Virginia in 1684, he made a brief visit to New York City, where he saw the urban infrastructure that Governor Sir Edmund Andros had built. "This place is very delightfull," Effingham opined, particularly the "Methodiseing in all places everything so prudently for the honor of the Government." Over the next few years, he worked to "methodize" Jamestown in a similar fashion. Individual buildings in the destroyed city had been restored, but Effingham increased the pace of redevelopment.[32] He also began using the capital more deliberately as part of an expanded calendar of imperial ceremonies, particularly to mark events trumpeting Stuart power, such as the ascension of James II and the suppression of Monmouth's Rebellion. Proclamations of official celebration emphasized that ceremonies would be led by Effingham at Jamestown before being replicated across the colony at a later date, reinforcing the capital's place in a spatial hierarchy. Effingham even promoted the establishment of an annual "Cockney Feast" in Jamestown: a social event intended to bring together self-identified Londoners (likely agents and allies of the metropolis's major tobacco merchants). The inaugural feast featured a sermon by Reverend Duell Pead focusing on the paramount importance of loyalty to the Crown. Through all these innovations, Effingham made Jamestown a model for the type of urban development that would bind Virginia residents to the Stuart state.[33]

Implementing this vision across the colony, however, proved far more difficult. Effingham got this larger project off to an inauspicious start when he opened his first General Assembly in April 1684. The first item on his agenda was urban development, but, rather than seeking compromise, he chided the delegates as "deficient to your-selves" for their lack of towns and in need of imperial guidance to understand their own best interests. By doing so, he ignored the burgesses' efforts over the past four years and the fact that it had been the Crown's vacillation on the issue that had provoked a violent uprising. However, reframing the town question this way allowed Effingham to claim that the king's concern for the well-being of Virginia, in the face of planter obstinacy, necessitated unilateral action to establish a limited number of official port towns. Unlike Culpeper, he had no intention of haggling over the plan. In fact, because the legislation was merely suspended, Effingham felt that he could simply demand that the planters comply with his orders, rather than giving them free rein to formulate a new act.[34]

Unsurprisingly, Effingham's opening gambit sparked an immediate impasse. The burgesses held to their version of the town plan and were determined that Effingham would not pick and choose elements of it that benefited the Crown. They were not interested in reorganizing commerce through towns if Effingham insisted that these places be solely "for the preventing of frauds and better securing his Majesties revenue." In response, they offered a revised proposal that demoted the locations to the status of "portes" while more than doubling their number across the colony, effectively neutering their influence. The costs of building this many towns and the impracticality of appointing imperial officials to oversee trade at each site made the plan obviously unworkable for the empire's purposes. However, as with earlier proposals, the burgesses justified their plan in populist terms, arguing that more locations were vital because poor planters would be hurt by the cost of shipping tobacco to more distant sites. (This, of course, had not concerned them in 1680 when they advocated a smaller number of locations under their control.) The purpose of the burgesses' new plan was clearly to show their determination that urban development would happen on their terms or not at all.[35]

Effingham saw through this maneuver and excoriated the burgesses' proposal. The 1680 plan "to raise Twenty Townes out of Noe Townes did seem Impracticable," Effingham fumed. If that plan was doomed to failure, how much more so was this new proposal to appoint two or three per county? Effingham then explained that he had never intended the burgesses to draft new legislation, but only to spur planters to invest their funds at the existing town sites to construct facilities of a sufficient standard that he, London's merchants, and the king would all find acceptable. He envisioned new urban development that would require planters to contribute more funds but exercise less control. Effingham once again sought to claim the populist mantel for this position, claiming that "the Country in Generall is now most desirous of" implementing the new imperial plan. He suggested that the real problem was the squabbling elites, divided between those who had "laide out great sums of money" on town development and those who feared towns would deprive them of the "opportunity to Engrosse the Trade as now they do." This argument provided further justification for the imperial centralization of trade regulation, underlining the fact that the real division lay between the governor and the burgesses in general.[36]

The session ended without resolution, but when the burgesses gathered again in 1685, they were united in their determination to revive the town plan on their terms. The burgesses were responding to the empire's continued assault on their political and economic autonomy. The recent news of James II's ascension to the throne had been accompanied by details of an increase in tobacco duties, which were more than doubled to five pence per pound; although some of this increase would be passed on to consumers rather than being borne by planters, the implication was that the imperial state had unilateral authority to control the tobacco market. Effingham had also received royal instructions to restrict counties' powers to draft bylaws, and he announced this change at the start of the new assembly session. Delegates quickly responded by demanding that Effingham approve a "new" town plan similar to the proposal the governor had dismissed the previous year.[37]

Though Effingham initially seemed receptive, negotiations soon erupted into a full-scale constitutional standoff. When the Virginia Council, acting as the upper chamber of the General Assembly, initially assented to the town measure, Effingham attached a loose sheet of paper to the draft legislation with a series of amendments intended to reinforce royal authority over the new towns by clarifying the responsibilities of imperial customs officers. If the burgesses had consented to these additions, Effingham would have had a funded network of placemen to oversee trade at each port town. However, Robert Beverley, as clerk of the assembly, saw an opportunity; he detached the unsigned amendment sheet, describing it as a "certain paper no waies authenticated," and entered the unamended act as an approved statute awaiting the governor's signature. When Effingham reviewed the acts a few days later, he noticed the omission and refused to sign the law, sparking an acerbic war of words. The dispute raised key questions about assembly procedures; it made the burgesses more defensive about their legislative autonomy and forced Effingham to clarify how much power he had to shape legislation. It was no coincidence, though, that this constitutional showdown occurred around the town issue that had been simmering for half a decade. For both sides, the content of the disputed amendments was what animated the struggle. Beverley resorted to a legal technicality in rejecting the unsigned amendments because control over this legislation was crucial. The burgesses refused to add Effingham's provisions for customs collection to the act, despite their stated determination to see it pass, and Effingham refused to agree to the unamended act. With no resolution in sight, Effingham angrily dismissed the General Assembly. Town development was once again the major fault line in Virginia's relations with the empire.[38]

Faced with this conflict, Effingham abandoned urban development in favor of a straightforward assertion of royal control. This was especially true after James II's ascension, when maintaining the flow of tobacco duties became the top priority for the new king as he sought to fund the growth of the English army. A report from the customs commissioners in 1687 noted that "especially considering the greatness of the New Impost on Tobacco," they could not risk further economic improvement projects that might lead to "the disturbance of that Trade, and prejudice of his Mats Revenue." Although the burgesses returned to town planning again in 1686 and 1688, Effingham persistently sidestepped the issue that he and his masters in London had once considered their top priority.[39]

Both the burgesses and the governor still supported urbanization, but in a series of seemingly minor legislative squabbles, they had confronted the issue's fundamental conflict. Urban development, now informed by increasingly sophisticated theories of political economy, offered concrete ways to appeal to common planters and thereby justify the authority of either local elites or imperial officials. The initial plans of both planters and imperial officials were more practical than any that had gone before, which explains the partial progress made toward establishing towns. However, planters, merchants, and officials were all now more cognizant of their particular interests. They were careful not to invest resources in the physical infrastructure of towns—warehouses, residences, and wharves—without concrete guarantees that they would serve their purposes. Stuart urban policy rejected the kinds of concessions requisite to encourage planters to build town infrastructure of their own volition; the burgesses resisted the imperial bureaucracy that might leverage state power to construct such infrastructure; and finally, leading tobacco merchants, who might have been interested in the efficiency savings of centralized trade, had little need to invest in or do business through a vast network of notional towns in empty fields. The result was a network of false starts, with surveys, lot markings, and a few hastily constructed wooden structures. More significantly, though, the contest over urban development had helped to clarify the particular interests and objectives of all those involved in the plantation economy. This was a crucial step toward finding compromises and accommodations that would allow the Chesapeake elite to intensify their brutal plantation system and cement its role within the new centralized and commercialized empire. Equally, the struggle during the 1680s also enhanced the planter gentry's self-perception as civic guardians of their local county communities, capable of negotiating the details of imperial political economy for their poorer neighbors and articulating a local vision for an economic order that would benefit all white men.

"TO PROMOTE THE TRADE OF HIS SUBJECTS"

Maryland had been unstable during Bacon's Rebellion, but it had not fallen into outright revolt. Yet Lord Baltimore still found himself subject to imperial investigations and to the Crown's new town plans, which were expanded to embrace Maryland. As the proprietor scrambled to make sure that he retained authority over potential urban development, he left himself open to renewed accusations of corrupt and arbitrary government. As a result, while Effingham was able to shelve the issue of town development in the mid-1680s, in Maryland it became a potent symbol of Baltimore's authority over planters' livelihoods and a key factor in the uprising against his rule in 1689.

The economic and political situation at the north end of the Chesapeake Bay was even more fraught than in Virginia. Maryland's tobacco producers were entirely focused upon the lower-priced Orinoco strain, and they also struggled with more marginal land not suited to tobacco at all. As a result, the colony was hit even harder by low tobacco prices. The tensions inspired by the ongoing threat of native attacks along the western frontier also lingered longer in Maryland, spurred on by increasing anti-Catholic fears imported from England. Fears of an alliance between the Iroquois, the French, and Maryland's Catholics reflected both of these economic and religious concerns in isolated frontier communities. On the other end of the social scale, a Protestant gentry had begun to coalesce during the 1670s. They dominated Maryland's assembly and challenged Baltimore on constitutional issues.[40]

Complicating matters further, the Plantation Duty Act had, for the first time, imposed royal customs officers on the colony. The most controversial of these figures was Christopher Rousby, a local merchant who had been appointed royal collector for the Patuxent River. Rousby demanded that ship captains consult him upon entering and leaving the colony, preempting the proprietor's oversight. Baltimore clearly felt threatened by this shift in commercial oversight, complaining that "at Rousbys house . . . the Comanders of London ships are much treated" and made party to their host's "lewd debaucht swearing," in contrast to the "Civill society" at St. Mary's City. Baltimore described Rousby as an "insolent and Knavish Collector who presumes dayly to Nose me and my Government." The Crown's newfound penchant for rescinding charters, however, meant that men such as Rousby who claimed to be safeguarding royal prerogative held real power to undermine the proprietorship with their reports. In this context, Baltimore realized that he had to pay closer attention to imperial edicts, including orders that he cooperate with Virginia governor Culpeper "to promote the trade of His [Majesty's] Subjects . . . and to encourage their industry."[41]

These circumstances explain why, despite having suggested just a few years before that urban development would require divine intervention, Baltimore decided to embark on a new urban plan in 1682. Whereas his previous efforts had focused on restructuring local authority to benefit his allies, Baltimore's new proposals reflected the same concern with claiming legitimacy through improvement that characterized Virginia's debate. He hoped to deploy appreciation from Maryland's marginal planters to bolster his position against both the local gentry and the imperial bureaucracy. Baltimore had reviewed the state of the colony's economy and concluded that "if some expedient be not speedily found," then "the inhabitants will be reduced to great straights." The *Complaint from Heaven* had suggested that, if framed correctly, urbanization might earn him the appreciation of poorer planters.[42]

The turn toward populist improvement meant that, where he had previously acted by proprietary fiat, Baltimore now sought assembly legislation, but this immediately established town development as a locus for the battle over legitimacy within the province. Both Baltimore and the delegates in the lower house were eager to demonstrate that they understood and were seeking to address the needs of struggling planters. Baltimore claimed to be interceding with the delegates on behalf of poorer planters, claiming that town development was "earnestly Desired by the Generallity of the Inhabitants," but delegates described the proprietor's proposal as "much desired by his Lordship and Upper house" and claimed that, by contrast, they sought a solution "well respecting The ease Commodity and Benefitt of the Commonalty." By allowing both Baltimore and his opponents to claim to represent the public interest in crucial economic questions, the debate brought issues of political economy into conversation with other politico-religious concerns about Baltimore's authority and inscribed these fears onto specific urban spaces.[43]

Debate over the details of the new town plan during the General Assembly of 1682 was shaped by competing invocations of the interests of poorer planters. The core of the proprietor's proposal was another effort to restrict trade to specified locations, which were nominated by the councillors of the assembly's upper house, who were overwhelmingly loyal to him. Political enfranchisement for the new towns was hinted at—in keeping with Baltimore's 1660s plans for St. Mary's City—and potential town residents were promised trading privileges. The proposal also appointed proprietary revenue collectors, but it notably made no mention of the royal customs service. Baltimore's intention was clearly to turn the imperial town plans to his own advantage.[44] The delegates in the lower house agreed that the plan would "tend much to the Honour Saefty and Security of the Province and Advancement of Trade," but they demanded that Baltimore "take the Advice of this house, or the Commissioners of the respective Counties" in selecting locations that would "Suit with the Conveniency of the Inhabitants."[45] The delegates drew up a list of locations containing thirty sites spread over Maryland's ten counties. The high number of sites partly reflected factionalism among the delegates. However, much like the situation in Virginia, it was also part of an effort to water down the impact of proprietary oversight and to bolster delegates' claims to be mitigating the inconvenience for ordinary planters.[46] The rhetoric of civic concern also informed delegates' complaints about Baltimore's proposal to restrict the size of town lots; the proprietor intended the rule to prevent speculators buying up large portions of new towns, but the delegates portrayed it as an effort to privilege warehouses and mercantile infrastructure rather than lots large enough to build residential structures. Similarly, the delegates pushed for rules allowing only local residents to transport tobacco from outlying plantations into towns in order to prevent Atlantic merchants from continuing their current dispersed trade and then simply touching cargoes down at town sites merely to comply with the act. Through these amendments, delegates articulated a populist vision of towns inhabited by individual freeholders employed as local boatmen and petty merchants.[47]

Equally, however, the proposals from the lower house also demonstrated that they, as local gentry, anticipated using the new towns to reinforce their local authority. The delegates argued that some of the changes that Baltimore's plan would impose upon the tobacco trade were "Enough to sett the Inhabitants together by the Eares"; in other words, they would disrupt the commercial hierarchies within local communities. Delegates worked to limit this effect wherever possible. The lower house initially demanded clarification about "how, by whom, in whose Name, and for whose use such places shall be purchased." Previous town land had been

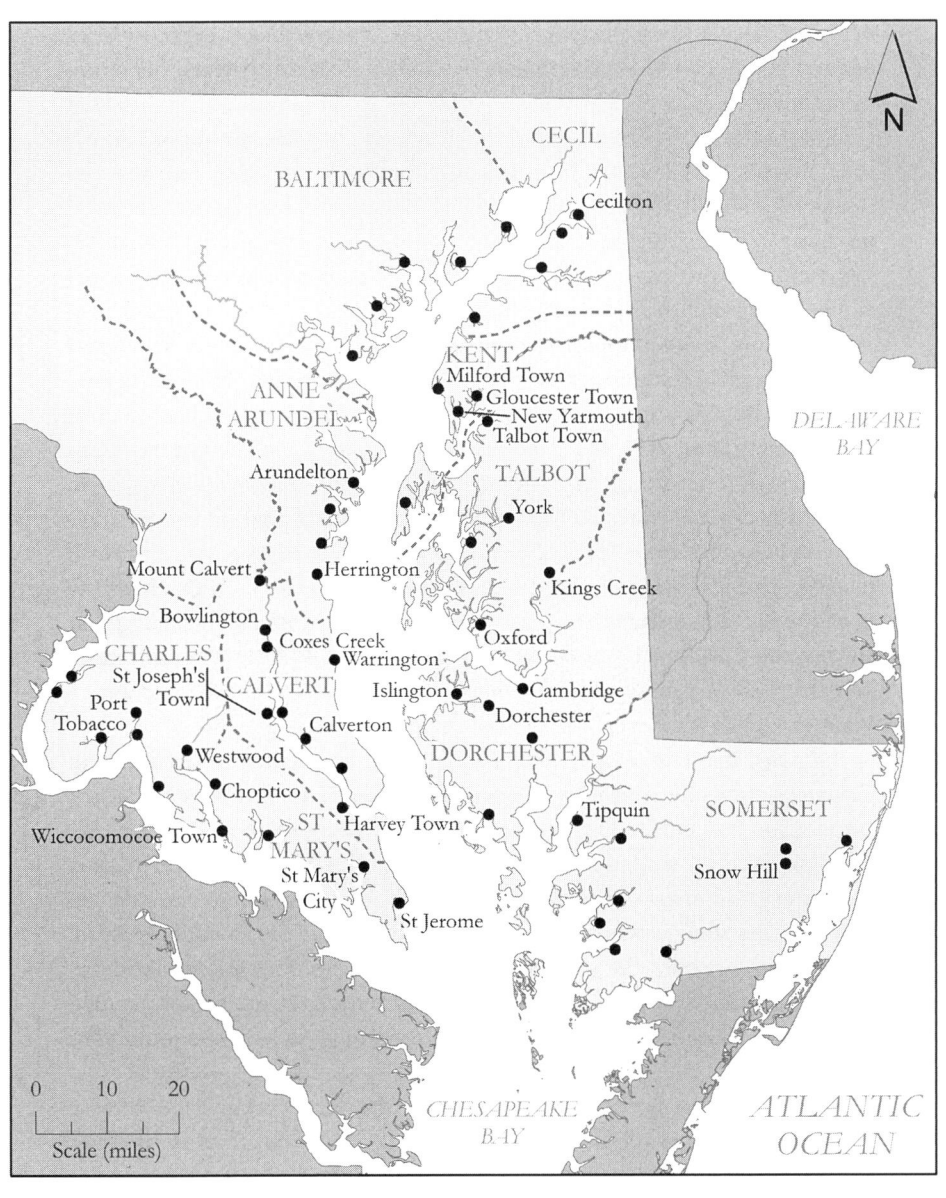

5.2 Map of Maryland town locations, 1683–1688
This map shows all of the identifiable locations of the towns established by the Maryland Assembly in acts from 1683, 1684, 1686, and 1688. Names are only given for sites where clear contemporary evidence of naming exists, and using the original spelling, even if the town site later developed a recognized name. (Some information adapted from Shomette, *Lost Towns of Tidewater Maryland* [Centreville, MD: Tidewater, 2000], appendix.)

held in trust by the proprietor until the lots were sold, but the delegates refused to replicate this system and demanded the right to designate trustees like those appointed in Virginia. They also proposed that proprietary revenue collectors in the towns would report to the county courts. Finally, they added a provision for building churches and public buildings in the towns, thereby allowing local leaders to bolster their authority by erecting new county courthouses and also to reinforce Protestant ecclesiastic structure, which was especially significant in a colony where confessional and political loyalties were intertwined.[48]

Baltimore was anxious to retain the image of champion of the interests of common planters, so he quickly approved many of the delegates' amendments, but on issues of authority, he dug in his heels. He stuck to the original list of "places for Towns Nominated by his Lordship and Upper house"—at least half of which belonged to proprietary allies or Baltimore himself. Delegates from Somerset and Anne Arundel Counties appealed the location choices, only to be told that "the Appoynting places for Townes &c is Affirm'd by the upper house to be the prerogative of the Lord Proprietary." The upper house underlined the point by insisting that a clause be added to the town act giving Baltimore sole right "at any time hereafter to Nominate any new place or Places where the People are in Want of Town or Townes."[49]

Neither side was prepared to compromise on these crucial issues of authority, and soon the legislation was at the center of a bitter political standoff. In the late 1670s, Baltimore had exercised his prerogative to reduce county representation in the lower house from four to two delegates per county. Members of the lower house had repeatedly sought to overturn this decision, and they now decided to tie the issue to the town legislation. They refused to pass the proprietor's town plan, even after negotiating so many compromises, until he agreed to reverse the decision on county representation. This maneuver was more than simply a cynical trade-off. The delegates chose the town plan for leverage because they saw the two issues as connected; both addressed how the proprietor related to ordinary planters. Delegates were determined to reinforce the rights of their existing power structure before any new urban spaces were established that might disrupt county hierarchies. Tellingly, even as they sought to double the size of county delegations, they also petitioned against potential town representatives because they might "prove Burthensome to the Publique by Increasing the number of Burgesses in Assemblyes." A stalemate ensued, leading Baltimore to prorogue the assembly.[50] The key to breaking the deadlock the following year was Baltimore's escalation of populist rhetoric. He harangued the delegates, insisting that the town proposal contained nothing of "any Particular Advantage to my Self," and he challenged them that if they genuinely opposed the town plan, they should "go to your house and accordingly Vote it so, That so it may be known where and at whose Doores it Lyeth." Their bluff called by this appeal to popular support for towns, the delegates approved the act that same afternoon.[51]

But uncertainty about proprietary authority over new towns lingered and came to hinder the act's implementation. Over the next few years, the town sites became the focus for local battles over who really spoke for the economic interests of local communities. When Baltimore gathered another assembly in 1684, a flood of appeals demanding the relocation of towns arrived. Some of these requests arose in the upper house and focused on transferring town sites to the land of reliable proprietary allies. One such case involved the addition of Calverton, a small town in Calvert County that had emerged from the earlier efforts at town development in the 1660s; its chief resident was proprietary ally Michael Taney.[52] In other cases, it was the lower house who proposed relocations on the basis of requests ostensibly from the "inhabitants" of each county. Baltimore was anxious to settle these issues, and so he approved most of the changes, but his concessions did not put all dispute to rest. Within county communities, towns continued to provide concrete stakes for local rivalries and partisan battles between proprietary supporters and opponents.[53]

The first major confrontation occurred in Somerset County. The General Assembly had legislated for a town at "Barrows Ridge" on the Pocomoke River in Somerset, but in the summer of 1684, the county's town commissioners visited a location near Barrows, called Snow Hill, where they were confronted by "a considerable number of the most ablest of the Inhabitants of the Sea Side [of the county]," who requested that they "take a view of the Conveniency" of the place. When they then moved on to the Barrows site, "the Inhabitants aforesaid" followed them to "earnestly request" that they relocate the town. The browbeaten commissioners ultimately recommended the move to Snow Hill. It is impossible to know how big the crowd was, but the story suggests either a sizable concerned citizenry who were taking urban development very seriously or an effort to legitimize a preplanned relocation of the town site with reference to mass public appeal. Either way, the events demonstrate how popular concern with political economy was being used to justify local authority.[54]

An even clearer example of town development propagating local political identity came in Calvert County. Lower house delegates had suggested a town at "Coxes Creek" in 1683, but Baltimore overruled them.

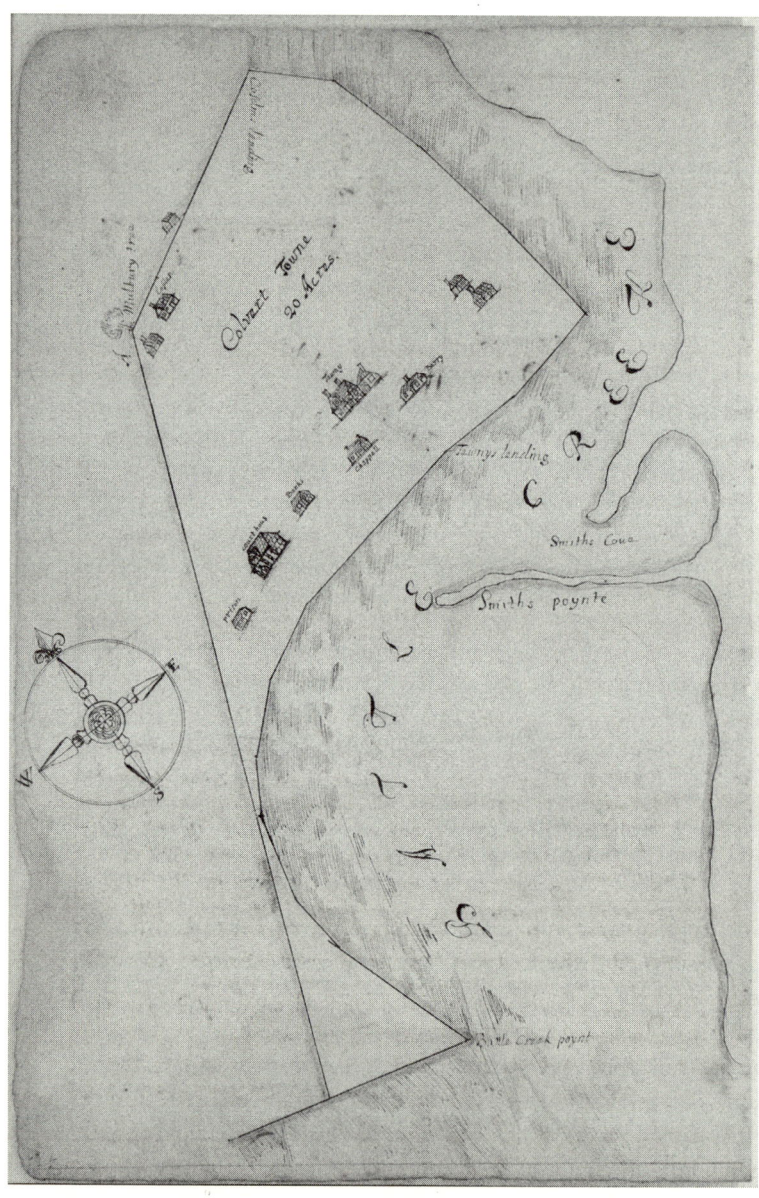

5.3 Surveyor's plat of the town of Calverton, Calvert County, 1682
The town of Calverton was established by the 1660s and was recognized by Lord Baltimore in his 1668 town proclamation. Residents of the community petitioned the Maryland Assembly in 1682, seeking to secure the title to the land on which the town was built. The case resulted in a new survey of the town site, which provides a unique contemporary depiction of the size and layout of a Chesapeake town. (Courtesy of the Maryland Historical Society.)

The following year, the provincial council agreed to a petition to add an additional town at Coxes Creek.⁵⁵ This decision, however, elicited a vitriolic response in the county. In 1685, residents drew up a petition with fifty-eight signatures, claiming that Coxes Creek had been promoted by "malitious suggestions" and that it was "altogether to us inconvenient." Instead of simply ignoring the town act's provisions, local planters went to the trouble of collecting signatures. Petitioning was a technique that was growing in popularity in the partisan political climate of contemporary England, and in Calvert County it helped to mobilize popular opinion to establish the authority of community leaders. County leaders would build on this system of petitioning as a means of mobilizing popular opinion four years later in their revolution against Baltimore in 1689.⁵⁶

Events in Charles County linked town building directly to the confessional tensions that would eventually spark revolution in Maryland. Charles County was the poorest part of Maryland's western shore, and it was also the home of Josias Fendall, a proprietary opponent who was periodically rumored to be plotting against the colony's government. Therefore, Baltimore was particularly eager to realize the transformative potential of town development there in order to reimpose his authority. The provincial council believed that the "Inhabitants of [Charles] County . . . were willing to build and promote soe good a worke."⁵⁷ However, widespread antiproprietary sentiment in Charles County meant that town development there inevitably acquired a factional dimension. Baltimore's efforts to site one of the county's towns only enflamed the situation. He first located it on land belonging to the Catholic Church on Port Tobacco Creek; he could scarcely have found a more divisive place, and it was quietly abandoned in 1684. The new location, on the land of proprietary ally William Chandler, was only slightly less problematic. By March 1685, the lack of action to implement the town act in the county had attracted the provincial council's attention, with reports that "ill affected persons to the good and wellfare of this Province have raised and spread abroad scandalous speeches" about the town plans and ejected the surveyor, the Catholic Randolph Brandt, before he could lay out the towns. For suspicious Protestant leaders, the triumvirate of Brandt, Chandler, and the Catholic Church made urban development seem like a "popish" conspiracy as threatening to their trade as the rumors of Catholic-inspired Indian attacks were to their frontier safety. The council ordered Brandt to complete the survey, threatening to punish "all such as shall endeavour to obstruct impede or prevent" his work. All but two of the sixteen men eventually involved in laying out the towns were proprietary allies who would remain loyal to Baltimore during the revolution of 1689. Events in Charles County clearly demonstrated the way that urban development plans could tap into local rivalries and economic problems and tie them to the broader divisions opening within the colony over the legitimacy of Baltimore's authority.[58]

Internal political factionalism, though, was only half the problem with town development; the proprietor's plans were also challenged by imperial authorities. The already tense relationship between proprietary officials and the royal customs service, which had partly ignited Baltimore's renewed interest in town development, took a macabre turn on the evening of October 31, 1684, when Baltimore's cousin, councillor George Talbot, murdered customs officer Christopher Rousby. Making this insult to imperial authority worse, the provincial council quickly appointed three of their number to replace Rousby. In response, Thomas Allen, the captain of the vessel on which the murder occurred, arrested Talbot and asserted temporary authority over customs enforcement in the province. He sailed the upper Chesapeake Bay all winter, enforcing the Navigation Acts and destroying papers issued by proprietary authorities. By February 1685, the council was writing frantically to Baltimore in London that Allen was "continually infesting the severall Ports here" and "Lording it over them, in a most insufferable manner." Not only would the trade of the province be ruined by this challenge to the authority of the new port towns, the council claimed, but also Baltimore's "Government here [would be] rendred ridiculous and ineffectuall."[59]

The provincial council was incensed by Allen's actions, but Baltimore, who had returned to London, felt under increasing pressure to conform the town plan to imperial designs. In the spring of 1685, the council issued a proclamation chastising opponents of town building, who had broached "severall seeming difficulties, which they pretend may be grounded upon the designe of Townes, and endeavour to amuse & pswade the vulgar that the Townes aforesaid will not goe forward to the great prejudice of the good people of this Province." The councillors were returning to the civic theme of public welfare, which Baltimore had used so effectively in 1683 to secure passage of the legislation.[60] But by this point, Baltimore had learned enough about imperial political economy back in London to begin trimming his sails to royal expectations. He rubbed shoulders with Stuart courtiers and tobacco merchants as they discussed Virginia's urban legislation, getting a better sense of the empire's limited objectives for towns.[61] Baltimore was also under pressure because news of Christopher Rousby's murder had severely damaged his reputation with imperial officials. Baltimore clearly had good reasons to rethink his urban plans for Maryland

and to demonstrate his loyalty to the empire. In the summer of 1685, he wrote to an official in Maryland to insist upon changes to the town act to allow ships from outside the colony "to lade transport and carry to such Townes" any tobacco produced at outlying plantations. This change neutered the key provision that had prevented Atlantic merchants from merely making a token "landing" of their goods at towns to pay duties. It undermined the local control of trade that the provincial council had reemphasized earlier that year, and it brought the colony's nascent towns into line with narrowing imperial goals that wanted them to be merely spaces for the enforcement of mercantile restrictions and taxes.[62]

This restricted vision of urban development was never likely to be popular with planters back in Maryland, and the way that Baltimore chose to implement it generated even greater resentment. Under pressure from imperial officials to make rapid progress with the network of port towns, Baltimore instructed the provincial council to nominate "meet and fitt persons living convenient to the respective Townes" who should "take especiall care to see the said Acts observed." This created a new cadre of officers who would track all shipping, much as Effingham had hoped to do in Virginia. It would provide Baltimore with a regulatory infrastructure that could appear credible to imperial officials but would nevertheless remain under proprietary oversight.[63] The list of men appointed to fill these roles bore this out. Less than half of the appointees had been selected as town commissioners by assembly delegates in 1683, suggesting their independence from the county elites. A number were drawn directly from the provincial council's ranks, and barely 10 percent would go on to join the revolution against Baltimore.[64] These proprietary placemen were a direct threat to the commercial independence of the planter hierarchy. They could not have been more precisely calibrated to raise fears about Baltimore's arbitrary power over commerce. When a new General Assembly met in October 1686, delegates immediately took action. They drew up fresh legislation to reinforce the status of the counties' previously appointed town commissioners, granting them "As full & ample Authority" and a broad remit "as to the doeing & performeing of all and every other things . . . relateing to the new Townes."[65]

The assembly's efforts were in vain, however, because Baltimore, facing mounting pressure in London, and desperate to shore up his authority in Maryland, had decided to give up on the town-building plan. He had dispatched a new governor, William Joseph, with instructions "to dispence with the penalties" in the town act and allow full trading rights to all "vessels belonging to the port of London." According to Baltimore, "the traders and dealers to my Country" had explained to him "that the planters there are not in a condicon as yet to bring their Tobaccoes to Townes." London's merchants had been careful to emphasize that "they were very much for Townes themselves, but the want of those conveniences . . . rendred the way prescribed by the Act as yet utterly unpracticable." But the crux of the matter, as Baltimore candidly noted, was that he feared "that should this Act be pressed too hard upon the Traders it might prove a fit Subject of Complaint for my Enemies to the King against me." In short, Baltimore was now beholden to a new set of imperial economic forces.[66]

The problem, however, was that, in what was now a bitterly divided colony, he could not abandon a plan that he had weighted with such populist significance without attracting indignation. Thanks to the new layers of debate over political economy that Baltimore himself had introduced, improvement had become an important part of any claim to political legitimacy in Maryland. When Governor Joseph gathered a new General Assembly in 1688, the delegates immediately vented their anger about the town plan.[67] They claimed that Baltimore had no right to selectively suspend parts of a legislative act. On a more pragmatic economic level, they also asked why Baltimore's appointed town officers should still be allowed to collect fees if towns were no longer to be marketing centers. The changes were a "great Greivance to the People" and "of fatall Consequence to their Posterity." These complaints seethed with barely concealed anger that the urban project had been subtly transmuted from a public economic improvement into a proprietary revenue system.[68]

This anger became a crucial part of the case against Baltimore's proprietorship the following year. In the early spring of 1689, reports arrived from England of the Glorious Revolution that had overthrown James II and replaced him with his daughter Queen Mary and her husband, William of Orange. Without word from Baltimore, though, Governor Joseph took no action to declare the new Protestant monarchs. In response to Joseph's vacillation, a coalition of local county elites from across the colony formed the self-styled Protestant Association, marched to St. Mary's City, and forced Joseph to surrender his government, effectively overthrowing proprietary authority. Antipopery fueled the revolutionaries' case against Baltimore, leading them to find evidence of tyrannical arbitrary authority in all the proprietor's actions. One element of this fear related to rumors that Joseph and Baltimore were in league with the French and Indians and were planning attacks on the colony's frontier communities. But the recent debacle over towns was equally critical, because it linked antipopery, local gentry influence in their counties, and the topic nearest to most planters' hearts: their economic security in an increasingly complex commercial empire.[69] In their manifesto justifying the revolution, the rebels drew attention to the town-planning process, the appointment of town officers, and Baltimore's selective suspension of parts of the act. A major part of their indictment of Baltimore's supposed malevolent tyranny related to the way he had transformed the town plan from a project designed to address the needs of poor planters into a system to exploit his subjects' fragile economic status. The town plan was an example of "how fatall and of what pernicious consequence that unlimited and arbitary pretended authority may be to the Inhabitants," and especially to their "liberties and properties." The Maryland rebels perceived proprietary prerogative's most dangerous characteristic to be its paternalistic claim to address economic problems; for the Protestant provincial elites who drafted the document and who would go on to consolidate their own status on the basis of property in land and labor over the next decade, security of both "liberty" and "property" was of paramount importance to local legitimacy.[70]

Given their role in justifying rebellion, it is hardly surprising that Maryland's towns featured disproportionately in the uprising itself. Rebellious planters purposefully gathered at town sites to stake claims to the mantle of community interest. In March 1689, the sheriff of Charles County, Robert Doyne, was confronted by "much Company" who had gathered at Charles Town to present him with a petition. Later that year, when Governor Joseph had been deposed and the Protestant Associators sent word to the counties about their successful usurpation, crowds gathered in the colony's towns. In Talbot County, proprietary loyalist Peter Sayer was appalled by such a gathering at the town of York, describing it as a "poor silly mobile." A few weeks later, Sayer rode down to Oxford, another town at the southern end of the county, to witness representatives departing for the Associators' new assembly. Crowded along the quayside was "a great Company of people" who gathered to see them off.[71]

Not all the colony's civic spaces fell under rebel control though. In Somerset County, opposition to Baltimore's overthrow was voiced in Snow Hill, where the former county sheriff publicly read letters from Baltimore's deposed councillors. Likewise, over the next few years, Peter Sayer returned to Oxford in Talbot County many times, and instead of a revolutionary crowd, he met with a stubborn network of merchants and sailors who expressed pro-Baltimore and Jacobite sentiments. Oxford's allegiances may have been fickle, but it was clear that new towns had become key sites of public political action. In notable contrast to the events of the previous revolt against Baltimore's father during the 1650s, when the colony's spatial order was completely overturned, the events of 1689 involved a struggle between rival factions to control recognized port towns that legitimated local leadership.[72]

Despite Baltimore's frantic lobbying in London, the new monarchs stripped him of his political authority and converted Maryland into a royal colony. Baltimore was clearly the victim of the intensifying confessional politics of the English Atlantic; antipopery had dogged both him and his father for half a century, but new anxieties animated this fear in particularly revolutionary ways in 1689. It is certainly true, as scholars have noted, that part of the explanation lay in shifting native geopolitics across the mid-Atlantic, which raised suspicions about the proprietor's diplomacy.[73] However, a parallel transformation was occurring within the political economy of empire that made Baltimore's commercial policies as suspicious as his diplomatic ones. He was caught between the interests of consolidating London merchants, imperial officials, an increasingly differentiated class of local elites, and a community of marginal planters struggling with a glutted tobacco market. This intersection of forces demanded that Baltimore reconceptualize the political economy of his province and turn toward urban improvement as a means of cultivating opportunity for the province's white population. But the increasingly self-conscious Protestant elites in Maryland's county communities understood that if they could steer town development, then they could use it to legitimate their leadership. Urban development during the 1680s thus provided a catalyst for local leaders to claim greater authority over their communities by offering a more compelling and consistent vision of how they would integrate Maryland into the Atlantic imperial economy. The new improvement agenda therefore set up a confrontation between the proprietor and the Protestant gentry over who could best deliver these objectives. When Baltimore was squeezed by the fiscal and commercial pressures of James II's reign, he was forced to reshape his town plan to save his charter, but in doing so, he played into the narratives of Catholic conspiracy. He lost the battle of political-economic legitimacy on the local level—and with it, his colony.

∴

Between 1680 and 1688, more than sixty towns were established in the Chesapeake region. This was urban development on an unprecedented scale. It reflected contemporary recognition that the region faced fundamental problems, which Bacon's Rebellion had highlighted. More land was under cultivation, being farmed with increasingly ruthless efficiency through the exploitation of enslaved labor; the tobacco produced was being traded by a consolidated merchant nexus increasingly centered on London and being taxed more heavily and more adeptly by imperial authorities. These economic conditions had led to the emergence of a new class of poor and landless colonists and had heightened the sense of social crisis in both colonies. Urban development had held long-standing appeal for civic market regulation, but towns now appeared to be a way to foster local improvement projects within the imperial system and thereby forge alliances, exercise patronage, and win loyalty. Towns were now considered "a Remedy to all persons and greevances."[74]

It was the Stuart Crown that first grasped this opportunity, importing ideas from its approach to English boroughs and pursuing a vision of urban growth under tight political authority. This royal approach, though, quickly elicited hostility from members of the Chesapeake local elites keen to make town development serve their own purposes. This confrontation demarcated new fault lines over who would shape provincial political economy between the Crown, colonial elites, and, in Maryland, the proprietor. While Stuart officials around the English Atlantic in these years battled with colonists over particular mercantile policies that affected their established economic structures, in the Chesapeake, the first issue remained towns, because they bore directly on the much broader— and still unresolved—question of what the region's economy should look like and where and how legitimate authority could be established over it.[75]

The difficulty of tackling such questions ultimately hobbled all of the town legislation and ensured that very little actual urban growth was generated in the Chesapeake during these years. Yet the battles were a crucial catalyst in helping the planter elite in both colonies to find their place within the mercantilist and imperial system. On the county level, techniques such as the petitioning over town locations in Calvert County, Maryland, and Robert Beverley's rabble-rousing in Middlesex County, Virginia, gave local leaders the opportunity to build (or rebuild) their authority by mediating between their white neighbors' personal hardships and the increasingly complex Atlantic economy. On the provincial level, negotiations over town development also allowed planter elites to develop new forms of provincial political leadership. The lower houses of both colonies' assemblies claimed new authority to speak for the common good of their constituents and to negotiate on behalf of distinct provincial interests, most obviously when they engaged in horse trading with governors and proprietors over each piece of legislation. In both colonies, town debates bolstered the planter elites' civic claim to represent popular economic concerns, just as they were simultaneously intensifying their slaveholding and tobacco production and increasing the social disparities within their communities. And Baltimore's loss of Maryland, of course, offered a dramatic lesson in how powerful this local claim to legitimacy could be.

The other crucial lesson of the town-planning boom, though, was the true extent of the power now held by well-connected English merchants. By the mid-1680s, London's leading tobacco merchants brought in huge revenues and had the ear of the king. They were only prepared to countenance urban development that did not inconvenience the close working relationships they had built with particular members of the planter elite and the imperial bureaucracy. Previously, civic efforts had sought to rein in the influence of leading merchants and private interests, but they were now too powerful to be eliminated. Instead, any further adjustments to the political economy of the tobacco plantation system would require triangulating between the clearly articulated interests of the planters, the empire, and the English merchant community. After the Glorious Revolution, it would be the task of the new English monarchs, William and Mary, and particularly their most proactive servant in the Chesapeake region, Francis Nicholson, to find a form of urban development that could satisfy the interests of planters, merchants, and an overtly commercial empire.

CHAPTER SIX

The Imperial City and the Solidifying of the Plantation System

The two decades around the turn of the eighteenth century witnessed a profound intensification of the slave-powered tobacco plantation system in the Chesapeake. Racial slavery was firmly entrenched by the importation of nearly twenty thousand enslaved laborers and by the passage of new slave codes. The wealthiest planters further reinforced their dominance by patenting huge estates, averaging nearly twelve thousand acres in Virginia.[1] A stable and powerful plantation elite finally solidified. The timing of this transformation was no mere coincidence; it was not a result of long-term gradual changes or a long-delayed response to the events of Bacon's Rebellion. It was, in fact, a result of changes in the political economy of empire that offered elite planters new opportunities to reinforce their power within the structures of empire. The best-connected elite planters learned to utilize metropolitan ties to gain advantages in shipping and access to labor and cheap land.[2] Working out the contours of this new integration within empire was not straightforward though. It involved wrestling with the complex political-economic legacies of the Glorious Revolution. It was another bout of bitterly contested urban development that framed the region's debate over these issues, pitting the new narrower elite against their gentry neighbors and also against grandiose visions of the new imperial governor, Francis Nicholson. In their struggle to wrest control of these new urban spaces, members of the elite developed a new definition of urban civic virtue that was built upon polite sociability rather than the older tradition of urban corporate community. Ultimately, it was this revised vision of urbanity that undergirded their new relationship with the interests and lobbies of the empire and laid the civic foundation for the critical consolidation of the intensive and integrated plantation system.

Across the Atlantic world in the aftermath of the Glorious Revolution, English officials altered their approach to commercial empire. A faction within the new Whig leadership rejected the Stuart monarchy's focus on direct control and focused on liberalizing trade and increasing access to credit in order to maximize labor productivity and stimulate growth.[3] The new focus on efficiency drew renewed imperial attention to the perennial problems in the Chesapeake. Tobacco prices remained in their long-term slump, and the onset of war with France only increased shipping costs and further depressed profits. One report described the Chesapeake as "the poorest, miserablest, and worst" part of the English Empire.[4] But instead of seeking to address these problems, as the Stuarts had, by controlling the tobacco trade through a narrow clique of merchants, the new Whig leadership actually sought ways to expand tobacco production even further to make productive use of the whole labor force and generate more customs revenue. They hoped to liberalize the market to ensure that this increased production sold at a viable price, and they also wanted to improve the region's infrastructure to facilitate faster, safer, and more efficient commerce. In its purest form, the Whig vision was an ever-expanding world of small-scale tobacco farmers trading within a liberal network of English commerce and loyal to imperial institutions that guaranteed their commercial freedom.[5]

Urban development was once again central to this new vision, but the plans differed sharply from the projects that had come before. The person who took the lead in enacting urban reform in the Chesapeake was Francis Nicholson, a former soldier and official under James II who had quickly changed his allegiances after 1688. Nicholson served as lieutenant governor of Virginia in the early 1690s, before being promoted to the governorship of Maryland in 1694 and then returning to Virginia in 1698 as the de facto executive of the colony under the Earl of Orkney, whose appointment as governor was purely honorary.[6] During these years, he developed an ambitious vision for reordering Chesapeake society, the lynchpin of which was the establishment of three self-consciously imperial cities: Annapolis, Williamstadt, and Williamsburg, which would facilitate small-scale tobacco production and bind ordinary planters to the empire through new religious and cultural institutions. During Nicholson's tenure, elite planters faced the necessity—and the opportunity—to defend their place within the liberalized commercial empire and justify their authority; a key part of that challenge was responding to his drive for urban development.

The responses of Chesapeake leaders, though, revealed new divisions among the planter class. Nicholson was initially able to win support for his agenda in both colonies, but the consensus behind his schemes quickly fell apart, playing a crucial role in his unpopularity in Maryland during the late 1690s and in his ejection from office in Virginia in 1705. Even as Nicholson's coalitions dissolved, though, his new cities forced planters to stake out discrete positions on the region's place within the commercial empire. One faction of planters turned decisively back to a local civic vision, mocking Nicholson's pretensions to being "the Founder of a new City" and advocating the establishment of small incorporated towns across the region.[7] By contrast, the experience of the Nicholson years led the most powerful and well-connected elites to fully reject this provincial vision. They embraced the informal imperial bonds manifest in Annapolis and Williamsburg. They rejected Nicholson's aim of using the cities as hubs for a small-planter society but nevertheless cultivated them as spaces where they could practice the polite sociability and consumption of imperial goods that bound them to the larger empire. Ultimately, this latter vision prevailed, laying the foundations for a new social, cultural, and political organization of planter society that rested upon a different kind of urban virtue, one that privileged manners, patriarchy, and commercialism over the selfless pursuit of the common good. The consolidation of the elite was less advanced in Maryland, but the overall pattern of debate between imperial officials and diverging planter interests was similar in both colonies. The struggle over urban development reveals that a self-conscious adjustment of vision and adaptation to imperial political economy lay behind what might otherwise appear to be no more than a series of pragmatic lobbying efforts and commercial connections, finally cementing the position of the narrow planter elite within the empire.

"NIC OF ANNAPOLIS"

Francis Nicholson arrived in Virginia in 1690 as lieutenant governor, but with Governor Effingham back in England with no intention of returning to the Chesapeake, he was effectively the colony's chief executive. He had been appointed by the new Williamite regime, but his instructions scarcely differed from those issued to Effingham in 1683. He was to control shipping and reinforce imperial order. Circumstances in Virginia, though, soon forced Nicholson to confront core questions of political economy that Effingham had worked hard to ignore during the later years of his tenure. During his postings around the Chesapeake over the next decade, he developed, in coordination with officials in England and the colonies, a novel plan for colonial capital cities that would serve as cornerstones of a remodeled society built around small landowners united through overarching imperial institutions.

The Glorious Revolution had incited a war with France, and the fiscal burdens of the Nine Years' War made William and Mary's administration eager to secure revenues, but Nicholson and other imperial officials now had a more nuanced sense of how to elicit those funds. While the Stuart empire had sought to maximize tax revenue, they saw the plantation economy in static terms, conforming to the long-standing belief that the market for tobacco was finite; they therefore believed that they needed to squeeze revenue from its production while pursuing other crops and manufactures in their effort to win the loyalty of struggling colonists. Nicholson, by contrast, promised to "doe all yt in mee lies to Encourage ye Planting" of unlimited quantities of tobacco in order to bring in the largest crop and generate the highest tax revenue.[8]

Nicholson certainly still saw troubles with tobacco, but they were not the same troubles his predecessors had seen. Soon after arriving in the Chesapeake, he noted that the root of the region's unrest and inefficiency was the monopolistic control of London merchants and elite planters. Because of wartime disruption, merchants were not sending enough ships to the region, and therefore many colonists lacked basic necessities and were converting from tobacco production to the production of hemp and flax for clothing, which competed with English woolens. Elite planters still shipped their tobacco because of their connections with London merchants, and merchants profited from higher tobacco prices in London because of restricted supply, but half the region's crop was rotting in the tidewater, impoverishing middling planters and imperial coffers.[9] Even more troublingly, when this tobacco did find a market, it was through smuggling, which surged in the 1690s with the influx of Scottish interlopers who ignored the Navigation Acts. Imperial observers concluded that elite planters were also to blame for smuggling; the surveyor general of customs for North America, Edward Randolph, complained that elite planters who served as customs inspectors actively colluded with smuggling.[10] Nor was it just the mercantile system that worked against ordinary planters and the empire alike. Nicholson and Randolph also condemned the large land grants Chesapeake elites were patenting; by acquiring vast acreages they could not yet farm, elites took high-quality land off the market, leaving it uncultivated and pushing poorer planters to the periphery, where they could not as easily contribute to the imperial economy. Nicholson lamented that he had "observed great quantityes of Lands" lying vacant due to elite planters' speculation, and he noted that they might be used to people the colony with prospective foot soldiers for the struggle against France.[11]

For Nicholson, the key to resolving these issues lay in reorganizing the economic and political structure of the region. He was particularly concerned about strengthening imperial bonds, exemplified by his unprecedented practice of touring the colony, talking to ordinary farmers, and inspecting their farms. Nicholson's itinerancy was about making imperial government visible and linking the interests of the empire with the concerns of individual planters. One of these long-standing concerns was Indian relations, and Nicholson was particularly unyielding in his native diplomacy, which likely made his tours reassuring for frontier planters. "I often visit ye Country," he later explained, "that I may keep up their drooping Spirits, and incourage them in planting, assuring them of his Ma[jes]tys Royal Intentions for their Good & Wellfair."[12] Beyond their public-relations benefits, Nicholson's tours also allowed him to provide astonishingly detailed reports on the colony's situation to London, rich with the kinds of data coveted by the new science of political arithmetic, which might serve as the basis for targeted imperial reforms. He tracked the extent of elite land speculation and the size of middling plantations. He logged the crops being grown, noting the increase in hemp and flax, alerting officials to the threat it posed to the English woolen trade, and encouraging small farmers to plant more tobacco. He also recorded the structure of Anglican parishes and the nature of religious observance and education, suggesting changes in parish and county boundaries to rationalize local institutions.[13] All of these observations were about economic and social improvements that could be carefully tailored to reinforce loyalty to the empire, reducing the influence of elite planters, liberalizing the market in land and tobacco, and building new physical and institutional infrastructure. Nicholson recognized that "the Great Men being concern'd," he dared not act too rashly, but he was determined to act to reshape the political economy of the region, promoting a world of small-scale agriculture and strong imperial bonds that seemed to require new imperial hubs and local trading infrastructure.[14]

Nicholson also had other concerns that went beyond Chesapeake political economy. The context of the Nine Years' War and the threat of French attacks meant Nicholson also had to bolster defenses. He thought Virginians were especially vulnerable, "not living together in Towns as other places doe" and having "no places to secure shipps." Mere defensive infrastructure was not sufficient, though, because the empire also had to protect the tobacco fleet once it left the Chesapeake. During the 1690s, imperial officials developed a convoy system in which ships gathered to sail the Atlantic together under naval escort. But this system also highlighted the problems with the Chesapeake region's spatial organization. If ships needed to be marshaled into a convoy, their rambling trade around the Chesapeake would waste time and naval resources, with the escort waiting for weeks while the disparate ships assembled. Developing hubs to accelerate turnaround was thus crucial.[15]

If all of these factors convinced Nicholson that urban development was an immediate priority, his instincts also aligned with the priorities of the planter gentry in the early 1690s. The regime change in England meant that planters unhappy with Stuart rule were hoping for a reversal of imperial economic policies. In summer 1690, just as Nicholson arrived, the Middlesex County bench was attempting to revive the development of the county's town site that had been hindered by local rivalries during the 1680s. The justices of Lower Norfolk County were also reporting by May 1691 that the "usual place for holding Courts" was now in Norfolk Town, which had been established under the 1680 act and was now described as "the Towne of the said County." Colonists had taken advantage of the brief hiatus in imperial control to reignite urban development. As soon as Nicholson gathered the General Assembly in the spring of 1691, the burgesses proposed a new town-building plan almost identical to those consistently stymied by Effingham.[16]

Although his instructions had not included any orders about town development, Nicholson saw the burgesses' proposal as an opportunity to embark on broader reforms. He enthusiastically backed the plan but added some innovations. First, pleading wartime pressures, he argued that some sites did not allow for shipping to "be Secured at by ffortifications." He suggested these places be merely "towns" for local exchange, whereas thirteen more defensible sites would serve as "ports" where Atlantic trade could be administered by imperial officials. This represented a compromise between local economic development and broader imperial goals that had evaded Effingham.[17] Second, the governor aimed to strengthen the authority of customs collectors in the ports. Considering the difficulties Effingham had encountered with this objective, he seemed doomed to founder. However, Nicholson volunteered something Effingham had not been at liberty to offer—plans to plow the revenue back into the colony to fund defense, the Anglican Church, and a new college. Establishing educational, military, and ecclesiastical infrastructure became a hallmark of Nicholson's tenure in the Chesapeake, and from this early stage, he tied

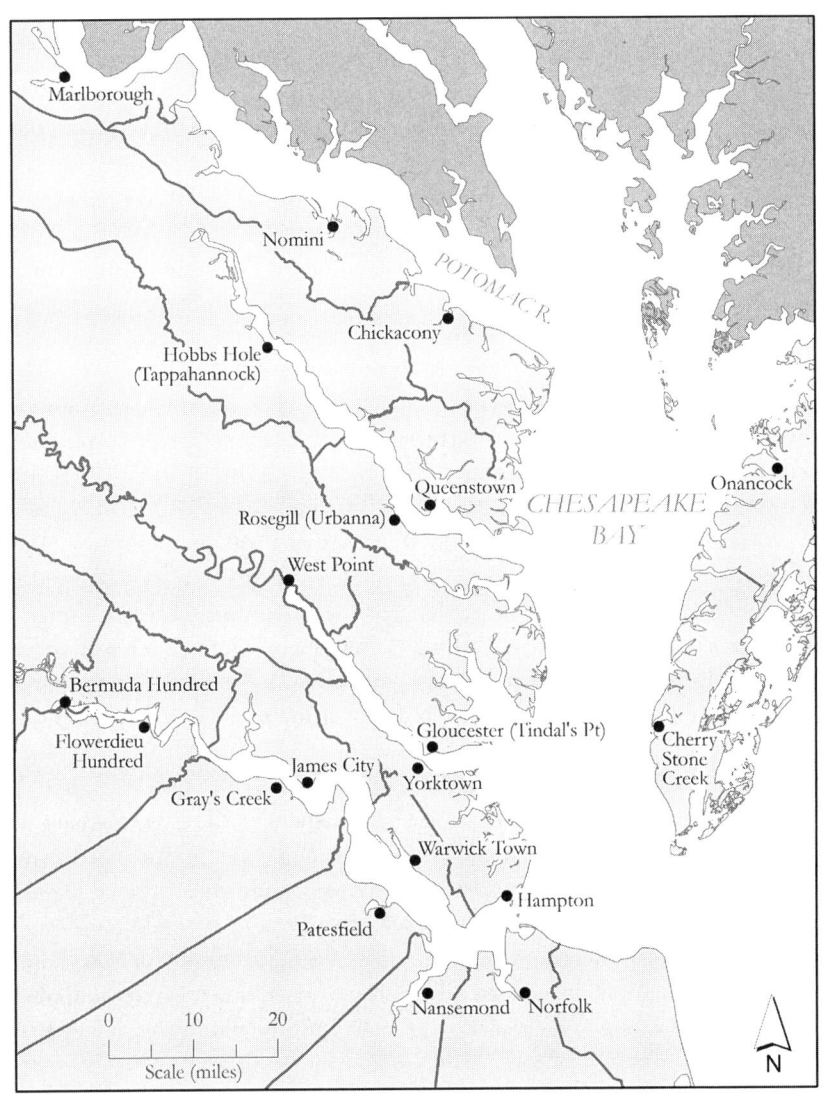

6.1 Map of Virginia town locations, 1691
This map shows the locations of all the port towns established by the Virginia General Assembly in 1691.

this effort to urban development and imperial oversight of trade. Nicholson envisioned port towns as sites for panimperial institutions designed to expand the definition of the public good by equating it with the broader success of the English Protestant empire, while also supporting the imperial state's financial needs.[18]

Nicholson was extremely pleased with the finished act, but he recognized that its passage through the General Assembly was only half the battle. He confidently noted to officials in London that "the Act for Ports is agreeable to his Maties Instructions," but he begged that "if any of ye Merchants oppose itt, I humbly move . . . yt wee may bee heard about itt" before the king took any decision to disallow the act. The governor recognized that the biggest opposition to his plan had come from the colony's royal council, which consisted of the most elite planters, and he feared that their allies among the London merchant community would seek to get the act overturned. The following year, he implored the House of Burgesses to pay a lobbyist to advocate for the town act as a way of combining "the advancement of Religion & Learning, their Mats Interest, the Countreys great advantage & increase of Trade." He also sought to reinforce support for the act within the colony, leading by example when he purchased three lots at Yorktown and pushed the councillors to do likewise.[19] As he predicted, though, Nicholson encountered opposition to the town plan in London, marshaled by an increasingly powerful lobby of tobacco merchants and their allies among the upper echelons of the planter elite. Because of this well-organized opposition, the Crown suspended the new town act in 1693. The lesson Nicholson took from this defeat, though, was not to shy away from town building but instead to focus on a limited number of sites where he could personally oversee development.[20]

Early in 1694, when he was promoted to the governorship of Maryland, Nicholson embarked on even more ambitious plans. He now presided over a colony that was just as wracked by economic problems and subject to even looser imperial oversight. Poverty in Maryland, particularly in marginal tobacco lands on the Eastern Shore, was leading planters to convert to local flax and linen production and smuggling, and in some cases even pushing migration out of the region to other parts of English America. Maryland's first royal governor, Lionel Copley, had overlooked these problems and cultivated alliances with the Protestant gentry who had overthrown Lord Baltimore. Sir Thomas Lawrence, an English gentleman dispatched to Maryland as the new colonial secretary, and Edward Randolph, the surveyor general of customs in America, had both reported on Copley's corruption and mismanagement, and Nicholson concurred, suggesting

Maryland was "not very well settled either in ye Church, Civil or Military Government."[21] Within days of arriving, Nicholson began a comprehensive effort to ascertain the "State of the constitution of the Government." He revived his practice of touring the colony and also demanded that sheriffs gather details about each county's militia, local government, parish structures, and population—the start of a regular survey, imposing imperial oversight over local community structures that the planter gentry had cultivated as their sphere. Nicholson ordered that county courts meet on a regular schedule, that militias form organized units, and that Anglican parishes be demarcated.[22]

These actions laid the groundwork for the reorganization of Maryland around two port cities. In autumn 1694, Nicholson presented the Maryland Assembly with a letter from Queen Mary "concerning Ports" and suggested that they consider a plan for town development.[23] There was continued support for urban development among Maryland planters, and so the assembly quickly produced a predictable reworking of their 1680s town-building legislation. However, following his experience in Virginia, Nicholson knew better than to support this kind of project. He developed an alternative plan to establish two port towns that would centralize customs enforcement, trade, justice, and governance—one at Arundelton on the Severn River, in Anne Arundel County, to serve the Western Shore and act as the provincial capital, and another at Oxford, in Talbot County, to serve the Eastern Shore. Nicholson may have always intended to steer the delegates toward this vision, or he may have developed the plan as a compromise, but either way it demonstrated a break with previous town legislation. Despite opposition from St. Mary's City, the ploy worked. The two new urban spaces, renamed Annapolis and Williamstadt respectively, were approved by the assembly because they represented a step toward their larger goal and also because they allowed the relocation of the provincial capital to a site more convenient for most colonists, but the overall plan was unmistakably Nicholson's solution for the region's political-economic problems.[24]

Nicholson's first objective for Annapolis and Williamstadt was to centralize administration. He relocated customs officials and naval officers to the cities and ordered all ships trading in the northern half of Maryland to report to them. Since his days in Virginia, Nicholson had complained about the difficulty of gathering officials for meetings, and he hoped the new cities would alleviate these problems. Proximity to Annapolis became a test of suitability for his nominations to provincial offices, and all county officials in Anne Arundel and Talbot were instructed to reside in the towns. To some extent, this policy worked. A group of recent immigrants who were able young lawyers and administrators established themselves in Annapolis, and by 1700, they began buying urban real estate. Among the new arrivals was recent immigrant William Bladen, who won Nicholson's patronage and quickly ascended to the offices of customs collector, clerk to the council, and attorney general.[25]

Nicholson's second and more ambitious objective was for his cities to attract poor and middling planters in order to counteract the deeper regional economic problems observed on his tours. He pushed a plan to grant new town residents legal immunity from debt cases in Maryland's county courts, making the prospect of relocation appealing to those in financial trouble. In addition, he advocated incentives for establishing new crafts and carved out space for a marketplace at the heart of Annapolis. He also allocated common land for the capital. This common land was not intended to be a symbol of corporate shared interest, as it had been for Sir Edwin Sandys's Virginia Company boroughs a century before; instead, it would allow city residents to graze livestock and maintain a measure of self-sufficiency while practicing their trades.[26] Nicholson was particularly concerned about the rapid growth of Philadelphia, which he believed was fueled by illegal trade, and he hoped his new towns would provide the same commercial opportunities for their surrounding hinterlands, only under the watchful eye of the empire rather than the lax oversight of William Penn. Annapolis was, in many respects, intended as the imperial anti-Philadelphia.[27]

These two objectives—administrative centralization and the cultivation of imperial bonds with middling colonists—were manifested in space. The most distinctive feature of Nicholson's new cities was their elaborate layouts that the governor personally oversaw. The plan for Annapolis took advantage of two hills at the site, which Nicholson capped with the new statehouse and parish church, symbols of the colony's temporal and spiritual government. Streets fanned out from these buildings to ensure all parts of the new city had direct sightlines to the organs of the state. Similarly, in his plan for Williamstadt, Nicholson located the public buildings on a prominent headland that dominated the harbor entrance. Unlike Baltimore's St. Mary's City plan, which emphasized the exclusive relationship between the city's corporate community and proprietary institutions built around it, the radial perspective in Annapolis placed imperial institutions at the core of the design, emphasizing the centrality of the imperial state but also its accessibility for all colonists. Nicholson's support for the establishment of King William's School in Annapolis, the colony's first educational institution, also linked planters with the civil structures

6.2 James Stoddert, *A ground platt of the citty and port of Anapolis* (1718)
This contemporary ground plat of the city of Annapolis clearly
depicts the elaborate radial layout of the city designed by Governor
Francis Nicholson. (Courtesy of the Maryland State Archives.)

of religion and culture that underpinned the new Protestant empire.[28] The use Nicholson made of this space further emphasized imperial bonds. In autumn 1695, when the General Assembly gathered in Annapolis, Nicholson opened the session by inviting residents and visitors to "walk down [to the quayside] towards the Dusk of the Evening for to Drink his Ma[jes]ts health at which time he would cause a bone fire to be made for the Joyfull news of his ma^{ts} Success ag[ains]t the ffrench." It is unclear how much of Annapolis's street layout was visible by this point (just a year after the capital was moved), but amid the staked-out streets, Nicholson established the empire's virtual presence in Annapolis by treating colonists to a celebration of its successes.[29]

The lynchpin of this imperial planning was Nicholson himself. He carefully supervised the building work in both Annapolis and Williamstadt, dismissing the first builder for the statehouse because of his slow progress. In 1696, when a survey of the town was completed, Nicholson had the delegates witness as he set his personal seal to the plats. The Annapolis plan also featured a large town lot that was reserved for a governor's residence right in the jaws of the harbor, allowing Nicholson to see, and be seen by, all shipping. Unsatisfied by this informal control and influence, he also pushed through "An Act for Keeping Good Rules and Orders in the Port of Annapolis" in 1696 that named himself and Secretary Thomas Lawrence as two of the seven commissioners charged with governing the town.[30]

In summarizing the governor's effort, Lawrence lauded him as "the fairest . . . of all his Majestys Governors" for having built at Annapolis "homes churches and free schools . . . and bringing at ye same time a poor Country out of debt." Nicholson was practicing a novel kind of imperial urbanity, combining incentives for economic development with a new imperial nexus of state, church, and educational institutions and an aspiring network of imperially oriented officials. None of Nicholson's pursuits individually challenged the hegemonic position of the wealthiest planters, but as a whole, they did seek to reorient the center of not only commercial but also political and social order. After Nicholson left Maryland in 1698, his successors, particularly Governor John Seymour, who took office in 1704, continued to pursue this vision.[31]

The effect of Nicholson's ideas also reached beyond Maryland; they resonated with elements of the imperial leadership in London who were seeking to remodel the empire. The pressures of wartime finance inspired debate in the metropolis about how to control spiraling debt and inflation, and this eventually led to the formation of a new advisory committee of experts on trade, the Board of Trade. The Board came into existence in May 1696, with responsibility for policing Atlantic commerce and also formulating plans "for ye better Employing & setting on work the poore of this kingdom." A faction on the new board, led by John Locke, favored active measures to stimulate colonial development and liberalize access to land and credit in the colonies.[32] These individuals were extremely interested in Nicholson's reforms in the Chesapeake. Soon after the Board was established, it began receiving reports of customs evasion and corrupt elites amassing land grants in Virginia, which contrasted starkly with Nicholson's reports from Maryland, leading them to press Virginia's new governor, Sir Edmund Andros, over his failure to reinvigorate town development there in the same way that Nicholson was doing in Maryland.[33] In fact, such was their enthusiasm that they ordered Secretary Lawrence in Maryland to send them copies of all orders related to Annapolis and Williamstadt, and they also sought out information from Virginians visiting the metropolis. During summer 1697, they questioned three men: Virginia gentlemen Edward Chilton and Henry Hartwell and Virginia's Anglican commissary and president of the new College of William and Mary, the Reverend James Blair. The Board quizzed them about Virginia's land policies and the failure of urban development. In their lengthy report, the Virginians underscored the Board's favorable impression of Nicholson's approach in Maryland by emphasizing the need for economic reform and urban development.[34]

The Board of Trade's queries were the first sign that Locke and the more radical members of the Board were developing a larger reforming project for Virginia in which urban development was crucial. Over the winter of 1697/8, Locke lobbied for Nicholson to replace Andros in Virginia and created radical proposals to empower the new governor's reforming agenda. He drew on the detailed information furnished by Blair, Hartwell, and Chilton, but where they had lamented "the Obstinacy of the People" in resisting towns and economic improvement, Locke's analysis aligned with Nicholson and Lawrence in blaming the elite's monopolization of land as the root cause of Virginia's failure to foster "the great Company of Citizens and Tradesmen that are in other Countrys." He agreed with Nicholson that the key was to craft a new expansive economy that generated increasing quantities of tobacco and other commodities useful for the empire, but did so through widespread landownership and the creation of a class of productive small farmers.[35] To help lay the basis for this new Chesapeake society, Locke hoped to end the headright system of land grants for those importing slaves, which had been abused by leading planters to vastly expand their estates. This change, as Holly Brewer has noted, was also intended to disincentivize the expansion of slavery. Locke hoped to promote, in its place, an influx of European skilled laborers. He suggested establishing new towns with "weekly markets and some few fairs in a year" and granting free passage for craftsmen traveling to Virginia, "upon Condition that they follow their Trades in some of these townes." He also proposed (reflecting Nicholson's actions in Maryland) that "the Governour, and other principal officers of the Government . . . reside at the chief of these Towns." Locke's plans were more radical than what Nicholson had attempted, especially in their efforts to scale back slave imports, but they shared a faith in the combination of land and urban reforms to reduce the influence of slaveholding elites and make the region's commercial development subservient to England's imperial project.[36]

Nicholson remained informed about Locke's plans through his London correspondents, so he was ready for immediate action when his transfer to Virginia was confirmed late in 1698. Although conflict between Locke and his fellow Board member William Blathwayt meant that Locke's ambitious plans for towns were actually left out of Nicholson's finalized instructions, events in Virginia conspired to clear the way for radical action by the new lieutenant governor anyway. Just a few months before Nicholson's transfer, the statehouse at Jamestown burned to the ground. The conflagration gave Nicholson the perfect opportunity to relocate another capital city as a starting point for broader reform.[37] He threw himself into this endeavor. He ignored calls to revive the 1691 act, preferring instead to concentrate his efforts on moving the capital and creating an urban culture there that might match his vision for Annapolis and Williamstadt and fit with the ambitions of Locke at the Board of Trade. This, Nicholson explained, was a project that would "tend to Gods Glory, his Majesties Service, and the welfare and Prosperity of yor Country in Generall."[38] By selecting Middle Plantation for the new capital, Nicholson immediately won crucial support. The site, lying inland along the spine of the James-York peninsula, was already home to the College of William and Mary, and thus it was the favored choice of college president James Blair. More broadly, the area was already known for its well-drained land and comparatively moderate climate; it had an unusual preponderance of high-status buildings in the late seventeenth century, suggesting that it constituted an elite neighborhood. By selecting this space, then, Nicholson was ensuring a base of support for the capital relocation among a portion of the planter elite. In spring 1699, the General Assembly quickly approved his plans for the new capital city, christened Williamsburg.[39]

Nicholson's plans for Williamsburg brought together imperial urban development and broader political-economic reform. He eagerly devised another elaborate street plan that emphasized the institutions of church, state, and education. This time the main symbol was a central avenue (named Duke of Gloucester Street, in honor of the heir to the throne) running from the recently erected college building past the parish church to the site of the planned statehouse. In the middle of this central boulevard, Nicholson designed a diamond-shaped alignment of streets "in the form of a cypher, made of W. and M.," that would emphasize the centrality of the monarchs and the empire.[40] While working on these stylistic details, Nicholson also pursued the Board of Trade's other suggested reforms. He pushed through restrictions to limit plural office holding at the provincial level and to directly control the appointment of county-level officials. He also instituted reforms to the headright system in line with Locke's proposals, ending grants for slave imports. Although he continued to issue land grants more liberally than his strict instructions required, most of these were small grants to middling planters. Furthermore, as he attempted to break down the hierarchical structure of landownership, he also proposed to the burgesses "that Some Speedy care be taken to make all the Countyes in this Colony and Especially those between James River and York River [where Williamsburg was located] . . . more Compact then now they are by Devideing and bounding them in Some other manner." In other words, Nicholson envisioned Williamsburg as a grand imperial city at the center of a rationalized administrative hierarchy overseeing compact communities of small farmers.[41]

Making this reorganization work also meant appealing to middling planters, who were essential to Locke's plans for Virginia. To make the new capital a center for provincial trade that could create new economic opportunities, Nicholson used his own gubernatorial funds to erect wharves on two creeks near Williamsburg, linking the town to both the James and the York Rivers. These creeks were too small for oceangoing vessels but suitable for small intra- and intercolonial trading vessels. They were intended to provide economic opportunities for middling men and women, as a first step to the kind of internal commercial development Locke had planned. To ensure that this purpose was not diverted, Nicholson insisted that wharves remain in common hands to prevent them from being monopolized by wealthy Atlantic merchants.[42]

Nicholson also sought to appeal to middling men and women who might not move to Williamsburg but might still visit the new capital and encounter the empire through its streets. A timely opportunity to target

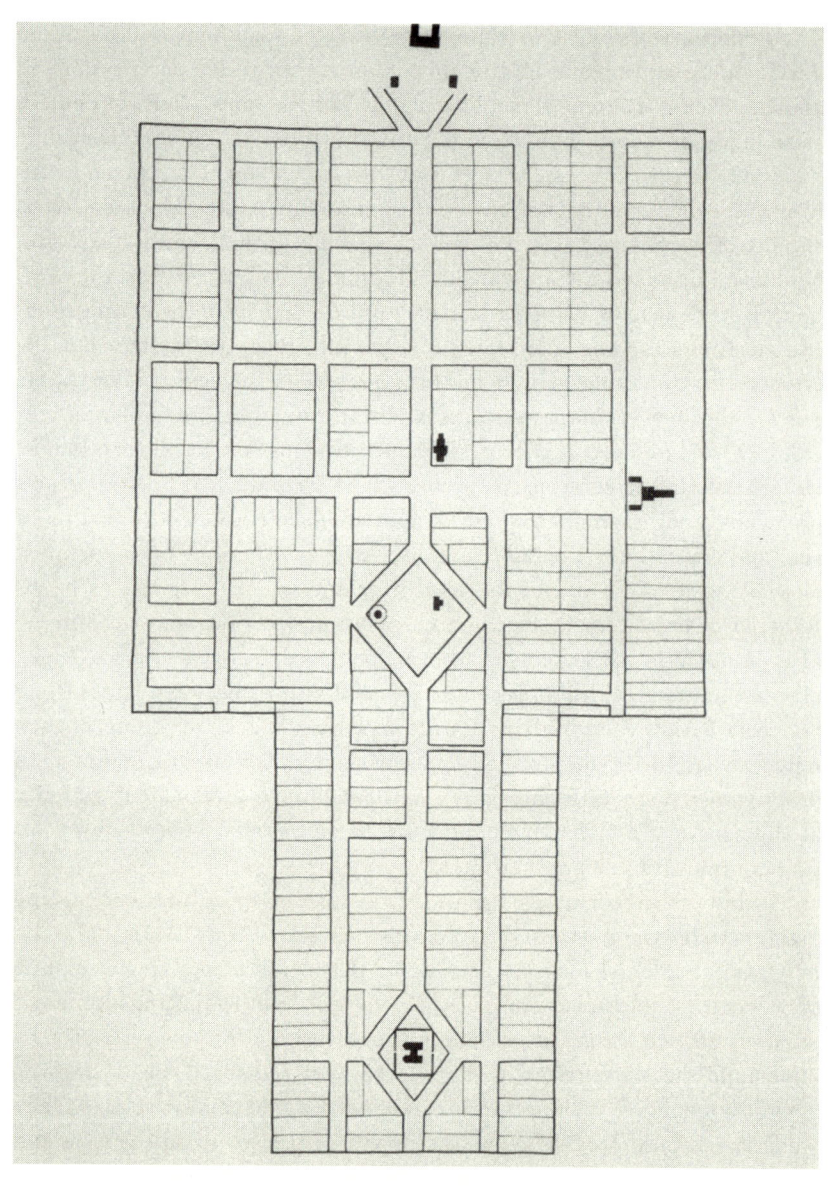

6.3 Conjectural plan of Williamsburg, 1699, by John W. Reps
The ambitious plan for Williamsburg was anchored by key public buildings and was centered on the diagonal streets that formed a cypher of the letters *W* and *M* around the market square. (Courtesy of the Colonial Williamsburg Foundation.)

these planters arose with the ascension of Queen Anne in 1702. Work on the statehouse was not complete, but the city's streets were laid out, and Nicholson was eager to reinforce the status of his new metropolis. He hosted a coronation celebration in Williamsburg involving the militia of "York & James City, Troop of New Kent County, horse & dragoons of Charles City . . . and of Warwick & Elizth City." This amounted to almost the entire free white male population of the James-York peninsula. These men were treated to a bacchanalia that marked Williamsburg as a place where the fruits of empire could be enjoyed by all.[43] They were plied with punch, marched back and forth behind the lavishly attired governor, serenaded by bugles, oboes, and violins, and addressed with sermons and poems lauding the empire. After dark, they were treated to a fireworks display. Nicholson also distributed copies of the addresses honoring the new queen that had been issued by English cities, underscoring the point that Williamsburg, as the provincial urban hub, should emulate those cities. He subsequently made arrangements for Williamsburg's celebration to be reported in the *London Gazette*. The ceremony encapsulated the relationship Nicholson hoped to build with ordinary Virginians through Williamsburg.[44]

To some extent Nicholson's plan succeeded. Williamsburg became a more vital urban center than Jamestown ever was. More importantly for Nicholson's broader objectives, his policies won him support among middling planters. The burgesses expressed public thanks for the festivities honoring Queen Anne. Three years later, when the planter elite succeeded in getting Nicholson ousted from office, the residents of New Kent County drafted a petition demanding "that no Thanks but Rather a Check be given" to reprimand those who had lobbied against him. For middling planters, many of whom had probably visited Williamsburg and enjoyed the governor's hospitality, Nicholson's attempts to remodel the colony's place within the empire, anchored in the new capital city, were appealing.[45]

Nicholson saw his efforts at Williamsburg, Annapolis, and Williamstadt as part of a larger project to redefine the English Empire in a new era. Scholars have largely viewed his cities as elite oases of refinement for a maturing planter class, but their principal planner never imagined them in this way.[46] It was imperative, Nicholson wrote in 1699, that "Commanders in Chief, may each live where ye seat of Government is," but it was equally vital that he "go into several parts of ye Country" so that he could meet ordinary colonists and be "esteemed by ye people . . . to be a lover of them and their country."[47] Nicholson's objective was to build a world of productive tobacco planters all bound to the empire through the imperial institutions he fostered. Institutions and practices—including the church, education, and pageantry, all centered in the capital—were intended to tie the local, provincial, and imperial together.

Unsurprisingly, Nicholson's bold agenda attracted considerable resistance. His urban plans were central to the furious transatlantic lobbying that eventually led to his removal from office in Virginia in 1705. Yet by emphasizing imperial institutions and refined urban spaces, Nicholson had permanently recast the Chesapeake debate over urban development and planter political economy. His opponents were now divided into two camps over the issue of urban development and its ramifications for the future relationship of the plantation system to the empire: those still fighting the battles of the 1680s, who sought a return to local urban improvement, and those who sought to co-opt Nicholson's cities and make them hubs for a civic culture of politeness and a nexus of transatlantic political and commercial bonds. The struggle over how to respond to Nicholson's vision came to define the ideology of the planter elite in the eighteenth century.

"A TOWNSHIP OR BURGH"

Opposition to Nicholson's plans was fiercest among those planters who still harbored aspirations for local, decentralized authority over commerce and society. These individuals were leading investors in the small towns that had been developed over the previous decade and had led the resistance to Baltimore and Effingham during the 1680s, but they had generally done so because they were not as well connected to elite London merchant networks or as fully invested in the intensification of tobacco production through the acquisition of enslaved laborers. These differences were not merely a product of regional divergences in the Chesapeake economy; some of those most eager to return to local urban development lived in regions, such as the Eastern Shore, where tobacco production was withering away, but others were in the heart of Virginia's sweet-scented tobacco region, where the escalation of the large-scale slave plantation system was advanced. Nor can we teleologically view these individuals as simply falling behind in an inevitable race toward elite consolidation; they were all successful planters and merchants proactively seeking fortunes within the commercial empire, but they envisioned the political-economic future of the region differently. They remained committed to a local civic vision of the political and commercial relationships that held the empire together, and this commitment became more and more vehement as it diverged from their increasingly well-connected neighbors who began to think in broader imperial terms.

The most predictable resistance to Nicholson in Maryland came from the colony's only existing corporation, St. Mary's City. As soon as the governor announced his plans for Annapolis in October 1694, a group of seventy men representing "the Mayor Recorder Aldermen Common Council men and ffreemen of the City of St. Maries" petitioned him to reconsider. Harkening back to the city's patronage relationship with the proprietor, they made their "Humble Address" to Nicholson, rather than to the representatives, who ultimately voted on the relocation. They pleaded for his "grace and ffavour in granting and Continuing to them their antient ffranchises rights & priviledges," indicating that they believed their greatest leverage lay in their long-standing exchange of privileges for civic responsibilities. As citizens of the corporation, they explained, they had invested in "meane indifferent lands" and erected public buildings, a governor's residence, and a civic community. Now they even offered to foot the bill for dedicated coach services linking their city with other regions of the colony. This exchange, in which corporate citizens took on public responsibilities in return for specific privileges, was rooted in the logic of early modern civic corporations. None of this rhetoric carried any weight with Nicholson, who saw the public good within a panimperial framework. He passed the petition along to the General Assembly, undermining the special relationship the corporate citizens claimed, and it elicited a sarcastic response from the delegates.[48]

Resistance to Nicholson, however, did not end there. In Talbot County, local justices blocked plans to relocate public offices to Williamstadt, and the parish vestry sued the sheriff for attempting—as required by the legislation—to use tithes to pay for urban development.[49] Meanwhile, in St. Mary's County, John Coode, who led the revolution that overthrew Baltimore's government, and fellow county residents Philip Clarke, Robert Mason, and Gerard Slye, marshaled resistance. In 1697, they penned formal grievances, emphasizing that Nicholson "hath Erected a Town in a very ill remote place of the Province," putting "the Countrey to an unreasonable charge thereby to no purpose." Resentment became even more pronounced during Nicholson's final year in Maryland. Slye harangued the governor to his face, telling him that colonists resented the new capital and weaving in Maryland's rich tradition of antipopery by accusing him of being a Jacobite who planned to build a Catholic chapel in Annapolis. He summed up the disgruntled colonists' perceptions by describing the governor as "Nic of Annapolis," a nickname that captured their disdain for the governor's imperial urban pretensions.[50]

Even after Nicholson's departure from Maryland, Annapolis continued to attract resentment. The new capital created opportunities but also pitfalls for the men and women of Anne Arundel County, who now found themselves living in its hinterland. One such individual, Richard Clarke, gambled on being able to take advantage of Annapolis's development and launched a career as an attorney and land speculator. In many respects, this was precisely the kind of transformation Nicholson envisioned for middling white colonists, but it involved making connections in the imperial bureaucracy and relying upon new lines of credit, which were becoming central to the Atlantic economy. For some, such as Clarke, taking these risks did not pay off, and they quickly found that commercial imperial networks were less forgiving than local colonial communities. When Clarke's investments faltered, he was accused of forging bills of exchange (effectively drawing on credit he did not have in London) to meet merchant demands; he was then widely rumored to have set fire to the Annapolis statehouse in 1704 in an effort to destroy the records of his debts and criminal charges. From that point, Clarke became an outlaw. Rumors of his plans to incite a servant uprising and burn Annapolis to the ground were carefully cultivated by Maryland's new governor, John Seymour, who shared Nicholson's interest in imperial urban development. Seymour used the specter of rebellion to scare planters into supporting his plans. Nonetheless, Clarke's neighbors saw him as a man standing up to the imperial urban vision in defense of older norms of local exchange, credit, and trust. The whole crisis demonstrated the persistent gulf between the urban plans of imperial officials and the long-standing attitudes of ordinary planters.[51]

A similar gulf existed in Virginia, especially among those who had supported Nicholson's 1691 act and now felt betrayed by his focus on Williamsburg. Robert Beverley Jr., whose father had spearheaded town development in the 1680s, led this opposition. He possessed a far more established fortune than Richard Clarke and owned a substantial estate on the prosperous middle peninsula of Virginia, but he and his local allies still chafed at the influence of their wealthier and better-connected neighbors, and they sought greater influence in the tobacco trade. To that end, Beverley continued the family interest in developing a town in Middlesex County during the early 1690s, and his efforts there may have sparked the plans for the 1691 town act. When Nicholson returned to Virginia in 1698 and refused to revive the plan for local town development, Beverley became bitter. His frustration was exacerbated by the plan to relocate the capital because he also owned property at Jamestown that would inevitably lose value. The governor, he insisted, was now driven by "the fond Imagination, of being the Founder of a new City." To Beverley, Williamsburg was an ego-boosting folly that would not address the colony's fundamental problems.[52]

Correcting this error was one of the central objectives of Beverley's famous *History and Present State of Virginia* (1705). Towns "well executed," he argued, "would have answer'd all [Virginia's] Desires." However, the 1680 act had been "brought to nothing by the Opposition of the Merchants of London," and the 1691 plan had been undermined by Nicholson, who "tack'd about" at the behest of those same merchants. Beverley's attitudes bristled with provincial civic identity. He remained committed to local patronage of small towns as a way to remedy Virginia's dependence upon volatile tobacco markets. He also emphasized that Nicholson's Williamsburg plan used demagoguery that appealed to the worst instincts of poorer planters' "slothful Indolence," to drive a wedge between them and provincial leaders. Far from celebrating Virginia's "pastoral" abundance and agrarian simplicity, Beverley shared Nicholson's drive to make poor planters productive in new industries, but he sought to do so under the paternalistic care of county leaders.[53]

Another commentator who insisted on the need for locally managed urban development, in more radical terms than Beverley, was Francis Makemie, a Scottish Presbyterian clergyman from Virginia's Eastern Shore. Makemie owned property in Onancock, the town established in Accomack County in the 1680s, and he had links to the growing Caribbean trade in that region and to the clandestine Scottish trade that Nicholson and Randolph sought to eliminate. He outlined an alternative vision of the virtues of urban development in a lengthy treatise, *A Plain and Friendly Perswasive to the Inhabitants of Virginia and Maryland For Promoting Towns and Cohabitation*, which was intended to spur colonial legislators into action.[54] Makemie rejected Nicholson's plans because they imposed upon the poor "beyond their Strength," but argued that ordinary planters could build homes in small towns using the lumber that was abundant on every estate and the bricks that could "be made at every man's Door." He shared Beverley's faith in the capacity of local regulation in these smaller towns, but instead of relying on the county gentry, he returned to older civic traditions, emphasizing the governance of self-regulating urban communities. "Many who now carry on Fraud against Strangers, by trading in a corner, at private Plantations," he explained, "would soon be ashamed of such things at a publick Market" in an independent town. Makemie was not naive about the growing scale of the Atlantic economy or the challenges it posed for the region, but he believed that local civic communities were best placed to exploit commercial opportunities. He emphasized the new "ready Market" for selling provisions to the Caribbean (in which he was personally invested), but argued that merchants from other parts of English America were draining "from us the marrow of our Estates" because they exported wheat and produce and returned processed goods. The reason, he explained, was that without towns men "seldom meet to consult, form and contrive Designs" and therefore "entertain frequent jealousies of each other" rather than cooperating in local mercantile operations or investing in new trades. Makemie saw the cultivation of civil society in towns as crucial to the creation of new commercial opportunities, which would ultimately benefit the whole society by raising the value of land unsuitable for tobacco.[55]

As a Presbyterian clergyman, Makemie also criticized Nicholson's plan for an Anglican ecclesiastical hierarchy centered in Williamsburg. He argued that small towns would provide ideal locations for churches that would promote access to religious teaching and worship that reflected the faith of local communities, and not imperially sanctioned religious institutions; poor and middling planters, he argued, would have the "Privileges and Opportunities" of gathering in their own congregations. He insisted that it was the "example of a severe and Virtuous conversation" in towns, and not the structures of the imperial church, that would reform the community's morals. Although Makemie did not explicitly propose new corporate structures for the towns, his pamphlet nevertheless constituted the most overt return to the ideas of autonomous civic corporate communities from the early seventeenth century.[56]

While Nicholson was still in office, his critics had little chance to act on this alternative agenda, but when the governor was forced out in 1705, they advocated a return to local town development. Beverley and Makemie were both in London during the height of the campaign to oust Nicholson from office, and so it was not surprising that their urban vision was reflected in the instructions issued to the new governors dispatched to Virginia and Maryland, Lieutenant Governor Edward Nott and Governor John Seymour, respectively. Both Nott and Seymour were instructed to encourage urban development beyond the colonial capitals. Beverley and Makemie, intended to capitalize on the new opportunity that these instructions presented. They prepared carefully for the new governors' inaugural legislative sessions. Makemie had copies of his *Plain and Friendly Perswasive* printed and ready for circulation in the Chesapeake upon his return, and Beverley had his allies in Middlesex County, Virginia, prepare the ground for a new urban development plan.[57]

The result of their efforts was legislation that went far beyond the expectations of the Crown or the comfort of many of the region's best-connected elite planters. When the Virginia General Assembly met in 1705, Beverley and Makemie were both in attendance—the former as a burgess and the latter as a lobbyist distributing copies of his *Perswasive*.[58] Beverley, his brother Harry, and their Middlesex ally Christopher Robinson sat on the committee that drafted new town legislation. The plan they developed, which was eventually enacted by the General Assembly in 1706 following a winter recess, was the most elaborate urban project ever contemplated in the region. Like previous town plans, it restricted trade to a set number of locations, in this case sixteen. But restricting tobacco production was not a major part of this act, as it had been in the 1680s. Instead, it focused on the development of urban markets and fairs. No unauthorized trade was to be permitted within a five-mile radius of each town in order to encourage the development of urban commercial property and ensure that exchange fell under the scrutiny of the town's open market. The act also sought to shape the urban population by rewarding freehold residents with substantial tax breaks in order to encourage free white craftsmen to relocate, while specifically preventing slave owners from claiming the same tax breaks for their enslaved laborers in the towns; this confirmed the implicit assumption over the previous two decades that new towns were to function as spaces of economic opportunity for middling whites, compensating for opportunities lost because of the switch to enslaved African labor on large estates, and also reinforcing the racial distinction between African agricultural laborers and European urban craftsmen.[59]

Most radical of all, the legislation ordered that "a township or burgh be established at each of the places." When a town reached thirty families, it would be governed by a popularly elected corporate body of eight "benchers of the guild hall," and once it reached sixty families, it would gain a common council and a burgess in the General Assembly. The towns were expected to develop "a merchant guild and community with all customs and libertys belonging to a free burgh" and were empowered to maintain a militia, a treasury, a court, and a corpus of bylaws. This independent corporate structure clearly diverged from the centralized imperial institutions that Nicholson had sought to impose. It also forced county elites to surrender more control than they had been prepared to do in the 1680s. It therefore represented a gamble by men such as the Beverley brothers, who

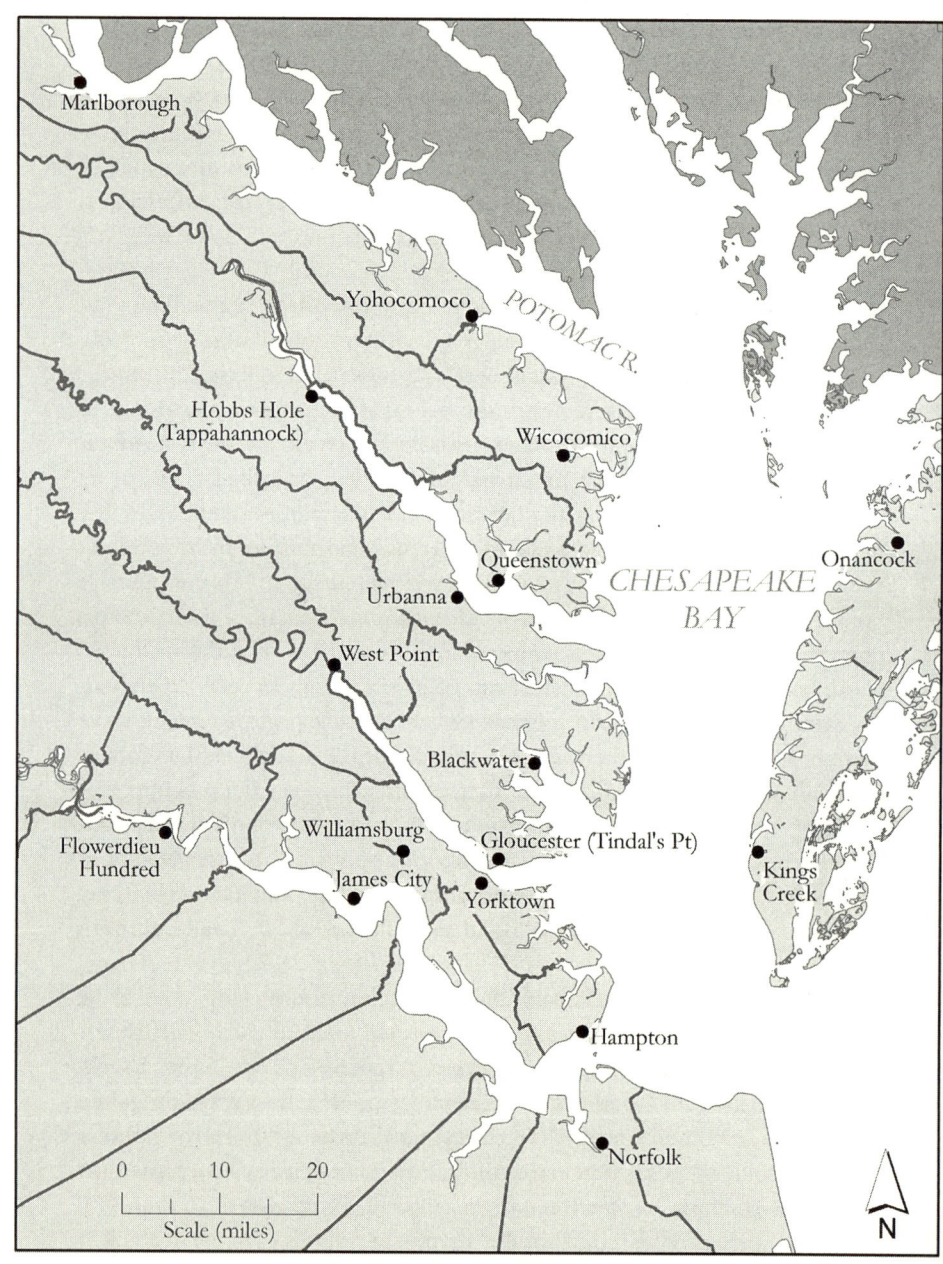

6.4 Map of Virginia town locations, 1706
This map shows the locations of all the towns established by the Virginia General Assembly in 1706.

hoped to assert their influence over new urban communities and benefit from the increased power in their struggle against better-connected neighbors. It also offered new opportunities for people such as Makemie, who operated outside the sphere of the large London merchant community. While undermining Nicholson's vision, then, the plan was also a tactical move in the ongoing struggle within the planter community over its place within the political economy of empire.[60]

Maryland's legislature also responded to the imperial urban vision. Governor John Seymour, who had arrived in Maryland in 1704, had initially supported Nicholson's plans to centralize administration and commerce through Annapolis, but when he presented the Board of Trade's new orders on town building to the assembly in 1706 (with Makemie in attendance again), he astutely framed the plan in the planters' interests; he suggested new towns would allow them to wrest control of their trade from English merchants who had made "your Land & Industrye a sure Monoplie to themselves, whereby You can never let the middle and lower Sorte of People reap any things from a very hard labour."[61] Given this open invitation, the delegates spent less than a week writing a bill that harkened back to the county-based urban development proposals of the 1680s. Although it established six customs districts, reflecting the Crown's objectives, beneath this structure it established nearly forty towns, diluting the effectiveness of customs oversight and ensuring local control. Furthermore, while imports of goods and enslaved people were restricted to towns, tobacco exports were allowed to continue from any wharf, neutering the entire imperial objective of consolidating, overseeing, and taxing exports. Instead of stimulating growth through commercial restrictions, the act offered new incentives for "Tradesmen and Artificers" to set up in towns. In addition, all male orphans were to be apprenticed to urban craftsmen, again reinforcing the connection between poor whites and urban craft labor. Finally, the legislation specifically restricted the elite speculation on urban lots that had characterized recent development in Annapolis; lots could only be sold to county residents, and no one could buy more than one lot within each town. This was a clear rejection of the imperial oversight of trade, which had been central to Nicholson's plans, but also of the influence of a narrow provincial elite. Just like the Virginia plan, the act returned control over political economy to local leadership.[62]

County leaders across Maryland wasted little time implementing the newly passed act in ways that demonstrated their support for its objectives. In Dorchester County, the town commissioners gathered just two months after the act's passage and traveled the county, purchasing the

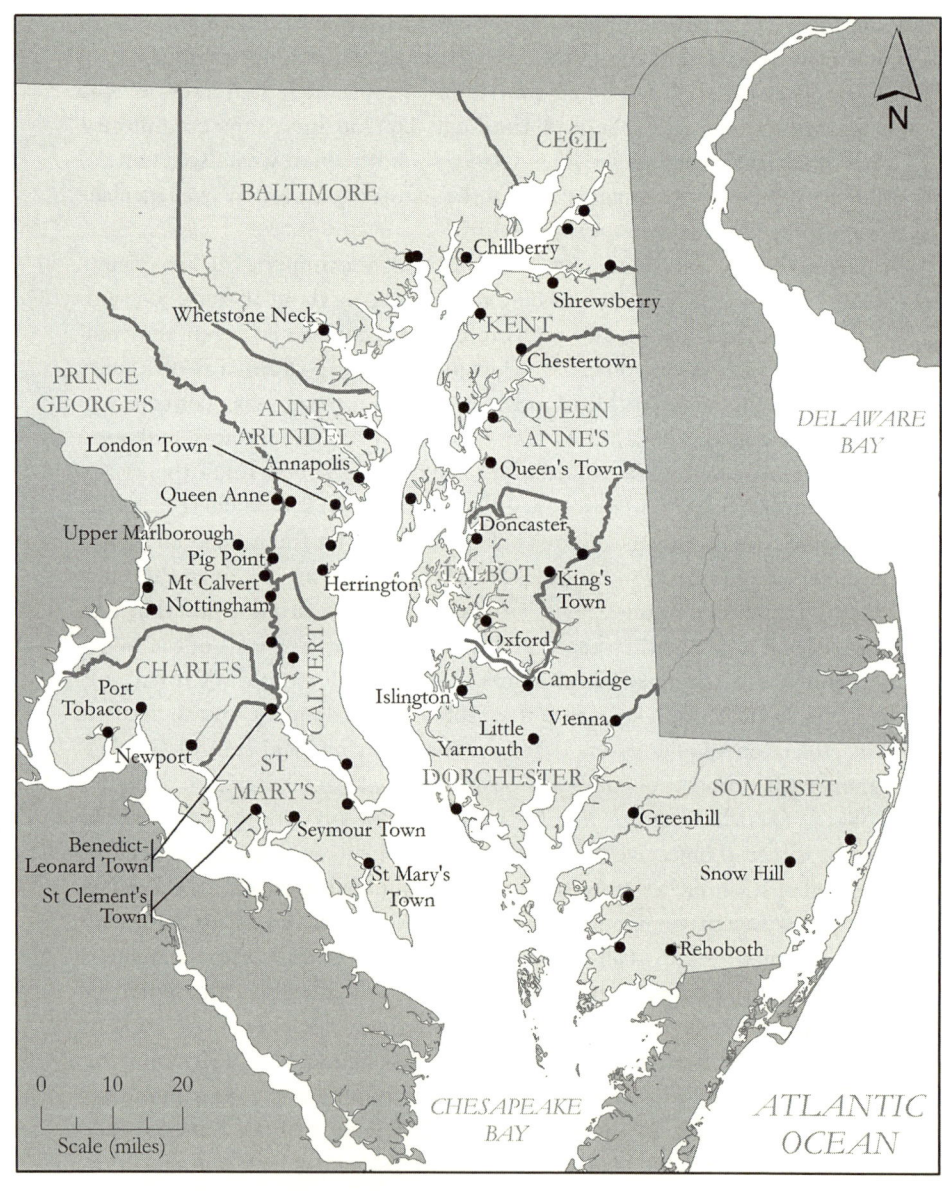

6.5 Map of Maryland town locations, 1706–1708
This map shows all of the identifiable locations of towns established by the Maryland Assembly in acts from 1706, 1707, and 1708. Names are only given for sites where clear contemporary evidence of naming exists, even if the town site later developed a recognized name. (Some information adapted from Shomette, *Lost Towns of Tidewater Maryland* [Centreville, MD: Tidewater, 2000], appendix.)

land, naming and surveying each town, and selling lots. Lot prices were extremely low, with some as cheap as fifty pounds of tobacco. The commissioners also loosely abided by the rules preventing speculation; the only outsiders among the initial thirty-one purchasers were two men from a neighboring county, and most of the sales were single lots to individuals, such as "Thomas Taylor, Butcher of Dorchester County," and Elizabeth Haynes, who purchased two lots in the town of Cambridge. The leadership in Dorchester County clearly saw the new act as an opportunity to stimulate local economic development under their oversight.[63]

The burst of activity in Dorchester County was part of a broader resistance to Nicholson's imperial urban vision among a portion of the region's planter gentry and petty merchants. This opposition ran the gamut from Makemie's and Beverley's reasoned treatises to Slye's angry outbursts and even Richard Clarke's potentially violent plotting. At its root, it shared a skepticism about Nicholson's imperial urban framework of institutions, networks, and rituals. These individuals sought to reassert the power of local civic communities as spaces of mediation with the larger Atlantic economy. Ultimately, though, these reactionaries were increasingly aligned not only against imperial officials but also against a rival faction of the most elite Chesapeake planters.

"THE PRINCIPAL INHABITANTS IN THE RESPECTIVE DISTRICTS"

For the upper echelons of Chesapeake planter elite, the prospect of new small towns around the region was increasingly unappealing. The dozen or so men who dominated the provincial councils in both Virginia and Maryland were the wealthiest planters, but what set them apart was their strong ties to consolidating English tobacco merchant consortiums and the imperial bureaucratic and lobbying system. Some members of this group—such as Virginia councillor Ralph Wormeley—had been skeptical about local efforts at new town development in the 1680s, but around the turn of the century, their interests further diverged from those of their fellow planters. They were increasingly able to achieve many of their objectives through merchant connections that allowed them to lobby the Board of Trade directly. As a result, they were anxious to embrace the imperial institutions that Nicholson's vision introduced, as a symbol of their membership within the polite civic culture emanating from contemporary London, while also rejecting Nicholson's plans—and the plans of their less well-off neighbors—for more egalitarian development and support for middling planters under imperial patronage. They did all they could to resist and undermine the urban plans of both Nicholson and Beverley.[64]

Amid the initial enthusiasm for renewed town development in the early 1690s, some members of the planter elite began to voice opposition. In Maryland, the leading Protestant planters who had helped to oust Lord Baltimore and had won seats on the colony's new provincial council forged an alliance with the first royal governor, Lionel Copley; they reinforced their influence in London by recruiting the influential tobacco and slave merchant Peter Paggan, who helped them to lobby the Board of Trade against officials such as Nicholson and Randolph, whom they felt were meddling too much in their trade. Having established these connections, Copley and his allies resisted reviving the urban plans. Many of the gentry leadership, for whom local urban development in the 1680s had been a potent symbol of local control against Baltimore, hoped to revive town development plans in the early 1690s, just as Virginians did in 1691. But in 1692, during the first official assembly under Crown government, Copley and the provincial councillors refused to consider the delegates' pleas for a new town plan.[65]

In Virginia, Nicholson's support had allowed the burgesses to pass the town act in 1691, but elite opposition was brewing there too. During the debate in 1691, the provincial council substantially altered the town act, making it harder for small-scale intracolonial traders to operate from the towns. They also had a major influence on the choice of locations and the implementation of the 1691 act. For example, Ralph Wormeley ensured that the town site on his estate in Middlesex was downgraded in the 1691 plan from the status of an official port of entry to that of a second-tier local market town.[66] Even after the downgrade, though, Wormeley told Middlesex County justices implementing the act that he would only sell the land in exchange for an annual symbolic tribute of an ear of corn, which would underscore his ultimate authority over the region's political and economic life. When the commissioners refused, he dispatched his servants to chase off the surveyors working at the site. In King and Queen County, the commissioners complained that they encountered similar resistance from dominant local landowner Colonel John West as they laid out the town at West Point.[67]

Elite resistance continued after implementation of the act began. Well-connected planters and their English merchant allies also lobbied against the legislation on both sides of the Atlantic. In the Chesapeake, they cast doubt on the chances of royal approval for the act. Nicholson acknowledged that "Severall Persons Resideing or Inhabiting in ye City of London

... pretend great Creditt is given to them by ye Comissioners of their Maties Customes & others" and that they used this influence to discourage development in Virginia. They then used this lack of development to claim in London that the act was impractical, because it was "unreasonable to Compel the Inhabitants & Planters to bring downe their Goods, before there are places Convenient for their Reception and Security." This combination created a self-fulfilling prophecy of failure. When the next General Assembly met, the burgesses were desperately seeking a "meanes to dishearten & put a Stop to the discouragers." The provincial council, however, who were doing most of the discouraging, rejected their appeals to make the rumor mongering a crime.[68] After Sir Edmund Andros replaced Nicholson in autumn 1692, the councillors redoubled their efforts to undermine the act. Andros immediately reported to London that all men of "good repute" hoped the act would be replaced. Later he added details about a ship that had arrived in the Rappahannock River, but "the Act for Towns and Ports being in force she intends for Maryland"—an anecdote passed along to him, unsurprisingly, by Ralph Wormeley.[69] Elite opposition did not aim to entirely undermine urban development, but it looked to radically redirect it. London merchants advised the customs commissioners that their allies, "the Principal Inhabitants in the respective districts," could advise Andros on how to remodel the act to focus purely upon customs inspection and mercantile convenience. Andros attempted to implement precisely such a plan. He announced the suspension of the act in 1693, but with the provincial council's support, he proposed a trimmed-down version that designated a small number of official ports. When the burgesses rejected the proposal as "very burthensome & inconvenient," the council concluded that no deal was preferable to a bad one. For the next five years, they repeatedly sidestepped the issue with the burgesses and with English officials.[70]

The reason for this new reticence was that, for well-connected elite planters, the promise of local control over political economy no longer held much appeal. Through their London connections, particularly with William Blathwayt, whom they described as their "patron" at the Board of Trade, Chesapeake (predominantly Virginia) planters were able to influence imperial policy. Douglas Bradburn has shown how leading London merchants negotiated the formalization of the wartime convoy system, which forced all ships to cross the Atlantic together under naval escort. Because the size and the timing of each year's fleet was negotiated in advance, well-connected merchants were able to limit competition from smaller traders and those who might preempt them to the year's tobacco market. This gave their elite planter allies far more control over commerce than locally incorporated towns ever would have offered. Furthermore, as William Pettigrew has demonstrated, the wealthiest Chesapeake planters played a decisive role in lobbying against the slave-trading monopoly of the Royal African Company, resulting in the 1698 Africa Trade Act that formally opened slave trading to any merchants. This liberalization led to an explosion in the number of enslaved men and women brought directly from Africa, thereby redoubling the influence of the elite faction with the capital to take advantage of this human windfall to expand their operations. In 1705, the Virginia General Assembly revised the slave code to reinforce elite planters' control over this growing enslaved population. Finally, merchants also attempted to use their lobbying power to gain access to the Russian tobacco market, which would have increased demand and thereby absorbed increases in tobacco output from expanding elite estates without further depressing prices.[71]

The ability to influence imperial policy was changing leading planters' sense of their place within the empire. They no longer viewed relationships through a local lens; rather, they framed their appeals by relating their commercial interests to the empire's broader wartime mission. In seeking access to the Russian trade, for example, influential London merchant Micajah Perry and elite planter William Byrd II framed their petition as an "Advantage to the Kingdom of England and the Plantacons" without any doubt that their mutual interests were consonant. Although a weaker economy delayed the development of this outlook among the Maryland elite, a few years later, they also petitioned the Crown to address low tobacco prices by embracing the imperial argument that whatever increased overall tobacco production was in the best interests of the imperial economy as a whole. Elites in both colonies had inculcated a new outlook, accepting that their economic role within the empire was primarily supplying tobacco but then using this role as leverage to demand influence over imperial policy.[72]

The Virginian author of *An Essay upon the Government of the English Plantations on the Continent of America*, likely the elite planter Benjamin Harrison III, captured this dynamic. He argued that the colonies ought to be integrated into the state much as England's shires were: through local elites closely bound to the metropolis. This meant rejecting intermediary institutions such as proprietorships or corporations in favor of panimperial Protestantism, a settled legal code, and an official lobbyist in London "to give an account from time to time, as he shall be thereto required, of all the Affaires and Transactions of the Plantation." This structure would highlight the natural commonalities between the interests of the leading planters and the broader empire, specifically in expanding—rather than restricting, as Locke and Nicholson suggested—the cheap supply of enslaved labor and land grants, both of which the author believed were crucial for imperial expansion westward in North America. The pamphlet made no mention of towns, which were not important to the author's view of American planters as landed aristocrats in the service of the empire.[73]

This vision found plenty of support in London among the faction at the Board of Trade who opposed Locke's plans. While Locke was developing his radical proposals for the reorganization of Virginia in 1697, William Blathwayt and other members of the Board developed a general report on imperial trade. It concluded that corporations and urban privileges needed to be reduced in England rather than increased in the colonies and that the plantations should be "plentifylly supplyd with Negroes" to increase production.[74]

For a crucial moment in the mid-1690s, these developing attitudes were able to coexist with Nicholson's vision for urban development. Virginia's councillors, who had blocked all efforts to revive the 1691 town plan, initially supported Nicholson's plans for Williamsburg. This temporary coexistence did not mean that the two parties shared the same vision for that city. Even in the moment of agreement, there were hints that the elite vision differed from Nicholson's. In 1697, James Blair, Henry Hartwell, and Edward Chilton (who were all connected to the highest echelons of the elite) had provided Locke with ample evidence of the need for urban development, laying the foundations for Nicholson's new instructions. Their testimonies to the Board of Trade, however, contained hints of the distinct elite ideas that remained beneath the surface. Blair, who was Nicholson's closest ally, readily admitted that port towns "might occasion a Market . . . for the advantage of the Country," but Hartwell's and Chilton's testimonies ignored local markets and instead emphasized the importance of strictly limiting urban development to benefit merchants and customs officials. In their coauthored *Present State of Virginia*, the three men lamented the lack of towns, but instead of blaming the likes of Wormeley, who had consistently blocked development, they attributed this shortcoming to "the Obstinacy of the People," who "having never seen a Town . . . cannot therefore imagine the Benefit of it, and are afraid of every Innovation that will put them to a present Charge." They ultimately agreed with Andros in recommending a restricted system of ports imposed from London but cautioned against promoting domestic exchange or the craft economy. As attorneys well positioned to serve as imperial bureaucrats,

Chilton and Hartwell favored the establishment of a single new capital city that could be both a "Seat of the Government, and Center of Business."[75] Their suggestions differed markedly from the market towns Locke proposed. Blathwayt, acting on their advice, undermined Locke's town-building provisions in the instructions that the Board eventually issued to Nicholson. The wave of enthusiasm for development that led to Nicholson's transfer to Virginia concealed profound underlying differences.[76]

The councillor elite initially made common cause with Nicholson's plans for Williamsburg by projecting their own aspirations for a polite imperial space onto the new city. Relocating the capital to the vicinity of the College of William and Mary naturally appealed to Blair, as president of the college, and the existing elite neighborhood at Middle Plantation made the site appealing to other members of the council. Blair assisted Nicholson's efforts to persuade the House of Burgesses by hosting a gathering at the college on May 1, 1699. The burgesses toured the town site, and some of the college scholars gave orations supporting the relocation. Likely authored by Blair, the speeches promoted a more elite version of urbanity than Nicholson (and certainly Locke) had in mind. They cast the new city as a place where the planter gentry could reinforce their status as English gentlemen. The speeches dwelt upon the virtue of locating the capital near the college, which was a key tool for training Virginians to rival the "old stock of English Gent." Furthermore, the "market" in the new capital would not regulate commerce but instead provide everything necessary for a "seat of polite Literature & the Liberal arts," which would cultivate civil society in Virginia and increase consumption of English manufactured goods, thereby benefiting the imperial economy. The new capital was to be an ideal compromise between the "Flesh potts of Egypt" available in London and the isolated provincial rurality of the planters' world; it would cultivate "good company and conversation."[77] These ideals drew upon the maturing urban renaissance in contemporary England, during which the ruling gentry transformed provincial towns into centers for polite sociability and nodes of a new national culture. In England, new ideals of politeness and manners within the emerging public sphere of these refined towns were replacing older corporate forms of civic identity. A new focus on politeness and consumerism also helped to more strictly define gender roles within planter society just as members of the elite sought to impose greater patriarchal authority over their wives and families. Like English provincial towns, Blair envisioned Williamsburg as a space where manners and politeness could be displayed and used to justify elite male authority exercised in an Atlantic imperial sphere, rather than a place where virtue could be cultivated through local compromises for the common good.[78]

Inevitably, once the full ramifications of Nicholson's plans became apparent, the unity among the governor and the Virginia elite dissolved. Nicholson's pretensions to patronage over Williamsburg particularly irked Blair, who felt that, as college president, local clergyman, and Anglican commissary, he should dominate the city's polite urban sphere. Blair cultivated a network of conversation and political debate by hosting Virginia's councillors at his lodgings "to drink Chocolate in the Morning, and may be Sometimes in the afternoon a Glass of wine," simultaneously encouraging them to shun the governor's hospitality. He also began circulating satirical verse and printed broadsides against the governor around Williamsburg's streets, nailing them to trees. The papers were another part of the embryonic effort to cultivate a public discourse akin to that developing in contemporary England, through which the elite could debate imperial policy and critique the governor.[79] This vision stood in stark contrast to Nicholson's vision for the city, and the clash of ideas came to a head following Nicholson's elaborate celebration of Queen Anne's coronation. The Williamsburg spectacle, lubricated with rum punch and centered on gubernatorial patronage, was anathema to Blair and the provincial council. True to the culture of politeness they sought to establish, they framed their critique of Nicholson in moral terms. They marshaled witnesses to testify that they "saw five hundred drunk for one sober" and suggested that the governor was corrupting the manners of the country by encouraging debauched masculinity among the militia and subverting their effort to establish a more refined patriarchy. However, the councillors' true concern lay in what the celebration implied about the relationship between the empire, the governor, and Virginia's common planter. They wrote to London that Nicholson was "endeavouring not only to regain the good opinion of the Common people" but also to set them against the provincial leadership. They cultivated reports that ordinary militiamen in attendance "Cursed" Nicholson for his extravagance, but no matter how much they protested, the councillors could not shake the conviction that the governor's tactics had worked. After all, the burgesses had publicly thanked him for the celebrations.[80]

This episode resonated with deeper divergences between Nicholson and the provincial council over the nature and control of political and economic power in the region that inspired intense lobbying to oust the governor. Nicholson's effort to restrict large land grants and expand the class of middling planters was intimately connected to his effort to make

Williamsburg a populous and popular imperial center. The councillors came to realize that his work confronted rather than complemented the informal networks of influence they were building within the empire. By 1703, their merchant allies began spreading rumors that Nicholson's plan for Williamsburg had been vetoed in London in order to undermine the governor's position in the colony. Williamsburg also played a crucial role in Blair's subsequent lobbying to unseat Nicholson; he repeatedly emphasized Nicholson's ill-tempered demands for control over the building process and even suggested that the governor was anxious to control the city as part of a plan to lead an uprising of urban laborers against the landed classes, taking "all the Servts as Cromwell took the Apprentices of London into his Army." Nicholson was obviously no Cromwell, but Blair's comment demonstrated that concerns about the potential power of independent and self-conscious urban communities lingered from the era of the Civil War and that the Virginia elite recognized the danger that urban populism, under Nicholson's direction, could pose to their authority. Blair's rhetoric may have been overblown, but with many of Nicholson's allies in London displaced by political upheaval at court, it eventually worked to get the governor removed in 1705.[81]

Unseating Nicholson was just the start of the Chesapeake planter elites' efforts to gain control over the imperial cities he had created. Following Nicholson's removal, direct authority over Williamsburg largely fell to the provincial council, who dominated the development process through the 1710s. When Lieutenant Governor Alexander Spotswood arrived in Virginia in 1710 and sought to erect a grandiose official residence in the city, the councillors and burgesses insisted on inspecting the work and withheld funds for it to reinforce their influence over the city's development.[82]

In Maryland the battle for control of Annapolis was just as tense. In 1708, Governor Seymour sought to reinforce his authority over the capital by replacing the original city trustees with a closed self-perpetuating corporation consisting of his most trusted allies. His actions sparked outrage in the General Assembly. Delegates contested his authority to issue urban charters. After several months of acrimony, Seymour was forced to issue a new corporate charter that allowed for popular election of the city's common councillors and delegates to the assembly. The new charter retained an elite structure, and many of Seymour's allies were still appointed as aldermen, but the assembly insisted upon passing an "Act Confirming and Explaining the Charter of Annapolis" that asserted the ultimate authority of the planter class over the city.[83]

From this point through the mid-eighteenth century, Annapolis and

Williamsburg remained firmly under the control of the provincial planter elite and became centers for refined sociability. Their clubs, bowling greens, horse races, and literary culture allowed planters visiting the city to demonstrate their ties to the empire through fashion and consumption. This world was satirized by Annapolis resident Dr. Alexander Hamilton in his *History of the Ancient and Honorable Tuesday Club*, the mock history of an elite social club in Annapolis, and by the pseudonymous author Tim Pastimes in an essay lampooning the social world of midcentury Williamsburg in which town residents "sift out each other's affairs . . . and if they can't discern a foible, will with the utmost facility make one." Of course, satire was itself part of the culture of the polite public sphere that helped to reinforce elite identity. Polite society promoted a version of civic virtue that privileged appropriate behavior and decorous consumption of the empire's fruits rather than civic corporate independence. The real business of regulating commercial interests was privatized through the elite planters' relationships with British merchants.[84] Though similar polite cultures developed in other English Atlantic port cities, none were as consciously constructed or as fully dominant. In other places, such as Kingston, Jamaica, and Charleston, South Carolina, the authority of the planter elite over urban life was directly challenged by distinct groups of merchants, middling whites, and enslaved workers.[85]

Inevitably, this new urban ideal also diverged from the local civic vision advanced by Beverley and Makemie. In their efforts to remove Nicholson, the councillors had briefly made common cause with these men. During a visit to London that coincided with Nicholson's downfall, council president Edmund Jenings had supported Beverley's proposals, leading to the instructions that pushed Nott and Seymour to reinvigorate urban development. In reality, though, their ideas differed considerably. Jenings and his merchant allies had approached the customs commissioners with a proposal to establish ports, similar to the plan proposed under Andros's governorship. They claimed it would prevent illegal trade and speed up shipping—all things that might benefit large-scale planters as much as imperial coffers. But they noted that they opposed more ambitious plans in order that "no hardship be put on any, beyond the shiping and unshiping of goods." Jenings's ports were to be little more than warehousing facilities where elite planters and merchants could streamline and integrate their operations with the imperial state.[86]

These goals were ultimately irreconcilable with the expectations of many burgesses back in the Chesapeake who favored Beverley and Makemie's more ambitious plans. When the Virginia Assembly passed their

1706 urban development plan, the provincial council were skeptical: "it was with no little difficulty," they noted, "that this Bill received its passage [through the upper house]." They advised Governor Nott that, although they had misgivings about the act, it was all he would get from the truculent burgesses. They likely anticipated that their allies in London could ensure the act's rejection even if the governor signed it. Writing to merchant Thomas Corbin a few months after the act's passage, councillor and preeminent planter Robert "King" Carter entreated him to find an alternate way to raise tobacco prices that would undermine the case for towns, because "all who really desig[n the Queen's] Service will think this the best way to keep us upon G[enerally follo]wing the Trade of Tobacco as now we do."[87]

All of the town legislation from Maryland and Virginia was scrutinized by the Board of Trade for three years between 1706 and 1709, and the full force of the elite lobbying network was deployed against it. Despite evidence to the contrary, the merchants again suggested that proposed towns had not progressed beyond the surveyors' books and that insufficient development made trade restrictions impractical. For support, they recruited a delegate from the Maryland Assembly who happened to be in London— John Bradford, a merchant-factor in the colony's wealthiest region. Bradford claimed that ten towns had been laid out on the Patuxent River but that there were "but few houses built." In Virginia, he "understood that nothing at all had been done there towards the Building of Towns."[88] The most decisive argument of the merchants and elite planters, though, focused on the Virginia plan's creation of new urban corporations. Following the merchants' testimony, the customs commissioners reported that the corporate plans were especially troubling because they were a dangerous alternative form of political authority that would hinder the expansion of the large-scale plantation complex. The elite planter-merchant nexus had now come full circle, using their own rhetoric of civic virtue and commitment to the empire's broader common good to explicitly reject the urban corporate structure that had been seen (and still was by the authors of the 1706 act) as the bulwark of local civic virtue in the world of commerce. Their arguments worked. The Board particularly emphasized the Virginia act's corporate provisions in their recommendation that both colonies' town plans be vetoed by the Crown.[89]

The royal rejection of the 1706 town plans signaled the end of a century of large-scale urban development legislation. The Chesapeake's elite planters had definitively turned against an urban vision for their political economy. As soon as word of the Board's decision to annul the town legislation reached the colonies, Virginia's councillors drafted a proposal in keeping with their intentions all along. They presented the House of Burgesses with "an Act Establishing ports Ware houses Rowling houses and Publick Landings" that supported the construction of simple commercial infrastructure without providing for any urban lots or granting any special privileges. After some debate, the measure passed in 1712. With their victory over Nicholson and Seymour for control of the region's imperial capitals, their successful lobbying to replace Beverley's town plan with a more limited alternative, and passage of their new slave code, the planter elite finally had a political-economic system that could legitimize and secure their control over the volatile tobacco market and its enslaved labor force.[90]

∴

Official news of the royal rejection of town legislation only reached the Chesapeake in 1710. Contrary to the claims of London merchants, the four-year delay had encouraged considerable investment at town sites in both colonies. At Vienna in Dorchester County, Maryland, more than half of the one hundred lots were sold before news of the legislation's repeal. In Middlesex County, Virginia, the town on Rosegill Creek was finally laid out and named Urbanna; it quickly attracted the investment the Beverleys had longed for—small-time coastal merchants who competed with factors for big London trading houses. This investment laid the basis for mid-eighteenth-century growth in Urbanna and Vienna, and also in places such as Cambridge, Mount Calvert, and Londontown in Maryland and Norfolk, Hampton, Yorktown, and Tappahannock in Virginia.[91]

Crucially, however, these slowly emerging towns were no longer seen as civic communities. The legislation that created them had been annulled, and most were left without a political identity for the remainder of the colonial period. They were now spaces within a commercial empire, the labor and commodity markets of which were negotiated through the planter elites' ties to broader institutional structures. The urban institutions that had seemed so vital to Edwin Sandys's vision and that had continued to resonate through the 1706 Virginia legislation were now considered dangerous hindrances by the politico-commercial networks that structured the Atlantic empire. During the last sixty-six years of colonial rule, despite renewed periods of economic depression, there was no further general legislative action to promote urban development that approached the level of ambition reflected in the 1706 Virginia act. The end of political action to promote towns coincided with the consolidation of the tobacco trade and the rapid rise in the use of enslaved labor.

But it would be a mistake to see the attitude toward towns as just a barometer of planters' transition to intensive slave-driven production and consolidation of political power. In fact, conflicting urban visions in the two decades around the turn of the eighteenth century catalyzed the consolidation of interest groups and the articulation of the new civic ideals that undergirded this process. Nicholson's imperial cities, replete with ecclesiastical, educational, and bureaucratic institutions, had pointed the way toward a more integrated empire in which cities were not a locus for local authority but a key interface with the larger empire. The planter elite adopted this idea and embraced the new capital cities' imperial and polite culture, but they rejected the populist elements of Nicholson's vision that threatened their hegemonic dominance of the slave-powered tobacco economy. In both Williamsburg and Annapolis over the next few decades, elites crafted a world of informal connections to the empire through office holding, consumerism, and a planter public sphere that flourished each year when grandees gathered in the cities. In these spaces, as one contemporary noted, "compleat gentlemen" could "dwell comfortably, genteely, pleasantly, and plentifully." The process of establishing new capital cities had thus allowed the Chesapeake planter elite to forge a civic identity built around a patriarchal culture of manners and politeness rather than corporate common property and cooperative stability. Over the next few decades, this elite vision of gentry sociability and authority would inform a new approach to urban development in the rapidly expanding and diversifying world of the eighteenth-century Chesapeake—an approach that would allow them to participate in an intensifying capitalist market economy while maintaining a uniquely firm commitment to "country" ideals.[92]

CHAPTER SEVEN

Urban Growth and Country Thought in the Planters' Golden Age

By 1720, the Chesapeake planter elite could look with satisfaction upon a political and economic structure that finally seemed settled. Everyone in positions of power now agreed that tobacco was the region's key contribution to imperial prosperity; elite planters had access to larger numbers of enslaved laborers and larger estates on which they were forced to work. But these halcyon days would not last. The brief economic boom gave way to another dramatic downturn and a new era of introspection in the Chesapeake. Economic pressures meant that metropolitan alliances the planters had cultivated became frayed. One Marylander even suggested that London merchants were "Enemies to our being in any other Condition but Bondage and Slavery."[1] Yet for the first time when faced with an economic crisis, planters did not turn to urban development legislation. They hatched plans to reduce tobacco production, cut taxes, and print paper money, and invested in private speculative projects, but from 1709 until the American Revolution, no one proposed any legislation to establish multiple new towns, in the ways that had been so common for a century.

For anyone familiar with the typical picture of eighteenth-century Chesapeake planters, this rejection of urban development seems unsurprising. Scholars have reconstructed the social rituals that pervaded Chesapeake life in this period, from horse races to county court sessions and militia musters. These events reinforced elite hegemony in an explicitly rural society. This elite pastoralism was encapsulated by William Byrd II's assessment that "we are very happy in our Canaan," far from the "fogg and smoak . . . of dirty London," in a land "where milk and honey flow; where peace and plenty abound." This perspective, moreover, has seemed a natural extension of so-called country rhetoric in contemporary Britain. The increasing intersection of expanding commercial and state institutions in

London, particularly during the administration of Sir Robert Walpole, was attracting the ire of the British political opposition and giving rise to a new strain of thought that emphasized the country gentry's virtue against the corruption and private interests of urban merchants and court elites. Chesapeake planters were also increasingly influenced by European ideas about scientific agricultural reform that emphasized the foundational importance of the agrarian contribution to the economy. In this context, it hardly seems surprising that planters would shun urban development.[2]

Ironically, though, between the 1730s and the 1750s, in the midst of the planter elites' golden age, urbanization took off in the Chesapeake. Town sites that had lain moribund since the 1680s sprang to life. The elites' commitment to agricultural improvement, funded by easier access to credit, spurred urban growth. Norfolk and Baltimore boomed after midcentury, but equally significant was the growth in smaller places such as Petersburg, Dumfries, and Winchester in Virginia and Upper Marlborough, Frederick, and Charlestown in Maryland, which all became bustling ports or market towns with busy streets, warehouses, and recognizable town identities.[3]

At the heart of this seeming paradox was a new definition of urban development that was central to the evolution of the planter elites' distinct "country" ideology. Wary after a century of struggle over urban political and commercial power that had shaped their parents' and grandparents' rise, elites adopted a new privatized vision of town growth. Between 1727 and 1762, a total of fifty-seven legislative acts recognized the foundations of new towns, but none offered incentives or privileges.[4] While burgesses still considered these centers important for the regional economy, their legislation became about restricting the power of urban communities rather than facilitating their growth. Lots were sold and warehouses were erected, frequently by elite planters themselves, but the authority to regulate the tobacco trade was closely guarded by the gentry. The planter elites' efforts to restrict urban institutions did not represent a rejection of commerce or a retreat into a pastoral precapitalist idyll; instead, they were a conscious effort, built on generations of experience, to retain and reinforce their authority by claiming virtuous oversight of the marketplace. This was an effort that stood in marked contrast to the emerging cities elsewhere in the British plantation world. Ultimately, this process of structuring town development during the mid-eighteenth century gave the Chesapeake planter gentry crucial experience in deploying their country ideology in answer to practical questions of commerce and the common good. Their particular vision for political economy was a product of this long-running regional debate rather than a reflection of imported European ideas. In the third quarter of the century, elites would deploy this vision of rural virtue and urban corruption, honed in response to local questions about town development, to frame the commercial tensions that drew the Chesapeake into the American Revolution.

"THE GUARDIANS OF OUR TRADE AND PROPERTY"

After two decades of disrupted wartime trade, the Peace of Utrecht in 1713 seemed to promise the Chesapeake elite an opportunity to finally cash in on the close bonds they had built with English merchants. Peace meant that European markets reopened and freight rates were reduced. One merchant noted in 1715 that "Tobo now with us is at a great Price as I have known it in my time." With improved economic conditions and the growing complexity of the Atlantic commerce, the Chesapeake planters began focusing their efforts exclusively on agriculture and relying on their system of alliances with London merchant houses. Merchants also continued to serve planters' political interests, establishing a well-organized tobacco lobby in London. In 1715, William Byrd II traveled to London as Virginia's agent in the metropolis and the effective head of this lobbying operation. In consort with friends and merchant allies, he was able to overturn Lieutenant Governor Alexander Spotswood's plans to regulate the tobacco and Indian trades in ways that would have limited elite planter authority. This was precisely how the system envisioned by leading planters was supposed to work, to shape policy according to the shared interests of planters and merchants. In this context, there was little need for dramatic new legislation to reshape the region's commercial infrastructure. Such consensus, though, masked the changing outlook of the planter elite. When political-economic questions resurfaced in the 1730s, they returned to contesting with merchants and imperial officials for control over their trade, but they now did so in new rural civic terms.[5]

The root of the new problems lay in the fact that the planters' newfound influence after 1713 had inspired overconfidence. Despite numerous warnings from their merchant allies to proceed cautiously, the Chesapeake planters embraced the economic upswing of the late 1710s as an opportunity to expand at breakneck speed. They rapidly increased their demand for enslaved labor. In the four years from 1718 to 1721, nearly twice as many enslaved people arrived in the Chesapeake as over the preceding decade. The horrors of slavery condemned some of these men, women, and children to early deaths, but the enslaved population still rose dramatically. In just ten years, between 1714 and 1724, the laboring population of Virginia rose nearly 40 percent.[6] This staggering expansion was facilitated by treaties with indigenous peoples that opened new land grants in the piedmont regions. In the early 1720s, the Virginia elite persuaded Governor Spotswood to relax land-granting rules, and on the day the regulations changed, nearly 100,000 acres were patented. Although Maryland lacked a piedmont on the same scale, the early eighteenth century did see a dramatic rise in settlement in the western regions of Prince George's County (present-day Montgomery and Frederick Counties).[7] This expansion reinforced the position of the Chesapeake gentry, but it also glutted the tobacco market. Increased production, combined with a credit contraction after the bursting of the South Sea Bubble, caused a drop in tobacco prices in the 1720s.

Both the Virginia and Maryland assemblies felt compelled to take action to reduce production and stabilize prices. They returned to the oft-tried strategy of legislating a limit, or "stint," on the number of tobacco plants that each worker could cultivate. They also sought to restrict the labor supply by placing a heavy duty on the importation of enslaved people. However, throughout the economic downturn of the 1720s, no legislators or petitioners in either Virginia or Maryland ever proposed plans to devolve economic regulation upon new towns. Their plans were exclusively focused on requiring planters to control their production on an individual basis.[8]

These reforms, though, drove a wedge between elite planters and their merchant allies. The colonial assemblies needed the merchant lobby in London to secure approval for the legislation from the Board of Trade. Councillor Robert "King" Carter wrote to London to encourage merchant allies to stand behind the acts. "You and all lovers of Virginia," he hoped, "will bend your Utmost Strength to Nurse this Child of our Assembly's bringing forth." But the merchants proved negligent nursemaids. The merchants, who had made common cause with the planter elite over wartime convoys and liberalizing the slave trade, now rebuffed their appeals and actively organized to overturn the duty on slaves. Carter noted that the planters' plans had "mett with great discouragemts."[9]

Planters' relations with the merchant community soured further over the next decade. Merchants colluded on plans to increase freight rates for goods sent to the colonies. Maryland's governor, Benedict Leonard Calvert, admitted that the tobacco trade "seems to be of all other, most lyable and Subject to frauds" by merchants, while "the Planter can scarce get a living." A definitive manifestation of the divisions between planters and merchants came in 1732 when they fundamentally differed over proposals to convert tobacco customs duties into an internal English excise tax on tobacco retailing. Planters favored the plan because they suspected that merchants had long manipulated the customs system to defraud them, but opposition from tobacco merchants in Parliament proved enough to derail it. It now seemed that English merchants were united against the planter interests, and they accused their former allies of "Scurrilous libels." They even arranged a boycott of merchant Micajah Perry's business, because of his role in stalling the excise bill, driving him to the brink of bankruptcy.[10]

The tensions partly owed to the fact that the planter-merchant alliance, which had weathered other economic downturns over the previous thirty years, was now being tested by new competition. Merchants in other English and Scottish ports, particularly Glasgow (after the 1707 Act of Union allowed Scots access to the imperial market), were encroaching on the tobacco trade. Not only did these competitors claim an increasing share of the total trade, but they also traded differently, dispatching goods to the Chesapeake and using them to purchase tobacco directly rather than relying on elite planters consigning cargoes. This meant they could trade with smaller producers, undercutting the personal ties between planter elites and leading merchants. The simplified system also gave them an advantage in selling wholesale tobacco in Europe, meaning that they could offer higher prices by dealing in bulk. By 1718, King Carter was already lamenting that he could not match the prices the Scots were offering for mediocre leaf.[11] The volume of this alternative trade increased only gradually from the 1720s, but the effects were bitterly felt from the outset because it struck at the heart of the network of shared interests between leading planters and merchants. London merchants felt compelled to resist economic reforms and call in debts because they faced growing commercial competition. In an open letter to Marylanders in 1729, they excused their increasingly intractable attitude toward planters' debts by explaining that "London used formerly to have a much greater Share of the Trade . . . than in late Years it has had, and consequently, it was then much more in the Power of the Merchants of London to govern the Market." They claimed that while they had control of the trade, they had been able to accommodate planters, but because half the tobacco now flowed elsewhere, they had lost that flexibility. "That," they insisted, "is not at all for your Interest."[12]

Despite the merchants' protestations, though, the planters' patience was wearing thin, and they increasingly articulated a new vision of economic regulation. Instead of reverting to urban civic models, they began asserting their own unique capacity to manage the market. A particularly clear example of this shift came in Maryland in 1729. The colony's attention was grabbed by Maryland planter and merchant Henry Darnall's *A Just and Impartial Account of the Transactions of the Merchants in London . . .* (1728), an account of his efforts to organize London's tobacco merchants to agree on minimum prices. Darnall's pamphlet was suffused with civic language, describing the way in which merchants had agreed to contribute to a common stock, enter into "Society," and lay aside private interests, which "if not sacrificed to the Publick Good, no Society can prosper." Another anonymous author claimed that Darnall's scheme was based on "Reason and calculated for the GOOD and SAFETY of the People." This was a rigorous defense of the civic principles that had originally driven urban plans but that, since the turn of the century, had been delegated to merchant-planter networks.[13] However, soon after the publication of the pamphlet, news arrived that Darnall's agreement had been broken by Samuel Hyde, one of the most influential tobacco merchants trading to Maryland. Accounts in the *Maryland Gazette* labeled Hyde "an Enemy to the Trade" and a "Rascal" who "deserved to be kicked thro London." A list of Hyde's clients circulated, in an effort to shame those who continued to trade with him.[14] The implication was that wealthy planters should act as community guardians by monitoring their commercial relationships; they were to judge the character of their trading partners, keep careful account of the fees on each transaction, and avoid debts. Darnall also suggested that planters respond by forming county committees to regulate prices; other letters in the *Maryland Gazette* over the next few months reinforced the planters' essential civic duty to work together to manage the trade. The publication of the pamphlet and the letters was, in itself, an important step in facilitating this process, allowing a dispersed elite to maintain, through the newly established local press, a virtuous dialogue that would facilitate regulation. The planter gentry were no longer called to build new towns; instead, they intended to collectively exercise civic virtue on their private estates, connected by printed discourse.[15]

Over the following three years, further output from the Annapolis printing press reinforced these ideas. In 1730, the local poet Ebenezer Cook published *Sotweed Redivivus, Or the Planters Looking-Glass*, focusing on the problems with the tobacco trade, corrupt merchants, and the need for economic reform to address "the lingering State of Common-weal," in the colony. Cook's prescription of economic diversification was a predictable return to the discourse of the past century, but the onus for achieving it was now placed upon the planter gentry; the work's subtitle encouraged planters to engage in the humanist process of self-reflection in order to generate agrarian virtue, and the entire poem was structured around a series of these planter conversations. Cook had not entirely given up on urban development, suggesting that "we ought conveniently to dwell / In Towns and Cities, buy and sell / Our Merchandize at public Scales," but he believed this would only be realistic once planters had converted to a diversified agricultural economy.[16] Annapolis schoolmaster Richard Lewis took the theme of agrarian virtue even further two years later in his poem *Carmen Seculare*, which surveyed Maryland's natural bounty and rural hospitality. Lewis's solution to the economic crises was to incentivize further immigration so that "Artists will appear / And quitting crowded Towns, inhabit here. / Well please'd, would they employ their gainful hands / To purchase and improve your vacant Lands." Lewis's direct rejection of urban life came closest to the contemporary European trend toward the valorization of rural pastoral simplicity against modern urban corruption. For Lewis, Maryland had fully embraced the status of a pastoral haven, where men and women laid the groundwork for civic virtue through industrious agricultural improvement.[17]

Virginia clergyman Hugh Jones had fleshed out a similar sentiment in his 1724 *Present State of Virginia*. Jones was well connected within Virginia's planter elite, and his survey of the colony was laudatory and optimistic. He acknowledged the depressed tobacco market but emphasized that the gentry had laid the foundations for "Arts, Sciences, Trades, and useful Inventions." In stark contrast to almost all previous accounts, he praised the Chesapeake region's rurality, noting that even main roads were "not unlike the Walks in Greenwich Park" and emphasizing the grandeur of the "Gentlemen's Seats." Without the scorn of previous authors, Jones noted that these men had "neither the Interest nor Inclination . . . to cohabit in Towns" because their private estates offered "the Provisions of a little Market." Even those who had settled in Williamsburg "behave themselves exactly as the *Gentry in London*" rather than like London merchants and artisans. He admitted that this lifestyle made some gentlemen overly wary of innovation, but these characteristics meant they were unlikely to "have been imposed upon" by the "monstrous Bubbles" that had recently gripped London. According to Jones, the key to improvement lay in tapping the region's natural abundance, and no group was better placed to pursue improvement than the gentry. "The common Planters," he observed, "don't much admire Labour" and could hardly be counted upon to turn the colony's fortunes around, and London's tobacco merchants were barely acknowledged in Jones's text. His essay, ostensibly aimed at an English audience, thus read as an encomium directed toward the colony's planter elite, celebrating their rural virtues and reminding them of their civic duty.[18]

Over the next few decades, the planter gentry sought to realize this civic ideal of regulation and innovation on their private estates. Elite planters were careful to remain sensitive to the issues and concerns of their poorer neighbors and to self-consciously represent what they perceived to be local interests at the provincial level.[19] They also attempted to lead by example in reforming the economy. Some of the wealthiest planters converted their plantations into diversified farming operations that, while still focused on tobacco, sought to bring the modern skills of European husbandry and science to bear on grain farming, livestock, and other more exotic crops. These innovations were not just intended to generate profit; they were to provide a model to neighbors and, as Landon Carter termed it, to "endeavour to serve mankind." Whereas seventeenth-century efforts at improvement and diversification had been focused on town development and converting poor freemen into artisans, Carter's innovations were undertaken on his private estates by his enslaved workforce.[20]

The planter gentry also developed an etiquette of debt that was based on their rural civic vision. Elite planters mostly borrowed and lent among themselves and extended small amounts of credit to their poorer neighbors. However, they came to see ongoing commercial debt as a symbol of dangerous dependence upon untrustworthy merchants. Although they faced economic challenges, this fear of systemic mercantile debt was not entirely a product of genuine financial desperation. As Trevor Burnard has argued, the extent of debt never truly matched the heightened rhetoric surrounding it for eighteenth-century planter elites, and planters in other parts of the British Atlantic never developed a similar phobia of indebtedness. This was because the ethics of debt were crucial to the construction of a rural planter form of civic community. They understood moderate debts as expected symbols of mutual obligation that held their communities together, but larger external debts compromised their ability to retain their civic authority within the local community. These attitudes stood in contrast to planters elsewhere in British America, who were increasingly comfortable with extended credit networks. The Chesapeake's elite planters strove to be virtuously restrained consumers and careful managers of their business accounts; they also aspired to be lenient county magistrates in the adjudication of their neighbors' debt suits. These ethics were a local rural effort to preserve civic ethics that had been forged over a century of debate about urban regulation of commerce.[21]

The best example of the planter elite's commitment to personally regulate and improve the economy without civic urbanism was the creation of the tobacco inspection system. In 1730, under the guidance of new lieutenant governor William Gooch, Virginia's General Assembly enacted the Tobacco Inspection Act, which revolutionized trade. The act required that all tobacco be brought to designated inspection warehouses, where salaried inspectors, selected from among the community's planters, would assess the quality of the product. Inferior, or "trash," tobacco would be burned, but hogsheads adjudged fit for market would be branded with an official mark, and their owners would receive paper notes that (backed by these quality controls) could subsequently be used as a stable currency. The system promised to reduce supply to the glutted market and raise quality, lifting prices while providing a reliable medium for local exchange.[22] Furthermore, it would standardize quality, making it easier for planters to deal with new merchants without needing to slowly establish the trust necessary to vouch for their product's quality. Planters could thus be more discerning about their trading partners. In introducing the scheme to officials in London, Gooch claimed that it was designed to address the frauds committed by "Agents and Sailors" who manipulated the tobacco trade to the planters' detriment. Significantly, none of the leading traders in London could be prevailed upon to support the proposal before the Board of Trade, despite their recent support for inspection in London under Darnall's scheme. The merchants understood the Tobacco Inspection Act for what it was: an effort to reassert provincial control over the political economy of tobacco.[23]

The inspection system was defined by the planter elites' self-image as bastions of civic virtue in their communities. It was built upon the premise that only planters themselves could be impartial judges of tobacco quality and that their neighbors would submit to the costs and public scrutiny of this system.[24] In contrast to a similar proposal advanced fifteen years before by former Lieutenant Governor Spotswood, which was designed to create a network of patronage offices under the governor's control, the 1730 act specifically required that all inspectors be selected by the planter elite themselves and that they be barred from elected office during their appointments. These provisions were designed to demonstrate that the act was grounded on rural virtue and disinterest.[25]

The gentry civic vision underpinning the inspection system was laid bare during Gooch's efforts to defend the plan against opposition from poor and middling planters. In 1732, the lieutenant governor published a pamphlet defending the act that was structured as a fictional dialogue between two common planters, Thomas Sweet-Scented and William Oronoco, and their local county magistrate, Justice Love-Country. The two planters begin by expressing their anger at seeing their tobacco burned by the inspector, but during their conversation, the justice convinces them of the virtues of the legislation. The format gave the lieutenant governor the opportunity to refute misconceptions about the act, but his aim was equally to remind men like Justice Love-Country of their responsibilities under the new system. Rather than simply overawing his neighbors, the gentleman magistrate wins them over with his knowledge of commerce and his virtue. "What have we, who sell our Tobacco in the Country, to do with the Markets Abroad?" asks Tom Sweet-Scented, and the justice explains the relationship between European marketing and tobacco prices paid in the Chesapeake. Love-Country goes on to explain the way in which new tobacco notes would undermine the scheming of local storekeepers who were "very sharp in the Sale of their Goods." Gooch's justice deploys his solid grasp of commerce to convince his neighbors that "a private Stake . . . must be given up to the Good of the Publick."[26]

Gooch called on the planter elite, though, to go beyond rhetorically defending the common good. Justice Love-Country counsels his neighbors to look to the gentlemen gathered in the General Assembly as "the Guardians of our Trade and Property" and argues that local justices would monitor inspectors' performance. On an individual level, Love-Country also gives his word that the rich will not exploit the inspection system to destroy the poor's tobacco while flouting the rules themselves. Most boldly of all, the justice even soothes his neighbors' worries about short-term losses (before the promised rise in tobacco prices) by putting his own fortune on the line. If the two poor planters produce 2,000 pounds of tobacco but can only get 1,200 pounds past the inspection, Love-Country commits "to give you more, in Money or Goods, for the 1200, than you could sell the 2000 for." The gentleman justice is careful to note that, "tho' I am no Dealer," he is prepared to make the commitment "to shew you what you may do." Where urban corporations or merchant alliances might have previously stood as guarantors for this kind of price-fixing endeavor, individual members of the virtuous planter gentry were now being cited as the bedrock of tobacco inspection in a new civic vision.[27]

Although there is little evidence to suggest that many of the planter elite replicated Love-Country's generous commitment, Gooch's scheme did prevail. Early protests were suppressed by the local militia, and the support of the upper echelons of the planter gentry foiled efforts to overturn the legislation. In 1747, when legislators in Maryland were convinced to institute their own inspection system, the plan was notably supported by members of the elite who focused exclusively on planting, against the opposition of those with greater mercantile connections. The inspection system became a powerful tool in reinforcing elite planters' power over their local economies.[28]

It is important to appreciate, however, that this was neither a coincidence nor a simple power grab by the wealthiest planters. The inspection system was a self-conscious manifestation of their growing "country" perspective—their deepening conviction that their planter gentry status made them virtuous disinterested leaders, not because they were cut off from commerce but because they understood its complexity without being entangled in its corruption. This was a political-economic vision nurtured in the Chesapeake and built upon decades of debate over towns and tobacco. Well-governed urban spaces no longer seemed crucial to the defense of the common good, but prudently managed plantations had stepped into their place.

THE URBAN CHESAPEAKE

None of the discussion surrounding the tobacco inspection scheme ever mentioned town development. Nonetheless, the new network of inspection warehouses that suddenly appeared across the tidewater proved to be a crucial ingredient in the dramatic transformation of the region's settlement system. Numerous towns were established during the second quarter of the eighteenth century, and new investment simultaneously poured into existing town sites that had lain practically dormant for a generation. These places, however, had to be reconciled with the planters' maturing vision of commercial and civic order.

Inspection warehouses necessarily created new nuclei for the Chesapeake economy. Anyone hoping to sell tobacco (still the majority of white men) was forced to visit the warehouse at least once a year to have their crop assessed. This captive market quickly made inspection warehouses ideal places for taverns and stores to cluster. Outport merchants had already experimented with a store system rather than accepting consignments, and the ability for storekeepers to accept notes for crops that were already inspected and stored at quaysides made these transactions easier. Gradually this system morphed into a network of permanent stores, located near inspection warehouses and stocked year-round with manufactured goods. Planters who had just had their crops inspected could be relieved of their newly acquired tobacco notes, and those notes could be quickly converted back into hogsheads of tobacco when the annual fleet arrived.[29] Glaswegian merchants in particular perfected the store system. The Scots primarily operated in Virginia along the Potomac and upper Rappahannock Rivers, in a number of newly established towns, such as Dumfries, Alexandria, Port Royal, and Falmouth, and also in the upper James River region. More than four-fifths of the Scottish merchants whose Chesapeake residences can be identified lived in towns. By midcentury, they actively identified themselves with these urban locations. For example, the Glaswegian merchant Robert Bogle, writing in 1760, understood his market in terms of "friends in Port Royal" and "Acquaintances in Falmouth."[30] The urbanizing effect of inspection warehouses was particularly acute at the fall line, where the major rivers ceased to be navigable for oceangoing vessels. Settlement had expanded rapidly in the piedmont region, but tobacco produced on these new plantations had to be brought down to the falls and then transshipped onto larger vessels, which already encouraged clustering of goods and services. The siting of inspection warehouses at particular points around these falls reinforced this development and spurred the growth of Fredericksburg and the establishment of both Richmond and Petersburg.[31]

The inspection system thus guided and reinforced a process of urbanization that was driven by the expansion of settlement and credit networks. In Virginia, besides the warehouses that were appointed at town sites surviving from previous town legislation, at least nine of the inspection locations later requested recognition as towns. These included places such as Bray's Church in King George's County, which had become the town of Leeds by 1742, and Constance's Warehouse, which was designated as the town of Suffolk in that same year. The circumstances in Maryland were subtly distinct because the tobacco inspection system was not established until 1747, after the growth of new towns in the colony over the previous two decades. However, when inspection was established in the colony, the link between inspection and towns took hold there as well, with almost a third of the seventy-six warehouses being located in existing towns.[32]

Beyond providing a boost to particular town sites, the inspection system reinforced long-term economic diversification, which also stimulated urban growth. By driving marginal planters, who could not produce inspection-grade tobacco, out of the market, the system encouraged these individuals to pursue new crops, particularly wheat for the Caribbean trade. This process began in northern Maryland and the Eastern Shore and spread to other subregions, including Virginia south of the James River. Wheat cultivation also dominated away from the tidewater in western

Maryland and the Shenandoah Valley.³³ Wheat required milling, which forced planters to develop centralized facilities that tobacco had never needed, and the development of grain mills played a central role in the growth of Baltimore, Charlestown, and Chestertown, in the Maryland grain trade, and of Norfolk, Virginia.³⁴

The combined result of these trends was that by the third quarter of the century, the Chesapeake had a developed urban network. At its apex were the exponentially growing cities of Norfolk and Baltimore, which were each bustling ports with populations of over six thousand by 1776. They had recognizable eighteenth-century urban landscapes of densely packed streets and increasingly diverse populations of merchants, artisans, and enslaved laborers. Below this level were the region's two refined capital cities, Williamsburg and Annapolis, and also a wide range of smaller commercial centers that boasted populations ranging from a few hundred to a couple of thousand. Yorktown, for example, had nearly two hundred buildings, divided between a commercial quarter along the waterside and larger merchant homes arrayed along the river bluff. Other port towns—such as Urbanna, Petersburg, and Alexandria in Virginia and Oxford on

7.1 "View of the Town of Yorktown, 1755," from John Gauntlett, *Voyage of HMS Success and HMS Norwich to Nova Scotia and Virginia, 1754–56*
In the mid-eighteenth century, Yorktown was one of many thriving small port towns in the Chesapeake. (Courtesy of the Mariners' Museum, Newport News.)

Maryland's Eastern Shore—had a handful of streets marked by merchant stores and residences. Inland commercial centers, particularly Winchester in the Shenandoah Valley, also flourished. By the 1750s, it had at least five merchant stores, seven taverns or ordinaries, and at least nine artisan's workshops. Even smaller towns, such as Suffolk, in the nontobacco region of Virginia's south side, had about one hundred houses by 1770, but one contemporary commentator noted that they were only single-story buildings scattered along sandy unmaintained streets.[35]

Urban development of the mid-eighteenth century was clearly not a process the planter gentry could easily ignore. Gentlemen like Justice Love-Country, who prided themselves on knowledge of the market, were confronted with a new network of traders who understood their identity as merchants of Falmouth or Chestertown and who used distinct commercial systems and marketing networks. The cognitive disjuncture provoked by these changes can be glimpsed through the experience of William Byrd II. When he visited the town of Norfolk in 1728, he encountered a burgeoning port city that exported an "abundance of beef, pork, flour and lumber," and, even as one of the colony's highest-ranking officials, he had little knowledge of or control over this commerce. Local merchants, he lamented, imported too much rum, but he felt powerless to address this threat to social order, as he might have through the consignment trade. Byrd also felt out of place in this urban space. When he attended worship at the parish church, he noted in his secret diary that he had distracted worshippers because they "could not attend their devotion for staring at us, just as if we had come from China or Japan." Although exaggerated for satirical effect, Byrd's sense of discomfort is palpable. This refined gentleman, who had spent so many years navigating London's social and political circles, felt out of place in a rapidly expanding Atlantic port city in his own colony. Norfolk did not quite fit his pastoral understanding of his homeland as a land of "milk and honey"; nor did it sit comfortably within the "country" structures of political and economic authority that framed his authority over it.[36]

The planter gentry did not simply retreat into a precommercial agrarian paradise though; they actively engaged with the urbanization process, but they did so in a strictly private fashion. Elite planters quickly realized that there were profits to be made in urban real estate, and they invested in new town lots even though they had little intention of residing in the towns themselves. Despite efforts to prevent this kind of speculation, there were a number of examples of planters buying up urban lots and then waiting to sell them at a profit once the towns developed.[37] The most successful speculator was Charles Carroll of Annapolis, who in 1736 purchased twenty-six lots in the newly established town of Baltimore; he held on to the property until the late 1740s when the grain trade began to boom, and he was able to sell the lots at a healthy profit. Another investment strategy, used in Norfolk and Williamsburg, was to purchase acreage adjacent to growing towns and then subdivide it into lots.[38]

The potential for these kinds of profits led to even greater speculation in the third quarter of the eighteenth century, driven in particular by a new craze for urban land lotteries. William Byrd III, in a desperate effort to salvage his fortune, promoted the most ambitious of these schemes. He offered 417 urban lots adjacent to the growing city of Richmond; potential investors purchased tickets, and when the drawing occurred, approximately ten percent of ticket holders would win urban lots, nearby land, or fisheries on islands in the James River. The lottery format drummed up interest in a society where gambling was famously popular, but it was also predicated upon the speculative impulse; the system did not allow individuals to assess the quality of particular lots or make considered judgments about long-term development at certain locations. Some planters even banded together to buy multiple tickets in ways that replicated the speculation of western land companies in the backcountry. Although Byrd struggled to sell all the tickets immediately, the popularity of the lottery format was clear: in 1767, the *Virginia Gazette* carried advertisements for three different urban lotteries running concurrently. In Maryland, Charles Carroll replicated the lottery system in 1770 to sell lots in a new town named Carrollsburg, on Anacostia Creek within what later became the District of Columbia. These investments represented a greater capital outlay than any seventeenth-century planters had been prepared to risk privately. They bore witness to a transformation in the speed and scope of urbanization. The men behind them were now pure speculators who viewed urban property as simply one part of a diversifying portfolio of land.[39]

"WITH REMARKABLE REGARD TO JUSTICE"

In keeping with this distinct pattern of development, the Chesapeake's new towns had a completely different relationship to the imperial and provincial state than seventeenth-century planners had envisioned. Urbanization occurred without legislative encouragement and support, and when legislation was generated, it was deeply inflected by the planters' developing "country" thought; it sought to restrict, rather than enable, the bestowal of political and commercial power on new urban places. The dozens of acts

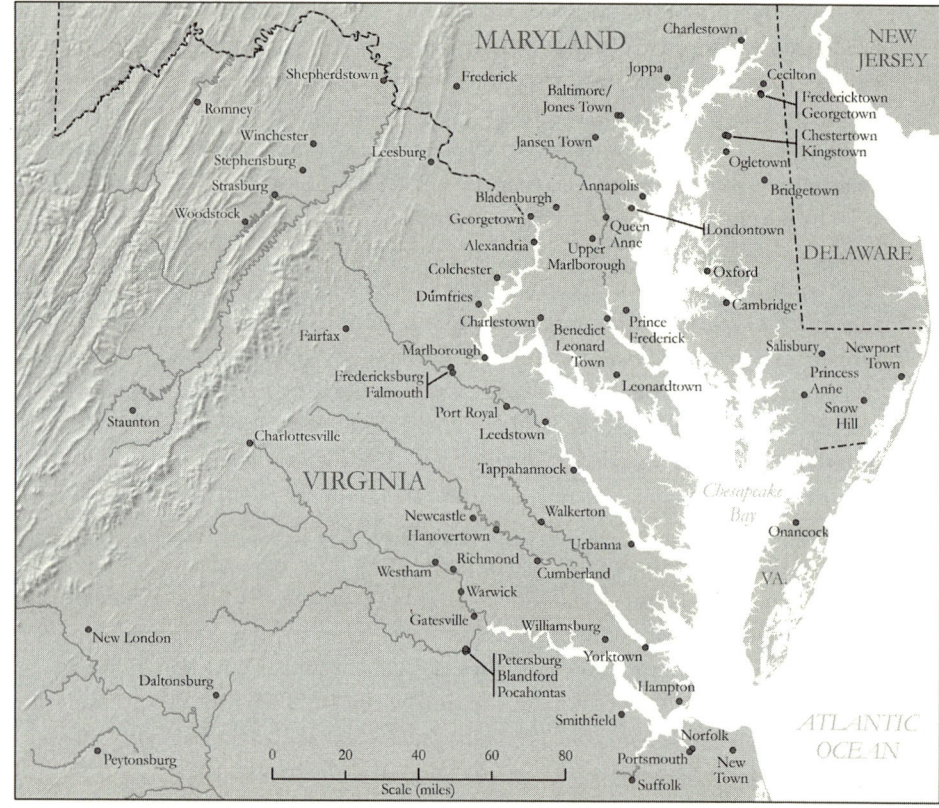

7.2 Map of legislated towns and cities in the Chesapeake, 1710 and 1763
This map shows the locations of all towns and cities that were the subject of provincial legislation of any sort in Virginia and Maryland between 1710 and 1763. The town of Frederick, Maryland, was established by a proprietary charter from Lord Baltimore.

passed in both Maryland and Virginia between the 1730s and 1760s were entirely piecemeal and specific to particular towns. These new plans were almost always the result of local or private petitions that understood urban development purely in terms of the subdivision of land, and the planter gentry sought to use this legislation to control the impact of commerce on their communities.[40]

This change in attitude can be observed through one of the earliest of these town plans, the 1727 act recognizing Fredericksburg and Falmouth. That year, the House of Burgesses received a petition from the residents of Spotsylvania County requesting official sanction for two new towns. Whereas previous petitions during moments of economic depression had inspired broad-ranging debates about urban development, in this case the burgesses simply drafted limited legislation granting groups of trustees (consisting primarily of elite planters, headed by John Robinson, president of the provincial council) the right to lay out lots at each site. There were no trade restrictions or urban privileges, and the trustees' only responsibility was to oversee the land sale. This move was grounded upon a novel underlying rationale. "Great numbers of people have of late seated themselves and their families, upon and near the river Rappahannock," the act began, and "it is necessary, that the poorer part of the said inhabitants should be supplied from thence." However, a lack of facilities meant that people were being exploited because "such supplies are not to be had, without great disadvantages." In essence, the General Assembly conceived the problem for the Rappahannock settlers in terms of infrastructure; the lack of facilities left planters at the mercy of a few factors, and the subdivision of urban lots under elite supervision would liberalize trade under the watchful eye of the local gentry. In summarizing the act, Lieutenant Governor Gooch made this position clear. He explained that the land near the falls of the Rappahannock was "held by private persons," that they "exacted exorbitant prices for storage" from those forced to bring their crops down from the piedmont, and that they even "endeavoured to engross the whole trade themselves." The legislation was intended to "remove these inconveniences" by compulsorily purchasing the land and opening the market to all, and Gooch opined that the burgesses "had no other means to relieve the hardships of the Frontier people, and what they have now done is, with remarkable regard to justice." Urban development was no longer a process of devolving regulatory authority or using privileges to stimulate economic improvement, but of allowing the gentry, as civic-minded guardians of their community's common good, to rein in the corrupting influence of merchants.[41]

Numerous examples of this same procedure occurred over the next two decades in both colonies. In 1742, residents in Nansemond County, Virginia, expressed a desire to develop infrastructure around the local tobacco warehouse as a place "for traders to cohabit in, and bring their goods to," and they received similarly limited legislative permission to divide up the land and refund the original owner when the lots were sold. A few years later, the residents of Fairfax and Frederick Counties lobbied for comparable permission to acquire the land around the tobacco warehouse at Hunting Creek to prevent the monopolization of the prime trading site on the Potomac River. In this case, the landowner, Philip Alexander, tried to fight the legislation, but he did not prevail. In 1749, the delegates opted to allow the subdivision of the site, only saving Alexander's pride by insisting that the new town be named Alexandria. In Somerset County, Maryland, petitioners sought to minimize opposition by waiting until the nascent commercial site they coveted was in the possession of a minor, making it easier for them to acquire the site that later became Salisbury.[42]

Of course not all landowners were unhappy to see their land targeted for this kind of development. As Gooch had observed at the foundation of Fredericksburg, the landowners had little reason to complain because the "present recompence is very sufficient, and the future value of their adjacent lands will be considerably augmented." Moreover, the attention that could be gained through a public sale of this type might attract a better market for lots than an individual private speculator could achieve. This was certainly the case in Alexandria, where the initial auction for lots attracted interest from across the region, and eighty lots were sold within six months. Planter Augustine Washington, observing the sale, noted that Alexander had little reason to complain because he would "not have made half the Sum" through a private sale.[43] As the potential of warehouse sites became clear, landholders increasingly preempted public petition by agreeing to legislation on their own terms. In Kent County, Maryland, for example, Gideon Pearce teamed up with other local inhabitants to request that eighty acres of his plantation along the Sassafras River be subdivided as George Town—the General Assembly was debating a parallel measure for a town on the opposite bank of the river, which was likely why Pearce rushed to seek public approval.[44]

Even when private individuals undertook their own subdivision, they sometimes came to the General Assembly seeking to rubber-stamp their actions. The most well-known example of this process was the formal recognition of William Byrd II's new town of Richmond in 1742. Byrd owned a large estate at the falls of the James River, and as early as 1729, he had recognized the threat posed by a potential petition to have his land forcibly laid out as a town, protesting "the grea[t injus]tice of this proceeding." Byrd was determined that if a town was needed, he would lay it out himself. Four years later, he began planning, and by 1737, he was advertising lots for sale. However, once the city was laid out, he brought the plan before the burgesses and elicited an act to validate his actions. The legislation guaranteed his title and thereby offered security to anyone who purchased lots from him—they could not be swindled by a future public project to seize the land and resurvey it under public auspices. Aside from offering the right to host semiannual fairs, though, the act offered no other urban privileges. It was purely intended to protect Byrd's investment by cloaking it in a veil of approval from his fellow planter gentry.[45]

Because all of these legislative proposals were considered individually, the planter elite were consistently able to reassert their role in arbitrating the public good. Some proposals, such as those for Bladensburg in Maryland or Port Royal in Virginia, flew through the legislature with little debate, while others, such as those of Virginia merchants Peter Aylett and John Cocke for towns near their tobacco warehouses in King William and Surry Counties, respectively, were dismissed. Such rejections were almost certainly influenced by private interests—for example, the powerful Carroll family in Maryland appear to have repeatedly derailed plans for the town of Upper Marlborough near their estate. However, the planter elite had established themselves as the ultimate authority deciding which individuals and which sites were legitimized as serving the public interest and which were dismissed as private projects that granted too much influence to particular merchants. It was the planters who sat in the House of Burgesses who decided that the town of Fredericksburg was vital to liberalizing the market of the upper Rappahannock, but that Peter Aylett's proposal was merely a private scheme to inflate the value of his lands.[46]

This power was particularly important to the Virginia gentry in their struggle against the growing influence of Scottish merchant-factors. The Scottish store system was a direct challenge to the elite planters' consignment trade and their relationships with their poorer neighbors. Scottish factors were also unpopular with local planters because of their determination to reject social ties to the local elite that might cloud their business judgment. For these reasons, legislators were far more reluctant to allow towns to be laid out in places where the Scots were well established. Despite repeated petitions, it took ten years for the burgesses to recognize a town on Quantico Creek, because the site was controlled by John Graham, an agent for the Glaswegian Bogle firm. When the town was eventually laid out, Graham had it named in honor of the Scottish town of Dumfries, where he had begun his career.[47]

The Maryland Assembly's claim to adjudicate locations was framed in relation to a different challenge to planter authority. The restoration of the Calvert proprietorship in 1715 reintroduced an alternative source of power. Over the next half century, explicit parties developed supporting and opposing the Calverts' prerogatives and interests. Although town development did not become overtly entangled in these struggles as it had in the seventeenth century, competing claims to authority did arise occasionally. For example, in the early 1730s, when the pace of town establishment was picking up in Maryland, the provincial council (generally loyal to the proprietor's interests), began demanding amendments to town legislation requiring lot holders to pay proprietary quitrents. In another case, the proprietor's allies objected to the proposed location of a town at Elk Ridge in Anne Arundel County, and they only backed down when the delegates consented to allow Baltimore to name the town after his trusted adviser Sir Theodore Janssen.[48] Finally, in the late 1740s, the proprietor reasserted his authority to establish towns without assembly input, beginning with a grant to his ally Daniel Dulany to establish the town of Frederick. Dulany subdivided more than three hundred lots and demanded annual quitrents from Frederick's lot holders; Baltimore also allowed Dulany to establish and administer fairs and collect tolls. After Dulany's grant, the Maryland Assembly stopped all legislation establishing new towns until the Revolution. Further development at places such as Carrollsburg and Hamburg on the Potomac River was supported by similar proprietary grants, which likely contributed to the growing rift between the Calverts and their subjects.[49]

Beyond permitting or prohibiting the subdivision of land, the planters' legislatures were careful to restrict any potential independent urban authority. Almost all of the legislation in both colonies did nothing beyond permitting the public supervision of lot sales. In places where urban lots had already been laid out, particularly by the 1750s and 1760s, the trustees were reduced to the role of building inspectors with the power merely to "settle and establish such rules and orders for the more regular and orderly building of the houses in the said towns." Even these limited powers were also granted overwhelmingly to local planter grandees, and the Maryland acts explicitly required that the records be lodged with the clerk of the county court, giving county justices jurisdiction over urban land disputes. A petition in 1745 from the town residents of Suffolk, Virginia, asking that planter trustees from distant corners of Nansemond County be replaced with town residents, was rejected without debate.[50]

Because the communities had no powers to establish bylaws, undertake public works, or regulate local markets, they were also forced to repeatedly petition the assemblies over every minor issue, further reinforcing elite authority.[51] Both assemblies were bombarded with specific requests for legislation to regulate common eighteenth-century urban problems, such as hogs roaming the streets and the dangerous prevalence of wooden chimneys. Rather than despairing under the weight of this minor business, the burgesses embraced their role as arbiters of the public good. They enthusiastically parsed the details of various minor urban proposals; for example, they approved a ban on livestock in Norfolk and Fredericksburg but rejected one for Tappahannock, and they specified that in the town of Port Royal hogs could be outlawed but not sheep. Towns even lacked the capacity to act in emergencies; in 1750, the residents of Queen Anne Town petitioned the Maryland Assembly because a creek had overflowed across the main street and they needed legislative approval to fund repairs. The Chesapeake's experience in this respect was not completely unique. A similar rise in urban petitions and particular legislation occurred in eighteenth-century Britain, but towns and boroughs had far more direct representatives in Parliament, and so the power dynamics of petitioning were different. In the Chesapeake, the planter gentry used urban petitions to carefully circumscribe town authority.[52]

The most obvious authority that delegates jealously guarded was the power to establish urban markets and fairs. Some towns did successfully petition for the right to host markets and fairs, but these specific grants were carefully constrained and strictly limited to two or four years, after which they needed to be reviewed and renewed by the burgesses. The town of Suffolk, Virginia, had been granted the right to hold fairs for a few years when, in 1748, the town residents requested that the "Directors of the said Town be enabled to establish such Orders for the better Regulation of the Markets in the said Town as they shall think reasonable." The General Assembly rejected the petition. Marketplace courts, known as "courts of piepowder," had been commonplace in seventeenth-century town legislation, but they no longer fit with the planter gentry's vision for economic regulation. In an effort to place strict boundaries around the power of urban market regulation in the growing town of Baltimore, the Maryland Assembly granted the town commissioners the right to host fairs only on the understanding this not "extend, or be construed to extend, to enable or capacitate the said Commissioners or Inhabitants of the said Town, to elect or choose Delegates or Burgesses." So determined were they on this point that they repeated the provision twice in the finished act. As Baltimore grew into a major port city during the third quarter of the eighteenth century, its governing structure remained strictly under the supervision of the planters in the assembly.[53] Virginia's leaders were even forthright about their intention to limit urban commercial jurisdiction. Imperial officials overturned a number of Virginia town acts from the 1748 assembly, arguing that the towns should instead have received corporate charters from the Crown that would grant them jurisdiction over the local marketplace; but assembly members responded by claiming that there was a "Want of

Persons properly qualify'd to constitute a Corporation" and that "Neither do the People desire a Court of Piepowder" because "their monthly County Courts" were "sufficient to determine their Differences." The planter elite were determined to ensure that the county court remained the primary site for commercial regulation.[54]

Another symbol of urban identity and independence that was notably absent from eighteenth-century plans was common land. Only in a couple of exceptional cases did either assembly allow a town to have a common. In 1736, the inhabitants of Williamsburg requested funds to purchase land, claiming that the lack of common land was "a great Hardship upon the poorer Sort of Inhabitants," but the burgesses refused. The residents of Baltimore encountered the same response from the Maryland Assembly in 1742 and again in 1744. These common spaces were likely only intended as pasture for residents' animals, but their establishment would have reinforced local collective identity and raised questions about jurisdiction. The same principles applied to situations where the common land was a wharf or quayside and thus directly tied to commercial regulation and access to trade. The Virginia burgesses supported Yorktown residents in purchasing common land along the town's quayside, which derived from the provisions of the original town plans from the 1690s, but when Tappahannock citizens sought to establish a similar common ownership over their waterfront, the burgesses rejected the plea. In the most extreme case, in Chestertown, Maryland, the delegates even facilitated the subdivision and privatization of common waterfront land that had been established under an earlier plan.[55]

The planters' lack of interest in public spaces or urban institutions carried over into the physical layout of the spaces themselves. Some of the legislation made provision for public buildings but provided few details on how to site them or pay for their development. These limited instructions led to a proliferation of towns designed on undifferentiated grids with no orientation around public spaces. When planters privately subdivided their property into urban lots, the neglect of public institutions could be even more startling. In 1739, William Meriwether laid out part of his estate in Hanover County, Virginia, as the town of Newcastle, but after the land had been surveyed and the lots sold, he realized that "no Provision was made for Streets." He astutely noted that "if not remedied," the error would "entirely render the carrying on of Business there impractical," and he was forced to advertise in the *Virginia Gazette* to request that lot owners surrender a portion of their property for streets. The contrast with the early years of Jamestown, when public streets had been the highest priority, could not be starker.[56]

Meriwether had inadvertently revealed the underlying logic of the new urban vision. Town lots were now atomistic gateways to a larger Atlantic marketplace that were created, shuffled, and even gambled for by the provincial planter class, rather than shares in a local civic community that mediated commercial exchange. Instead of being governed by distinct urban institutions, the ordering and shuffling of these homogenized town lots was now merely overseen by the neighboring planters as an extension of their civic responsibility for the larger county community.

"PROPER IMMUNITIES AND PRIVILEGES"

Despite this general trend in favor of a strictly limited model of urban development, there were two exceptions during the mid-eighteenth century. The towns of Charlestown, Maryland, and Norfolk, Virginia, received extensive urban privileges. The circumstances surrounding these grants demonstrate the continued resonance of urban civic ideals in the Chesapeake region after generations of debate. Their experiences, though, proved that they were now exceptions in a world in which civic virtue was defined by the planter class.

The distinctive plan of Charlestown in northern Maryland was the product of the unique geopolitical circumstances into which the town was born. Charlestown was established in the early 1740s at the height of renewed tensions between the Calvert and Penn families over the border between Maryland and Pennsylvania. It was located on the North East River in Cecil County, at the heart of the contested border zone. The Maryland Assembly's unambiguous intention was to lure merchants and settlers from Pennsylvania with the promise of "proper Immunities and Privileges" and have them settle around a town that could be clearly identified with Maryland authority. Charlestown received unique authority. It was to consist of five hundred acres (twenty times larger than most of Maryland's other contemporary town grants), including a three-hundred-acre common, and land was to be reserved for public marketplaces and churches. Charlestown inhabitants soon petitioned for and received permission to establish a public wharf and shipyard and to popularly elect town commissioners with the power to regulate the burgeoning grain trade. These exceptional provisions were clearly focused on winning loyalty and trade in the battle with Pennsylvania, and they were likely encouraged by proprietor Charles Calvert (after whom the town was named). Calvert received regular reports about the threat Charlestown posed to Philadelphia merchants and the fact that it would soon be "a thorn in their sides." The Charlestown plan demonstrates that the planter community had not forgotten the arsenal of civic privileges that might aid town development and that these provisions had not lost their potential appeal to would-be town residents. Unless nudged by geopolitics, however, they refused to offer anything like these provisions to other new towns.[57]

The most significant deviation from the planters' established policy was the incorporation of the Borough of Norfolk in 1736. By the mid-1730s, Norfolk was a thriving port town that embodied the Chesapeake's economic diversification. Despite their reluctance to grant self-government elsewhere (besides the provincial capitals that were already firmly under gentry control), the burgesses agreed to a petition from the town's residents requesting incorporation. They did so for a number of reasons. As the petitioners pointed out, the costs of much-needed urban infrastructure were falling upon planters in Norfolk County, and a charter would free rural residents from these expensive commitments. The burgesses were also aware of the large transient population of sailors, servants, and escaped slaves who moved through the growing port town, and they appreciated that a stronger local government might better police this underclass who were outside the bounds of their rural slave system. Leading planters' anxiety had been dramatically escalated just a few years before when enslaved people across the colony had planned an uprising, the epicenter of which had been in the Norfolk area. These actions of the enslaved made establishing tight control over Norfolk critical. Strict regulation of taverns and the establishment of a workhouse became key responsibilities of the corporation that were referenced repeatedly in correspondence between the General Assembly and the borough. Finally, the terms of Norfolk's charter ensured that it would remain as tightly bound to planter interests as possible. The corporation was designed as a closed and self-perpetuating oligarchy without popular elections, and it was stocked with local planter-merchants who had strong ties to the neighboring counties and few connections to Scottish networks. If these men could keep power in their hands, then the elite had less reason to fear Norfolk's political and commercial independence.[58]

As restrictive as the burgesses sought to make it, though, Norfolk's corporate identity inevitably conflicted with their own aspirations for political-economic authority. From the outset, it was clear that the corporation was not beholden to the General Assembly. Although the burgesses initially agreed to the charter, their progress on drafting it ground to a halt when Lieutenant Governor Gooch pointed out that only he, as the Crown's representative, could grant urban charters. Gooch issued the charter, but, mindful to preserve their claim to authority, the House of Burgesses insisted upon drafting an "Act to confirm the Charter of the Borough of Norfolk." The legislation summarized the key provisions of the charter and then merely declared "that the said charter . . . be and are hereby confirmed unto the said borough of Norfolk."[59] Despite this legislative effort, though, direct allegiance to the imperial state still constituted an alternate path to authority for Norfolk's corporate leadership. Over the next two decades, the borough's close relationship with imperial official Robert Dinwiddie demonstrated this fact. Dinwiddie was appointed surveyor general for customs for the southern district of America in 1738 and chose Virginia as a base of operations. He quickly became embroiled in a dispute with the colony's planter leadership, but in the midst of this conflict, the Norfolk corporation made him an honorary burgher, a distinction that he reciprocated by presenting the borough with an official seal. The borough's association with Dinwiddie continued when he advanced to the office of lieutenant governor of Virginia, and he presented the town with a "very handsome silver mace . . . as a Token of his great Regard and Affection for the said Borough." This relationship had the potential to significantly shape the region's commercial structure: Norfolk was engaged in a struggle to relocate the customs office for the southern region of the James River away from the rival port of Hampton, and Dinwiddie potentially had the power to institute this change. In later decades, Norfolk's corporation continued to seek gubernatorial patronage—in 1767, the aldermen greeted the arrival of Governor Botetourt with a formal address that noted, "This infant Borough entirely supported by Commerce, with all humility, craves your Lordships Patronage."[60]

Keenly aware of the potential of this alternative authority, the Virginia House of Burgesses did everything in its power to restrict Norfolk's independence. When, in 1749, the corporation sought authority to expand the boundaries of the borough and survey new streets, the burgesses refused the request. They were not opposed to the expansion of the city's infrastructure, but they insisted that the power to undertake the development be vested in a committee of local planters. Dinwiddie, possibly acting in defense of his client borough, refused to countenance this plan, and the planter gentry were forced into a compromise that granted the corporation authority over the land. However, it was another sixteen years before the House of Burgesses agreed to the corporation's other request to expand their legal jurisdiction over debt suits. The burgesses were also careful to circumscribe every grant of tax-raising powers that the Norfolk corporation received, earmarking its specific purpose and thus ensuring that every time the corporation needed to raise a new levy, it required fresh approval from the provincial gentry.[61]

The common thread running through the exceptional stories of Charlestown and Norfolk was the persistent appeal of civic corporate independence. In both towns, residents, traders, and artisans demonstrated repeatedly that they still valued the ideals of urban self-government and sought to expand their privileges. The planners of Charlestown were particularly keen to emphasize that urban public projects, such as building a municipal shipyard, were "so public a Good." Despite the decline of civic corporatism around the British Atlantic in the eighteenth century, there was still a market for these ideas in the Chesapeake. The region's ruling class, however, were careful to utilize this appeal very selectively. The planter gentry now consciously and deliberately rejected urban political authority and market regulation as a path to civic virtue.[62] The experiences of Norfolk and Charlestown were very much the exceptions that proved, and reinforced, the rule. Being repeatedly confronted by the petitions of the Norfolk burghers probably only served to remind the planter gentry of the dangers of urban commercial authority and the potential power of trading interests and patronage relationships within the wider empire that lay beyond their control.

As economic forces reshaped the region and created new opportunities for town development in the second quarter of the eighteenth century, the broad political-economic questions about urban networks cut from whole cloth had given way to more prosaic questions, such as the width of new streets or whether to keep hogs confined to their pens. Nevertheless, these debates still provided a crucial venue for reinforcing the planter gentry's understanding of their status and authority. They were certainly not opposed to town development or naive about commercial forces and arrangements, and many welcomed the chance to invest and speculate in the expanding world of mercantile exchange. But, as county justices and elected burgesses, these men now saw it as their duty to use their independent private estates and their local offices to maintain the civic virtue that the tobacco trade had always seemed to threaten. Towns were now a necessary evil rather than a positive good.

"[N]O TOWNS OF ANY CONSEQUENCE"

By the 1760s, diversification, territorial expansion, and marketing innovations had transformed Chesapeake society. Cities such as Norfolk and Baltimore stood witness to this reality. Yet the planter gentry clung to authority over this world and continued to espouse the importance of civic virtue. They were now convinced that their private, rural, slave-powered estates provided the safest defense against corruption. Spending every legislative session debating the cases of countless new towns reinforced this country perspective. So when commercial and imperial crisis hit in the 1760s, the ideas deployed against the British Empire were not simply a rhetorical strategy borrowed from English opposition thought. They were at the heart of the Chesapeake elites' understanding of their political-economic status, which had been a century and a half in the making and which finally led them to contemplate revolution.

The fundamental problems with Chesapeake political economy had never gone away. Planters were still reliant on agricultural exports with a small local merchant population, and competition for the best prices was still fierce. The rural gentry ideal had been sustained by the expansion of the economy and credit networks in the first half of the eighteenth century. With rising demand in Europe, Scottish merchants had invested heavily in the store system, and English financiers had loaned to local merchants. While credit was easy, planters could convince themselves that their gentry hierarchy warded off the worst excesses of commercialization and private interest, but the effect was to increase borrowing to the point where the planters' total debt of almost £1.7 million was equal to nearly twice the annual export value of all Chesapeake commodities combined. County oligarchs had refined their ethics of credit in the face of this expansion, becoming increasingly conscious of the dangers of debt but also acutely aware of the honor involved in debt that made it ignoble to challenge a fellow planter's capacity to repay. This system, however, which reinforced the planter elites' civic role within their communities, was undermined by the major financial crises that beset the Atlantic economy during the 1760s and 1770s. By 1764, postwar depression led merchants to begin calling in Chesapeake debts. This shift particularly hurt the larger planters who still consigned their tobacco to English factors and who were already losing out to the expanding Scottish traders in the piedmont.[63]

Faced with this fresh crisis, planters once again reexamined their economy. They focused much of the blame upon merchants and the burgeoning network of towns in which they established their stores. Despite the economic contraction hitting planters, the region's towns and merchant communities were growing. A wave of Scottish storekeepers and factors arrived in the 1760s, and the towns in the grain-producing regions, especially Baltimore, witnessed continued growth through these turbulent economic times, shifting the balance of commercial and political power. Even locally based merchants involved in the wheat trade seemed to have diverging interests from the majority of planters. In Baltimore, the traditional planter-merchants, who had built the town but continued to live on their rural estates, were giving way to a new generation of urban resident merchants. In a scathing critique of the merchant class, one planter oligarch opined that "our being so much incumbered arises wholly from their own Conduct" and that, even with the "strictest Frugality & Œconomy," it was impossible for planters to escape debt.[64]

Using vivid civic rhetoric, planters accused merchants of betraying the common good of the community for their own private ends. "A Planter," writing in the *Virginia Gazette*, insisted that they "neither value you, or your country, any farther than to serve their present wants and purposes; for no sooner are they feathered, than (like birds of migration) they fly away, and laugh at the silly sheep whom they have fleeced." In language rich with references to tyranny, dependence, and bondage, the planters argued that their local capacity to regulate the economy was being undermined by the powerful private interests of merchants.[65] The most egregious example of this came in 1764 when British merchants, angered by Chesapeake planters using county courts to hinder debt collection and control exchange rates, had lobbied Parliament for the Currency Act, which prevented debts from being paid in depreciated colonial paper money and cut off one of the few routes planters had left to lessen the burden of debt in their communities. The Virginia gentry reacted violently to this collusion between merchants and imperial authorities, describing it as "too tyrannical for a free born People." They increasingly came to see imperial authority itself as a threat to their visions of rural civic community.[66]

The planters' response to this threat was not simply an increase in agrarian antagonism in the decade before the American Revolution; it also involved an intertwined effort to once again reimagine the region's political economy. Chesapeake planters in the 1760s returned to the conviction that their dependence upon tobacco agriculture was their cardinal sin, which had allowed merchants to exploit them. The plantation system powered by enslaved labor, they argued, had also made planters lazy and overly fond of luxury. "States that cultivated and improved their commerce," one planter noted, "became respectable in proportion as that succeeded," but the tobacco trade could never deliver these rewards because it was dominated by British merchants and could not "so properly be called the trade of this colony as of Great Britain."⁶⁷

Similar arguments throughout the seventeenth century had inspired planters to embark on new urban development, but the revolutionary generation sought to meet these challenges by extending their agrarian reforms. After 1763, only eight towns received legislative sanction in Virginia (none in Maryland) in the thirteen years before the Revolution, compared to thirty-five over the previous fifteen years. It was not that planters had forgotten the potential advantages of urban development. One essayist writing in the *Virginia Gazette* in 1770 praised the recent towns "judiciously laid out" but then lamented the difficulty of persuading anyone to invest in them. Nonetheless, the author did not even stop to contemplate granting particular commercial privileges to encourage investment. Urban development still seemed essential for commercial and political reasons, but planters were skeptical about being able to safely nurture a commercial community in their midst. The economic development plans they did pursue sought to achieve the same civic ends by "country" means. Some planters began putting these ideas into action by converting more of their fields to wheat and testing out other crops and manufactures, such as hemp, which could be used to make rope. Beyond these private initiatives, the focus was on empowering rural networks of the planter gentry. An essay in the *Virginia Gazette* in 1771 encouraged planters to "all meet at our several court houses" and agree to local regulation of the tobacco trade, pinning hopes on the civic capacity of the rural county community. "Academicus," writing in 1773, praised the establishment of a society dedicated to scientific agriculture in Virginia that would stoke innovation and civil discourse. The author noted that the best "Means of the Association" was "populous Cities, where Men of Genius, from Motives of Amusement and Business, reside together," but because such cities were "a very distant Prospect indeed" for the Chesapeake, the new society would provide an effective rural substitute. Societies for scientific agriculture proliferated across America after the Revolution, laying the foundations of agrarian republicanism, but in Virginia their birth was tied to planters' ongoing efforts to reconcile urban civil discourse with their dispersed and hierarchical rural community.⁶⁸

The planter elite built upon this rural gentry structure when they began to protest British policies through nonimportation agreements. In response to the empire's imposition of the Stamp Act and later the Townshend duties, Chesapeake planters joined the movement to boycott British goods, recognizing that it also provided an effective means to pay down their accumulated debts and stimulate the domestic manufacturing economy. In keeping with their agrarian civic vision for diversification, though, the planter gentry leaned heavily upon their decentralized county communities to administer the nonimportation agreements. County committees were charged with forming local nonimportation associations, relying on local gentry leadership. Furthermore, the vast majority of those who joined were planters. Local merchants of all affiliations in the region's towns (particularly factors for major British merchants) refused to participate. One observer believed that no more than two Norfolk merchants agreed to sign the nonimportation agreement.[69]

When the boycott crumbled in the face of weak enforcement, the planter elite were quick to blame the region's towns. The Fauquier County committee wrote to Peyton Randolph, who was coordinating the Virginia association, to complain that merchants in Dumfries and Falmouth were importing goods in defiance of the agreement. When challenged, they excused themselves by citing "the general example of Fredericksburg, Port Royal, and even Williamsburg itself, where, they say, the association is paid no manner of regard." Prominent Maryland planter Charles Carroll, of Annapolis, suggested that a similar combination of towns along the north shore of the Potomac, "from Portobacco to Geo; Towne," had conspired to undermine the agreement. In both cases, the use of the town names rather than those of specific merchants suggests that the urban communities were perceived to work as coherent political and economic interests. The Fauquier committee noted the contrast between town merchants and the individual traders from elsewhere in their county, who were lauded for their faithfulness to the association. The town merchants were working in "combination" as part of a "premeditated scheme . . . to aid the Parliament of Great-Britain in fixing the yoke of slavery on America." To the planter class, urban association, so long perceived as the safeguard of virtue in a commercial society, now represented a threat to the genuine civic community manifest in the counties.[70]

Antimerchant rhetoric was less pronounced in Maryland, but concern about urban governance still played a part in the evolution of revolutionary protest. The immediate prerevolutionary years witnessed a growing divergence between Maryland and Virginia, owing to the transition to wheat agriculture in much of the northern Chesapeake and the connected rise of the city of Baltimore. From scarcely a few hundred homes at midcentury, Baltimore had almost surpassed Norfolk, Virginia, as the Chesapeake's largest city by 1776. This growing influence made Baltimore's merchant community an important force in provincial politics. Planter leaders who opposed imperial measures established an informal alliance with Baltimore merchants who shared their antipathy to the Stamp Act, but during the protests against the Townshend duties later in the decade, the city's traders were far less enthusiastic than the planters about renewing the boycott on British goods. Although the rift was healed over the next few years as Maryland's revolutionary leadership coalesced, the political status of Baltimore was still a sensitive issue. In 1771, the General Assembly sought to address what it described as "dishonorable unmanly and deceitful Dispositions" practiced by Baltimore's millers and merchants, and, rather than empowering the city's commissioners to regulate their own market, the planter representatives themselves passed a set of regulations to be imposed upon the city. Concerns about Baltimore's influence were still present in 1776, when Maryland's revolutionary leadership forged a new constitution that granted Baltimore representation in the state legislature but permanently restricted it to two delegates—half of the voting power granted to each of the state's counties.[71]

Burgesses in Virginia went further than their neighbors to the north in seeking ways to restrict the authority and independence of towns in the prerevolutionary years. Although the planter elite had long enjoyed a cordial relationship with the corporation of Williamsburg, which was composed of members of prominent planter families, during the late 1760s, they came to see the commercial deals of the merchant community and the settling of debts that took place in the capital city as a threat to their county authority. Of particular concern was the right of the Hustings Court in Williamsburg to hear cases in chancery and common law that arose anywhere within the province. This charter provision allowed merchants to sue in Williamsburg for debts contracted anywhere in the colony and receive justice more quickly than might have been possible in the debtor's county court. This privilege dated back to the 1730s, and planters had long had concerns about it, as suggested by their repeated refusal to extend a similar privilege to the Borough of Norfolk. In 1769, faced with rising debt and concerns about control over trade, the burgesses rescinded the privilege and reduced Williamsburg's jurisdiction to cases arising within the city. This decision was ultimately overturned in London, as the Board of Trade concluded that the city's authority was "highly useful to the Trade of this Kingdom," but the reversal only further underscored the fact that the Chesapeake's cities were serving the interests of the broader commercial empire rather than the local planter community.[72]

By comparison with Norfolk, however, Williamsburg got off lightly.

Over the course of the revolutionary protests, the borough at the mouth of the Chesapeake Bay came to represent to Virginia's planter leadership the apogee of imperial-commercial collusion and self-interest that they sought to throw off. Norfolk's corporate leaders initially played an active role in the resistance to the Stamp Act and naval impressment during the mid-1760s. However, corporate officials were always careful to insist that they were defending the rights of the borough, defining themselves as members of one of the "large commercial towns of this continent" and not as citizens of the planter commonwealth of Virginia. They became increasingly concerned that the nonimportation associations managed by the planter gentry undermined the borough's "opportunity to regulate their trade," which was the ultimate purpose of their corporate existence. For their part, planters became convinced that Norfolk's Scottish merchants were betraying the interests of the colony by breaking nonimportation agreements. They became even more embittered against the borough in 1775 over its negotiations with the royal governor, the Earl of Dunmore, who had fled Williamsburg and was patrolling the Chesapeake Bay with a naval fleet. The corporation's negotiations with Dunmore led Richard Henry Lee to suggest that Norfolk was not sufficiently committed to the revolutionary cause. It was, he claimed, merely a "nest of Tories." Provincial militias that had amassed in Williamsburg marched toward Norfolk to prevent it from falling into Dunmore's hands. Faced with this threat, the corporation petitioned Dunmore for his assistance. By obliging, Dunmore effectively sealed Norfolk's fate, making it the front line in the first major military engagement of the Revolution in Virginia. After losing a skirmish with the Virginia forces in December 1775, Dunmore was forced to withdraw to his ships, and the Virginia militia torched the entire town to keep it out of loyalist hands. Long before the Declaration of Independence was signed, in their first major military action, Virginians decimated their largest city.[73]

The charred remains of Norfolk were a testament to decades of conflict over political economy in the region. The character and status of the Chesapeake's largest urban center had become a flashpoint in the revolutionary Chesapeake because it was—as the urban question had always been—a local manifestation of the debate about what constituted the common good of the colony and the empire and how the economy should be regulated to achieve it. As imperial officials and merchants in the metropolis moved to assert greater control in the 1760s, the planter elite looked with growing suspicion at the towns in their midst and the distinct networks of interests that they represented. They now saw these communities as the sites of informal "combinations" of factors and outsiders that owed their loyalty to a larger imperial commercial world. The Chesapeake planter class had always adapted and reinforced their claims to authority in new imperial and commercial circumstances through debate over urban development, and in this culminating imperial crisis, they fully embraced a country version of civic virtue by painting their region's towns as the ultimate symbols of private interest in contrast with their own rural virtue. The reversal from the era of Sir Edwin Sandys was complete.

∴

In his *Notes on the State of Virginia*, Thomas Jefferson observed that his home state had "no towns of any consequence." Yet any cursory glance at a contemporary map or a merchant's letter book by the time of the American Revolution revealed a very different picture of the Chesapeake, pockmarked with growing urban centers, such as Alexandria, Georgetown, and Petersburg, and anchored in the two major Atlantic port cities of Norfolk and Baltimore. The fact that Jefferson still believed these towns to be inconsequential was a product of careful efforts to keep them so. The planter elite now justified their rural hegemony by claiming that it was capable of providing the civic safeguards against corrupting commerce that had always seemed so elusive in the Chesapeake. For a variety of reasons (some of the planters' own making), towns and cities rapidly took shape across the region during the mid-eighteenth century, but provincial politicians now sought to restrict a process that their fathers and grandfathers had desperately sought to stimulate. Through these decades, therefore, as wharves and warehouses were built in growing towns, planters were also constructing an alternative, rural civic vision that was as much a product of bitter experience as it was of ideas imported from Europe.[74]

The plantation system in the Chesapeake had grown in dialogue with the urban idea. Planters had revered, resisted, and replicated the role of the urban community as a mediator between civic society and the commercial world, even as that role was being challenged by urban growth and class dynamics elsewhere around the Atlantic world. In other British plantation regions, large cities, such as Charleston and Kingston, did grow, and these unincorporated communities became more economically, socially, and racially diverse. They became typical eighteenth-century British Atlantic cities with a distinct middling class who challenged the status of the planters. The planter elite in the Chesapeake resisted these innovations. They retained direct control over urban space, and when prosperity in Norfolk made similar developments likely, they sought to constrain them within an oligarchic corporate structure. Significantly, though, in these other plantation regions, elites exhibited far fewer concerns about the relationship between commerce, slavery, and the development of civic society. It was in the city-obsessed region of the Chesapeake where planters most fully embraced classical republican and country thought during the revolutionary era as they continued to struggle to legitimize their authority over a capitalist agricultural society.[75]

Ultimately, despite their confidence in their rural civic virtue, the eighteenth-century planter gentry proved no more successful than their forefathers at stabilizing the Chesapeake economy. The shortcomings of their short-lived vision were exposed by the economic crises of the 1760s, and angry planters struck out at the towns in their midst as the most potent symbols of the oppression of imperial political economy. However, the planters of this era also came to recognize the same fundamental fact that their predecessors throughout the seventeenth century had appreciated: that tobacco monoculture could not be the basis for a stable economic or political order. This realization led them to break the bonds of empire that had constrained their political-economic vision. In the first decades of the new nation, Chesapeake planters revived urban development, but their two-century-long struggle with town building would still inform the way they understood the relationship between political and commercial power.

Epilogue: "This little Common wealth"

Having inaugurated their campaign against the British Empire by burning their largest city, Virginia's revolutionary planter class made a seemingly curious decision three years later: they established two new urban corporations. The creation of the corporate cities of Alexandria and Winchester was quickly followed by grants of corporate status to Fredericksburg, Yorktown, Petersburg, and Richmond all within four years. Maryland's new state government also debated the status of the booming city of Baltimore. These were the first major expansions of urban jurisdiction in the Chesapeake in forty years. This abrupt volte-face was a powerful reminder that the city as a civic institution remained crucial to the way Chesapeake planters thought about political economy. During the 1780s, as they sought to define their place within the new nation and the transformed Atlantic economy, they engaged in a renewed debate about towns and cities that rehashed, in a transformed political context, many of the questions about urban development, identity, and authority that had occupied them since 1607.

Having thrown off British imperial authority, the Chesapeake debate over urban space was now played out on the state level, but it still drove to the heart of the region's political-economic structure. Independence had cut the region off from markets in other parts of the British Empire while doing little to combat the British merchants' dominance in the tobacco trade, leading to severe economic depression and raising political-economic questions about the new nation's relationship to the Atlantic economy. During the 1780s, politicians throughout the United States debated whether the solution to these problems lay in opening the nation up to free trade to stimulate European demand or whether the states should embrace a neomercantilist policy designed to directly restrict British trade and support domestic merchants and manufacturers. Scholars have focused on the broad intellectual underpinnings of these positions and the ways they spurred inter- and intrastate rivalry in the new nation. Within the Chesapeake, and especially in Virginia, however, planters concretized these broad policy positions by renewing traditional debates over urban spaces. Chesapeake planters continued to believe that urban communities and institutional structures could shape how their states integrated with the postrevolutionary American economy. Their return to urban development and debate in the 1780s informed the way that nascent ideas about agrarian republicanism became reconciled with the plantation system.[1]

For members of the Chesapeake planter gentry, revolution against the British Crown had also promised the opportunity to throw off the tyrannical control of British merchants in the region's small towns. When these British factors were forced out of the Chesapeake at the outbreak of hostilities and the region's trade was thrown open to the commerce of the world, some leaders believed they would be able to liberalize the market, bringing in a diverse array of foreign and domestic merchants. Thomas Jefferson famously projected that the natural bounty of the Chesapeake, liberated from the British mercantile system, would support a flourishing agrarian society without the entanglements of trading restrictions and debts. With its many rivers penetrating westward toward the mountains, and particularly the Potomac that seemed destined to be the main conduit into the interior, the region appeared poised for economic transformation.[2] The chastening experience of the war and postwar years, though, complicated these ideals. Direct trade with continental Europe failed to materialize, so competition remained limited. Some planters endeavored to fill the commercial vacuum. For example, Richard Adams proposed to establish trading companies of "Principal Gentlemen," to assert local control over the export of the region's goods. Most of the Chesapeake elite, though, were struggling with wartime taxes, depressed tobacco prices, and the loss of many enslaved laborers who escaped to the British. They lacked the capital to set up as merchants. During the 1780s, a significant portion of the tobacco trade was redirected to Philadelphia merchants without addressing the centuries-old problem of commerce on the tobacco coast itself. After the Peace of Paris in 1783, planters faced the even more galling proposition of a renewed British stranglehold over the Chesapeake tobacco trade. To make matters worse, the protests of poor and middling planters against wartime economic conditions weakened the traditional gentry grip on county-level authority and presaged the emergence of an egalitarian vision of a yeoman farmer republic. All of these factors chipped away at the planter gentry's capacity to regulate the local market and legitimize their civic leadership.[3]

Faced with these profound challenges to their political and economic system, Chesapeake planters once again turned to the establishment and reorganization of urban spaces. The rise of small towns in the region in the mid-eighteenth century meant that the Chesapeake now had an urban network, and in Baltimore it boasted a legitimate metropolis. Nonetheless, establishing more towns became an immediate priority. Virginia's new state government made legislative provisions for the establishment of fifty-two new towns between 1776 and 1788, a notable departure from the slow pace of town establishment during the previous two decades of imperial tension. Some of these new towns lay far to the west in Kentucky, reflecting Virginian aspirations to lead the western expansion of the new nation. However, a significant number, such as Kempsville in Princess Anne County and Kinsale in Westmoreland County, were established in long-settled tidewater regions. The sudden burst of activity was clearly aimed at encouraging domestic merchants and artisans by expanding the network of small towns.[4] Even more significant than establishing new towns was the drive to endow existing urban centers with greater control over the local market. George Washington, who was a particularly vocal proponent of commercial development of the Potomac valley as the primary gateway to the trans-Appalachian west, sought to spur the development of Alexandria. He argued that the problem for the young port city was that it consisted only of "small dealers" who effectively continued to operate as factors for major British merchant houses. Planters across the region were therefore "in a manner driven" to these large external merchant networks based in Philadelphia and Baltimore because local towns lacked independent merchants who possessed both common interests with the neighboring planter community and sufficient capital to invest in "large whole-sale Stores." In order to rectify this situation, Washington worked tirelessly to promote improved navigation along the Potomac that would allow local merchants to grow their operations, and he also played a role in expanding access to commercial banking in northern Virginia. The ultimate symbol of Virginians' ambition for the Potomac, of course, would be the new federal capital of Washington, DC, which George Washington helped locate along the river in 1790. The Virginian president was committed to the idea that the city would be a commercial entrepôt as well as a political hub for the nation as it expanded westward.[5]

These efforts clearly reflected increasingly sophisticated attitudes toward banking and commercial infrastructure, yet they also relied upon the revival of older civic corporate ideals. Alongside private initiatives in Alexandria, the General Assembly also incorporated the town in 1779, under the leadership of a mayor, recorder, four aldermen, and six common councillors. As "a body corporate and politick," Alexandria received the right to invest in land and pursue improvement projects for the common good, such as jails, workhouses, and marketplaces. Its leaders received wide-ranging legal jurisdiction and the power to draft their own bylaws. The legislation encouraged the town residents to envision themselves as a civic community under the title of the "commonalty of the town of Alexandria" rather than merely as the representatives of individual property holders in a municipal space. Alexandria's powers were strikingly similar to the traditional corporate authority granted to the Borough of Norfolk forty years earlier, emphasizing the potential for incorporation to facilitate public regulation of commodities and labor. Although planters had been deeply suspicious of Norfolk as a corporate borough chartered by the royal governor, a majority of the legislators were now prepared to charter their own corporate communities directly dependent upon the sovereignty of the state government. In keeping with the republican principles of the new nation, corporate officers were to be annually elected instead of serving for life as a perpetual closed oligarchy. Nonetheless, civic assumptions still underpinned the perception that stable urban corporate communities would serve the common good of Chesapeake society in the postrevolutionary Atlantic economy, by regulating prices and collectively raising capital for public projects.[6]

The civic corporate principles behind Alexandria's charter became even clearer over the next few years. Alexandria and Winchester were joined by Richmond, Petersburg, Yorktown, and Fredericksburg in the ranks of Virginia's new incorporated towns. In the new nation, only Massachusetts, which had an even richer early seventeenth-century heritage of urban civic ideology, was more proactive in incorporating towns and cities.[7] Fredericksburg's corporation provides the clearest example of the assertion of civic identity. The General Assembly's initial charter for Fredericksburg, issued in 1781, was practically identical to those granted to Alexandria and Winchester, but the following year, the state's delegates received a petition from the "Mayor and commonality" of Fredericksburg requesting expanded corporate authority. They hoped to enlarge the town boundaries to one square mile in order to encompass "some ill disposed persons" who had "already set themselves down Just without the present limits to carry on those bad practices" of avoiding local market regulation. Furthermore, they sought permission to levy taxes in order to maintain public buildings and wharf facilities. Granting their urban community these expansive powers would, they claimed, be "for the better government of this little *Common wealth* and consistent with the true policy of the State." The General Assembly agreed to the expansion of the city's limits, but they balked at granting corporate authority to levy imposts. Nonetheless, the Fredericksburg petition demonstrated the renewed faith in the "little Common wealth" of the corporate borough, as the best way of regulating local political economy within a new world of postindependence free trade.[8]

No new urban corporations were established in Maryland during the 1780s, but the state's only existing corporate town did reinforce and reinvigorate its authority. Annapolis had already undergone an urban political renaissance when revolutionary leader and city resident Samuel Chase had campaigned for more assertive corporate governance in the city during the late 1760s. It made sense, therefore, that the corporate borough would be seen as the key agent in helping the city recover from the disruption of war and compete with the growing dominance of Baltimore. In the aftermath of the war, the corporation embarked on a number of ambitious public projects, such as erecting a new market house and a public wharf.[9] The Maryland Assembly also repeatedly offered to incorporate Baltimore in the early 1780s, but in keeping with the planters' commitment to traditional civic corporate structures, the proposals were "organised like other old corporations" and were consequently opposed by the growing population of artisans and small merchants in Maryland's metropolis, who feared being excluded from the city's government.[10]

The apogee of efforts to use port towns to maintain civic order over the world of liberalized trade came in 1784, with a Virginia scheme to centralize commerce through port towns. James Madison, serving as head of the Virginia General Assembly's committee on commerce, took the lead in drafting the proposal, initially planning to make Norfolk "the only port of entry and clearance" for the state. This was a bold scheme because the city was only just recovering from its destruction at the hands of the patriot army.[11] Madison, though, hoped to use the borough as the basis for a new system of state regulation in a plan starkly reminiscent of the hopes of Chesapeake urban planners in the seventeenth century. As he later explained to Jefferson, his vision was to force all goods to be unloaded in Norfolk, thereby separating the Atlantic wholesale trade from the local intrastate retail trade and helping to cultivate a diverse mercantile world anchored in the borough. Madison believed that this restructuring would make it easier for domestic merchants to compete against British traders for the pared-down wholesale trade and would force all crop transactions and credit arrangements on the local retail side to be negotiated in Norfolk's regulated marketplace. Madison consistently lamented that his fellow planters did not understand the crucial "utility of establishing a Philad[elphi]a. or a Baltimore among ourselves." Scholars have struggled to make sense of Madison's scheme because it does not appear to fit within the framework of either liberal free-trade policies or a neomercantilist embrace of American protectionism. He was fiercely critical of proposed amendments that would exempt Virginia-based merchants from the restrictions, suggesting that he was not strictly mercantilist in his goals, but he also decried those who believed "that trade ought in all cases to be left to regulate itself." In fact, to understand Madison's position, we must see it as a more sophisticated resurgence of the corporate civic humanist solution to the planters' dilemma that stretched back to the thinking of Sir Edwin Sandys, emphasizing the civic-minded self-regulation of a well-capitalized local merchant community, only now under the patronage of the republican state rather than the Crown. Restricting all trade to selected ports was intended to bring it under the supervision of local civic communities that would act to check the worst excesses of merchants without establishing draconian state regulations.[12]

However, Madison's plan and the whole wave of urban incorporations quickly encountered opposition. Predictably, the state's other regions and towns immediately protested the restrictions, and Madison was forced to expand the number of designated wholesale port cities to five: Norfolk, Alexandria, Yorktown, Tappahannock, and Bermuda, just below the falls of the James. Even so, anxious petitions soon followed from other neglected towns and regions, including Fredericksburg and Petersburg. Critics also insisted that ships owned entirely by Virginians should be exempt from the provisions—a mercantilist restriction that Madison believed "departs from its [the act's] principle" but which was "a necessary concession to prevailing sentiments." One final amendment specified that the designated export cities would be charged with collecting duties, thereby reducing the need for land taxes on farmers. These changes to Madison's original plan were enough to narrowly win passage of the act by sixty-four votes to fifty-eight, but they undercut the particular civic responsibilities of corporate boroughs, reducing the cities to the status of mere revenue collection sites for the state. Neutered in this way, the legislation took effect in 1786, but it still met with continued resistance and Madison's attention had turned to a bolder solution to the economic crisis, which he would pursue at the constitutional convention the following summer. Just as Madison was returning from Philadelphia in October 1787, the act was repealed.[13]

Resistance to urban institutions and regulation was rooted in two distinct sets of ideas about commerce and the state in the new republic. First, the hostility was a product of new republican resistance to any special privileges or restrictions on free trade. This critique was built upon the vocal opposition to corporate privileges articulated by the thinkers of the Scottish Enlightenment, such as David Hume and Adam Smith, who saw them as inefficient and an infringement upon individual rights. Efforts to incorporate urban communities across the new nation, including in Philadelphia and Boston, faced opposition on the grounds that oligarchic corporate charters were cover for efforts to reestablish aristocracy and restrict the rights of ordinary townspeople. Opponents of the plan to incorporate Philadelphia argued that granting privileges to particular cities was "repugnant to the genius and spirit of our constitution" and a "manifest abridgement of . . . our rights and possessions." The mechanics of Baltimore reflected this discourse. They objected to the efforts of the Maryland Assembly to impose an oligarchic corporate charter on the city, arguing that it was the effort of "a *few persons* to steal a corporation upon the town, which is to affect the liberty and property" of the city's eight thousand citizens.[14]

Outside the towns and cities themselves, new urban corporations conflicted with the ethos of agrarian republicanism that valorized the independent yeoman farmer who traded his produce freely without the entanglements of particular commercial privileges and credit networks. This vision borrowed from the ideas of the contemporary French physiocrats, who argued that all true economic value derived from land and that urban institutions did little but hinder the efficiency of individual farmers. These ideas were, of course, most famously articulated by Thomas Jefferson, who envisioned small independent farmers as the foundation of the nation's future. In his *Notes on the State of Virginia*, Jefferson argued that the Chesapeake's rurality was a product of its natural bounty, which made it ideally suited for building an egalitarian agrarian society unencumbered by cities and towns. While he had initially supported Madison's port plan, Jefferson had done so to help raise revenues for the state and thereby reduce burdens on the small-farmer class. The plans that he himself developed through the 1780s to address the imbalance in Virginia's commerce rejected Madison's reliance on urban regulation. Jefferson hoped to strip away particular local privileges for individuals and corporate communities by negotiating a liberalized tobacco trade with France that would allow individual planters to cut out merchants and commercial middlemen. Part of the resistance to the new wave of urban development, then, was rooted in a new liberal republican vision of free trade and yeoman independence.[15]

Second, though, the debate over new urban institutions also drew upon the planter elite's early eighteenth-century commitment to a rural vision of civic order. The most vocal critic of the effort to reinvigorate urban corporate governance was Fairfax County planter and prominent Virginia revolutionary George Mason. Mason is famous for his strident republicanism and his commitment to natural rights, but he was also one of Virginia's wealthiest planters, who retained a profound suspicion of urban development rooted in the region's long struggle over civic authority. As early as 1782, Mason began expressing grave concerns about the corporation of Alexandria, which lay just upriver from his Gunston Hall plantation. His criticism increased dramatically after the passage of Madison's port plan. Mason was particularly concerned that the legitimacy and virtue of the county court, the bedrock of Virginia's planter society, was being compromised by the overlapping presence of new corporate officers. When Alexandria officials were allowed to also serve as county justices, their "private Interest, instead of being connected, as it ought to be, will frequently be contrasted with that of the People." Corporate towns, Mason argued, could not be expected to promote civic virtue and certainly could not be trusted to regulate commerce, because unlike the county oligarchs, they "have not that common Interest and fellow-feeling with the People of the County, so indispensibly necessary to produce Attention, Moderation, and Frugality."[16]

For Mason, the common interest that corporate officers lacked was rooted in two characteristics of the planter elite. First, each planter was bound to a plantation, which defined his status in the market and the local community by "the natural advantages accruing from the situation of his estate." His status as a trader relied upon the natural convenience of the river frontage of his estate. It was therefore inherent and stable, and not dependent on artificial state privileges. Plans to centralize trade in corporate towns compromised the God-given role of large planters with prime riverside estates as mediators between the Atlantic economy and the local community. This theory was built upon the new physiocratic conception that all value lay in land and hence all commercial order should be derived from the particular qualities of the land, but instead of supporting an egalitarian agrarian republic, Mason marshaled these ideas to reinforce the position of a planter elite to hold the most naturally advantageous estates. Rather than articulating an agrarian ideal that landownership liberated individuals to engage in free trade, Mason echoed the argument of planters through the mid-eighteenth century that their private wharves made them natural civic leaders within the Atlantic marketplace.[17]

The second key feature of planters' estates that Mason suggested made them more reflective of the common interest than corporate towns was their labor force. Towns, Mason argued, were reservoirs of "Idleness, Ease and Plenty," where labor was wasted. Again echoing the physiocrats, he rejected the idea that labor could be productive in any sphere other than agriculture, and he was particularly critical of the erection of a workhouse for the county poor in Alexandria, "where such of the Poor [resident there] as are able to earn their Living or Part of it, by their Labour, are without Employment, for Want of Ground." The large planters, by contrast, were dependent upon enslaved labor and thus had a shared interest in reducing the tax burden on productive agricultural labor, which Mason believed was in the interest of the whole community. "The Inhabitants of the Town generally having very few Tytheables," Mason wrote, "particepate little in the Burdens they lay upon others." The main source of tithables on rural estates was, of course, enslaved laborers. Small independent farmers therefore also had few tithables compared to their slave-owning neighbors, but according to Mason, large planters in the county court, precisely because of their many enslaved tithables, were the guarantors of orderly labor that served the interest of the whole community. Despite the fact that Mason had well-documented misgivings about slavery and its effect on Virginia's economy, he nonetheless saw the slaveholding planter as the defender of the common good against the private interests of the corporate town.[18]

Mason fully articulated his rationale in 1789 when he led a new campaign to have the Fairfax County courthouse removed from Alexandria to a new site in the center of the county, away from the "notorious unfitness, and partiality of Town Jurys." Mason drafted a petition to the General Assembly claiming that "Country Gentlemen, and Reputable Farmers and planters" were deprived of justice in the town, and he collected 558 signatures of men who claimed to speak "in behalf of themselves, and other Inhabitants of the County." When Alexandria's leaders drafted their own counterpetition that attracted more than one thousand signers, Mason cried foul. His petition, he claimed, was signed by "the principal Gentlemen of the County," and although "the Alexandrians boast that they have a great many more *Names*," he alleged that they had been amassed by making what he termed "Threats" and "Promises" to the county population; although these signatures were likely a reflection of many county residents' recognition of the town's importance in their commercial lives, for Mason that merely proved its corrupting influence. Furthermore, he claimed that the town petition was also padded out with the signatures of "a great Number of Sailors, & other Itinerant People," who, he implied, had no status in the county community. His commitment to the voice of the yeoman farmer only extended as far as his neighbors were prepared to accede to his leadership. Mason's argument was that the bonds of interest that allowed leaders to speak for the community's common good were those between local county oligarchs and the mass of ordinary farmers, which were predicated upon landownership and a shared stake in enslaved labor, rather than those fostered by corporate towns that linked and reconciled competing interests in Atlantic commerce.[19]

Ultimately, Mason's crusade against the revival of the corporate town was an assertion of the planter's role as the lynchpin of a county-based civic structure for the new agrarian republic. Mason had been a leading proponent of reforming Virginia's economy away from tobacco and slavery during the 1760s, and he was careful to note that he was not opposed to all commerce and wished "to promote the honest Interest, and real Prosperity of the Town of Alexandria." However, he argued that planter control through the county community and the state legislature was the only means to "prevent the apprehended Evils, and promote the Good of the Community at large, without injuring, or affecting the Interest of a growing Town."[20] In a 1786 broadside against the port act, he urged that planters find an alternative solution to the problems of economic dependence. He hoped for personal reformation on the part of his fellow planters, who were to make "honest payment of our debts" as an example for the community. Mason pinned his hopes for reforming the political economy of plantation society upon the virtues of planters and the natural endowments of their sizable estates and enslaved labor forces. In doing so, he combined the new vision of agrarian republicanism and the theories of the physiocrats with the long-standing planter civic vision that had emerged over two centuries of battles over urban development and plantation agriculture.[21]

As he repeatedly reminded his readers, Mason was not alone in expressing these sentiments. He consciously crafted a popular alliance to undermine urban institutional development. In addition to the hundreds of men in Fairfax County who signed Mason's petitions, there were also challenges to the status of Petersburg, Winchester, and Fredericksburg. This opposition reached a crescendo in the election of 1787. Delegates committed to debt relief and paper money were swept into power. Mason was opposed to these debtor schemes, and he worked to subvert them through the session, but at the same time, he marshaled the support of the new General Assembly to repeal Madison's port act and to pass an act "for regulating the rights of cities, towns, and boroughs, and the jurisdiction of corporation courts." The new legislation barred corporate officers from serving as county justices, limited the jurisdiction of town courts to cases arising both "between the respective inhabitants" and within the bounds of the town, and prevented residents of enfranchised boroughs from voting in county elections. Implementation of these new rules led to a vicious battle in Norfolk, where town-based county justices refused to resign their positions and squared off against the community of rural planters. A local petition railed against the men who had "formerly Belonged to the County, but have Since [de facto] withdrawn themselves from it" through their loyalty to the corporation. The corporation and county of Norfolk had (tensely) coexisted for more than fifty years as overlapping forms of jurisdiction and community, but in the planters' republic, they were becoming mutually exclusive local authorities. Mason had maneuvered to ensure that the popular clamor for debt relief was combined with the traditional authority of the region's more conservative planter elites, to ensure that corporations now appeared to be a fundamental threat to county communities and rural civic virtue.[22]

The ultimate result of the urban debate in Virginia during the 1780s was to definitively reinforce the perception of towns and cities as distinct and potentially disruptive interests that the planter republic needed to contain. The 1787 legislation prohibiting corporate officers from serving in county courts began a process of constitutionally separating Virginia's cities from their hinterlands, giving them separate but limited authority. Instead of empowering urban spaces, this reduced them to minor administrative units subsumed within the structure of the republican state, under the authority of a Richmond elite that retained close ties to major planter families.[23] Although the importance of urban centers to the economic future of the young republic was clear, their political influence was quarantined within their own attenuated spheres. As merely divisions within a unitary republican state, cities were endowed with the authority to maintain civil order in their atypically heterogeneous communities but not with an independent jurisdictional authority over commerce or common property. Virginia continued to create corporations—for municipalities, public works, and businesses—in the nineteenth century, but they were carefully controlled and circumscribed by the state's narrow governing clique. This theoretically shielded the world of independent yeoman farmers from the corrupting dependence on urban networks, but it also effectively reinforced the elites' hegemonic claims to virtuous regulation of the local economy.[24]

The Chesapeake's towns and cities ultimately paid a price for this quarantining of urban authority within the planters' world. In the early republic, Virginia's cities stagnated under the limited independent status imposed on them. Baltimore, which eventually did establish a powerful corporate government in 1796, thrived, but investment in Richmond and Norfolk stalled. The gradual decline in the Chesapeake region's tobacco economy played a role, but economic factors alone cannot explain the cities' sluggish growth—especially as historical geographers have argued that the transition away from tobacco stimulated urbanization. Politically and culturally quarantined from its surrounding hinterlands, Virginia's new capital of Richmond particularly struggled to recruit corporate officers or raise money for public infrastructure and improvement projects during the early nineteenth century. Even Washington, DC, which Virginians such as George Washington had projected as a bustling commercial city, remained a backwater; it was jurisdictionally confined by the federal district and limited to the status of a local social hub for tidewater planters. In fact, all of Virginia's largest towns were among the slowest growing in the nation in the early nineteenth century.[25]

Faced with the challenges of charting a commercial future for their new republican society, Chesapeake leaders had once again thought with towns. To some, new urban spaces and institutions drew upon a rich civic corporate heritage and seemed to again offer a way to encourage local economic development that would go hand in hand with civic-minded regulation of the region's commerce. However, these developments catalyzed a debate about where, how, and under whose authority economic regulation should occur in the planters' republic. More than particular issues that flared during these years of economic depression, such as debt relief and paper money, the dispute over urban spaces played a critical role in shaping and legitimizing the institutional infrastructure of the region's postindependence economy. It provided a crucial space for men such as George Mason to reframe the ideal of rural civic leadership, combining prerevolutionary country thought with the new physiocratic and agrarian republican ideas. They thereby reconciled their political-economic outlook, forged through decades of urban debates, with the ideas of the new nation. This was part of an effort to reinvigorate the Chesapeake economy and empower ordinary farmers while maintaining the planters' claims to local authority over the market. Ultimately, though, it laid the foundation for a republican planter political economy that combined rural capitalism with agrarian conservatism.²⁶

:::

The postrevolutionary moment of introspection and crisis in the Chesapeake provides a fitting end point for this study. Much had changed in the region with independence, yet the debate over towns and cities retained its potency. This book has demonstrated that the continuing relevance of urban plans should not be a surprise. Conflicting ideas about urban development had persisted over nearly two centuries, as the plantation economy and the British Empire emerged and changed. They had been critical to the way Chesapeake planters had shaped their place within these systems. By charting this persistence, this study makes several arguments about the colonial Chesapeake and the emergence of the plantation system in the British Atlantic empire.

The persistence of urban debate in the face of shifting circumstances after the Revolution underlines the fact that environmental and economic factors alone cannot explain the lack of towns and cities along the tobacco coast. Scholars going all the way back to Thomas Jefferson have contended that the region's many rivers and its dependence upon tobacco prevented urban development and that only the transition to wheat farming in the eighteenth century encouraged the growth of towns and cities. Yet, throughout the twists and turns of the Chesapeake economy, during eras when economic diversification was pursued with varying degrees of success, and even once the transition to wheat production and western settlement began in earnest in the mid-eighteenth century, planters in the region regarded the development of towns as a critical issue. Urban spaces were shaped by people, not simply by commodities or geography. Their limited development in the Chesapeake was far from inevitable, and their relative significance at different moments in different parts of the region —and of the British plantation world more generally—was part of the process of consciously crafting plantation political economy.²⁷

Equally, the fact that the Chesapeake's negotiation over urbanization extended beyond the American Revolution attests that it cannot be explained as a simple center-periphery debate within the British Empire over mercantilism. Some scholars have seen the lack of towns as a symptom of a rigid British policy that nixed proposals for colonial development and forced the periphery to produce raw materials for metropolitan industrialization. In reality, though, mercantilism was never a simple and coherent set of policy positions propounded by authorities in London; rather, it was a complex, contradictory, and evolving set of theories and ideas. At no point did imperial officials purposefully pursue a policy of discouraging or restricting all efforts at urban development in the plantation colonies.[28]

In the place of a monolithic mercantilism, this study has sought to reconstruct the multiple, overlapping institutional structures and sources of sovereignty that existed in the English Atlantic, of which towns and cities were a particularly critical variant in the crafting of commercial policy.[29] More than simply collections of buildings or agglomerations of commercial functions, urban spaces were distinct civic communities, often with a corporate identity. They were part of the patchwork of structures that included county courts, Crown offices, joint-stock companies, and manorial lordships, all of which claimed different shares of authority. Among these various sources of sovereignty, urban communities were especially crucial to commercial empire because they were charged with reconciling economic expansion with the civic humanist focus on virtue and the common good. Assumptions about what this process of reconciliation entailed and how it related to other claims to authority on the part of planters, merchant companies, and the imperial state did not remain static, but neither did they simply dissolve into an imperial leviathan: everyone involved in Atlantic commerce continued to recognize that certain kinds of urban spaces created certain kinds of commercial authority, which could shape the economy around different definitions of the common good. Economic regulation was therefore the result of perpetual negotiation, and urban spaces and institutions were essential to establishing how and where restrictions and incentives would be deployed. Factions that combined colonists, merchants, and officials formed conflicting alliances in response to these questions, advocating towns and cities with distinctive relationships to the empire and the Atlantic economy. The nature of Britain's commercial empire was defined by these contests over political and legal geography. The fact that this process in the Chesapeake resulted in anemic urban development until the mid-eighteenth century while other colonies, including other plantation colonies, developed bustling towns can elucidate the precise ways in which imperial authority and Atlantic commerce intersected in this particular region to create a plantation system built around a rural civic structure.

By understanding the way in which Chesapeake political economy was debated through urban development, we can also better understand the complex and often seemingly contradictory morass of political ideas that managed to coexist in early America. Ideas about economic growth and the individualistic pursuit of improvement projects can be traced back to the early seventeenth century, but equally, civic humanist principles that emphasized virtue and the common good over private profit have long been recognized as critical to revolutionary and postrevolutionary thought. Exploring the distinct institutional spaces that chafed against each other in the English/British Empire, and the political-economic paths not taken, illuminates how these different strains of thought could be held in tension. The imperial state did not relate to the emerging market economy in just one way; instead, it operated through many different projects, institutions, and policies, offering a variety of mechanisms for encouraging private investment while promising to constrain and check the dangerous impulses of those private interests—hence, why the English Commonwealth state in the early 1650s could push for state regulation through the Navigation Act while also promoting the establishment of corporate communities or why the planter elite of mid-eighteenth-century Virginia saw no conflict between investing in urban land and simultaneously claiming to be the guardians of their county communities against merchant influence. These multifaceted and multisited local discourses demonstrate that no straightforward ideological position was simply imported to the Chesapeake region in tracts and pamphlets. Ideas about political authority and political economy were primarily generated in the process of ironing out the tensions and contradictions between overlapping jurisdictions that the empire projected into the Atlantic world. It was not until after the American Revolution, in the construction of a unitary republican state, that the variable statuses of institutions and political spaces became completely incompatible with the authority of the planters' republic.[30]

Ultimately, this book explains the way in which, in the Chesapeake, capitalism, the state, and the plantation complex were born together. The plantation system of staple agriculture using bound labor and relying on Atlantic commercial connections was nakedly exploitative, driven by the self-interest of a consolidating planter class, who secured their political status and their authority over land and labor with the support of the imperial state. Compared to other British plantation colonies, the planter class in the Chesapeake produced a less reliably profitable commodity and had less of a monopoly over landownership and the supply of labor. Therefore, the establishment and maintenance of this system in the tidewater was not inevitable, but rather highly contingent; it required the most political-economic work on the part of planters, merchants, and officials. This made the Chesapeake a generative frontier of the plantation system. For the Chesapeake planter elite, constructing their political economy required negotiation within an imperial political-economic framework that sought to balance commercial interests with the pursuit of the common good. Urban development consistently provided the catalyst for this negotiation. Each stage of urban debate was about defining the terms on which the factors of production would be distributed and contesting the control of the mechanisms that would regulate them. Through this process, the small class of white men who came to control tidewater society gradually co-opted the civic authority of urban corporate institutions and used it to reinforce their own position within the complex nexus of imperial state power. Only in this way were the agricultural capitalist slave owners of the eighteenth-century Chesapeake able to portray themselves as classical republicans and thereby maintain their hegemony in a plantation society with an unusually large number of poor and middling whites and a consistently unreliable staple commodity.

The result of this process was not a plantation system incompatible with urbanization but one in which the relationship between the planter and the city was fraught. Far from being antithetical to urbanization, the plantation system was intimately tied to the network of Atlantic port cities, and the institution of slavery was readily compatible with urban spaces. Yet this compatibility does not mean that leading planters had the same relationships to urban institutions and markets as European gentry or independent family farmers in the northern regions of British America.[31] Planter elites in the Chesapeake always recognized that their power, both locally and in the broader Atlantic world, needed to be justified and defended against competing claims to power on the part of states, merchants, and their poorer neighbors. Their solution was to restrict and carefully oversee local towns and marketplaces, keeping them under the broader control of the planters' republic.

This was a structure that defined the economically declining antebellum Chesapeake, but it was also a pattern that the region's planter-migrants took with them as they began to flee the crumbling tobacco economy and relocate to the cotton belt. Although New Orleans became a boom town for the cotton economy, smaller local towns and cities were limited across the region. The Mississippi River port city blossomed as an export hub filled with British and New York factors, but the descendants of Chesapeake planters who had become cotton kingpins were wary of devolving local exchange to urban centers in their neighborhoods, and because their expanding enslaved labor force was generally kept outside the legal consumer economy, there was little incentive for local retailing to drive urban development. These antebellum planters were following a long tradition as they became deeply enmeshed in an exploitative global capitalist market but held the cities and merchants who anchored that market at arm's length. Understood in light of Chesapeake planters' long conflicted relationship with urbanization, this seeming dichotomy was not a sign of feudal premodern resistance to modernity but a conscious calculus to retain local authority when dependent upon a global commodity market.[32]

The city, though, still represented a manifestation of the commercial and political power that the planter class was always worried that they lacked. Unsurprisingly, when the cotton boom faded, Virginians led the southern United States in a new crusade to throw off their dependence on New York merchants and pursue "direct trade" with Europe through a program of urban development. "Building up Virginia's cities," the Richmond *Daily Dispatch* proclaimed in 1851, "will save the South from an indelible brand of degradation." Chesapeake planters never lost their fixation with "cities in the air" because those aspirations defined who they were and everything they aspired to be.[33]

ABBREVIATIONS

APC	W. L. Grant, James Munro, and Almeric W. Fitzroy, eds., *Acts of the Privy Council*, Colonial Series (London: HMSO, 1908–12).
Archives	William Hand Browne et al., eds., *Archives of Maryland* (Baltimore: Maryland Historical Society, 1883–1972).
BL	British Library, London
CSPC	William Noël Sainsbury et al., eds., *Calendar of State Papers*, Colonial Series (London, 1860–1926).
EJC	H. R. McIlwaine, ed., *Executive Journal of the Council of Colonial Virginia*, 6 vols. (Richmond, VA, 1925–66).
HP	M. Greengrass, M. Leslie, and M. Hannon, eds., *The Hartlib Papers* (Sheffield: HRI Online Publications, 2013), http://www.hrionline.ac.uk/hartlib.
HS	William Waller Hening, ed., *Statutes at Large; Being a Collection of All the Laws of Virginia, from the First Session of the Legislature in the Year 1619*, 13 vols. (Charlottesville, VA, 1969).
JHB	H. R. McIlwaine, ed., *Journals of the House of Burgesses of Virginia*, 13 vols. (Richmond, VA, 1905–1915).
LJC	H. R. McIlwaine, ed., *Legislative Journals of the Council of Colonial Virginia*, 2nd ed. (Richmond, VA, 1979).
LVA	Library of Virginia, Richmond
MHM	*Maryland Historical Magazine*
RVC	Susan Myra Kingsbury, ed., *The Records of the Virginia Company*, 4 vols. (Washington, DC, 1906–1935).
TNA	The National Archives of the United Kingdom, Kew
VMHB	*Virginia Magazine of History & Biography*
WMQ	*William & Mary Quarterly*

NOTES

Note on dates: Until 1752, Britain and its empire used the Julian Calendar (known as Old Style), with the year beginning on March 25. All dates in this study before 1752 are shown in Old Style, but the year is assumed to have begun on January 1.

INTRODUCTION

1. Francis Makemie, "A Plain and Friendly Perswasive to the Inhabitants of Virginia and Maryland For Promoting Towns and Cohabitation," reprinted in *VMHB* 4 (1896): 255–71 (quotes, 255, 256, 258–59).

2. "Governor Harvey and Council of Virginia to the Privy Council, Jan 18, 1639," TNA CO 1/10, #5; *Archives*, 5:137; Louis B. Wright, ed., *The Prose Works of William Byrd of Westover: Narratives of a Colonial Virginian* (Cambridge, MA: Belknap, 1966), 388.

3. Bernard C. Steiner, *Early Maryland Poetry* (Baltimore: Maryland Historical Society, 1900), 30; Thomas Jefferson, *Notes on the State of Virginia*, ed. David Waldstreicher (New York: Bedford, 2002), 153.

4. Edmund Morgan, *American Slavery, American Freedom: The Ordeal of Colonial Virginia* (New York: Norton, 1975), chaps. 4–6; T. H. Breen, "Looking Out for Number One: The Cultural Limits on Public Policy in Early Virginia," in Breen, *Puritans and Adventurers: Change and Persistence in Early America* (New York: Oxford University Press, 1980). For rational adaptation, see Russell R. Menard, "Plantation Empire: How Sugar and Tobacco Planters Built Their Industries and Raised an Empire," *Agricultural History* 81 (2007): 309–32; Lorena S. Walsh, *Motives of Honor, Pleasure, and Profit: Plantation Management in the Colonial Chesapeake, 1607–1763* (Chapel Hill: University of North Carolina Press, 2010).

5. Winthrop D. Jordan, *White over Black: American Attitudes toward the Negro, 1550–1812* (Baltimore: Penguin, 1969); Anthony S. Parent, *Foul Means: The Formation of a Slave Society in Virginia, 1660–1740* (Chapel Hill: University of North Carolina Press, 2003).

6. For the center-periphery model, see Jack P. Greene, *Peripheries and Center:*

Constitutional Development in the Extended Polities of the British Empire and the United States, 1607–1788 (Athens: University of Georgia Press, 1987); Christian J. Koot, *Empire at the Periphery: British Colonists, Anglo-Dutch Trade, and the Development of the British Atlantic, 1621–1713* (New York: New York University Press, 2011). Recent exceptions are William Pettigrew, *Freedom's Debt: The Royal African Company and the Politics of the Atlantic Slave Trade, 1672–1752* (Chapel Hill: University of North Carolina Press, 2013); Douglas Bradburn, "The Visible Fist: The Chesapeake Tobacco Trade in War and the Purpose of Empire, 1690–1715," *WMQ*, 3rd ser., 68, no. 3 (July 2011): 361–86; Peter Thompson, "The Thief, the Householder, and the Commons: Languages of Class in Seventeenth-Century Virginia," *WMQ*, 3rd ser., 63 (2006): 253–80. Older scholarship addressed planter relations with English merchants in nonideological terms. See David Alan Williams, "Political Alignments in Colonial Virginia Politics, 1698–1750" (PhD diss., Northwestern University, 1959); Peter V. Bergstrom, *Markets and Merchants: Economic Diversification in Colonial Virginia, 1700–1775* (New York: Garland, 1985); John Mickle Hemphill, *Virginia and the English Commercial System 1689–1733: Studies in the Development and Fluctuations of a Colonial Economy under Imperial Control* (New York: Garland, 1985).

7. Steve Pincus, "Rethinking Mercantilism: Political Economy, the British Empire, and the Atlantic World in the Seventeenth and Eighteenth Centuries," *WMQ*, 3rd ser., 69, no. 1 (Jan. 2012): 3–34; Philip J. Stern and Carl Wennerlind, eds., *Mercantilism Reimagined: Political Economy in Early Modern Britain and Its Empire* (New York: Oxford University Press, 2014).

8. New scholarship on slavery and capitalism has largely focused on the nineteenth-century United States, with the exception of S. Max Edelson, *Plantation Enterprise in Colonial South Carolina* (Cambridge, MA: Harvard University Press, 2006); Trevor Burnard, *Planters, Merchants, and Slaves: Plantation Societies in British America, 1650–1820* (Chicago: University of Chicago Press, 2015). The classic discussion of slavery and capitalism is Eric Williams, *Capitalism and Slavery* (Chapel Hill: University of North Carolina Press, 1944).

9. Makemie, "Plain and Friendly," 259; "Ashley to Sayle, 10 Apr. 71," in *The Shaftesbury Papers* (Charleston: South Carolina Historical Society, 1897, repr. 2000), 310–12.

10. The best overall account of Chesapeake social and economic development is Walsh, *Motives of Honor*. See also Carville Earle, *The Evolution of a Tidewater Settlement System: All Hallow's Parish, Maryland, 1650–1783* (Chicago: University of Chicago, Dept. of Geography, 1975); Kevin Kelly, *Economic and Social Development of Seventeenth-Century Surry County, Virginia* (New York: Garland, 1989), chap. 3; James Horn, *Adapting to a New World: English Society in the Seventeenth-Century Chesapeake* (Chapel Hill: University of North Carolina Press, 1996), chap. 3; Lorena S. Walsh, "Land Use, Settlement Patterns, and the Impact of European Agriculture, 1620–1820," in *Discovering the Chesapeake: The History of an Ecosystem*, ed. Philip D. Curtin, Grace S. Brush, and George W. Fisher (Baltimore: Johns Hopkins University Press, 2001), 220–48. For comparison with rural/urban settlement density in the west of England, where many early colonists originated, see Carl B. Estabrook, *Urbane and Rustic England: Cultural Ties and Social Spheres in the Provinces, 1660–1780* (Stanford, CA: Stanford University Press, 1998), 45–47.

11. Kathleen Bragdon, Edward Chappell, and William Graham, "A Scant Urbanity: Jamestown in the 17th Century," in *The Archaeology of 17th-Century Virginia*, ed. Theodore R. Reinhart and Dennis J. Pogue (Richmond, VA: Dietz Press, 1993), 223–49; Audrey Horning, "'A Verie Fit Place to Erect a Great Cittie': Comparative Contextual Analysis of Archaeological Jamestown" (PhD diss., University of Pennsylvania, 1995); Cary Carson, Joanne Bowen, Willie Graham, Martha McCartney, and Lorena Walsh, "New World, Real World: Improvising English Culture in Seventeenth-Century Virginia," *Journal of Southern History* 74 (2008): 63–85; Silas D. Hurry, ". . . *once the Metropolis of Maryland": The History and Archaeology of Maryland's First Capital* (St. Mary's, MD: Historic St. Mary's City Commission, 2001).

12. Dennis J. Pogue, "Calverton, Calvert County, Maryland: 1668–1725," *MHM* 80 (1985): 271–76; Joseph Brown Thomas, "Settlement, Community, and Economy: The Development of Towns on Maryland's Lower Eastern Shore, 1660–1775" (PhD diss., University of Maryland, 1994); Donald G. Shomette, *Lost Towns of Tidewater Maryland* (Centreville, MD: Tidewater, 2000).

13. "Urbanization in the Tidewater South, Part II: The Growth and Development of Williamsburg and Yorktown," NEH Report, 1988, Rockefeller Library, Colonial Williamsburg; Jane Wilson McWilliams, *Annapolis, City on the Severn: A History* (Baltimore: Johns Hopkins University Press, 2011).

14. John W. Reps, *Tidewater Towns: City Planning in Colonial Virginia and Maryland* (Williamsburg, VA: Colonial Williamsburg, 1972), chaps. 9–11; Clarence P. Gould, "The Economic Causes of the Rise of Baltimore," in *Essays in Colonial History* (New Haven, CT: Yale University Press, 1931), 225–51; Thomas J. Wertenbaker, *Norfolk: Historic Southern Port* (Durham, NC: Duke University Press, 1931), chap. 2.

15. Wright, *Prose Works*, 52; Jefferson, *Notes on the State of Virginia*, 152–53.

16. Carville Earle and Ronald Hoffman, "Staple Crops and Urban Development in the Eighteenth Century South," *Perspectives in American History* 10 (1976): 7–78; Ronald E. Grim, "The Absence of Towns in Seventeenth Century Virginia: The Emergence of Service Centers in York County" (PhD diss., University of Maryland, 1977); James O'Mara, *An Historical Geography of Urban System Development: Tidewater Virginia in the Eighteenth Century* (Downsview, ON: York University, Dept. of Geography, 1983). For a review of this debate, see Robert D. Mitchell, "Metropolitan Chesapeake: Reflections on Town Formation in Colonial Virginia and Maryland," in *Lois Green Carr: The Chesapeake and Beyond—A Celebration: A Collection of Discussion Papers Presented at a Conference May 22–23, 1992 . . .* (Crownsville: Maryland Historical and Cultural Publications, 1992), 105–25. For broader functional comparisons, see Joseph A. Ernst and H. Roy Merrens, "'Camden's Turrets Pierce the Skies!': The Urban Process in the Southern Colonies during the Eighteenth Century," *WMQ*, 3rd ser., 30 (1973): 549–74; Jacob Price, "Economic Function and the Growth of American Port Towns in the Eighteenth Century," *Perspectives in American History* 8 (1974): 123–86.

17. David Hackett Fischer, *Albion's Seed: Four British Folkways in America* (New York: Oxford University Press, 1989), 207–418; Christopher Tomlins, *Freedom Bound: Law, Labor, and Civic Identity in Colonizing English America, 1580–1865* (Cambridge: Cambridge University Press, 2010).

18. Lois Green Carr, "County Government in Maryland, 1689–1709" (PhD diss.,

Harvard University, 1968); Lorena Seebach Walsh, "Charles County, Maryland, 1658–1705: A Study of Chesapeake Social and Political Structure" (PhD diss., Michigan State University, 1977); Robert Wheeler, "The County Court in Colonial Virginia," in *Town and County: Essays on the Structure of Local Government in the American Colonies*, ed. Bruce C. Daniels (Middletown, CT: Wesleyan University Press, 1978), 111–33; Williams H. Seiler, "The Anglican Church: A Basic Institution of Local Government in Colonial Virginia," in Daniels, *Town and County*, 134–59; Horn, *Adapting to a New World*, chap. 4.

19. Rhys Isaac, *Transformation of Virginia, 1740–1790* (Chapel Hill: University of North Carolina Press, 1982); Aubrey C. Land, *Colonial Maryland: A History* (Millwood, NY: KTO Press, 1981), 182–98; Wilson Somerville, *The Tuesday Club of Annapolis (1745–1756) as Cultural Performance* (Athens: University of Georgia Press, 1996); Paul A. Shackel, "Town Planning, and Everyday Material Culture: An Archaeology of Social Relations in Colonial Maryland's Capital Cities," in *Historical Archaeology of the Chesapeake*, ed. Paul A. Shackel and Barbara J. Little (Washington, DC: Smithsonian Institution Press, 1994), 85–96.

20. Wertenbaker, *Norfolk*, 26.

21. Trever Burnard, "Towns in Plantation Societies in Eighteenth-Century British America," *Early American Studies* 15 (2017): 835–59.

22. The only studies of town legislation are Edward M. Riley, "The Town Acts of Colonial Virginia," *Journal of Southern History* 16 (1950): 306–23; Reps, *Tidewater Towns*; John C. Rainbolt, "Absence of Towns in Seventeenth-Century Virginia," *Journal of Southern History* 35 (1969): 343–60; John C. Rainbolt, *From Prescription to Persuasion: Manipulation of Eighteenth Century Virginia Economy* (Port Washington, NY: Kennikat, 1974).

23. Andrew Fitzmaurice, *Humanism and America: An Intellectual History of English Colonization, 1500–1625* (Cambridge: Cambridge University Press, 2003); Alexander B. Haskell, *For God, King, and People: Forging Commonwealth Bonds in Renaissance Virginia* (Chapel Hill: University of North Carolina Press, 2017).

24. Keith Wrightson, *Earthly Necessities: Economic Lives in Early Modern Britain* (New Haven, CT: Yale University Press, 2002); Joan Thirsk, *Economic Policy and Projects: The Development of a Consumer Society in Early Modern England* (Oxford: Clarendon, 1978); Andrew McRae, *God Speed the Plough: The Representation of Agrarian England, 1500–1660* (Cambridge: Cambridge University Press, 1996).

25. TNA CO 1/4, #32.

26. Morgan, *American Slavery*, chaps. 6–10; Horn, *Adapting to a New World*, 141–46; Walsh, *Motives of Honor*, 91–121.

27. For the Caribbean, see Koot, *Empire at the Periphery*; Abigail Swingen, *Competing Visions of Empire: Labor, Slavery, and the Origins of the British Atlantic Empire* (New Haven, CT: Yale University Press, 2015). For Carolina, see Joyce Chaplin, *An Anxious Pursuit: Agricultural Innovation and Modernity in the Lower South, 1730–1815* (Chapel Hill: University of North Carolina Press, 1993).

28. For rapid plantation consolidation, see Burnard, *Planters, Merchants, and Slaves*, chaps. 1–2.

29. Morgan, *American Slavery*; Russell R. Menard, "From Servants to Slaves: The

Transformation of the Chesapeake Labor System," *Southern Studies* 16 (1977): 355–90. For the debate about the transition to slavery, see John C. Coombs, "Beyond the 'Origins Debate': Rethinking the Rise of Virginia Slavery," in *Early Modern Virginia: Reconsidering the Old Dominion*, ed. Douglas Bradburn and John C. Coombs (Charlottesville: University of Virginia Press, 2011), 239–78. Winthrop Jordan long ago noted that the very gradual emergence of the plantation system in the Chesapeake made it particularly useful for understanding the evolution of ideas about race and slavery, see Jordan, *White over Black*, 72.

30. John C. Coombs, "The Phases of Conversion: A New Chronology for the Rise of Slavery in Early Virginia," *WMQ*, 3rd ser., 68 (2011): 332–60.

31. Walsh, *Motives of Honor*, chaps. 4–7; Lorena S. Walsh, "Summing the Parts: Implications for Estimating Chesapeake Output and Income Subregionally," *WMQ*, 3rd ser., 56 (1999): 53–94.

32. Chesapeake scholarship has long focused on poor and middling planters (see, for example, Lois Green Carr, Russell R. Menard, and Lorena S. Walsh, *Robert Cole's World: Agriculture and Society in Early Maryland* [Chapel Hill: University of North Carolina Press, 1991]), but it has almost exclusively portrayed them as rational economic actors, not as people with distinct political or economic visions.

33. There has been a wealth of recent literature on urban slavery in the early modern Atlantic world, upon which this study depends; see Philip D. Morgan, "Black Life in Eighteenth-Century Charleston," *Perspectives in American History*, n.s., 1 (1984): 187–332; Pedro Welch, *Slave Society in the City: Bridgetown, Barbados, 1680–1834* (Kingston, Jamaica: Ian Randle, 2003); Seth Rockman, *Scraping By: Wage Labor, Slavery, and Survival in Early Republican Baltimore* (Baltimore: Johns Hopkins University Press, 2008); Mariana L. R. Dantas, *Black Townsmen: Urban Slavery and Freedom in the Eighteenth-Century Americas* (New York: Palgrave Macmillan, 2008); Jorge Cañizares-Esguerra, Matt D. Childs, and James Sidbury, eds., *The Black Urban Atlantic in the Age of the Slave Trade* (Philadelphia: University of Pennsylvania Press, 2013); Rashauna Johnson, *Slavery's Metropolis: Unfree Labor in New Orleans during the Age of Revolutions* (Cambridge: Cambridge University Press, 2016); Marisa J. Fuentes, *Dispossessed Lives: Enslaved Women, Violence, and the Archive* (Philadelphia: University of Pennsylvania Press, 2016).

34. Previous scholarship has focused on the Chesapeake as a whole, minimizing the role of politics. A few recent works have bucked this trend. See Jean B. Russo and J. Elliott Russo, *Planting an Empire: The Early Chesapeake in British North America* (Baltimore: Johns Hopkins University Press, 2012); James D. Rice, *Tales from a Revolution: Bacon's Rebellion and the Transformation of Early America* (New York: Oxford University Press, 2012).

35. Jordan, *White over Black*, chap. 2.

36. For the importance of tracing connections between the local and global in early America, see Christopher Grasso and Karin Wulf, "Nothing Says 'Democracy' like a Visit from the Queen: Reflections on Empire and Nation in Early American Histories," *Journal of American History* 95, no. 3 (Dec. 2008): 764–81; Christopher Grasso and Peter C. Mancall, "World and Ground," *WMQ*, 3rd. ser., 74, no. 2 (2017): 195–202.

37. "A Discourse of the names and first causes of the institution of Cities and

peopled townes," in John Stow, *A Survey of London* (London, 1603), 547–68 (quote, 550); for the identification of Dalton, see John Stow, *A Survey of London*, ed. Charles Lethbridge Kingsford, 2 vols. (Oxford: Clarendon, 1971), 2:387. For cities and states, see Charles Tilly, *Coercion, Capital, and European States, AD 990–1990* (Oxford: Basil Blackwell, 1990); Charles Tilly and Wim P. Blockmans, eds., *Cities and the Rise of States in Europe, A.D. 1000 to 1800* (Boulder, CO: Westview Press, 1994); Almut Höfert, "States, Cities, and Citizens in the Later Middle Ages," in *States and Citizens: History, Theory, Prospects*, ed. Quentin Skinner and Bo Stråth (Cambridge: Cambridge University Press, 2003).

38. Peter Clark, *European Cities and Towns 400–2000* (Oxford: Oxford University Press, 2009), chaps. 2–6; Hans Baron, *The Crisis of the Early Italian Renaissance: Civic Humanist and Republican Liberty in the Age of Classicism and Tyranny* (Princeton, NJ: Princeton University Press, 1955); Quentin Skinner, *The Foundations of Modern Political Thought* (Cambridge: Cambridge University Press, 1978), vol. 1, chaps. 4 and 6; J. G. A. Pocock, *The Machiavellian Moment: Florentine Political Thought and the Atlantic Republican Tradition* (Princeton, NJ: Princeton University Press, 1975), 83–330; Eco O. G. Haitsma Mulier, *The Myth of Venice and Dutch Republican Thought in the Seventeenth Century* (Assen, Neth.: Van Gorcum, 1980).

39. Lewis Mumford, *The City in History: Its Origins, Its Transformations, and Its Prospects* (New York: Harcourt, 1961), chaps. 12–13; Richard Mackenney, *The City-State, 1500–1700: Republican Liberty in an Age of Princely Power* (Atlantic Highlands, NJ: Humanities Press International, 1989), chap. 2.

40. Giovanni Botero, *On the Causes of the Greatness and Magnificence of Cities*, trans. Geoffrey Symcox (Toronto: University of Toronto Press, 2012). The first English translation of Botero's work appeared in 1606, just as the Virginia Company was first established; see Giovanni Botero, *A treatise, concerning the causes of the magnificencie and greatnes of cities . . .* (London, 1606). For the rise of princely sovereignty, see Skinner, *Foundations of Modern Political Thought*, vol. 1, chap. 5. For Botero's integration of commerce into the pursuit of greatness, see Andrew Fitzmaurice, "The Commercial Ideology of Colonization in Jacobean England: Robert Johnson, Giovanni Botero, and the Pursuit of Greatness," *WMQ*, 3rd ser., 64 (2007): 791–820; see also Istvan Hont, *Jealousy of Trade: International Competition and the Nation-State in Historical Perspective* (Cambridge, MA: Harvard University Press, 2010), 5–17.

41. Pablo Fernández Albaladejo, "Cities and the State in Spain," in Tilly and Blockmans, *Cities and the Rise of States*, 168–83; Francesco Somaini, "The Collapse of City-States and the Role of Urban Centres in the New Political Geography of Renaissance Italy," in *The Italian Renaissance State*, ed. Andrea Gamberini and Isabella Lazzarini (Cambridge: Cambridge University Press, 2012).

42. Jay Kinsbruner, *The Colonial Spanish American City: Urban Life in the Age of Atlantic Capitalism* (Austin: University of Texas Press, 2005), esp. 33–38; Felipe Fernández-Armesto, "Latin America," in *The Oxford Handbook of Cities in World History*, ed. Peter Clark (Oxford: Oxford University Press, 2013), 364–84. Angel Rama, *The Lettered City* (Durham, NC: Duke University Press, 1996), chap. 1. For English and Dutch interest in Spanish American cities, see Richard L. Kagan, *Urban Images of the Hispanic World, 1493–1793* (New Haven, CT: Yale University Press, 2000),

chap. 4; Peter C. Mancall, *Hakluyt's Promise: An Elizabethan's Obsession for an English America* (New Haven, CT: Yale University Press, 2007), 32–33; María Fernanda Valencia-Suárez, "Tenochtitlan and the Aztecs in the English Atlantic World, 1500–1603," *Atlantic Studies* 6 (2009): 277–301.

43. Jan de Vries, *European Urbanization, 1500–1800* (Cambridge, MA: Harvard University Press, 1984), 39; for London, see Jeremy Boulton, "London, 1540–1700," in *The Cambridge Urban History of Britain*, vol. 2, ed. Peter Clark (Cambridge: Cambridge University Press, 2000), 315–46; Vanessa Harding, "City, Capital, and Metropolis: The Changing Shape of Seventeenth-Century London," in *Imagining Early Modern London: Perceptions and Portrayals of the City from Stow to Strype, 1598–1720*, ed. J. F. Merritt (Cambridge: Cambridge University Press, 2001), 117–43. For provincial towns, see Alan Dyer, "Small Market Towns, 1540–1700," in *Cambridge Urban History*, 2:425–49. Older scholarship characterized 1550 to 1700 as an era of decay in English towns, but this characterization has been significantly challenged; see Phil Withington, *The Politics of Commonwealth: Citizens and Freemen in Early Modern England* (Cambridge: Cambridge University Press, 2005), 3–8.

44. Robert Tittler, *The Reformation and the Towns in England: Politics and Political Culture, c. 1540–1640* (Oxford: Clarendon, 1998); Withington, *Politics of Commonwealth*, chap. 2.

45. Sir Thomas Smith, *De Republica Anglorum*, 41–42; E. Boulton, *The Cities Advocate, in this case or question of Honor or Armes; Whether Apprentiship extinguisheth Gentry?* (London, 1629), a2v; Stow, *Survey of London*. For new civic building projects, see Robert Tittler, *Architecture and Power: The Town Hall and the English Urban Community, c. 1500–1640* (Oxford: Clarendon, 1991); Robert Tittler, *Townspeople and Nation: English Urban Experience, 1540–1640* (Stanford, CA: Stanford University Press, 2001).

46. Withington, *Politics of Commonwealth*, 10; Jonathan Barry, "Civility and Civic Culture in Early Modern England: The Meanings of Urban Freedom," in *Civil Histories: Essays Presented to Sir Keith Thomas*, ed. Peter Burke, Brian Harrison, and Paul Slack (Oxford: Oxford University Press, 2000), 181–97; Jonathan Barry, "Bourgeois Collectivism? Urban Associations and the Middle Sort," in *The Middling Sort of People: Culture, Society and Politics in England 1550–1800*, ed. Jonathan Barry and Colin Brooks (New York: St. Martin's, 1994), 84–113; David Harris Sacks, *The Widening Gate: Bristol and the Atlantic, 1450–1700* (Berkeley: University of California Press, 1993); Sacks, "Freedom to, Freedom from, Freedom of: Urban Life and Political Participation in Early Modern England," *Citizenship Studies* 11 (2007): 135–50; Maarten Prak, "Urban Governments and Their Citizens in Early Modern Europe," in *London and Beyond: Essays in Honour of Derek Keene*, ed. Matthew Davis and James A. Galloway (London: Institute of Historical Research, 2012), 269–86.

47. For the idea of commonwealth, see Paul Slack, *From Reformation to Improvement: Public Welfare in Early Modern England* (Oxford: Oxford University Press, 1999), chap. 1; Wrightson, *Earthly Necessities*, chaps. 6 and 9; Henry S. Turner, *The Corporate Commonwealth: Pluralism and Political Fictions in England, 1516–1651* (Chicago: University of Chicago Press, 2016); Noah Dauber, *State and Commonwealth: The Theory of the State in Early Modern England, 1549–1640* (Princeton, NJ: Princeton University

Press, 2016). For office holding and participatory politics, see Patrick Collinson, "The Monarchical Republic of Queen Elizabeth I," *Bulletin of the John Rylands University Library of Manchester* 69 (1987): 394–424; Mark Goldie, "The Unacknowledged Republic: Officeholding in Early Modern England," in *The Politics of the Excluded, c. 1500–1850*, ed. Tim Harris (New York: Palgrave, 2001), 153–94.

48. William Scott, *An Essay of Drapery, or The Compleate Citizen* (1635); Keith Roberts, "Citizen Soldiers: The Military Power of the City of London," in *London and the Civil War*, ed. Stephen Porter (London: Palgrave Macmillan, 1996), 89–111.

49. Lawrence Manley, *Literature and Culture in Early Modern London* (Cambridge: Cambridge University Press, 1995), 258–93; Ian Archer, *The Pursuit of Stability: Social Relations in Elizabethan London* (Cambridge: Cambridge University Press, 1991); Gail Kern Paster, *The Idea of the City in the Age of Shakespeare* (Athens: University of Georgia Press, 1985).

50. John Goodwin, *M.S. to A.S.* (1644), 72–73, quoted in Manley, *Literature and Culture*, 549; Withington, *Politics of Commonwealth*, chap. 8; Tittler, *Reformation and the Towns*; Slack, *From Reformation to Improvement*, chap. 2; David Underdown, *Fire from Heaven: Life in an English Town in the Seventeenth Century* (New Haven, CT: Yale University Press, 1994); Margo Todd, *Christian Humanism and the Puritan Social Order* (Cambridge: Cambridge University Press, 1987). For the influence of these ideas in New England, see Barry Levy, *Town Born: The Political Economy of New England from Its Foundation to the Revolution* (Philadelphia: University of Pennsylvania Press, 2011); David D. Hall, *A Reforming People: Puritanism and the Transformation of Public Life in New England* (New York: Knopf, 2011), chap. 2.

51. Tittler, *Reformation and the Towns*.

52. Stow, *Survey of London*, 556, 558. Catherine Patterson, *Urban Patronage in Early Modern England: Corporate Boroughs, the Landed Elite, and the Crown, 1580–1640* (Stanford, CA: Stanford University Press, 1999); John Cramsie, *Kingship and Crown Finance under James VI and I, 1603–1625* (London: Boydell and Brewer, 2002).

53. Peter Clark and Paul Slack, eds., *Crisis and Order in English Towns, 1500–1700: Essays in Urban History* (London: Routledge, 1972); Clark and Slack, *English Towns in Transition, 1500–1700* (Oxford: Oxford University Press, 1976). For ritual, see Michael Berlin, "Reordering Ritual: Ceremony and the Parish, 1520–1640," in *Londinopolis, c. 1500–c. 1750: Essays in the Cultural and Social History of Early Modern London*, ed. Mark S. R. Jenner and Paul Griffiths (Manchester, UK: Manchester University Press, 2000), 47–67; David Harris Sacks, "Celebrating Authority in Bristol, 1475–1640," in *Urban Life in the Renaissance*, ed. Susan Zimmerman and Ronald F. E. Weissman (Newark: University of Delaware Press, 1989), 187–223. For city comedy, see Manley, *Literature and Culture*, chap. 8.

54. Robert Ashton, *The City and the Court, 1603–1643* (Cambridge: Cambridge University Press, 1979).

55. Boulton, *The Cities Advocate*, 51.

56. David Harris Sacks, "The Corporate Town and the English State: Bristol's 'Little Businesses,' 1625–1641," *Past and Present* 110 (1986): 69–105.

57. Robert Brady, *An Historical Treatise of Cities and Burghs or Boroughs* (1690), i; Withington, *Politics of Commonwealth*; Paul Halliday, *Dismembering the Body Poli-*

tic: Partisan Politics in England's Towns, 1650–1730 (Cambridge: Cambridge University Press, 1998); Gary S. De Krey, London and the Restoration, 1659–1683 (Cambridge: Cambridge University Press, 2005). Urban corporations also existed in tension with ecclesiastical institutions; see Carl B. Estabrook, "In the Mist of Ceremony: Cathedral and Community in Seventeenth-Century Wells," in Political Culture and Cultural Politics in Early Modern England: Essays Presented to David Underdown, ed. Susan D. Amussen and Mark A. Kishlansky (Manchester, UK: Manchester University Press, 1995), 133–61.

58. Haskell, For God, King, and People, chap. 1.

59. Edmund Spenser, A View of the Present State of Ireland, ed. W. L. Renwick (Oxford: Clarendon, 1970), 165.

60. Hiram Morgan, "The Colonial Venture of Sir Thomas Smith in Ulster, 1571–1575," Historical Journal 28 (1985): 261–78 (esp. 274–78); Raymond Gillespie, "War and the Irish Town: The Early Modern Experience," in Conquest and Resistance, 293–316; Raymond Gillespie, Colonial Ulster: The Settlement of East Ulster, 1600–1641 (Cork: Cork University Press, 1985); Nicholas Canny, Making Ireland British, 1580–1650 (Oxford: Oxford University Press, 2001), 121–34, 187–205; Phil Withington, Society in Early Modern England: The Vernacular Origins of Some Powerful Ideas (Cambridge: Polity Press, 2010), chap. 8; Audrey Horning, Ireland in the Virginian Sea: Colonialism in the British Atlantic (Chapel Hill: University of North Carolina Press, 2013), esp. 60–84.

61. David Beers Quinn, ed., The Roanoke Voyages, 1584–1590, 2 vols. (London: Hakluyt Society, 1955), 2:506–12.

62. Virginia Company, "Instructions given by way of Advice," 1606, in The Jamestown Voyages under the First Charter, 1606–1609, 2 vols., ed. Philip Barbour (London: Hakluyt Society, 1969), 1:49–54; Philip L. Barbour, ed., The Complete Works of Captain John Smith (Chapel Hill: University of North Carolina Press, 1986), 1:29.

63. Levy, Town Born; Simon Middleton, From Privileges to Rights: Work and Politics in Colonial New York City (Philadelphia: University of Pennsylvania Press, 2006); Jessica C. Roney, Governed by a Spirit of Opposition: The Origins of American Political Practice in Colonial Philadelphia (Baltimore: Johns Hopkins University Press, 2014); Emma Hart, Building Charleston: Town and Society in the Eighteenth-Century British Atlantic World (Charlottesville: University of Virginia Press, 2010).

64. Archives, 5:148.

65. On state and empire in British history, see David Armitage, The Ideological Origins of the British Empire (Cambridge: Cambridge University Press, 2000), 1–23.

66. Wright, Prose Works, 388.

67. Lauren Benton and Richard J. Ross, "Empires and Legal Pluralism: Jurisdiction, Sovereignty, and Political Imagination in the Early Modern World," in Legal Pluralism and Empires, 1500–1850, ed. Benton and Ross (New York: New York University Press, 2013), 1–20 (quote, 5–6). See also Michael J. Braddick, State Formation in Early Modern England, c. 1550–1700 (Cambridge: Cambridge University Press, 2000); Lauren Benton, A Search for Sovereignty: Law and Geography in European Empires, 1400–1900 (Cambridge: Cambridge University Press, 2010); Philip J. Stern, "'Bundles of Hyphens': Corporations and Legal Communities in the Early Modern British Empire," in Legal

Pluralism and Empires, 1500–1850, ed. Benton and Ross (New York: New York University Press, 2013), 21–48.

68. T. H. Breen, *Tobacco Culture: The Mentality of Great Tidewater Planters on the Eve of Revolution* (Princeton, NJ: Princeton University Press, 1985); Drew R. McCoy, *The Elusive Republic: Political Economy in Jeffersonian America* (Chapel Hill: University of North Carolina Press, 1980); Bruce A. Ragsdale, *A Planters' Republic: The Search for Economic Independence in Revolutionary Virginia* (Madison, WI: Madison House, 1996).

CHAPTER ONE

1. Virginia Company, "Instructions given by way of Advice," 1606, in Barbour, *Jamestown Voyages*, 1:49–54.

2. Robert Johnson, *Noua Britannia Offring most excellent fruites by planting in Virginia. Exciting all such as be well affected to further the same* (London, 1609), 25.

3. Haskell, *For God, King, and People*, chap. 2; Phil Withington, "Two Renaissances: Urban Political Culture in Post-Reformation England Reconsidered," *Historical Journal* 44 (2001): 239–67.

4. Accounts of early Virginia that emphasize local exigencies include Morgan, *American Slavery*; Horn, *Adapting to a New World*, chap. 3; Lorena Walsh, *Motives of Honor*, chap. 1. For a recent exception, which takes the role of urban development seriously, see Horning, *Ireland in the Virginian Sea*.

5. For the factional interpretation, see Wesley Frank Craven, *The Dissolution of the Virginia Company: The Failure of a Colonial Experiment* (Oxford: Oxford University Press, 1932).

6. Haskell, *For God, King, and People*, chap. 3; Andrew Fitzmaurice, "The Company-Commonwealth," in *Virginia 1619*, ed. Paul Musselwhite, Peter C. Mancall, and James Horn (Chapel Hill: University of North Carolina Press, forthcoming).

7. Turner, *Corporate Commonwealth*, 100.

8. Ralph Lane to Richard Hakluyt, 1585, in *The Original Writings and Correspondence of the Two Richard Hakluyts*, 2 vols., ed. E. G. R. Taylor (London: Hakluyt Society, 1935), 2:347; Karen Ordahl Kupperman, *Indians and English: Facing Off in Early America* (Ithaca, NY: Cornell University Press, 2000), 97–102, 155–56; Alison Games, *The Web of Empire: English Cosmopolitans in an Age of Expansion, 1560–1660* (Oxford: Oxford University Press, 2008), chap. 4; David Harris Sacks, "The True Temper of Empire: Dominion, Friendship and Exchange in the English Atlantic, c. 1575–1625," *Renaissance Studies* 26 (2012): 531–58.

9. Virginia Company, "Instructions given by way of Advice," in Barbour, *Jamestown Voyages*, 1:49–54 (quote, 54).

10. Philip L. Barbour, ed., *The Complete Works of Captain John Smith* (Chapel Hill: University of North Carolina Press, 1986), 1:29. Botero, *A treatise*; see also, Karen Ordahl Kupperman, *The Jamestown Project* (Cambridge, MA: Belknap, 2007), 217–28; Games, *Web of Empire*, chap. 4. For the provisions regarding trade, see "First Charter of Virginia, April 10, 1606," http://avalon.law.yale.edu/17th_century/va01.asp. For the connection between urban design and urban order, see Kagan, *Urban Images*, chap. 1.

11. Helen Rountree, "The Powhatan and the English: A Case of Multiple Conflict-

ing Agendas," in *Powhatan Foreign Relations*, ed. Helen Rountree (Charlottesville: University of Virginia Press, 1993), 173–205, esp. 173–84; J. Frederick Fausz, "'An Abundance of Blood Shed on Both Sides': England's First Indian War, 1609–1614," *VMHB* 98 (1990): 3–56. For James Fort, see William M. Kelso, *Jamestown: The Buried Truth* (Charlottesville: University of Virginia Press, 2006), esp. 80–114.

12. Barbour, *Complete Works*, 1:211, 273 (see also 264–65). For the martial civic tradition in Elizabethan England, see Rory Rapple, *Martial Power and Elizabethan Political Culture: Military Men in England and Ireland, 1558–1594* (Cambridge: Cambridge University Press, 2009).

13. William Strachey's account of the Starving Time also emphasized that the lack of civic order meant that "privie factionaries" could eschew public oversight; see Samuel Purchas, *Hakluytus Posthumus* (London, 1625), 19:46, 50–51.

14. Fitzmaurice, *Humanism and America*, chap. 3.

15. Robert Gray, *A Good Speed to Virginia* (London, 1609), E; William Crashaw, *A Sermon Preached in London before the Right Honorable Lord Lawarre...* (London, 1610), E2–F; Virginia Company, *A True Declaration of the estate of the Colonie in Virginia* (London, 1610), 15. Giovanni Botero cited this same story of Tarantum and Autium, in a chapter on colonization, printed as an appendix to the 1606 English translation of his treatise on cities; see Botero, *Greatness of Cities*, 101.

16. David Thomas Konig, "'Dale's Laws' and the Non-Common Law Origins of Criminal Justice in Virginia," *American Journal of Legal History* 26 (Oct. 1982): 354–75.

17. *RVC* 3:17; *Lawes Divine, Morall and Martiall*, in *Tracts and Other Papers Relating Principally to the Origin, Settlement, and Progress of the Colonies in North America*, 4 vols., ed. Peter Force (New York: P. Force, 1836–46), vol. 3, no. 2, 10, 28, 39. On the connection between new towns and the imposition of martial law, see also Ancient Planters of Virginia, "A Brief Declaration of the Plantation of Virginia duringe the first Twelve Yeares...," in *Jamestown Narratives: Eyewitness Accounts of the Virginia Colony, The First Decade: 1607–1617*, ed. Edward Wright Haile (Champlain, VA: RoundHouse, 1998), 900–901.

18. Ralph Hamor, *A True Discourse of the Present State of Virginia* (London, 1615), 19, 29–32; James Horn, *A Land as God Made It: Jamestown and the Birth of America* (New York: Basic Books, 2008), chaps. 6 and 7.

19. Fausz, "'An Abundance of Blood Shed on Both Sides'"; Carville V. Earle, "Environment, Disease, and Mortality in Early Virginia," in *The Chesapeake in the Seventeenth Century: Essays on Anglo-American Society*, ed. Thad W. Tate and David L. Ammerman (New York: Norton, 1979), 96–125.

20. Hamor, *True Discourse*, 25.

21. "Thomas Dale, Letter from Henrico, 10 Jun 1613," in Haile, *Jamestown Narratives*, 778–83 (quote, 779). Hamor, *True Discourse*, 18. Although corporate status was only granted to Bermuda City, Dale did also refer to Henrico as "our commonwealth of Henryco," suggesting that he also viewed it as a nascent city commonwealth; see Haile, *Jamestown Narratives*, 778.

22. Hamor, *True Discourse*, 16–18, 30–33 (quote, 31); John Rolfe, *A True Relation of the state of Virginia lefte by Sir Thomas Dale Knight in May last 1616* (New Haven, CT: Yale University Press, 1951), 38–39; see also, "A Brief Declaration," in Haile, *James-

town Narratives, 902-3. The model of a seven-year term of service and a promise of private land was made in Johnson, *Nova Britannia,* D4r.

23. Thomas Blenerhasset, *A Direction for the Plantation in Ulster* (London, 1610), A3v, A4v, C1v, C3r; Withington, *Society in Early Modern England,* 214-15. Blenerhasset's plans were never fully implemented, but they informed the "Project of the Ulster Plantation," which also proposed to establish twenty-five corporate towns; see "Ulster Plantation Papers," no. 74, *Analecta Hibernica* 8 (1938): 286-96. See also, R. J. Hunter, "Towns in the Ulster Plantation," *Studia Hibernica* 11 (1971): 40-79; Philip S. Robinson, *The Plantation of Ulster: British Settlement in an Irish Landscape, 1600-1670* (Dublin: Gill and Macmillan, 1984), chap. 7 (esp. 157-58). For the close connections between the Ulster and Virginia plantations, see Horning, *Ireland in the Virginian Sea,* chap. 4 (esp. 289-313).

24. Craven, *Dissolution,* chap. 2 (esp. 33-34).

25. David Harris Sacks, "The Greed of Judas: Avarice, Monopoly, and the Moral Economy in England, ca. 1350-ca. 1600," *Journal of Medieval and Early Modern Studies* 28 (1998): 263-307.

26. Philip J. Stern, "Companies: Monopoly, Sovereignty, and the East Indies," in *Mercantilism Reimagined: Political Economy in Early Modern Britain and its Empire,* ed. Philip J. Stern and Carl Wennerlind (New York: Oxford University Press, 2014), 177-95; Turner, *Corporate Commonwealth,* chap. 4 (esp. 88).

27. *RVC* 3:163; although evidence of the terms agreed to by Argall and Martin have not survived, an agreement made by Lord Zouche in 1617 was likely modeled on these earlier agreements; see *RVC* 3:77. For Martin's estate, see Aaron K. Slater, "The Ideological Origins of the Imperial State" (PhD diss., New York University, 2011), 174-85.

28. J. H. Lefroy, *Memorials of the Discovery and Early Settlement of the Bermudas or Somers Islands, 1515-1685,* vol. 1 (London: Longmans, 1877), 83-98, 109.

29. *RVC* 3:71, 73, 91-92. For complaints against Argall, see *RVC* 2:53-54, 400-405 (esp. 401); 3:252.

30. *RVC* 2:51-55, 284-85; 3:119-20, 175-76, 247, 255-56; Henry Chandlee Forman, "The Bygone 'Subberbs of James Cittie,'" *WMQ,* 2nd ser., 20 (1940): 475-86; Alain Charles Outlaw, *Governor's Land: Archaeology of Early Seventeenth-Century Virginia Settlements* (Charlottesville: University of Virginia Press, 1990), 3-9; Charles E. Hatch, *The First Seventeen Years: Virginia, 1607-1624* (Williamsburg: Virginia 350th Anniversary Celebration Corporation, 1957), 36-37. For Argall's efforts to frustrate rival settlements, see Ivor Noel Hume and Audrey Noel Hume, *The Archaeology of Martin's Hundred,* 2 vols. (Williamsburg, VA: Colonial Williamsburg, 2001), 1:18-21.

31. Hunter, "Towns in the Ulster Plantation," 42-51; Raymond Gillespie, "The Origins and Development of an Ulster Urban Network, 1600-1641," *Irish Historical Studies* 24 (1984): 15-29; Horning, *Ireland in the Virginian Sea,* 210-15. The distinction between patronage and corporate organization could be hazy, because many English towns also had wealthy humanistic patrons; see Patterson, *Urban Patronage.*

32. Sir Thomas Smith, *De Republica Anglorum: A Discourse on the Commonwealth of England,* ed. L. Alston (Cambridge: Cambridge University Press, 1906), 20; *RVC* 1:350.

33. *RVC* 3:98-109 (quotes, 98-100, 104). For previous discussion of the charter, see

Craven, *Dissolution*, chap. 3. For evidence that Sandys masterminded the reforms, see *Virginia Company Archives Online*, https://www.virginiacompanyarchives.amdigital.co.uk, FP93.

34. Theodore K. Rabb, *Jacobean Gentleman: Sir Edwin Sandys, 1561–1629* (Princeton, NJ: Princeton University Press, 1998). Sandys represented the boroughs of Plympton Earle, Stockbridge, Rochester, Sandwich, and Penryn, during various Parliaments; see ibid., 231–40.

35. Rolfe, *True Relation*, 21–24, 38; Council for Virginia, *A Brief Declaration* (London, 1616), 7; Nicholas Ferrar, *Sir Thomas Smith's Misgovernment of the Virginia Company*, ed. D. R. Ransome (Cambridge: Roxburghe Club, 1990), 8.

36. *RVC* 3:105; Yeardley had an urban heritage; see R. C. D. Baldwin, "Yeardley, Sir George (bap. 1588, d. 1627)," *Oxford Dictionary of National Biography* (Oxford: Oxford University Press, 2004), http://www.oxforddnb.com/view/article/30204. For further evidence that Yeardley's instructions were designed to counter Argall's actions, see *Virginia Company Archives Online*, FP92. See also Alexander B. Haskell, "Like 'the Roote and Body of a Tree': The Renaissance Ideal of the Public and the Creation of Virginia's General Assembly," in *Virginia 1619*, ed. Paul Musselwhite, Peter C. Mancall, and James Horn (Chapel Hill: University of North Carolina Press, forthcoming).

37. *RVC* 3:99–102; for the Fairefax grant, see J. Frederick Fausz, "Patterns of Settlement in the James River Basin, 1607–1642" (MA thesis, College of William and Mary, 1971), 71–72.

38. *RVC* 1:268; 3:99–102. For expansion of English borough estates, see Tittler, *Reformation and the Towns*; Withington, *Politics of Commonwealth*, chap. 2.

39. *RVC* 3:104–6; 1:268.

40. *Virginia Company Archives Online*, FP93.

41. *A Declaration of the State of the Colonie and Affaires in Virginia* (1620), 5, in Force, *Tracts and Other Papers*, vol. 3. The company also appealed for investment from England's boroughs; see *RVC* 1:418, 479, 489, 556.

42. Warren M. Billings, *A Little Parliament: The Virginia General Assembly in the Seventeenth Century* (Richmond: Library of Virginia, 2004), chap. 1. Withington, *Politics of Commonwealth*, 40. See also, David Harris Sacks, "Parliament, Liberty, and the Commonweal," in *Parliament and Liberty from the Reign of Elizabeth to the English Civil War*, ed. J. H. Hexter (Stanford, CA: Stanford University Press, 1992), 85–121. As Mark Goldie has noted, "historians' preoccupation with national parliaments" (or in Virginia's case, the General Assembly) "occludes the pervasiveness of the practice of deliberation and decision making in the assemblies of the parish republics"; see Goldie, "Unacknowledged Republic," 173.

43. *RVC* 3:99, 627. David Thomas Konig, "Colonization and the Common Law in Ireland and Virginia, 1569–1634," in *The Transformation of Early American History: Society, Authority and Ideology*, ed. James A. Henretta, Michael Kammen, and Stanley N. Katz (New York: Knopf, 1991), 70–92.

44. *RVC* 1:303, 394–96; 3:487. For Sandys's attitude toward monopolies, see Rabb, *Jacobean Gentleman*, esp. 86–97.

45. Sandys has been erroneously portrayed as an enabler of this system; see Edmund

Morgan, "The First American Boom: Virginia 1618–1630" *WMQ*, 3rd ser., 28 (1971): 169–98.

46. *RVC* 3:103; Gray, *Good Speed*, D3. For the role of artisans in Captain Nuce's plans for Virginia, see also *Virginia Company Archives Online*, FP336. For diversification, see Walsh, *Motives of Honor*, 63–68; Hume and Hume, *Archaeology of Martin's Hundred*, vol. 1, chap. 5; Keith Pluymers, "Atlantic Iron: Wood Scarcity and the Political Ecology of Early English Expansion," *WMQ*, 3rd ser., 73 (2016): 389–426.

47. *RVC* 3:275–80. For civic building in England, see Robert Tittler, *Architecture and Power*. For the exploitation of servants, see Morgan, "First American Boom."

48. *RVC* 3:441.

49. *RVC* 3:130, 197–200, 207–10. See also, Walsh, *Motives of Honor*, 49–51; Hume and Hume, *Archaeology of Martin's Hundred*, vol. 1, chap. 3. The leading investor in this scheme, John Smyth, had authored a description of the structure of authority in his home hundred of Berkeley in Gloucestershire, see John Smyth, *A Description of the Hundred of Berkeley in the County of Gloucester and of Its Inhabitants*, vol. 3 of *The Berkeley Manuscripts*, ed. Sir John Maclean (Gloucester, UK: J. Bellows, 1883–1885); see also Horn, *Adapting to a New World*, 78–80.

50. For the role of radical Protestantism in early Virginia, see Haskell, *For God, King, and People*, chap. 1; Douglas Bradburn, "The Eschatological Origins of the English Empire," in *Early Modern Virginia: Reconsidering the Old Dominion*, ed. Douglas Bradburn and John C. Coombs (Charlottesville: University of Virginia Press, 2011), 15–56. For puritans and corporate life in England, see above, introduction, note 49. For Christopher Lawne, see John Bennett Boddie, *Seventeenth Century Isle of Wight County Virginia* (Chicago: Chicago Law Printing, 1938), chap. 2.

51. Craven, *Dissolution*, chap. 10.

52. Walsh, *Motives of Honor*, 106–10; Morgan, "First American Boom."

53. *RVC* 3:160; *Virginia Company Archives Online*, FP336; for an earlier version of this plan, see *RVC* 1:226; for the company's response, see *RVC* 3:479, 489, 647.

54. *RVC* 4:104–6; Frederick Fausz, "Patterns of Settlement," 41; J. Frederick Fausz, "The Powhatan Uprising of 1622: A Historical Study of Ethnocentrism and Cultural Conflict" (PhD diss., College of William and Mary, 1977).

55. *RVC* 3:656, 669.

56. *RVC* 4:9–17 (quotes, 12), 70–75, 98–101.

57. Charles T. Hodges, "Private Fortifications in 17th Century Virginia," in *The Archaeology of 17th-Century Virginia*, ed. Theodore R. Reinhart and Dennis J. Pogue (Richmond, VA: Dietz Press, 1993), 183–221; Hume and Hume, *Archaeology of Martin's Hundred*, vol. 1, chap. 3 (esp. 135–38); Ivor Noël Hume, *Martin's Hundred* (New York: Knopf, 1982), 235–39; Fausz, "Powhatan Uprising," chap. 5 (esp. table V.1). Some less hierarchical communities continued to exist; see David R. Ransome, "Village Tensions in Early Virginia: Sex, Land, and Status at the Neck of Land in the 1620s," *Historical Journal* 43 (2000): 365–81.

58. Withington, *Politics of Commonwealth*, 61–66 (quote, 63).

59. "A Remembrance for my Hoble good Lord Chancellor of England," Ellesmere MSS7922, Huntington Library, Pasadena, CA; Theodore Rabb, *Jacobean Gentleman*, chaps. 8–9; Ashton, *City and the Court*, chaps. 3–5.

60. For monopoly negotiations, see Craven, *Dissolution*, chap. 8; for their significance to new ideas about empire, see Haskell, *For God, King, and People*, 191–95, 202–8. For attitudes toward monopolies in England, see Sacks, "The Greed of Judas." For Crown finance, see Cramsie, *Kingship and Crown Finance*.

61. E. M. Rose is currently engaged in a reconsideration of the distinct ideas and approaches of the company's factions during this period; see E. M. Rose, "The Pirate, the Planter and the Purveyor: Three Models of Colonial Investment," paper presented at the Shelby Cullom Davis Center, Princeton University, March 3, 2017 (a copy of which the author kindly shared with me).

62. *RVC* 3: 302.

63. *RVC* 2:373–76; 4:93, 135, 174–82.

64. *RVC* 4:194–95, 223–24, 408–35 (quotes, 194, 223, 422). Bargrave also envisioned a new form of monopoly, in which colonists and merchants would share an interest; see John Bargrave, "A Treatise shewing howe to erecte a publique and increasing Treasurie for Virginia," mssHM 962, Huntington Library, Pasadena, CA. For Bargrave, see Haskell, *For God, King, and People*, 224–32; Peter Thompson, "Aristotle and King Alfred in America" in *Thomas Jefferson, the Classical World, and Early America*, ed. Peter S. Onuf and Nicholas P. Cole (Charlottesville: University of Virginia Press, 2011), 193–218; Stephen Bann, *Under the Sign: John Bargrave as Collector, Traveler, and Witness* (Ann Arbor: University of Michigan Press, 1994).

65. *RVC* 3:231. For Caswell and Danvers's plans, see *Virginia Company Archives Online*, FP121; FP166.

66. *RVC* 3:707–10 (quotes, 708). See also Slater, "Ideological Origins," 181–85.

67. Ellesmere Manuscripts 7046–7058, Huntington Library, Pasadena, CA; Thomas Phillips, *Londonderry and the London Companies, 1609–1629: being a survey and other documents submitted to King Charles I* (Belfast: HMSO, 1928), esp. 17, 54, 79–84. See also T. W. Moody, *The Londonderry Plantation, 1609–1641: The City of London and the Plantation in Ulster* (Belfast: William Mullan and Son, 1939); Horning, *Ireland in the Virginian Sea*, 276–77.

68. Gillian T. Cell, *Newfoundland Discovered: English Attempts at Colonisation, 1610–1630* (London: Hakluyt Society, 1982), 258–69 (quotes, 265–67). For proprietorships, see Robert M. Bliss, *Revolution and Empire: English Politics and the American Colonies in the Seventeenth Century* (Manchester, UK: Manchester University Press, 1990), 23–28; Ken MacMillan, *Sovereignty and Possession in the English New World: The Legal Foundations of Empire, 1576–1640* (Cambridge: Cambridge University Press, 2006), 96–98.

69. *APC* 1:109, 112, 113, 154, 162. The company remained committed to the urban model until the end; see *RVC* 4:259–62.

CHAPTER TWO

1. Morgan, *American Slavery*, chap. 6; Bernard Bailyn, "Politics and Social Structure in Virginia," in *Seventeenth-Century America: Essays in Colonial History*, ed. James Morton Smith (Chapel Hill: University of North Carolina Press, 1959), 90–115; Breen, "Looking Out for Number One." Other scholars have contested this picture;

see especially Horn, *Adapting to a New World*; Ransome, "Village Tensions in Early Virginia," 365–81.

2. For royal attitudes toward urban corporations, see Ashton, *City and the Court*; Withington, *Politics of Commonwealth*, chap. 3; for provincialism in English politics during this era, see J. S. Morrill, *The Revolt of the Provinces: Conservatives and Radicals in the English Civil War, 1630–1650* (London: Allen and Unwin, 1976); Alan Everitt, *The Community of Kent and the Great Rebellion, 1640–1660* (Leicester, UK: Leicester University Press, 1966). For critiques of the focus on provincialism, see Clive Holmes, "The County Community in Stuart Historiography," *Journal of British Studies* 19 (1980): 54–73; Ann Hughes, "The King, the Parliament, and the Localities during the English Civil War," *Journal of British Studies* 24 (1985): 236–63.

3. For the growth of these networks, see Robert Brenner, *Merchants and Revolution: Commercial Change, Political Conflict, and London's Overseas Traders, 1550–1653* (Princeton, NJ: Princeton University Press, 1991), chap. 4; Sacks, *The Widening Gate*, chap. 8; J. Frederick Fausz, "Merging and Emerging Worlds: Anglo-Indian Interest Groups and the Development of the Seventeenth-Century Chesapeake," in *Colonial Chesapeake Society*, ed. Lois Green Carr, Philip D. Morgan, and Jean B. Russo (Chapel Hill: University of North Carolina Press, 1988).

4. Kevin Sharpe, *The Personal Rule of Charles I* (New Haven, CT: Yale University Press, 1992); for the impact of these ideas on the empire, see Bliss, *Revolution and Empire*, chap. 2; Ken Macmillan, *The Atlantic Imperial Constitution: Center and Periphery in the English Atlantic World* (New York: Palgrave Macmillan, 2011). For transatlantic patronage networks, see Louis H. Roper, *The English Empire in America, 1602–1658: Beyond Jamestown* (New York: Pickering and Chatto, 2009).

5. These ideas have been overlooked because Charles I's interest in Virginia has long been seen as largely pecuniary, and Baltimore's vision for Maryland has been solely attributed to his Catholicism. For crown attitudes, see Warren M. Billings, *Sir William Berkeley and the Forging of Colonial Virginia* (Baton Rouge: Louisiana State University Press, 2004), chap. 2; Roper, *English Empire in America*, 105–16; Haskell, *For God, King, and People*, 202–6; for the focus on the Calverts, see John Krugler, *English and Catholic: The Lords Baltimore in the Seventeenth Century* (Baltimore: Johns Hopkins University Press, 2004); Antoinette Sutto, *Loyal Protestants and Dangerous Papists: Maryland and the Politics of Religion in the English Atlantic, 1630–1690* (Charlottesville: University of Virginia Press, 2015).

6. For previous accounts of the origins of counties, see Warren M. Billings, "The Growth of Political Institutions in Virginia, 1634–1676," *WMQ*, 3rd ser., 31 (1974): 225–42; Robert Wheeler, "The County Court in Colonial Virginia"; Lois Green Carr, "The Foundations of Social Order: Local Government in Colonial Maryland," in *Town and County: Essays on the Structure of Local Government in the American Colonies*, ed. Bruce C. Daniels (Middletown, CT: Wesleyan University Press, 1978), 72–110; Horn, *Adapting to a New World*, 187–99; Robert D. Mitchell, "American Origins and Regional Institutions: The Seventeenth-Century Chesapeake," *Annals of the Association of American Geographers* 73, no. 3 (1983): 404–20. For interpretations that tie the region's county structure to a particular English rural subculture, see Fischer, *Albion's Seed*; Tomlins, *Freedom Bound*, 258–76.

7. *JHB* 1:26–27; TNA PC 2/33, f.296v; *APC* 1:92–95.

8. Haskell, *For God, King, and People*, 210–58.

9. *HS* 1:125. The council even proposed a new urban plan for the colony in the spring of 1623; see *RVC* 4:102–3. In 1624, Richard Barnes was publically ejected from Jamestown and "banished from James Cittye," suggesting that the corporate city limits continued to hold meaning; see H. R. McIlwaine, *Minutes of the Council and General Court of Virginia, 1622–1632, 1670–1676* (Richmond: Library of Virginia, 1924), 14.

10. McIlwaine, *Minutes of the Council*, 55; see also *JHB* 1:27.

11. Fausz, "Merging and Emerging Worlds"; Konig, "'Dale's Laws' and the Non-Common Law Origins," 371–75; Billings, "Growth of Political Institutions," 225–27; Paul D. Halliday, "Brase's Case: Making Slave Law as Customary Law in Virginia's General Court, 1619–1625," in *Virginia 1619*, ed. Paul Musselwhite, Peter C. Mancall, and James Horn (Chapel Hill: University of North Carolina Press, forthcoming).

12. Morgan, "First American Boom."

13. McIlwaine, *Minutes of the Council*, 5; for continued references to the Cape Merchant, see 39.

14. Brenner, *Merchants and Revolution*, chap. 4; Sacks, *The Widening Gate*, chap. 8.

15. *JHB* 1:27.

16. McIlwaine, *Minutes of the Council*, 28.

17. [John Ferrar], *A Perfect Description of Virginia* . . . (London, 1649), 15. Dutch merchant David De Vries provided a similar description of George Menefie's plantation; see DeVries, *Voyages from Holland to America*, trans. Henry C. Murphy (New York: New York Historical Society, 1853), 50. For the country-house genre, see Raymond Williams, *The Country and the City* (New York: Oxford University Press, 1973), chaps. 3–5; McRae, *God Speed the Plough*, chap. 9; Kari Boyd McBride, *Country House Discourse in Early Modern England* (Aldershot: Ashgate, 2001); Hugh Jenkins, *Feigned Commonwealths: The Country-House Poem and the Fashioning of the Ideal Community* (Pittsburgh: Duquesne University Press, 1998). For leading planters' preoccupation with land grants, see J. Mills Thornton, "The Thrusting Out of Governor Harvey: A Seventeenth-Century Rebellion," *VMHB* 76 (1968): 11–26.

18. James D. Rice, *Nature and History in the Potomac Country: From Hunter-Gatherers to the Age of Jefferson* (Baltimore: Johns Hopkins University Press, 2016), chap. 5; Fausz, "Merging and Emerging Worlds." The development of the fur trade was notably absent from royal discussions about diversifying the Chesapeake economy. This was likely because it was already being pursued by the merchant networks but was unlikely to ever serve the purpose that most concerned the Crown: the employment of large numbers of colonists as the basis for a permanent colonial commonwealth.

19. *JHB* 1:23. For Jamestown's recovery, see Horning, *Ireland in the Virginian Sea*, 318–32; Karen Bellinger Wehner, "Crafting Lives, Crafting Society in Seventeenth-Century Jamestown, Virginia" (PhD diss., New York University, 2006), 107–77, 427–53; Audrey Horning and Andrew C. Edwards, *Archaeology in New Towne, 1993–1995* (Williamsburg, VA: Colonial Williamsburg, 2000), chap. 13; Cary Carson, Audrey Horning, and Bly Straube, *Evaluation of Previous Archaeology* (Williamsburg, VA: Colonial Williamsburg, 2006), 45–47, 96–108; Martha W. McCartney, *James City County: Keystone of the Commonwealth* (Virginia Beach, VA: Donning, 1997), 45–46.

20. Martha W. McCartney, *Jamestown People to 1800: Landowners, Public Officials, Minorities, and Native Leaders* (Baltimore: Genealogical Publishing Company, 2012), 283; Horning, "'A Verie Fit Place,'" 152–55.

21. Sharpe, *Personal Rule*, 242–62 (quotes, 246, 247); see also Ashton, *City and the Court*, chap. 4.

22. TNA PC 2/33, f.240. The Privy Council repeatedly quizzed officials in the colony about what happened to the public stock left from the Virginia Company era; see TNA PC 2/36, f.76; *APC* 1:96–97; Morgan, *American Slavery*, 119–25. See also, TNA PC 2/32, f.342; 2/33, f.148, f.294; 2/38, f.373.

23. *APC* 1:103–4.

24. TNA CO 1/4, no. 32.

25. Quoted in Thomas Cogswell, "'In the Power of the State': Mr Anys's Project and the Tobacco Colonies, 1626–1628," *English Historical Review* 123 (2008): 35–64 (quote, 44).

26. TNA CO 1/4 f.84; Sharpe, *Personal Rule*, 257–62; for other perspectives on diversification schemes in England during this period, see Thirsk, *Economic Policy and Projects*; Wrightson, *Earthly Necessities*, chaps. 7 and 9. Contemporary merchants acknowledged that the king had encouraged diversification in the Chesapeake and that the region's dependence upon tobacco was not to be blamed upon him; see "Copy Speech To General Committee Of Virginia Company On Fraudulent Dealings In Tobacco, Undated," *HP* 61/2/3A.

27. TNA CO 1/5 no. 103; TNA PC 2/40, f.128; see also the Crown's sponsorship of a diversification project led by William Capps, TNA CO 1/4, no. 32; 1/5, no. 32.

28. TNA PC 2/33, f.147–48.

29. *APC* 1:92–95; TNA PC 2/33, f.296v.

30. Cogswell, "'In the Power of the State,'" 42, 49.

31. TNA PC 2/43, 63. For efforts to reestablish the Virginia Company, see Thornton, "Thrusting Out"; Brenner, *Merchants and Revolution*, 130–34.

32. The king returned to plans to establish a tobacco monopoly to fix prices for small planters; see TNA CO 1/9, 230–33; *JHB* 1: 57–65. For other interpretations of the tobacco debates, see L. H. Roper, "Charles I, Virginia, and the Idea of Atlantic History," *Itinerario* 30, no. 2 (2006): 33–53; MacMillan, *Atlantic Imperial Constitution*, 100–107.

33. Valerie Pearl, *London and the Outbreak of the Puritan Revolution: City Government and National Politics, 1625–1643* (Oxford: Oxford University Press, 1961), chaps. 1–3; Ashton, *City and the Court*, chap. 4; Sharpe, *Personal Rule*, 403–12. For Dover, see J. S. Kepler, *The Exchange of Christendom: The International Entrepôt at Dover, 1622–1641* (Leicester: Leicester University Press, 1976), chaps. 1–4.

34. TNA CO 1/4, no. 37 (quote, f.92v); see also CO 1/8, no. 12.

35. TNA CO 1/4, no. 55. For Harvey's commission in 1623, see TNA CO 1/3, no. 7.

36. Ashton, *City and the Court*, 121–49; Brenner, *Merchants and Revolution*, 219–39.

37. TNA CO 1/6, no. 54 (quote, f.135v). For Harvey's instructions, see TNA PC 2/38, f.373–77.

38. TNA CO 1/5, nos. 93–95; 1/6, no. 11 (quote, f.22r).

39. "Virginia in 1632–33–34," *VMHB* 8 (1900): 148; *HS* 1:208.

40. Horning, *Ireland in the Virginian Sea*, 335–38; Horning "'A Verie Fit Place,'" 146–87.

41. TNA CO 1/3, no. 7; PC 2/33, f.295r; "Decisions of the Virginia General Court 1626–1628," *VMHB* (Jan. 1897), 365–66. For Harvey's legislation, see *HS* 1:163.

42. Rice, *Nature and History*, 95–96. For Harvey's attitude toward Dutch trade, see "Virginia in 1632–33–34," *VMHB* 8 (1900): 149–50; "Virginia in 1635: The Deposing of Governor Harvey (Continued)," *VMHB* 8 (1901): 405.

43. For Harvey's merchant committee, see TNA CO 1/10, no. 15. For the customs office, see TNA CO 1/9, nos. 9, 20. For domestic customs, see Ashton, *City and the Court*, 147–56.

44. TNA CO 1/10, no. 5 (quotes, f.9v–10r, 10v).

45. "Virginia in 1632–33–34," 150.

46. Clayton Coleman Hall, ed., *Narratives of Early Maryland, 1633–1684* (New York: Charles Scribner's Sons, 1910), 60–61.

47. "Virginia in 1632–33–34," 157; "Sir Thomas Wyatt, Governor: Documents, 1624–1626," *WMQ*, 2nd ser., 8 (1924): 164–67; *HS* 1:208. A lack of genuine enthusiasm among Virginia's elite for a mixed pastoral landscape may explain why the palisade quickly fell into disrepair; see Philip Levy, "A New Look at an Old Wall: Indians, Englishmen, Landscape, and the 1634 Palisade at Middle Plantation," *VMHB* 112 (2004): 226–65; Virginia DeJohn Anderson, "Animals into the Wilderness: The Development of Livestock Husbandry in the Seventeenth-Century Chesapeake," *WMQ*, 3rd ser., 59 (2002): 377–408; Virginia DeJohn Anderson, *Creatures of Empire: How Domestic Animals Transformed Early America* (Oxford: Oxford University Press, 2004), 109–17.

48. TNA CO 1/5, no. 94; CO 1/4, no. 10 (f.28r–v).

49. Ferrar's marginalia on page 10 of William Bullock's *Virginia Impartially Examined* (1649), transcribed by Peter Thompson and available online at http://oieahc.wm.edu/wmq/Jan04/ThompsonWeb.pdf. The scholarship on the exploitation of bound labor and the origins of ideas about mastery in the plantation context is extensive; see Jordan, *White over Black*, chap. 2; Morgan, *American Slavery*, chap. 6; Tomlins, *Freedom Bound*, 262–69; Michael Guasco, *Slaves and Englishmen: Human Bondage in the Early Modern Atlantic World* (Philadelphia: University of Pennsylvania Press, 2014), chaps. 5–6.

50. McCartney, *Jamestown People*, 283. For Claiborne's commission, see Hale, *Virginia Venturer*, 140–46.

51. The efforts to reestablish the company were directed through the Dorset Commission, which was composed of staunch allies of the Virginia planters; for their recommendations for wide-ranging local powers, see "Virginia in 1631," *VMHB* 8 (1900): 36–39. For the 1632 draft order, see TNA CO 1/6, 70.

52. For the Maryland charter and the opposition in Virginia, see Krugler, *English and Catholic*, chaps. 5–6; Sutto, *Loyal Protestants*, chap. 1; Haskell, *For God, King, and People*, 246–58.

53. Rice, *Nature and History*, chap. 5; Fausz, "Merging and Emerging Worlds," 71–72.

54. Haskell, *For God, King, and People*, 260.

55. "Virginia in 1631," *VMHB* 8 (1900): 43–45; *HS* 1:161–64, 168–70, 185–94, 203–8.

56. The claim that Virginia's counties were established in 1634 is made in *HS* 1: 223–24. Jon Kukla has challenged the validity of this source; see Kukla, "The Founding of Virginia Counties—1634?" *Magazine of Virginia Genealogy* 22, no. 3 (1984): 3–6. However, a 1634 census of Virginia tithables was also divided by county; see TNA CO 1/8, no. 55.

57. Scholars have long asserted that the county system was established by the new royal commission established in 1634 under the leadership of Archbishop William Laud; see Thornton, "Thrusting Out," 25; Billings, "Growth of Political Institutions." However, it would have been impossible for instructions from the Laud Commission to have been debated, drafted, and implemented in Virginia before the 1634 Virginia census. I have not found any documents, or citations to documents, addressed to Virginia during this period that instruct the establishment of counties.

58. TNA CO 1/8, no. 61 (quotes, f.166r, 166v); for the concept of the county community, see Everitt, *The Community of Kent*.

59. TNA CO 1/8, no. 65 (quote, f.178v).

60. CO 1/32, no. 4. For accounts of Harvey's ouster, see Thornton, "Thrusting Out"; Billings, *A Little Parliament*, 20–22; Haskell, *For God, King, and People*, 258–71.

61. TNA CO 1/9, no. 9. Harvey's time in England saw a flurry of activity; see CO 1/9, nos. 17, 18, 20, 45, 47, 98.

62. T. H. Breen, "George Donne's 'Virginia Reviewed': A 1638 Plan to Reform Colonial Society," *WMQ*, 3rd ser., 30 (1973): 449–66 (quote, 462).

63. TNA CO 1/9, nos. 20, 47 (quotes, f.121r–v), 132.

64. "Virginia in 1636–38: Harvey's Second Administration," *VMHB* 10 (1902): 265, 272. Harvey did grant free urban lots; see "Virginia under Governor Harvey," *VMHB* 3 (1895): 29–30. For Kemp's property, see Carson, *Evaluation of Previous Archaeology*, 63–67.

65. *JHB* 1:57–63. Harvey's objectives were tied to the king's renewed plan of establishing a tobacco monopoly; see Roper, "Charles I, Virginia."

66. TNA PC 2/49, f.356; CO 1/9, no. 122; for Harvey's response, see TNA CO 1/10, no. 5, f.9r–10v. The Privy Council had reiterated support for rules restricting trade as recently as 1638; see TNA PC 2/49, f.356.

67. "Virginia in 1638–39," 54–57.

68. *Charter of Maryland: 1632*, see http://avalon.law.yale.edu/17th_century/ma01.asp. For the unusual extent of the powers conveyed by the Maryland charter, see MacMillan, *Sovereignty and Possession*, 98–99. For the Calverts' interest in colonial projects, see Krugler, *English and Catholic*; Sutto, *Loyal Protestants*, chaps. 1–2.

69. "Conditions of Plantation," in Hall, *Narratives*, 91–92. See Garry Wheeler Stone, "Manorial Maryland," *MHM* 82 (1987): 3–37; Carr, Menard, and Walsh, *Robert Cole's World*, 8–12.

70. Hall, *Narratives*, 17–22; Russell R. Menard, "Economy and Society in Early Colonial Maryland" (PhD diss., University of Iowa, 1975), 27. For Calvert's interest in the fur trade, see Fausz, "Merging and Emerging Worlds," 65–71; Rice, *Nature and History*, chap. 5 (esp. 97).

71. *Archives* 1: 4, 20, 75–76. For London, see Sharpe, *Personal Rule*, 404.

72. "Thomas Cornwaleys to Cecil Calvert, 14 April 1638," in *Calvert Papers*, no. 1,

Maryland Historical Society Fund Publication no. 28 (Baltimore: Maryland Historical Society, 1889), 169–81 (quotes, 176, 177, 179). For Cornwaleys, see Timothy B. Riordan, *The Plundering Time: Maryland and the English Civil War, 1645–1646* (Baltimore: Maryland Historical Society, 2003) 23–26, 194–97; Menard, "Economy and Society," 33–35, 86–89.

73. For town land, see Menard, "Economy and Society," 27, 57–66. For the factors hindering urban growth, see Lois Green Carr, "'The Metropolis of Maryland': A Comment on Town Development along the Tobacco Coast," *MHM* 69 (1974): 124–45. For the problems with manorial authority, see David W. Jordan, *Foundations of Representative Government* (Cambridge: Cambridge University Press, 1987), 15, 20. The situation was made worse when the supply of furs at St. Mary's dried up in the late 1630s as a result of shifts in indigenous geopolitics; see Rice, *Nature and History*, 97–102.

74. For Kent Island, see Fausz, "Merging and Emerging Worlds"; Brenner, *Merchants and Revolution*, 120–24; Russell Menard, "Maryland's 'Time of Troubles': Sources of Political Disorder in Early St. Mary's," *MHM* 76 (1981): 128–33.

75. Sutto, *Loyal Protestants*, chaps. 2–3.

76. For Calvert's commission, see Riordan, *Plundering Time*, 156–60; see also "An Act For publique ports" (1639) in *Archives* 1:76. For Calvert's efforts to impose this authority in Virginia, see Warren M. Billings, *The Papers of Sir William Berkeley, 1605–1677* (Richmond: Library of Virginia, 2007), 62–66.

77. Riordan, *Plundering Time* (for Ingle's connection with Claiborne, see 172, 185). See also Menard, "Maryland's 'Time of Troubles,'" 124–40.

78. Riordan, *Plundering Time*, 226–35, 271 (quote, 226).

79. TNA SP 16/508, 41–42.

80. TNA SP 16/508 (quote, 97). See also depositions recorded in TNA HCA 13/60, 13/119.

81. Riordan, *Plundering Time*, 236–38.

82. For the development of hundreds, see Menard, "Economy and Society," 58–60.

83. *Archives* 1:55–57, 129. During the enquiries into Ingle's uprising, two of the Calverts' allies provided contradictory information about the spatial organization of the colony; John Lewgar told officials that Maryland consisted "of two Counties," but Thomas Cornwallis described the colony's two jurisdictions using the urban monikers "Kent Towne" and "St. Maries"; see "Deposition of John Lewgar, 6 Aug. 1645" in TNA HCA 13/60; "Deposition of Thomas Cornwallis, 8 Aug. 1645" in TNA HCA 13/60.

84. For the assembly, see *Archives* 1:127–31, 146–47; this session also strengthened county jurisdiction; see *Archives* 1:147–64. For the Susquehannock threat, see Rice, *Nature and History*, 102–3. For the Kent Islanders' rebuffs to Claiborne, see Riordan, *Plundering Time*, 174–75, 290–91.

85. *Archives* 3:237–41, 256. Some scholars suggest that Brooke established a town on the Patuxent River named Battletown; see Stein, *A History of Calvert County*, 17–21. For the explicit analogy between Brooke's county grant and a Virginia county, see *Archives* 3:238.

86. *Archives* 3:257–58; Land, *Colonial Maryland*, 49–50; Hall, *Narratives*, 235. Al Luckenbach, *Providence 1649: The History and Archaeology of Anne Arundel County, Maryland's First European Settlement* (Annapolis: Maryland State Archives, 1995).

87. The predominant scholarly interpretation is that Ingle's rebellion spelled the end of Baltimore's manorial plans and inaugurated an era of small freehold landownership; see Menard, "Economy and Society," chap. 5 (quote, 213).

88. For a comparison to the process of county formation and state building in England and Ireland, see Braddick, *State Formation*; Jon G. Crawford, *Anglicizing the Government of Ireland: The Irish Privy Council and the Expansion of Tudor Rule, 1556–1578* (Dublin: Irish Academic Press, 1993), esp. 415; Annaleigh Margey, "Representing Plantation Landscapes: The Mapping of Ulster, c. 1560–1640," in *Plantation Ireland: Settlement and Material Culture, c. 1550–c. 1700*, ed. James Lyttleton and Colin Rynne (Dublin: Four Courts Press, 2009), 140–64 (esp. 144–46).

CHAPTER THREE

1. On this larger imperial project, see Bliss, *Revolution and Empire*, chap. 3; Brenner, *Merchants and Revolution*; Carla Gardina Pestana, *The English Atlantic in an Age of Revolution, 1640–1661* (Cambridge, MA: Harvard University Press, 2004), chap. 5; John Donoghue, *Fire under the Ashes: An Atlantic History of the English Revolution* (Chicago: University of Chicago Press, 2013).

2. William Bullock, *Virginia Impartially Examined* (London, 1649), 10.

3. The Navigation Act has a rich historiography; see Charles M. Andrews, *The Colonial Period of American History*, vol. 4, *England's Commercial and Colonial Policy* (New Haven, CT: Yale University Press, 1938), chap. 2 (esp. 34–49); R. W. K. Hinton, *The Eastland Trade and the Commonweal in the Seventeenth Century* (Cambridge: Cambridge University Press, 1959), chap. 7; Bliss, *Revolution and Empire*, chap. 3; Brenner, *Merchants and Revolution*, chap. 12; Steven C. A. Pincus, *Protestantism and Patriotism: Ideologies and the Making of English Foreign Policy, 1650–1668* (Cambridge: Cambridge University Press, 1996), part 1. Thomas Leng, "Commercial Conflict and Regulation in the Discourse of Trade in Seventeenth-Century England," *Historical Journal* 48 (2005): 933–54. For Worsley's crucial intellectual and practical contribution to the policy, see Thomas Leng, *Benjamin Worsley (1618–1677): Trade, Industry, and the Spirit in Revolutionary England* (Woodbridge, UK: Boydell, 2008), chap. 3. For contemporary concerns about the relationship between republicanism and empire, see David Armitage, "The Cromwellian Protectorate and the Languages of Empire," *Historical Journal* 35 (1992): 531–55; Armitage, *Ideological Origins*, chap. 5.

4. Billings, "Growth of Political Institutions"; Billings, *Sir William Berkeley*, chaps. 3 and 6; Carr, "The Foundations of Social Order."

5. *HS* 1:242, 252, 286, 300, 319, 362; Billings, *Papers of Sir William Berkeley*, 36, 66; De Vries, *Voyages from Holland*, 183. For Jamestown during the 1640s, see Carson et al., "New World, Real World," 71–72; Audrey J. Horning and Andrew C. Edwards, *Archaeology in New Towne, 1993–1995* (Williamsburg, VA: Colonial Williamsburg, 2000), 140–41; Carson et al., *Evaluation of Previous Archaeology*, 41–42, 48–51, 58–69, 147.

6. Billings, "Growth of Political Institutions"; Jon Kukla, *Political Institutions in Virginia, 1619–1660* (New York: Garland, 1989), chap. 4. For mercantile regulation, see *HS* 1:245–46.

7. *HS* 1:277, 285, 287, 292–93, 317–18, 326–27. For the Third Anglo-Powhatan War, see Rice, *Nature and History*, 121–29.

8. *HS* 1:240 (quote), 291, 309–10. For Berkeley's ecclesiastical policies, see Edward L. Bond, *Damned Souls in a Tobacco Colony: Religion in Seventeenth-Century Virginia* (Macon, GA: Mercer University Press, 2000), 146–57; see also, Haskell, *For God, King, and People*, 289–307.

9. DeVries, *Voyages from Holland*, 182; Victor Enthoven and Wim Klooster, "The Rise and Fall of the Virginia-Dutch Connection in the Seventeenth Century," in *Early Modern Virginia: Reconsidering the Old Dominion*, ed. Douglas Bradburn and John C. Coombs (Charlottesville: University of Virginia Press, 2011), 90–127. John R. Pagan, "Dutch Maritime and Commercial Activity in Mid-Seventeenth-Century Virginia," *VMHB* 90 (1982): 485–501; April Lee Hatfield, *Atlantic Virginia: Intercolonial Relations in the Seventeenth Century* (Philadelphia: University of Pennsylvania Press, 2004), chap. 2. For Berkeley's decision to cultivate Dutch trade, see Billings, *Sir William Berkeley*, chap. 6. For Charles I's efforts to block the Dutch trade, see Macmillan, *Atlantic Imperial Constitution*, chap. 4.

10. All of the legislation regulating tobacco from Harvey's governorship was allowed to lapse in 1643. The only regulation about tobacco passed by Berkeley related to trade with Maryland; see *HS* 1:276. For tobacco production and prices, see Walsh, *Motives of Honor*, chap. 2; Russell R. Menard, "The Tobacco Industry in the Chesapeake Colonies, 1617–1730: An Interpretation," *Research in Economic History* 5 (1980): 131–33.

11. Tomlins, *Freedom Bound*, 265–67 (quote, 265); Walsh, *Motives of Honor*, chap. 2 (esp. 134–37); Menard, "Economy and Society," chap. 5; Warren M. Billings, "The Law of Servants and Slaves in Seventeenth-Century Virginia," *VMHB* 99 (1991): 45–62. For the legislation, see *HS* 1:252–57, 74–75.

12. *HS* 1:245. For slave imports during the 1640s, see Walsh, *Motives of Honor*, 138–42; John Coombs, "Building 'The Machine': The Development of Slavery and Slave Society in Early Colonial Virginia" (PhD diss., College of William and Mary, 2003), chap. 2.

13. "Mr Johnson to John Ferrar, Mulberry Island, Va., 25 June 1650," *Virginia Company Archives Online*, FP1160.

14. Bullock, *Virginia Impartially Examined*, 17; Kukla, *Political Institutions*, 110–48; Billings, *Sir William Berkeley*, chap. 6.

15. *Archives* 3:237–41 (quote, 237).

16. For English concerns about Charles I's personal rule, see Sharpe, *Personal Rule*, chap. 9; Richard Cust, "The Collapse of Royal Power in England, 1637–1642," in *The Oxford Handbook of the English Revolution*, ed. Michael J. Braddick (Oxford: Oxford University Press, 2015). For Berkeley's opposition to Parliament, see Billings, *Sir William Berkeley*, chap. 6; Kukla, *Political Institutions*, 148–57. For Maryland, see Sutto, *Loyal Protestants*, 55–57; see also, *CSPC* 1:332–33, 344.

17. Charles Webster, *The Great Instauration: Science, Medicine and Reform 1626–1660* (Oxford: Lang, 2002); Mark Greengrass, Michael Leslie, and Timothy Raylor, eds., *Samuel Hartlib and Universal Reformation: Studies in Intellectual Communication* (Cambridge: Cambridge University Press, 1994); Ted McCormick, *William Petty and the Ambitions of Political Arithmetic* (Oxford: Oxford University Press, 2009), chap. 2; Carl Wennerlind, *Casualties of Credit: The English Financial Revolution, 1620–1720*

(Cambridge, MA: Harvard University Press, 2011), chap. 2; Blair Hoxby, *Mammon's Music: Literature and Economics in the Age of Milton* (New Haven, CT: Yale University Press, 2002), chap. 1.

18. "Benjamin Worsley to Samuel Hartlib, 13 Aug. 1649," *HP* 33/2/1B; "A Memorandum of the Virginia Plantation, undated," *HP* 61/5/1A–2B (quotes, 1A, 1B). The fact that Dutch competition caused Worsley to focus particularly on the Chesapeake trade is significant. English officials had long been concerned about Dutch trade with Barbados, which was also a royalist colony, but Worsley's surviving notes on imperial trade do not mention the Caribbean island apart from his praise for their efforts to diversify away from tobacco and pioneer agricultural innovations. Although sugar would come to dominate in the English Caribbean to the same extent that tobacco did in the Chesapeake, during the 1640s, as Caribbean planters experimented with indigo, cotton, sugar, and other commodities, it appeared to contemporaries as if the islands had achieved a level of economic maturation that the Chesapeake lacked; for this opinion in the 1630s, see TNA CO 1/9, no. 20. For the Hartlib circle's intense interest in the sugar industry, see Eric Otremba, "Enlightened Institutions: Science, Plantations, and Slavery in the English Atlantic, 1626–1700" (PhD diss., University of Minnesota, 2012), 39–51. For the sugar industry in Barbados during the 1640s, see Russell Menard, *Sweet Negotiations: Sugar, Slavery, and Plantation Agriculture in Early Barbados* (Charlottesville: University of Virginia Press, 2006); Simon P. Newman, *A New World of Labor: The Development of Plantation Slavery in the British Atlantic* (Philadelphia: University of Pennsylvania Press, 2016), chap. 3.

19. Bullock, *Virginia Impartially Examined*, 4, 10; Peter Thompson, ed., "Transcription of John Ferrar's Marginalia in the Bodleian Library's Copy of William Bullock's Virginia Impartially Examined," *WMQ* web supplement, http://oieahc.wm.edu/wmq/Jan04/ThompsonWeb.pdf, 2.

20. Todd, *Christian Humanism*; Tittler, *Reformation and the Towns*; Withington, *Politics of Commonwealth*, chap. 8. On corporate towns in the English Civil War, see Ian Roy, "The English Republic, 1649–1660: The View from the Town Hall," in *Republiken und Republikanismus im Europa der Frühen Neuzeit*, ed. Helmut G. Koenigsberger (Munich: R. Oldenbourg, 1988), 213–37; Stephen Porter, ed., *London and the Civil War* (London: Palgrave Macmillan, 1996).

21. Todd, *Christian Humanism*, chap. 5 (esp. 164–67); Underdown, *Fire from Heaven*; Paul Slack, "Poverty and Politics in Salisbury, 1597–1666," in *Crisis and Order in English Towns, 1500–1700: Essays in Urban History*, ed. Peter Clark and Paul Slack (London: Routledge, 1972), 164–203.

22. Barry Levy, *Town Born*, chap. 1. John Donoghue outlines a similar puritan program of transatlantic reform, see Donoghue, *Fire under the Ashes*, chaps. 1–2. For puritan conceptions of commerce, see Mark Valeri, *Heavenly Merchandize: How Religion Shaped Commerce in Puritan America* (Princeton, NJ: Princeton University Press, 2010).

23. Gabriel Plattes, *A Description of the Famous Kingdome of Macaria* (London, 1641), 11. For general scholarship on the Hartlib circle, see above n. 17.

24. Mark Jenner, "'Another epocha'? Hartlib, John Lanyon and the Improvement of London in the 1650s," in Greengrass, Leslie, and Raylor, *Samuel Hartlib and Universal*

Reformation, 343–56; Henry Robinson, *Briefe Considerations, Concerning the advancement of Trade and Navigation* . . . (London, 1649), 4, 9; Henry Robinson, *Certain Proposalls In order to the Peoples Freedome and Accomodation in some Particulars* . . . (London, 1652), 8. Robinson had articulated these ideas about urban development since the early 1640s; see also Henry Robinson, *Englands Safety In Trades Encrease* (London, 1641), esp. 5–7.

25. Walter W. Woodward, *Prospero's America: John Winthrop Jr., Alchemy, and the Creation of New England Culture, 1606–1676* (Chapel Hill: University of North Carolina Press, 2010), chap 3.

26. For Worsley's youth and his activities in the Netherlands, see Leng, *Benjamin Worsley*, chaps. 1–2. For Worsley's commitment to state unity, see Haskell, *For God, King, and People*, 310–14.

27. Bullock, *Virginia Impartially Examined*; see also Peter Thompson, "William Bullock's 'Strange Adventure': A Plan to Transform Seventeenth-Century Virginia," *WMQ*, 3rd ser., 61 (2004): 107–28.

28. Bullock, *Virginia Impartially Examined*, 44, 51–52. John Ferrar also sought to encourage tradesmen; see [John Ferrar], *A Perfect Description of Virginia* (London, 1649), 7–8.

29. Bullock, *Virginia Impartially Examined*, 10, 18–19.

30. "Benjamin Worsley to John Dury, 27th July 1649," *HP* 33/2/18A. Bradburn, "Eschatological Origins"; Kevin Butterfield, "Puritans and Religious Strife in the Early Chesapeake," *VMHB* 109 (2001): 5–36; Bond, *Damned Souls*, 147–48.

31. Anon., *New Englands First Fruits* (London, 1643), 9; Hatfield, *Atlantic Virginia*, chap. 5. For parish and county structure on the south side, see *HS* 1:228, 247, 250–51, 277–79, 404, 409. For the Lancaster project, see Horn, *Adapting to a New World*, 174–75n23.

32. John Bennett Boddie, *Seventeenth Century Isle of Wight County, Virginia* (Chicago: Chicago Law Printing, 1938), chap. 4.

33. "John Stirrup to John Ferrar, 26th Jan. 1650," *Virginia Company Archives Online*, FP1152; "Michael Upchurch to John Ferrar, 27th Mar. 1651," *Virginia Company Archives Online*, FP1204. For the character of the Providence settlement, see Luckenbach, *Providence 1649*; Jason D. Moser, Al Luckenbach, Sherri M. Marsh, and Donna Ware, "Impermanent Architecture in a Less Permanent Town: The Mid-Seventeenth-Century Architecture of Providence, Maryland," *Perspectives in Vernacular Architecture* 9 (2003): 197–214.

34. "Benjamin Worsley to Dury, 27th July 1649," *HP* 33/2/18A; "Benjamin Worsley to Samuel Hartlib, 13th Aug. 1649," *HP* 33/2/1A; see also "A Memorandum of the Virginia Plantation," *HP* 61/5/1A–2B.

35. Benjamin Worsley, "Memo on Virginia Plantation, Adapted from Worsley's letter to Dury, Undated," *HP* 33/2/22A–B (quotes, 22A, 22B); "Worsley to Hartlib, 13 Aug 1649," *HP* 33/2/1A–2B (quote, 2A); see also, "Further Animadversions About Virginia," *HP* 61/6/1A–2B.

36. "Worsley to Dury, 27 Aug 1649," *HP* 33/2/3A–4B (quote, 3B); Worsley, "Further Animadversions," *HP* 61/6/1A–2B (quotes, 1A, 2A). For the adaptation of the Virginia plans, see Leng, *Benjamin Worsley*, 57–60.

37. *CSPC* 1:361. For other interpretations of the commission, see Brenner, *Merchants and Revolution*, 595–98; Billings, *Sir William Berkeley*, 108–10.

38. "An Act for the Advancing and Regulating of the Trade of this Commonwealth," *Acts and Ordinances of the Interregnum, 1642–1660*, 2:403–6 (quote, 403), online at http://www.british-history.ac.uk/source.aspx?pubid=606.

39. While the free port plan was being considered, Parliament was already placing restrictions on colonial trade in the form of "An Act for prohibiting Trade with the Barbadoes, Virginia, Bermuda and Antego," *Acts and Ordinances of the Interregnum, 1642–1660*, 2:425–29, online at http://www.british-history.ac.uk/source.aspx?pubid=606. For the Navigation Act of 1651, see "An Act for Increase of Shipping, and Encouragement of the Navigation of this Nation," ibid., 2:559–62.

40. Leng, *Benjamin Worsley*, 60–70, 73–79; Leng, "Commercial Conflict and Regulation." The passage of the Navigation Act obviously involved a far broader range of interests from across the Commonwealth leadership; see Pincus, *Protestantism and Patriotism*, chaps. 3–4; Brenner, *Merchants and Revolution*, 613–28. Worsley's arguments were outlined in two pamphlets: B. W[orsley], *Free Ports, the nature and necessity of them stated* (London, 1652); Worsley, *The Advocate* (London, 1652).

41. "John Dury? To Benjamin Worsley?, Aug. 17, 1649," *HP* 1/2/11A; "A Memorandum of the Virginia Plantation," *HP* 61/5/1B.

42. Billings, *Sir William Berkeley*, 109–12; "Surrender of Virginia to the Parliamentary Commissioners, March 1651–2," *VMHB* 11 (1903): 32–41.

43. Warren M. Billings, "Some Acts Not in Hening's 'Statutes': The Acts of Assembly, April 1652, November 1652, and July 1653," *VMHB* 83 (1975): 22–76 (quotes, 70). Information about burgesses' service compiled by the author from *JHB* 1:vii–xx; see also Kukla, *Political Institutions*, 163. The dominant scholarly interpretation of these events has emphasized continuity; see Billings, *A Little Parliament*, 34; Kukla, *Political Institutions*, 158–69.

44. Billings, "Some Acts," 70. The authority of the new corporations over trade was likely intended to substitute for powers previously held by county courts, because regulation of the market was one of the few powers of the county court that was not recodified in 1652; see Kukla, *Political Institutions*, 164, 245n7.

45. "Worsley to Dury, 27th Aug. 1649," *HP* 33/2/3B.

46. "Worsley to Dury, 27th Aug. 1649," *HP* 33/2/3B.

47. For territorial expansion, see Horn, *Adapting to a New World*, 162, 174–87; Rice, *Nature and History*, 121–29. For Dutch trade, see Enthoven and Klooster, "Rise and Fall," 105–7. For the pattern of unfree labor migration, see Coombs, "Phases of Conversion," 341–48. For the stability of tobacco profits, see Russell R. Menard, "A Note on Chesapeake Tobacco Prices, 1618–1660," *VMHB* 84 (1976): 401–10.

48. *Virginia and Maryland; or, The Lord Baltimore's Printed Case Uncased and Answered* (London, 1655), in *Narratives of Early Maryland, 1633–1684*, ed. Clayton Coleman Hall (New York: Charles Scribner's Sons, 1910), 226; "Surrender of Virginia," 32–35. Sutto, *Loyal Protestants*, chap. 4.

49. For tensions between the puritans and Baltimore, see Sutto, *Loyal Protestants*, 61–67; Jordan, *Foundations*, 51–55.

50. C. Jane Cox, "Rediscovering the Lost Colonial Towns of Anne Arundel County,

Maryland," in *Urban Places in the Chesapeake*, ed. Julia King (forthcoming); Luckenbach, *Providence 1649*; Moser et al. "Impermanent Architecture." The existence of a nucleated settlement at Patuxent is attested by Leonard Strong, *Babylon's Fall in Maryland*... (London, 1655), esp. 4–5.

51. Jordan, *Foundations*, 53–54; Charles County, see *Archives* 3:308.

52. *Archives* 3:311–13 (quote, 312).

53. *Archives* 3:312; *Virginia and Maryland*, 226–28.

54. *Virginia and Maryland*, 199; Sutto, *Loyal Protestants*, 69–73.

55. *Virginia and Maryland*, 218–20 (my emphasis). A sympathetic pamphlet described Patuxent and Severn as "Ports," thus extending the presumption of local authority to also include commerce; see Roger Heaman, *An Additional brief Narrative Of a late Bloody Design Against The Protestants in Ann Arundel County, and Severn, in Maryland in the Country of Virginia*... (London, 1655), 7.

56. Strong, *Babylon's Fall*, 6–7; John Langford, *Refutation of Babylon's Fall* (London, 1655), in Hall, *Narratives*, 255; John Hammond, *Hammond versus Heamans, or An Answer*... (London, 1655), 11.

57. Strong, *Babylon's Fall*, 4; *Virginia and Maryland*, 228.

58. Strong, *Babylon's Fall*, 5, 10.

59. For commercial regulation, see *HS* 1:412–14 and also 469, 476. For the power of the county court, see Billings, "Growth of Political Institutions"; for expansion of counties, see Michael F. Doran, *Atlas of County Boundary Changes in Virginia, 1634–1895* (Athens, GA: Iberian, 1987), 6–15.

60. John Ruston Pagan, *Anne Orthwood's Bastard: Sex and Law in Early Virginia* (Oxford: Oxford University Press, 2003). Coombs, "Phases of Conversion," 346–47; for forced labor in the Revolutionary Atlantic, see Donohue, *Fire under the Ashes*. The establishment of "stability" in these years has been given many inflections by historians; see Morgan, *American Slavery*, chap. 8; Jack P. Greene, *Pursuits of Happiness: The Social Development of Early Modern British Colonies and the Formation of American Culture* (Chapel Hill: University of North Carolina Press, 2003), 13–18; Darrett B. Rutman and Anita H. Rutman, *A Place in Time: Middlesex County, Virginia, 1650–1750* (New York: Norton, 1984), chap. 2; Horn, *Adapting to a New World*, chap. 4.

61. Billings, *Papers of Sir William Berkeley*, 108–10. For Jamestown, see Carson et al., "New World, Real World," 73. For the Dutch trade, see Hatfield, *Atlantic Virginia*, chap. 2; Enthoven and Klooster, "Rise and Fall," 105–7; Koot, *Empire at the Periphery*, 73–82.

62. Billings, *Papers of Sir William Berkeley*, 95–97.

63. Hammond, *Hammond versus Heamans*, 2–3; John Hammond, *Leah and Rachel, or, the Two Fruitful Sisters Virginia and Mary-Land* (London, 1656), in Hall, *Narratives*, 281–308 (quotes, 287, 294, 296).

64. James Harrington, *The Commonwealth of Oceana and A System of Politics*, ed. J. G. A. Pocock (Cambridge: Cambridge University Press, 1992), 5; Armitage, "Cromwellian Protectorate"; Blair Worden, "James Harrington and 'The Commonwealth of Oceana,' 1656" in *Republicanism, Liberty, and Commercial Society, 1649–1776*, ed. David Wootton (Stanford, CA: Stanford University Press, 1994) 90–93; Pocock, *Machiavellian Moment*, chaps. 11–12; Steve Pincus, "Neither Machiavellian Moment nor Pos-

sessive Individualism: Commercial Society and the Defenders of the English Commonwealth," *American Historical Review* 103 (1998): 705–36.

65. Brenner, *Merchants and Revolution*; for Virginia, see Kukla, *Political Institutions*; Billings, *Sir William Berkeley*.

66. Hammond, *Leah and Rachel*, 296.

CHAPTER FOUR

1. J. M. Sosin, *English America and the Restoration Monarchy of Charles II* (Lincoln: University of Nebraska Press, 1980) chaps. 3–4; Bliss, *Revolution and Empire*, chaps. 5–6.

2. For Cromwellian skepticism about corporate governance, see "An Essaie or Overture for the regulating the Affaires of his Highness in the West Indies," Add. Mss. 11411, BL, f.11v–12v; William A. H. Schilling, "The Central Government and the Municipal Corporations in England, 1642–1663" (PhD diss., Vanderbilt University, 1970), chap. 3.

3. Thomas Hobbes, *Leviathan, or The Matter, Forme, & Power of a Commonwealth Ecclesiasticall or Civill*, ed. Richard Flathman and David Johnston (New York: Norton, 1997), 169. For towns in the English Civil War, see Roy, "The English Republic."

4. Chesapeake scholars have dismissed urban plans as a secondary part of diversification efforts; see Walsh, *Motives of Honor*, 181–90; Rainbolt, *From Prescription to Persuasion*; Sister Joan de Lourdes Leonard, "Operation Checkmate: The Birth and Death of a Virginia Blueprint for Progress, 1660–1676," *WMQ*, 3rd ser., 24 (1967): 44–74.

5. Morgan, *American Slavery*, chap. 10; for Maryland, see Lois Green Carr and Russell R. Menard, "Immigration and Opportunity: The Freedman in Early Colonial Maryland," in *The Chesapeake in the Seventeenth Century: Essays on Anglo-American Society*, ed. Thad W. Tate and David L. Ammerman (New York: Norton, 1979), 206–42; Russell R. Menard, "From Servant to Freeholder: Status Mobility and Property Accumulation in Seventeenth-Century Maryland," *WMQ*, 3rd ser., 30 (1973): 37–64; Jordan, *Foundations*, chap. 3.

6. Bliss, *Revolution and Empire*, 106–13; Hoxby, *Mammon's Music*, chap. 3; William J. Ashworth, *Customs and Excise: Trade, Production, and Consumption in England, 1640–1845* (Oxford: Oxford University Press, 2003), 103–11; for the new councils, see Charles M. Andrews, *British Committees, Commissions and Councils of Trade and Plantation, 1622–1675* (Baltimore: Johns Hopkins University Press, 1908): 49–53. Sosin, *English America*, chap. 3; for the role of merchants in advising the Crown, see Thomas Leng, "Epistemology: Expertise and Knowledge in the World of Commerce," in *Mercantilism Reimagined: Political Economy in Early Modern Britain and Its Empire*, ed. Philip J. Stern and Carl Wennerlind (New York: Oxford University Press, 2014), 97–116.

7. Thomas P. Slaughter, *Ideology and Politics on the Eve of Restoration: Newcastle's Advice to Charles II* (Philadelphia: American Philosophical Society, 1984), 44; "Marquess of Newcastle to Charles II," Clarendon MS 73, Bodleian Library, Oxford, f.359, quoted in Halliday, *Dismembering*, 84.

8. Halliday, *Dismembering*, 149–262 (quote, 54); J. H. Sacret, "The Restoration Government and Municipal Corporations," *English Historical Review* 45 (1930): 232–59;

John Miller, "The Crown and the Borough Charters in the Reign of Charles II," *English Historical Review* 100 (1985): 53–84.

9. These merchants included Martin Noell; see Edward Hughes, *Studies in Administration and Finance 1558–1825* (Manchester, UK: Manchester University Press, 1934), 129–34; and Sir John Robinson, see Christine Stevenson, *The City and the King: Architecture and Politics in Restoration London* (New Haven, CT: Yale University Press, 2013), 119–24.

10. Stevenson, *City and the King*, chaps. 4–5; Mark Jenner, "The Politics of London Air: John Evelyn's *Fumifugium* and the Restoration," *Historical Journal* 38 (1995): 535–51; Kate Mulry, "The King's Two Gardens: Cultivating Gardens, Aromas, and Political Subjects in the Late-Seventeenth Century English Atlantic," in *Empire of the Senses: Sensory Practices of Colonialism in Early America*, ed. Daniela Hacke and Paul Musselwhite (Boston: Brill, 2018), 257–99; T. F. Reddaway, *The Rebuilding of London after the Great Fire* (London: Jonathan Cape, 1940). Cynthia Wall, *The Literary and Cultural Spaces of Restoration London* (Cambridge: Cambridge University Press, 1999). See also James Robertson, "Stuart London and the Idea of a Royal Capital City," *Renaissance Studies* 15 (2001): 37–58.

11. Sir Matthew Hale, *A Treatise Relative to the Maritime Law of England* (London, 1787), 60. For the redefinition of commerce and the common good in this era, see Hoxby, *Mammon's Music*, chap. 3.

12. Robin Usher, *Protestant Dublin, 1660–1760: Architecture and Iconography* (New York: Palgrave Macmillan, 2012), chap. 1 (quote, 34). Tangier was established as a corporation but with a distinctly new character; see Tristan Stein, "Tangier in the Restoration Empire," *Historical Journal* 54 (2011): 985–1011; Games, *Web of Empire*, 293–98.

13. Michael Pawson and David Buisseret, *Port Royal, Jamaica* (Kingston, Jamaica: University of the West Indies Press, 2000); Swingen, *Competing Visions*, chap. 3; Leslie Theibert, "Making an English Caribbean, 1650–1688" (PhD diss., Yale University, 2013), chap. 4 (esp. 204–5).

14. *The Shaftesbury Papers* (Charleston: South Carolina Historical Society, 2000), 10–12, 16–18, 29–49, 93–117 (quote, 104), 119–23, 342–44 (quotes, 343, 344).

15. *The Speech of Sir Ellis Leighton to the Dublin Tholsel*, quoted in Usher, *Protestant Dublin*, 35; "Council for Foreign Plantations to Virginia, 17 February 1661," Egerton MS 2395, BL, f.335.

16. Jon Kukla, ed., "Some Acts Not in Hening's Statutes: The Acts of Assembly, October 1660," *VMHB* 83 (1975): 77–97 (quote, 88–89); Billings, *Papers of Sir William Berkeley*, 161–68 (quotes, 163, 165). For tobacco prices, see Menard, "A Note on Chesapeake Tobacco Prices."

17. Billings, *Sir William Berkeley*, 123–27, 130; *HS* 2:13, 20. *JHB* 2:8. For Jamestown, see Warren M. Billings, *Jamestown and the Founding of the Nation* (Gettysburg, PA: Thomas Publications, 1991), 79. The idea that Dutch trade would stimulate urban growth in these years was echoed by Virginia merchant John Bland; see "Virginia and the Act of Navigation," *VMHB* 1 (1893): 141–55 (esp. 151).

18. Sosin, *English America*, chap. 4.

19. "Proposalls concerning building of Towns," Egerton MS 2395, BL, f.666. There is

no definite evidence of authorship, but British Library cataloguers believe it to be in the handwriting of Martin Noell.

20. Billings, *Papers of Sir William Berkeley*, 161–68 (quotes, 163, 168).

21. R. G., *Virginia's Cure, or, An advisive narrative concerning Virginia* (London, 1662), quotes, 1, 3–4, 15. See also Bond, *Damned Souls*, 190–94.

22. R. G., *Virginia's Cure*, 10, 17. For Evelyn's garden, see Mulry, "The King's Two Gardens."

23. R. G., *Virginia's Cure*, 17. For Berkeley's instructions, see Billings, *Papers of Sir William Berkeley*, 177–78. William Cabell Brown, "Draft for the Creation of a Bishopric in Virginia," *VMHB* 36 (1928): 45–53; Bond, *Damned Souls*, 204–15 (esp. 214n80).

24. Billings, *Papers of Sir William Berkeley*, 269–70.

25. Billings, *Papers of Sir William Berkeley*, 189. *HS* 2:172–76. For the significance of brick, see Cary Carson, Norman F. Barka, William M. Kelso, Garry Wheeler Stone, and Dell Upton, "Impermanent Architecture in the Southern American Colonies," *Winterthur Portfolio* 16 (1981): 135–96 (esp. 161–63); Philip Levy, "Middle Plantation's Changing Landscape: Persistence, Continuity, and the Building of Community," in *Early Modern Virginia: Reconsidering the Old Dominion*, ed. Douglas Bradburn and John C. Coombs (Charlottesville: University of Virginia Press, 2011), 202n3.

26. Henning, *Statutes*, 2:176.

27. Billings, *Papers of Sir William Berkeley*, 291. Historians have tied this legislation to Berkeley's efforts to diversify the economy. The two were linked because he felt elite planters at Jamestown would have the authority to reshape the colony's economy. However, there is little evidence that the new urban buildings themselves were intended to house manufacturing, which in England remained a largely rural pursuit. See Billings, "Sir William Berkeley and the Diversification of the Virginia Economy," *VMHB* 104 (1996): 433–54; Horning, "'A Verie Fit Place,'" 263–321. For English manufacturing, see Paul Glennie and Ian Whyte, "Towns in an Agrarian Economy, 1540–1700," in *The Cambridge Urban History of Britain*, vol. 2, ed. Peter Clark (Cambridge: Cambridge University Press, 2000), 167–94 (esp. 181–84). County authority was also expanded to reinforce Berkeley's allies; see *HS* 2:18–21, 64, 73, 75, 83, 103, 171; Billings, "Growth of Political Institutions," 231–34.

28. *JHB* 2:27; "General Assembly accounts, September 1663," Clarendon MS 82, Bodleian Library, Oxford, f.275–78 (accessed through Virginia Colonial Records Project); [John Cotton], "The History of Bacon's and Ingram's Rebellion," in *Narratives of Insurrections, 1675–1690*, ed. Charles M. Andrews (New York: Charles Scribner's Sons, 1915), 69–70. For row houses, see Colonial Williamsburg Research Division, *Description and Analysis of Structure 144, Jamestown, Virginia* (Williamsburg, VA: Colonial Williamsburg, 2002); Billings, *Sir William Berkeley*, 179–83; Carson, Horning, and Straube, *Evaluation of Previous Archaeology*, 22–31, 110–16; Horning, "'A Verie Fit Place,'" 284–311.

29. TNA CO 1/19, f.75; Horning, "'A Verie Fit Place,'" 289–90.

30. Horning, "'A Verie Fit Place,'" 284–92; Billings, *Papers of Sir William Berkeley*, 326; *JHB* 2:27–28.

31. TNA CO 1/19, f.75. For Berkeley's ideas about organizing trade, see Billings, *Papers of Sir William Berkeley*, 269–70. For the tobacco stint, see Billings, *Sir William Berkeley*, 184–96; for slavery, see Coombs, "Phases of Conversion," 348; Russell

Menard, "From Servants to Slaves: The Transformation of the Chesapeake Labor System," *Southern Studies* 16 (1977): 355–90; David W. Galenson, *White Servitude in Colonial America: An Economic Analysis* (Cambridge: Cambridge University Press, 1981), 154–56.

32. Coombs, "Beyond the 'Origins Debate'"; C. S. Everett, "'They Shalbe Slaves for Their Lives': Indian Slavery in Colonial Virginia," in *Indian Slavery in Colonial America*, ed. Allan Gallay (Lincoln: University of Nebraska Press, 2009), 67–108.

33. Jacob M. Price and Paul G. E. Clemens, "A Revolution of Scale in Overseas Trade: British Firms in the Chesapeake Trade, 1675–1775," *Journal of Economic History* 47 (1987), 1–43. For marketplaces, see *JHB* 2:30; *HS* 1:412, 476; see also Billings, *Papers of Sir William Berkeley*, 281–83.

34. Billings, *Papers of Sir William Berkeley*, 278; Cary Carson, "Banqueting Houses and the 'Need of Society' among Slave-Owning Planters in the Chesapeake Colonies," *WMQ*, 3rd ser., 70 (2013): 725–80.

35. Billings, *Sir William Berkeley*, chap. 11; Morgan, *American Slavery*, chap. 10.

36. Sutto, *Loyal Protestants*, chaps. 6–7; Russell R. Menard, "Farm Prices of Maryland Tobacco, 1659–1710," *MHM* 68 (1973): 80–85; Walsh, "Summing the Parts." For imperial threats to Baltimore's charter, see *CSPC* 5, nos. 644, 809; *Archives* 5:45–47.

37. Augustine Herrman, *Journal of the Dutch Embassy to Maryland*, in *Narratives of Early Maryland, 1633–1684*, ed. Clayton Coleman Hall (New York: Charles Scribner's Sons, 1910), 309–33 (quotes, 316, 322). For the context of Herrman's mission and Anglo-Dutch trade in the Chesapeake, see Christian J. Koot, *A Biography of a Map in Motion: Augustine Herrman's Chesapeake* (New York: New York University Press, 2017), chap. 1. For New Amsterdam during the 1650s, see Cathy Matson, *Merchants and Empire: Trading in Colonial New York* (Baltimore: Johns Hopkins University Press, 1998), 25–35.

38. *Archives* 1:434, 436, 538–39; 2:50–51; 3:447–48, 459, 465, 490–94, 532.

39. *Archives* 1:538–39. See also Timothy B. Riordan, "Philip Calvert: Patron of St. Mary's City," *MHM* 99 (2004): 329–49; *Archives* 3:492.

40. Henry M. Miller, "Baroque Cities in the Wilderness: Archaeology and Urban Development in the Colonial Chesapeake," *Historical Archaeology* 22 (1987): 57–73; Riordan, "Philip Calvert," 341–48; Krugler, *English and Catholic*, 226–34.

41. *Archives* 51:567–70.

42. For Cecilton, see *Archives* 17:84; see also Koot, *Biography of a Map*, chap. 3. For Herrington, see Joseph B. Thomas and Anthony D. Lindauer, "Seeking Herrington: Settlement in a Very Early Maryland Town," *Maryland Archeology* 34, no. 2 (1998): 11–17. For Battletown, see Dennis J. Pogue, "Calverton, Calvert County, Maryland: 1668–1725," *MHM* 80 (1985): 271–76.

43. The 1668 proclamation was followed by two further proclamations adjusting the locations; see *Archives* 5:31–32, 47–48, 92–94 (quotes, 31, 47). For Lord Baltimore's involvement, see *Archives* 15:14–15.

44. *Archives* 5:46–47. For tax evasion, see Jordan, *Foundations*, 107; Sutto, *Loyal Protestants*, chap. 7.

45. *Archives* 5:47; "Philip Calvert to Gov. Richard Nichols, 23rd June 1668," Blathwayt Papers BL 60, Huntington Library, Pasadena, CA. For Baltimore's negotiations over slave imports, see Walsh, *Motives of Honor*, 140. For Sybery, see *Archives* 54:xxv.

46. Koot, *Biography of a Map*, chap. 4; Christian J. Koot, "The Merchant, the Map, and Empire: Augustine Herrman's Chesapeake and Interimperial Trade, 1644–73," *WMQ*, 3rd ser. 67 (2010): 603–44; Karel Kansky, "Augustine Herrman: The Leading Cartographer of the Seventeenth Century," *MHM* 73 (1978): 352–59. The towns may have been added after the map was completed: in 1672, Charles Calvert noted in a letter to his father that he would "observe yor Lordsh^{pps} Command about Inserting what you have directed"; see *Calvert Papers*, 1:272–73.

47. These statements contrasted with the disorganized way Ogilby described New England's towns; see John Ogilby, *America: Being the Latest, and Most Accurate Description of the New World* . . . (London, 1671), 159–62, 189–90. For Ogilby, see Katherine S. Van Eerde, *John Ogilby and the Taste of His Times* (Folkestone, UK: Dawson, 1976).

48. *Archives* 2:158–59, 163–73 (quote, 167).

49. *Archives* 2:168–69.

50. *Archives* 2:173–79 (quotes, 178).

51. The writ of *Quo Warranto* had begun to be used to revoke English municipal charters; this policy expanded in the early 1680s. See Halliday, *Dismembering*, chap. 6.

52. Hall, *Narratives*, 104. For an alternative analysis, see Sutto, *Loyal Protestants*, 114–15.

53. Although there is no evidence of development at most sites, later town proclamations did use the descriptor "the town land" when identifying sites, suggesting that some spaces developed well-known urban connections; see *Archives* 5:47. The 1683 act contained ten locations that implied preexisting urbanity; see *Archives* 7:609–10. Residents of one of the towns specifically self-identified as town citizens in 1682; see *Archives* 7:278. See also Pogue, "Calverton, Calvert County."

54. For economic adaptation, see Walsh, *Motives of Honor*, chap. 2. For county government, see *Archives* 2:255, 257–58, 260–61, 265. The importance of the 1671 sessions is noted in Carr, *County Government*, 321, 333, 359, 365, 423–44, 433. For the 1671 revenue provisions, see Jordan, *Foundations*, 110–11.

55. *Archives* 51:390–94.

56. Billings, *Papers of Sir William Berkeley*, 189–91 (quote, 189).

57. Anthony Langston, Undated Report, Egerton MS 2395, BL, f.366–68.

58. George Milner, "Proposals in order to the Improvement of the County of Albemarle in the Province of Carolina in point of Towns, Trade & Coyne," Egerton MS 2395, BL, f.661–65.

59. Langston may have been directly influenced by the 1650s puritan town plans, because he had been a servant to the Commonwealth-era governor Richard Bennett; see "Virginia in 1662–1665," *VMHB* 18 (1910): 412–13.

60. "Francis Moryson to Lord Clarendon, 1665," Clarendon MS 83, Bodleian Library, Oxford, f.390 (Virginia Colonial Records Project). Previous scholars have erroneously argued that poorer Virginians opposed all urban development; see Rainbolt, *From Prescription to Persuasion*, chap. 4; Angelo T. Angelis, "'By Consent of the People': Riot and Regulation in Seventeenth-Century Virginia," in *Colonial Chesapeake: New Perspectives*, ed. Debra Meyers and Melanie Perreault (Lanham, MD: Lexington Books, 2006), 117–40.

61. Andrews, *Narratives*, 40–41, 96. For native geopolitics, see Rice, *Tales from a Revolution*.

62. Billings, *Papers of Sir William Berkeley*, 293–95; Billings, *Sir William Berkeley*, 167–68. Drummond's governorship of Albemarle (1664–1667) corresponds with the date of Milner's proposal. For Drummond's Jamestown property, see McCartney, *Jamestown People*, 145; Anna Agbe-Davies, *Tobacco, Pipes, and Race in Colonial Virginia: Little Tubes of Mighty Power* (Walnut Creek, CA: Left Coast Press, 2015), 80–83, 102. For Scottish merchants, see Allan I. Macinnes, *Union and Empire: The Making of the United Kingdom in 1707* (Cambridge: Cambridge University Press, 2007), 161–62.

63. Andrews, *Narratives*, 27, 40–41, 96 (quotes, 40, 96); McIlwaine, *Minutes of the Council*, 371–72, 375; *JHB* 2:56; Martha McCartney, *Documentary History of Jamestown Island*, vol. 3, *Biographies of Owners and Residents* (Williamsburg, VA: Colonial Williamsburg, 2000), 215–16. It is notable, though, that Lawrence was not averse to using the law against his own servants when they ran away; see McIlwaine, *Minutes of the Council*, 375, 382–83. For Lawrence's activities as a lawyer, see McIlwaine, *Minutes of the Council*, 207, 218, 293, 297, 343–44. For Lawrence's English origins, see Paul Musselwhite, "Towns in Mind: Urban Plans, Political Culture, and Empire in the Colonial Chesapeake, 1607–1722" (PhD diss., College of William and Mary, 2011), 137. For the structure that was either Lawrence or Drummond's house, see http://historicjamestowne.org/archaeology/map-of-discoveries/drummonds-house/ (accessed July 10, 2017).

64. McIlwaine, *Minutes of the Council*, 313, 344; Andrews, *Narratives*, 40–41.

65. Andrews, *Narratives*, 40. For an overview of the rebellion, see Wilcomb Washburn, *The Governor and the Rebel: A History of Bacon's Rebellion in Virginia* (Chapel Hill: University of North Carolina Press, 1957).

66. *HS* 2:362; Billings, *A Little Parliament*, 42–47; Brent Tarter, "Bacon's Rebellion, the Grievances of the People, and the Political Culture of Seventeenth-Century Virginia," *VMHB* 119 (2011): 3–41.

67. McIlwaine, *Minutes of the Council*, 324. "Proclamations of Nathaniel Bacon," *VMHB* 1 (1893): 56, 59; "Bacon's Letter," TNA CO 5/1371 f.124–26. For small merchants who aligned with Bacon, see Billings, *Sir William Berkeley*, 234. George Milner, who wrote the Albermarle urban plan, may also have supported Bacon; see *HS* 2:372.

68. TNA CO 1/39, f.197–242 (quotes, 197, 209); see also Michael Oberg, *Samuel Wiseman's Book of Record: The Official Account of Bacon's Rebellion, 1676–1677* (Lanham, MD: Lexington Books, 2005), chap. 6; Tarter, "Bacon's Rebellion."

69. *Archives* 5:134–54 (quotes, 137, 140, 148, 152). Scholarly interpretations include Jordan, *Foundations*, 95–96; Antoinette Sutto, "Built upon Smoke: Politics and Political Culture in Maryland, 1630–1690" (PhD diss., Princeton University, 2008), 393–406; Rice, *Tales from a Revolution*, 137–39. The authors of the *Complaint* also dedicated their essay to the Corporation of London, which was significant given London's increasing opposition to royal authority; see Gary S. De Krey, *London and the Restoration, 1659–1683* (Cambridge: Cambridge University Press, 2005), chap. 3.

70. *Archives* 17:181–84. When a rebellion broke out in Maryland in 1681, resentment was also directed against St. Mary's City; see *Archives* 15:246, 355, 388–90; 17:51, 55–56, 117–18.

71. Billings, *Papers of Sir William Berkeley*, 572–73. Ann Cotton, "An Account of Our Late Troubles in Virginia, Written in 1676, By Mrs. An. Cotton, of Q. Creeke," 8 (my emphasis), in Force, *Tracts and Other Papers*, vol. 1. For the siege, see Andrews, *Narratives*, 129–36. The English playwright Aphra Behn also recognized the significance of urban space in the rebellion and emphasized this element in her fictional retelling of the rebellion; see Paul Musselwhite, "'What Town's this, Boy?': English Civic Politics, Virginia's Urban Debate, and Aphra Behn's *The Widow Ranter*," *Atlantic Studies* 8, no. 3 (September 2011): 1–21.

72. Thompson, "The Thief."

73. *Archives* 5:265–66.

74. Earle and Hoffman, "Staple Crops"; Carr, "'The Metropolis of Maryland.'"

CHAPTER FIVE

1. William Sherwood, "Virginia's Deploured Condition," in *Collections of the Massachusetts Historical Society*, 4th ser., 9 (1871): 162–65.

2. TNA CO 1/47, f.260v–62r (quote, 261v). Concerns about land prices and restricting opportunities also inspired revolt in Maryland in the early 1680s; see *Archives* 5: 280–81, 320–21.

3. TNA CO 1/45, f.189–90.

4. Morgan, *American Slavery*; Kathleen Brown, *Good Wives, Nasty Wenches, and Anxious Patriarchs: Gender, Race, and Power in Colonial Virginia* (Chapel Hill: University of North Carolina Press, 1996). See also Allan Kulikoff, *Tobacco and Slaves: The Development of Southern Cultures in the Chesapeake, 1680–1800* (Chapel Hill: University of North Carolina Press, 1986); Anthony S. Parent Jr., *Foul Means: The Formation of a Slave Society in Virginia, 1660–1740* (Chapel Hill: University of North Carolina Press, 2003). John Rainbolt offers a partial account of the elites' efforts to consolidate through economic policy; see Rainbolt, *From Prescription to Persuasion*, chap. 5.

5. For the imperial influence in Virginia, see Stephen Saunders Webb, *1676: The End of American Independence* (New York: Knopf, 1984). For Maryland and English politics, see Owen Stanwood, *The Empire Reformed: English America in the Age of the Glorious Revolution* (Philadelphia: University of Pennsylvania Press, 2011), chaps. 2 and 4; Sutto, *Loyal Protestants*, chap. 7.

6. Oberg, *Samuel Wiseman's Book*, 65–71 (quotes, 67, 69); see also Tarter, "Bacon's Rebellion." For the Crown's shifting policy, see also John C. Rainbolt, "A New Look at Stuart 'Tyranny': The Crown's Attack on the Virginia Assembly, 1676–1689," *VMHB* 75 (1967): 387–406.

7. TNA CO 5/1355, f.240–43; Culpeper quote, f.259. The plan is first mentioned in TNA CO 5/1355, f.258–62 and later in f.263–67. For Culpeper's instructions, see TNA CO 5/1355, f.326–56 (quotes, 345–47). For Blathwayt quote, see "Blathwayt, Reflections on a Paper concerning America, c. 1685," Blathwayt Papers BL416, Huntington Library. For events in England, see Tim Harris, *Politics under the Later Stuarts: Party Conflict in a Divided Society, 1660–1715* (London: Longman, 1993), chap. 4.

8. Thomas C. Barrow, *Trade and Empire: The British Customs Service in Colonial*

America, 1660–1775 (Cambridge, MA: Harvard University Press, 1967), chap. 2; Swingen, *Competing Visions*, 88–95; Sosin, *English America*, 63–68. For English customs reform, see R. C. Jarvis, "The Appointment of Ports," *Economic History Review* 11 (1959): 455–66; Ashworth, *Customs and Excise*, 110–16. See also, "Proposals for Reducing Smuggling," Dering Papers, Folger MS X.d.531 [19], Folger Shakespeare Library, Washington, DC.

9. Brady, *Historical Treatise*, i–ii. For *Quo Warranto* proceedings, see Halliday, *Dismembering*, chaps. 5–7; DeKrey, *London and the Restoration*, chap. 7; Tim Harris, *London Crowds in the Reign of Charles II: Propaganda and Politics from the Restoration until the Exclusion Crisis* (Cambridge: Cambridge University Press, 1987), chap. 6; Mark Knights, *Politics and Opinion in Crisis, 1678–81* (Cambridge: Cambridge University Press, 1994), chap. 9. Scholars have long acknowledged the connection between the *Quo Warranto* proceedings against English boroughs and the use of *Quo Warranto* against New England charters during the 1680s; see Philip S. Haffenden, "The Crown and the Colonial Charters, 1675–1688," pts. 1–2, *WMQ*, 3rd ser., 15 (1958): 298–311, 452–66.

10. TNA CO 391/2, f.275–78; CO 5/1355, f.345–47. The leading tobacco merchant in London politics was John Jeffreys; see DeKrey, *London and the Restoration*, 382–86; TNA CO 391/3, f.297–301, CO 1/47, f.252; Jacob M. Price, "Jeffreys, John," in *Oxford Dictionary of National Biography*, http://www.oxforddnb.com. For merchant influence in general, see Nuala Zahedieh, *The Capital and the Colonies: London and the Atlantic Economy, 1660–1700* (Cambridge: Cambridge University Press, 2010); Perry Gauci, *The Politics of Trade: The Overseas Merchant in State and Society, 1660–1720* (Oxford: Oxford University Press, 2001).

11. William Petty, *Political Arithmetick* (London, 1690), 72–73, 91–94 (quote, 117); see also Petty, *Another Essay in Political Arithmetick, Concerning the Growth of the City of London . . .* (London, 1682); McCormick, *William Petty*. Abigail Swingen, "Labor: Employment, Colonial Servitude, and Slavery in the Seventeenth-Century Atlantic," in *Mercantilism Reimagined: Political Economy in Early Modern Britain and Its Empire*, ed. Philip J. Stern and Carl Wennerlind (New York: Oxford University Press, 2014), 46–73.

12. Nicholas Barbon, *A Discourse Shewing The Great Advantages That New-Buildings, and the Enlarging of Towns and Cities Do bring to a Nation* (London, 1678), 2, 5; Petty, *Political Arithmetick*, 117. See also Paul Slack, *The Invention of Improvement: Information and Material Progress in Seventeenth-Century England* (Oxford: Oxford University Press, 2015).

13. Petty Papers, Add. MS 72867, BL, f.9–13, 22–28; some of these ideas were replicated in Petty, *Another Essay*, 27–43. Petty also considered urban improvement for Pennsylvania; see Petty Papers, Add. MS 72867, BL, f.48–51, 78–81, 86–89.

14. Middleton, *From Privileges to Rights*, 70–73; Matson, *Merchants and Empire*, 56–57; "Sir Richard Dutton to the Committee for Trade and Plantations," TNA CO 28/4/238, cited in Welch, *Slave Society in the City*, 22; Swingen, *Competing Visions*, 123.

15. Billings, *Sir William Berkeley*, chap. 14; Webb, *1676*, 127–64. For the February 1677 General Assembly, see *JHB* 2:68–80; *HS* 2:366–406; TNA CO 1/39, f.199; Coventry

Papers, Longleat House, vol. 78, f.44, 303 (Virginia Colonial Records Project). For the canton plan, see *HS* 2:448–54; Coventry Papers, vol. 78, f.398–400; TNA CO 1/44, f.398; "William Blathwayt to Lord Baltimore, 4th Nov. 1679," *Blathwayt Papers*, folder 18 Rockefeller Library Special Collections, Colonial Williamsburg, Williamsburg, VA. For new bylaw powers, see *HS* 2:441. For political divisions within the Virginia gentry, see Warren M. Billings, *Virginia's Viceroy: Their Majesties' Governor General: Francis Howard, Baron Howard of Effingham* (Fairfax, VA: George Mason University Press, 1991), 26–32.

16. TNA CO 1/45, f.188; CO 1/47, f.258–62. For coastal trade, see Hatfield, *Atlantic Virginia*, chap. 6. For consolidation of the tobacco trade, see Price and Clemens, "Revolution of Scale." For tobacco prices, see Menard, "Farm Prices," 80–85; for regional variations, see Walsh, "Summing the Parts."

17. *JHB* 2:148.

18. *JHB* 2:129–32, 135, 137–38; *LJC* 1:9; TNA CO 1/45, f.190.

19. *HS* 2:471–78.

20. Borsay, *English Urban Renaissance*; Estabrook, *Urbane and Rustic England*; Barry, "The Press and the Politics of Culture in Bristol 1660–1775," in *Culture, Politics and Society in Britain, 1660–1800*, ed. Jeremy Black and Jeremy Gregory (Manchester, UK: Manchester University Press, 1991), 49–81; Rosemary Sweet, *The Writing of Urban Histories in Eighteenth-Century England* (Oxford: Oxford University Press, 1997), chap. 6. For demographic and economic patterns in English small towns, see Alan Dyer, "Small Market Towns, 1540–1700," in *The Cambridge Urban History of Britain*, vol. 2, ed. Peter Clark (Cambridge: Cambridge University Press, 2000), 425–49. For Scottish burghs of barony, see Devine, "Scotland," in *Cambridge Urban History*, 2:151–64. For Whitehaven, see J. V. Beckett, *Coal and Tobacco: The Lowthers and the Economic Development of West Cumberland, 1660–1760* (Cambridge: Cambridge University Press, 1981), esp. 16–17, 189–200.

21. Andrew Yarranton, *England's Improvement by Sea and Land . . .*, 2 vols. (1677–1681), 25, 128, 132; Slack, *Invention of Improvement*, 161–63.

22. *HS* 2:473; Lower Norfolk County Court Order Book, 1675–1686, LVA, 185.

23. Accomack County Deeds and Wills, 1678–1682, LVA, 181; Accomack County Deeds and Wills, 1682–1697, LVA f.239r.

24. Middlesex County Court Order Book, 1680–1694, LVA, 41–42, 49–50, 193, 474, 509, 512–17. This dispute is fleshed out in Rutman and Rutman, *A Place in Time*, chap. 7. For Rosegill, see Carson et al., "Impermanent Architecture," 161–63. For another local conflict, see Surry County Court Orders 1671–1691, LVA, f.314r.

25. Middlesex County Court Order Book, 1680–1694, LVA, 60, 64. For Wharton, see Rutman and Rutman, *A Place in Time*, 110.

26. *EJC* 1:19; TNA CO 1/48, f.185–86.

27. TNA CO 1/48, f.228, 321; CO 1/51, f.316–18; CO 5/1356, f.175–87 (quote, 176); *JHB* 2:158–69; *EJC* 1:16, 19–21.

28. TNA CO 1/47, f.252–53; CO 5/1356, f.141. Because officials spent so long discussing the act, it remained in limbo in September 1681 when restrictions were to take effect, resulting in the uncertainty that provoked the Plant-Cutter Riots.

29. TNA CO 1/46, f.165–66; CO 1/47, f.180; CO 391/3, f.305–7; CO 5/1356, f.122–49.

30. TNA CO 1/47, f.252-53; CO 1/49, f.106, CO 391/4, f.194-99, 204-9; *EJC* 1:37.

31. Billings, *Virginia's Viceroy*, chaps. 1-2.

32. Warren M. Billings, *Papers of Francis Howard* (Richmond: Virginia State Library, 1989), 155; Richard Beale Davis, ed., *William Fitzhugh and His Chesapeake World, 1676-1701: The Fitzhugh Letters and Other Documents* (Chapel Hill: University of North Carolina Press, 1963), 94-95, 121-22, 177-78.

33. Paul Musselwhite, "Candlesticks and Cockney Feasts: The Politics of Urban Space in Imperial Jamestown, 1677-1688," in *Urban Places in the Chesapeake*, ed. Julia King (forthcoming).

34. *JHB* 2:240, 251-52; Billings, *Papers of Francis Howard*, 42.

35. *JHB* 2:213, 217, 222.

36. *JHB* 2:240; Billings, *Papers of Francis Howard*, 211. See also John Clayton, *A Letter from Mr John Clayton . . . to the Royal Society May 12, 1688*, 11, in Force, *Tracts and Other Papers*, vol. 3, no. 12.

37. TNA CO 391/4, f.194-99; Billings, *Papers of Francis Howard*, 228; Transcript of the House of Burgesses Journal, Effingham Papers, Library of Congress, f.5-6; *LJC* 1: 76-79. For tobacco prices, see Menard, "Farm Prices," 85. For duties, see George L. Beer, *The Old Colonial System, 1660-1746* (New York: Macmillan, 1958), pt. 1, vol. 1, 160-61.

38. *LJC* 1:95-105 (quote, 95). Copies of the act with Effingham's amendments can be found in Lord Howard of Effingham Papers, Library of Congress, and TNA CO 1/57, f.327-31. See also Billings, *A Little Parliament*, 184-88.

39. The only town that Effingham encouraged during the latter part of his tenure was Brenton, a private project directed by George Brent, a Catholic with links to Tory tobacco merchant John Jeffreys; support for Brenton, though, was persistently blocked by the burgesses. See Transcript of the House of Burgesses Journal, f.23; Davis, *William Fitzhugh*, 248-50, 259-60; "Robert Carter to John Carter, February 10, 1721," in *Robert Carter Papers Online*, http://carter.lib.virginia.edu. For the customs report, see TNA CO1/62, f.295.

40. For Maryland's economic variation, see Walsh, "Summing the Parts." For confessional politics and Indian policy, see Rice, *Tales from a Revolution*, chap. 8; Stanwood, *Empire Reformed*, 106-12. For the provincial Protestant elite, see Jordan, *Foundations*, chap. 3.

41. *Archives* 5:274-80, 344-46, 370-71 (quotes, 275-76, 370). See also Antoinette Sutto, "'You Dog . . . Give Me Your Hand': Lord Baltimore and the Death of Christopher Rousby," *MHM* 102 (2007): 240-257. For imperial efforts to push Baltimore to cooperate with Virginia's town plan, see also TNA CO 1/47, f.252-53; *CSPC* 11, no. 1007.

42. *Archives* 5:352. A petition from the small town of Calverton in early 1682 also suggested renewed interest in town development; see *Archives* 7:278-80. For Calverton, see Pogue, "Calverton, Calvert County."

43. *Archives* 7:368, 458-59. The previous interpretation has been that Maryland councillors pursued the plan entirely out of self-interest and that it was widely resented by ordinary planters. See Francis Edgar Sparks, *Causes of the Maryland Revolution of 1689* (Baltimore: Johns Hopkins University Press, 1896) 91-92; Michael Kammen, "Causes of the Maryland Revolution of 1689," *MHM* 55 (1960): 293-333 (esp. 311); Walsh,

Motives of Honor, 215–17; Lois Green Carr and David W. Jordan, *Maryland's Revolution of Government 1689–1692* (Ithaca, NY: Cornell University Press, 1974), 19.

44. I have reconstructed Baltimore's proposal by reading the finished act minus amendments; see *Archives* 7:609–19.

45. *Archives* 7:349–51; for Carvile and Rousby, see Edward C. Papenfuse et al., *A Biographical Dictionary of the Maryland Legislature, 1635–1789*, 2 vols. (Baltimore: Johns Hopkins University Press, 1985), 202, 705.

46. *Archives* 7:349–51, 369–70, 460–61.

47. *Archives* 7:369–70.

48. *Archives* 7:349–51, 369–70, 410–11, 609–19 (quotes, 369, 410, 612). For the importance of public spaces in early Maryland towns, see Michael T. Lucas, "Negotiating Public Landscapes: History, Archaeology, and the Material Culture of Colonial Chesapeake Towns, 1680–1720" (PhD diss., University of Maryland, 2008), chap. 6.

49. *Archives* 7:465–69.

50. *Archives* 7:360–85, 452, 473, 487–90 (quotes, 360, 552).

51. *Archives* 7:447–49, 492 (quotes, 492).

52. *Archives* 13:22.

53. *Archives* 13:22–27, 83–86, 89–91, 111–20. The council minutes assiduously distinguished between new locations proposed by the "inhabitants" of a region and those proposed by a particular county's assembly delegates.

54. *Archives* 13:25; 17:284–87.

55. *Archives* 7:460–61, 465–66; 13:26. Scholars have struggled to pinpoint these locations, but they were near each other on the Patuxent; see Reps, *Tidewater Towns*, 99; Shomette, *Lost Towns*, 299.

56. *Archives* 17:408–9. For petitioning in England, see Mark Knights, *Politics and Opinion*, chaps. 8–9. For the revolutionary-era petition in Calvert, see *Archives* 8: 110–11.

57. *Archives* 17:358. For Charles County, see Lorena Walsh, "Charles County, Maryland, 1658–1705: A Study of Chesapeake Social and Political Structure" (PhD diss., Michigan State University, 1977), 388–454. For town sites in Charles County, see Ethel Roby Hayden, "Port Tobacco, Lost Town of Maryland," *MHM* 40 (1945): 261–76; Shomette, *Lost Towns*, 195–202; Margaret Brown Klapthor and Paul Dennis Brown, *The History of Charles County, Maryland* (La Plata, MD: Charles County Tercentenary, 1958), 31–33.

58. *Archives* 7:465, 611; 13:29, 112 (quotes, 17:358); Papenfuse, *Biographical Dictionary*, 160, 209; Shomette, *Lost Towns*, 195–96, 200–201. For the sixteen men, see Charles County Court Records, 1685–1686, MSA C658-12, Maryland State Archives, f.4–5. These names were compared with those on the Charles County petition against Lord Baltimore (*Archives* 8:138).

59. Sutto, "'You Dog'"; *Archives* 5:436–41; 17:298–334, 339–43, 418–23 (quotes, 341, 342); *CSPC* 11, no. 1963.

60. *Archives* 17:362–63.

61. For Baltimore's interactions, see *CSPC* 12, nos. 317, 320, 332, 347, 385.

62. *Archives* 17:425.

63. *Archives* 5:495–98, 527–29 (quotes, 497, 528). The council later increased its control by enabling councillors to appoint and dismiss town officers at will.

64. Revolutionary loyalties were determined using contemporary petitions (*Archives* 8:110–11, 128–47), the tables in Carr and Jordan, *Maryland's Revolution*, and Lois Green Carr's notes, which are stored in the Maryland Hall of Records and were generously located for me by Jean Russo.

65. *Archives* 13:132–39 (quotes, 134).

66. *Archives* 8:42–43, 45–46.

67. *Archives* 13:147–53, 166.

68. *Archives* 13:171–73 (quote, 172).

69. Carr and Jordan, *Maryland's Revolution*; Sutto, *Loyal Protestants*, chap. 10; Stanwood, *Empire Reformed*, 106–12.

70. *Archives* 8:103.

71. *Archives* 8:76, 158–62. For Oxford's rapid growth, see Joseph Brown Thomas, "Small-Scale Settlement Development on Maryland's Eastern Shore, 1680s–1730s" (MA thesis, University of Maryland, 1990).

72. Carr and Jordan, *Maryland's Revolution*, 96; *Archives* 8:560–61; 13:343–44.

73. Rice, *Tales from a Revolution*, chaps. 8–10.

74. TNA CO 1/47, f.180.

75. Swingen, *Competing Visions*, chaps. 4–5; Koot, *Empire at the Periphery*, chaps. 3–5.

CHAPTER SIX

1. For slave imports, see Gregory E. O'Malley, *Final Passages: The Intercolonial Slave Trade of British America, 1619–1807* (Chapel Hill: University of North Carolina Press, 2014), 133; for new slave codes, see Parent, *Foul Means*, chap. 4; for land ownership, see Emory G. Evans, *"A Topping People": The Rise and Decline of Virginia's Old Political Elite, 1680–1790* (Charlottesville: University of Virginia Press, 2009), 14–16; see also Bailyn, "Politics and Social Structure in Virginia"; Morgan, *American Slavery*; Kulikoff, *Tobacco and Slaves*, chap. 7; David W. Jordan, "Political Stability and the Emergence of a Native Elite in Maryland," in *The Chesapeake in the Seventeenth Century: Essays on Anglo-American Society*, ed. Thad W. Tate and David L. Ammerman (New York: Norton, 1979), 243–73; Carole Shammas, "English-Born and Creole Elites in Turn-of-the-Century Virginia," in Tate and Ammerman, *The Chesapeake in the Seventeenth Century*, 274–96; Martin H. Quitt, "Immigrant Origins of the Virginia Gentry: A Study of Cultural Transmission and Innovation," *WMQ*, 3rd ser., 45 (1988): 630–55.

2. William A. Pettigrew, "Transatlantic Politics and the Africanization of Virginia's Labor Force, 1688–1712," in *Early Modern Virginia: Reconsidering the Old Dominion*, ed. Douglas Bradburn and John C. Coombs (Charlottesville: University of Virginia Press, 2011), 279–99; Bradburn, "Visible Fist."

3. Steven C. A. Pincus, *1688: The First Modern Revolution* (New Haven, CT: Yale University Press, 2009), chap. 12; Pincus, "Rethinking Mercantilism"; for new policies on the slave trade, see Pettigrew, *Freedom's Debt*; Swingen, *Competing Visions*.

4. Henry Hartwell, James Blair, and Edward Chilton, *The Present State of Virginia and the College*, ed. Hunter Dickinson Farish (Williamsburg, VA: Colonial Williamsburg, 1940), 4. For tobacco prices, see Russell R. Menard, "The Tobacco Industry in the Chesapeake Colonies, 1617–1730: An Interpretation," *Research in Economic History* 5 (1980): 109–77.

5. Poorer planters had increasingly diversified away from tobacco and toward subsistence crops, which officials now saw as a waste of labor; see Walsh, *Motives of Honor*, chap. 4. Officials were also concerned about illegal trade and piracy; see Mark Hanna, *Pirate Nests and the Origins of the British Empire* (Chapel Hill: University of North Carolina Press, 2015) chap. 6; Emma Hart, "'Naturally cut out . . . for unlawful trade': Colonial Economic Culture and the Enforcement of the Navigation Acts in the Mainland Colonies, 1690–1725," in *Governing the Sea in the Early Modern Era*, ed. Peter C. Mancall and Carole Shammas (San Marino, CA: Huntington Library Press, 2015), 223–52.

6. Bruce T. McCully, "From the North Riding to Morocco: The Early Years of Governor Francis Nicholson, 1655–1686," *WMQ*, 3rd ser., 19, no. 4 (Oct. 1962): 534–56; Stephen Saunders Webb, "The Strange Career of Francis Nicholson," *WMQ*, 3rd ser., 23, no. 4 (Oct. 1966): 513–48.

7. Robert Beverley, *The History and Present State of Virginia*, ed. Susan Scott Parrish (Chapel Hill: University of North Carolina Press, 2013), 79.

8. TNA CO 5/1306, f.466–69 (quote, 467r). For the contrasting outlooks of Whigs and Tories, see Pincus, *1688*, chaps. 12 and 14.

9. TNA CO 5/1305, f.158–67; 5/1306, f.35–36, 296–97, 378–82, 466–69.

10. For Randolph's report, see TNA CO 5/1306, f.439–44.

11. *LJC* 1:164 (quote); TNA CO 5/1309, f.9–10, 16; see also Parent, *Foul Means*, chap. 1.

12. TNA CO 5/713, f.300–303 (quote, 300v); CO 5/714, 46–51. For Nicholson and native diplomacy, see Rice, *Nature and History*, 166–67.

13. For the complete series of Nicholson's letters, see TNA CO 5/1305, f.158–67; CO 5/1306, f.35–36, 298–99, 378–82, 466–69; CO 5/1308, f.10–11. For the growing importance of political arithmetic, see McCormick, *William Petty*, chaps. 8–9.

14. TNA CO 5/1308, f.10–11 (quote, 11r). This vision had some commonalities with the Stuart plans to use towns to establish ties to poor planters, but the imperial bonds Nicholson envisioned were less about patronage of economic projects and more about shared commercial interests and imperial culture.

15. TNA CO 5/1305, f.158–67 (quote, 158); CO 5/713, f.304–5. For the convoy system, see Bradburn, "Visible Fist."

16. Middlesex County Court Order Book, 1680–94, LVA, f.474; *EJC* 1:179–80; *JHB* 2: 337–42, 345–46 (quote, 342).

17. *LJC* 1:138–39.

18. *LJC* 1:139; *HS* 3:61–64, 66–67. For Nicholson's religious and educational work, see Bruce T. McCully, "Governor Francis Nicholson, Patron 'Par Excellence' of Religion and Learning in Colonial America," *WMQ*, 3rd ser., 39 (1982): 310–33. For the broader context, see Stanwood, *Empire Reformed*, chap. 6.

19. TNA CO 5/1306, f.298–99; CO 5/714, f.46–51. For his investment in Yorktown,

see Edward Miles Riley, "The Founding and Development of Yorktown, Virginia, 1691–1781" (PhD diss., University of Southern California, 1942), 42.

20. TNA CO 5/1306, f.384–97; CO 391/7, f.63–65, 104–6. For Nicholson's response, see CO 5/1306, f.445–48.

21. For Nicholson's assessment, see TNA CO 5/714, f.46–51. For Copley's alliance with the revolutionary elite, see David W. Jordan, "The Royal Period of Colonial Maryland, 1689–1715" (PhD diss., Princeton University, 1966), 76–80, 88–97; Robert Noxon Toppan and Alfred Thomas Scrope Goodrick, eds., *Edward Randolph*, 7 vols. (Boston: Prince Society, 1898–1909), 5:77–104; 7:353–84, 397–98, 448–49, 451–53; CO 5/713, f.295–99; "Thomas Lawrence to William Blathwayt, 20th June 1694," Blathwayt Papers, folder 18, John D. Rockefeller Jr. Library, Colonial Williamsburg, Williamsburg, VA.

22. *Archives* 20:106, 113, 130, 133. For later reports, see *Archives* 20:283, 471, 538; 23:104; TNA CO 5/714, f.56.

23. *Archives* 19:33. The letter has not survived, but it likely argued that Virginia and Maryland should have a common urban policy; see TNA CO 5/1358, f.167–73; CO 391/7, f.104–6.

24. Annapolis was approved in 1694, and another town-founding act was diverted to establish Williamstadt the following year; see *Archives* 19:59, 83–88, 110–13, 178–80, 190. The choice of locations demonstrated Nicholson's effort to appeal to former proprietary allies. Arundelton was owned by Richard Hill, one of the most prominent Protestants to oppose the 1689 revolution, and Oxford, home to several critics of the revolutionary regime, had recently petitioned for a corporate charter to free it from the influence of Talbot County elites; for the relocation, see Edward C. Papenfuse, *"Doing Good To Posterity": The Move of the Capital of Maryland From St. Mary's City to Anne Arundell Towne, Now Called Annapolis* (Annapolis: Maryland State Archives, 1995), 10, 14; *Archives* 8:560; 13:343–44; 19:110–13. For the influence of the Protestant Associators in St. Mary's, see Jordan, "Royal Period," 104–7. John Scharf erroneously claimed the capital was relocated to move it away from Catholic influence; see Scharf, *History of Maryland* (Baltimore: J. B. Piet, 1879), 1:344–45. David Jordan dismissed a factional interpretation; see Jordan, "Royal Period," 148–49.

25. *Archives* 19:292, 320, 383; 20:388; CO 5/714, f.237. For Nicholson's concerns about distant councillors, see CO 5/1306, f.35–36. He also arranged for the post-stage route to run through both new towns; *Archives* 19:160–61. Besides William Bladen, this new group of Annapolis men included Amos Garrett, Charles Carroll, and Thomas Bordley. See Edward C. Papenfuse, *In Pursuit of Profit: Annapolis Merchants in the Era of the American Revolution, 1763–1805* (Baltimore: Johns Hopkins University Press, 1975), 8–10; Walsh, "Annapolis and Anne Arundel County," chap. 3, pp. 7–10; Nancy T. Baker, "Annapolis, Maryland, 1695–1730," *MHM* 81 (1986): 191–209. For Bladen, see C. Ashley Ellefson, "William Bladen of Annapolis, 1673?–1718: 'the most capable in all Respects' or 'Blockhead Booby'?," *Archives of Maryland Online*, vol. 747, http://aomol.msa.maryland.gov.

26. *Archives* 19:110, 211, 224, 228, 288–92, 301–8, 320–25, 498–504.

27. TNA CO 5/714, f.46–51.

28. Reps, *Tidewater Towns*, chap. 6; Mark Leone and Silas Hurry, "Seeing: The Power of Town Planning in the Chesapeake," *Historical Archaeology* 32 (1998): 34–62;

Mark Leone, *The Archaeology of Liberty in an American Capital: Excavations in Annapolis* (Berkeley: University of California Press, 2005), 83–99. For Williamstadt, see *Archives* 19:224. For King William's School, see McCully, "Governor Francis Nicholson," 318–19.

29. *Archives* 19:226.

30. *Archives* 19:470; 20:554–55, 589. Morris Radoff, *Buildings of the State of Maryland at Annapolis* (Annapolis, MD: Hall of Records Commission, 1954), 1–11. He also planned to erect a "Somerhouse" overlooking the overland route into the town and ordered that all tavern keepers provide him with lists of their customers; see *Archives* 19:498; 20:478.

31. TNA CO 5/714, f.40–41. Michael Lucas has revealed a similar emphasis on public spaces in Mount Calvert, suggesting that Nicholson was open to expanding the model beyond his initial hubs. See Lucas, "Negotiating Public Landscapes," 109–10. For Seymour, see Paul Musselwhite, "Annapolis Aflame: Richard Clarke's Conspiracy and the Imperial Urban Vision in Maryland, 1704–08," *WMQ*, 3rd ser., 71 (July 2014): 361–400.

32. Peter Laslett, "John Locke, the Great Recoinage, and the Origins of the Board of Trade: 1695–1698," *WMQ*, 3rd ser., 14 (1957): 370–402; I. K. Steele, *Politics of Colonial Policy: The Board of Trade in Colonial Administration, 1696–1720* (Oxford: Clarendon, 1968), chap. 1; Pincus, *1688*, chap. 14. For the Board of Trade's broader remit, see Slack, *Invention of Improvement*, 170–78.

33. "Earl of Bridgewater to Sir Thomas Lawrence, 30 Aug. 1697," MSS EL 9738, Egerton Papers, Huntington Library, Pasadena, CA. For Nicholson's alliance with other leading Whigs, see also MSS EL 9621, 9733. For Randolph's reports, see *CSPC* 15, nos. 46, 108, 120, 149, 176; for the board's response to Randolph, see *CSPC* 15:300; for their enquiries to Andros about towns, see *CSPC* 15: no. 956, 1295. For the board's contrasting opinions of Andros and Nicholson, see *CSPC* 15, nos. 1295, 1296.

34. TNA CO 5/714, f.331; CO 5/1309, f.75–82; CO 5/1359, f.89–109; CO 391/10, f.209–23, 263–67, 319, 324, 330; Hartwell, Blair, and Chilton, *Present State of Virginia*. See also Michael Kammen, "Virginia at the Close of the Seventeenth Century," *VMHB* 74 (1966): 141–69.

35. Locke's plan has erroneously been considered a draft of the *Present State of Virginia*; see Kammen, "Virginia at the Close," 141–53. However, Holly Brewer has demonstrated that the document (Locke MS e.9, Lovelace Collection, Bodleian Library, Oxford) was, in fact, a later composition, based on Locke's further investigations; see Holly Brewer, "Slavery, Sovereignty, and 'Inheritable Blood': Reconsidering John Locke and the Origins of American Slavery," *American Historical Review* 122 (2017): 1038–78. Hartwell, Blair, and Chilton, *Present State of Virginia*, 4–5. Kammen, "Virginia at the Close," 153–56 (quote, 155). For Locke's role in Nicholson's appointment, see Locke MS c.16, Lovelace Collection, Bodleian Library, Oxford, f.157; Randy Dunn, "Patronage and Governance in Francis Nicholson's Empire," in *English Atlantics Revisited: Essays Honouring Professor Ian K. Steele*, ed. Nancy L. Rhoden (Montreal: McGill-Queen's University Press, 2007), 59–80.

36. Kammen, "Virginia at the Close," 156–59 (quote, 157, 158). For this document's critique of slavery, see Brewer, "Slavery, Sovereignty, and 'Inheritable Blood.'" For prior

interpretation of these reforms, see Manning C. Voorhis, "Crown versus Council in Virginia Land Policy," *WMQ*, 3rd ser., 3 (1946): 499–514. Locke contributed to a similar debate about colonial labor occurring in Ireland; see Armitage, *Ideological Origins*, 165. For Locke's theory of empire as it relates to slavery and settler colonialism, see Barbara Arneil, *John Locke and America: The Defence of English Colonialism* (Oxford: Oxford University Press, 1996); David Armitage, "John Locke: Theorist of Empire?" in *Foundations of Modern International Thought*, ed. David Armitage (Cambridge: Cambridge University Press, 2013); Craig Yirush, *Settlers, Liberty, and Empire: The Roots of Early American Political Theory, 1675–1775* (Cambridge: Cambridge University Press, 2011).

37. TNA CO 324/25, f.26–80 (esp. 68). For the finalizing of Nicholson's instructions and the Locke-Blathwayt rivalry, see Steele, *Politics of Colonial Policy*, 23–24; Brewer, "Slavery, Sovereignty, and 'Inheritable Blood,'" 1065–67. For the fire at Jamestown's statehouse, see *EJC* 1:392–93, 397.

38. *JHB* 3:136–38, 149–52 (quote, 167).

39. TNA CO 5/1359, f.93–94. For Middle Plantation, see Philip Levy, "Middle Plantation's Changing Landscape: Persistence, Continuity, and the Building of Community," in *Early Modern Virginia: Reconsidering the Old Dominion*, ed. Douglas Bradburn and John C. Coombs (Charlottesville: University of Virginia Press, 2011), 185–206; Jennifer Agee Jones, "'The Very Heart and Centre of the Country': From Middle Plantation to Williamsburg," in *Williamsburg, Virginia: A City Before the State, 1699–1999*, ed. Robert P. McCubbin (Williamsburg, VA: City of Williamsburg, 2000), 15–24.

40. Hugh Jones, *The Present State of Virginia* (1724), quoted in Reps, *Tidewater Towns*, 156. For the cypher design, see ibid., chap. 7. See also Cathy Hellier, "The Character and Direction of Urban Expansion in Williamsburg," 7–12, in "Urbanization in the Tidewater South." For Nicholson's personal oversight of Williamsburg's development, see *EJC* 2:1–2, 29, 137, 181–83; Reps, *Tidewater Towns*, 154.

41. *JHB* 3:269, 279; *EJC* 2:181–82; Warren M. Billings, John E. Selby, and Thad W. Tate, *Colonial Virginia: A History* (White Plains, NY: KTO Press, 1986), 160–67; Evans, "A Topping People," 28.

42. *EJC* 2:107; *HS* 3:423; Reps, *Tidewater Towns*, 146–48. See also Hellier, "Character and Direction of Urban Expansion."

43. *EJC* 2:250–55; *JHB* 3:369–70.

44. "Peregrine Cony to the Bishop of London, 22nd July 1702," Fulham Palace Papers, vol. 15, no. 45, Lambeth Palace Library, London; TNA CO 5/1355, f.19–24; William J. Hinke, ed., "Report of the Journey of Francis Louis Michel from Berne, Switzerland, to Virginia, October 2, 1701–December 1, 1702, Part II," *VMHB* 24 (April 1916): 125–29. See also Paul Musselwhite, "'Like a Wild Desert': Building a Contested Urban Sensescape in the Atlantic World," in *Les cinq sens de la ville: Du Moyen Âge à nos jours*, ed. Robert Beck, Ulrike Krampl, and Emmanuelle Retaillaud-Bajac (Tours, France: Presses Universitaires François-Rabelais, 2013), 369–81.

45. *JHB* 4:147.

46. Cary Carson et al., "New World, Real World," 84–85. See also James D. Kornwolf, "'Doing Good for Posterity': Francis Nicholson, First Patron of Architecture, Landscape Design, and Town Planning in Virginia, Maryland, and South Carolina

1688–1726," *VMHB* 101 (1993): 333–74; Sylvia Doughty Fries, *The Urban Idea in Colonial America* (Philadelphia: Temple University Press, 1977), chap. 4.

47. TNA CO 5/1310, f.12–31.

48. *Archives* 19:71–78 (quotes, 71, 73); 20:147.

49. *Archives* 19:163, 224, 355; 20:363, 378, 387, 419–20, 426–28, 448.

50. *Archives* 23:375–78 (quote, 376–77), 446–55; for "Nic of Annapolis," see TNA CO 5/714, f.302; see also Jordan, "Royal Period," 176–96.

51. Musselwhite, "Annapolis Aflame."

52. Beverley, *History and Present State*, 79.

53. Beverley, *History and Present State*, 66–67, 72, 76, 252. Rainbolt, *From Prescription to Persuasion*, chap. 7. For the pastoral interpretation of Beverley's work, see J. A. Leo Lemay, "Robert Beverley's History and Present State of Virginia and the Emerging American Political Ideology," in *American Letters and the Historical Consciousness: Essays in Honor of Lewis P. Simpson*, ed. J. Gerald Kennedy and Daniel Mark Fogel (Baton Rouge: Louisiana State University Press, 1987), 67–111; Leo Marx, *Machine in the Garden: Technology and the Pastoral Ideal in America* (New York: Oxford University Press, 1964), 75–88; James L. Machor, *Pastoral Cities: Urban Ideals and the Symbolic Landscape of America* (Madison: University of Wisconsin Press, 1987), 74–81.

54. Boyd S. Schlenther, *The Life and Writings of Francis Makemie* (Philadelphia: Presbyterian Historical Society, 1971), 13–21; Ralph Whitelaw, *Virginia's Eastern Shore: A History of Northampton and Accomack Counties* (Gloucester, MA: P. Smith, 1968), 2:907; Francis Makemie, "A Plain and Friendly Perswasive to the Inhabitants of Virginia and Maryland For Promoting Towns and Cohabitation," reprinted in *VMHB* 4 (1896): 255–71.

55. Makemie, "A Plain and Friendly Perswasive," 257, 259, 261, 264, 266–67.

56. Ibid., 256, 264.

57. The new instructions resulted from a lobbying effort in London; see TNA CO 5/1314, f.315–19. For the instructions, see TNA CO 5/1337, f.54–55; CO 5/721, f.13–15. For Beverley's contact with his allies in Middlesex and their efforts to revive town development there, see *EJC* 1:403; Rutman and Rutman, *A Place in Time*, 218–25; *JHB* 4:92–100. Accomack (probably influenced by Makemie) and King and Queen Counties also sent petitions to renew town development during Nicholson's final years. See *JHB* 3:149; 4:109, 117, 119.

58. This assembly also reversed other elements of Nicholson's centralization agenda; see *EJC* 3:30; *JHB* 4:130, 165–66; Billings, Selby, and Tate, *Colonial Virginia*, 170–72.

59. *HS* 3:404–19. The legislation did encourage middling planters to invest in places such as Yorktown; see Riley, "Founding and Development," 64–68.

60. *HS* 3:405, 408. By this point, the word "burgh" had developed a narrow definition implying a small corporate town; see *Oxford English Dictionary*, http://www.oed.com, s.v. "borough," definitions 2–3.

61. For Seymour's initial attitude, see *CSPC* 22, no. 1210. For his reframing to the assembly, see *Archives* 26:523. See also *CSPC* 22, no. 1065; 23, nos. 160, 470. For a discussion of Seymour's plans, see Musselwhite, "Annapolis Aflame."

62. *Archives* 26:636–45 (quote, 643); for the legislative debate, see *Archives* 26:543–

48, 593, 598, 601, 605–6; for Makemie's presence at the session, *Archives* 25:212; 26:528. For speculative building in Annapolis, see Baker, "Annapolis, Maryland," 194–96. Seymour agreed to the legislation in order to have something to show London officials for his efforts. See *CSPC* 22, no. 470.

63. Proceedings of the Commissioners of Towns in Dorchester County, MD, 1706–09, MDSA M 12-1, Maryland State Archives, 50–65.

64. Evans, *"A Topping People,"* chap. 1.

65. For Paggan's relationship with Maryland's Protestant leaders, see "Maryland Council to Mr Peter Paggan, 21 December 1692," Ellesmere Americana, MSS EL 9572, 9694, Huntington Library; for the council's rejection of town development, see *Archives* 13:331, 341, 343–44.

66. The act established a two-tier system in which only a few locations were designated "ports" for clearing Atlantic shipping. For the council's efforts to water down the legislation, see *LJC* 1:138–40. For the finished act, see *HS* 3:53–69. Debate was so intense that one delegate later apologized for his conduct; *JHB* 2:347–49.

67. Middlesex County Court Order Book, 1680–1694, LVA, f.508–16; Rutman and Rutman, *A Place in Time*, 215–17; *JHB* 2:386, 397.

68. TNA CO 5/1306, f.384–97; CO 5/1306, f.445–48; *JHB* 2:396–407 (quote, 396). Nicholson compelled leading councillors to invest in lots in Yorktown, but they all quickly defaulted on the purchases; see Riley, "Founding and Development," 40–43, 49–51.

69. "Sir Edmund Andros to William Blathwayt, Nov. 3rd 1692," "Sir Edmund Andros to William Blathwayt, Jan. 16th 1692/3," Blathwayt Papers, folder 2, John D. Rockefeller Jr. Library, Colonial Williamsburg, Williamsburg, VA.

70. TNA CO 5/1306, f.384–97; "Sir Edmund Andros to William Blathwayt, Oct. 23rd 1693," "Sir Edmund Andros to William Blathwayt, Jan. 5th 1693/4," Blathwayt Papers, folder 3, John D. Rockefeller Jr. Library, Colonial Williamsburg, Williamsburg, VA; *JHB* 2:423, 450, 456–57, 470–71, 481; 3:93; *EJC* 1:296–97, 306, 385.

71. For the convoy system, see Bradburn, "Visible Fist," 361–86. For the slave trade, see Pettigrew, "Transatlantic Politics," 279–99. For the 1705 slave law, see Parent, *Foul Means*, chap. 4. For Russian trade, see Jacob M. Price, "The Tobacco Adventure to Russia: Enterprise, Politics, and Diplomacy in the Quest for a Northern Market for English Colonial Tobacco, 1676–1722," *Transactions of the American Philosophical Society* 51, no. 1 (1961): 1–120. For the development of interests in general, see Alison Olson, *Making the Empire Work: London and the American Interest Groups, 1690–1790* (Cambridge, MA: Harvard University Press, 1992), chaps. 4–6; Zahedieh, *Capital and the Colonies*, chap. 3; Gauci, *Politics of Trade*.

72. "Perry, Micajah & others, to William Blathwayt, Aug. 17 1697," Blathwayt Papers BL65, Huntington Library; TNA CO 5/717, f.221–22, 241.

73. *An Essay upon the Government of the English Plantations on the Continent of America* (London, 1701), 2, 78. See also Carole Shammas, "Benjamin Harrison III and the Authorship of An Essay upon the Government of the English Plantations on the Continent of America," *VMHB* 84 (1976): 166–73.

74. Add. Mss. 46542, BL, f.24–33 (esp. 26, 31).

75. TNA CO 391/10, f.215–23, 263–67; CO 5/1359, f.93–94; Hartwell, Blair, and Chilton, *Present State of Virginia*, 4–5, 12–14.

76. For the battle between Locke and Blathwayt, see Kammen, "Virginia at the Close," 150; Steele, *Politics of Colonial Policy*, 24.

77. "Speeches of Students of the College of William and Mary Delivered May 1, 1699," *WMQ*, 2nd ser., 10 (1930): 323–37 (quotes, 328, 329, 336; for reliance on English manufactures, see esp. 336).

78. Borsay, *English Urban Renaissance*; Joyce Ellis, "Regional and County Centres 1700–1840," in *The Cambridge Urban History of Britain*, vol. 2, ed. Peter Clark (Cambridge: Cambridge University Press, 2000), 673–704. For important qualifiers on the extent of the urban renaissance, see Estabrook, *Urbane and Rustic England*, chaps. 1–3. For the shifting civic focus toward manners and politeness, see Lawrence E. Klein, *Shaftesbury and the Culture of Politeness: Moral Discourse and Cultural Politics in Early Eighteenth-Century England* (Cambridge: Cambridge University Press, 1994); Pocock, *Machiavellian Moment*, 13–14. For the rise of patriarchy in Virginia, see Brown, *Good Wives*, chap. 8.

79. Reps, *Tidewater Towns*, 173–74; TNA CO 5/1314, f.305–12 (quote, 306). A few records of clubs in Williamsburg are preserved in the Francis Nicholson Papers, John D. Rockefeller Jr. Library, Colonial Williamsburg, Williamsburg, VA.

80. "Anonymous of 'Chelsey' to Francis Nicholson, Dec. 8th 1702," Francis Nicholson Papers, John D. Rockefeller Jr. Library, Colonial Williamsburg, Williamsburg, VA; TNA CO 5/1314, f.20–25. Customs official Robert Quarry confirmed that the councillors' anger was rooted in their jealousy of Nicholson's popularity; see TNA CO 323/5, f.50–56. Most accounts of Nicholson's rift with Blair revolve around the elites' self-interest and Nicholson's personal indiscretions; see Billings, Selby, and Tate, *Colonial Virginia*, 155–72; Evans, *"A Topping People,"* chap. 2. Kevin Hardwick demonstrates that the division revealed a broader rift over the nature of leadership; see Hardwick, "Narratives of Villainy and Virtue: Governor Francis Nicholson and the Character of the Good Ruler in Early Virginia," *Journal of Southern History* 72 (2006): 39–74.

81. *EJC* 1:323, 330; TNA CO 5/1314, f.20–25, 87–98; "James Blair to the Archbishop of Canterbury, Oct/Nov 1703," "Affidavit of James Blair, 25th April 1704," "Affidavit of James Blair, 1st May 1704," Francis Nicholson Papers, John D. Rockefeller Jr. Library, Colonial Williamsburg, Williamsburg, VA.

82. *JHB* 6:47–48, 60, 269, 273–74, 283, 297, 327, 331, 336, 341–48, 375, 382, 390–95; *EJC* 3:457–58. Spotswood only agreed to incorporate Williamsburg in 1722, after he repudiated his imperial instructions and aligned with the planter elite. For incorporation, see Robert Mangum Barrow, "Williamsburg and Norfolk: Municipal Government and Justice in Colonial Virginia" (MA thesis, College of William and Mary, 1960) chap. 2. For political alignments of the Spotswood era, see Williams, "Political Alignments," chaps. 5–6.

83. Chancery Record Book 2, MDSA S517-4, Maryland State Archives, 590–94; *Archives* 27:207–10, 218–21, 229–32, 358–59; *CSPC* 24, no. 290; C. Ashley Ellefson, "Governor John Seymour and the Charters of Annapolis," *Archives of Maryland Online*, vol. 749, http://aomol.msa.maryland.gov.

84. Alexander Hamilton, *The History of the Ancient and Honorable Tuesday Club*, ed. Robert Micklus (Chapel Hill: University of North Carolina Press, 1990); "Tim Pastimes to William Hunter, c. 1760/1" (quote. f.4), John D. Rockefeller Jr. Library, Colonial

Williamsburg, Williamsburg, VA. For Annapolis, see also Somerville, *The Tuesday Club*; Land, *Colonial Maryland*, 182–98; Jane Wilson McWilliams, *Annapolis, City on the Severn: A History* (Baltimore: Johns Hopkins University Press, 2011), chap. 2; Paul A. Shackel, "Maintenance Relationship in Early Colonial Annapolis," in *Annapolis Pasts: Historical Archaeology in Annapolis, Maryland*, ed. Paul A. Shackel, Paul R. Mullins, and Mark S. Warner (Knoxville: University of Tennessee Press, 1998), 97–118. For Williamsburg, see Rhys Isaac, *Transformation of Virginia, 1740–1790* (Chapel Hill: University of North Carolina Press, 1982), chap. 5; "Urbanization in the Tidewater South."

85. For Charleston, see Hart, *Building Charleston*. For Kingston, see Burnard, "'The Grand Mart of the Island': The Economic Function of Kingston, Jamaica in the Mid-Eighteenth Century," in *Jamaica in Slavery and Freedom: History, Heritage and Culture*, ed. Kathleen Monteith and Glen Richards (Kingston, Jamaica: University of the West Indies Press, 2002), 225–41; see also Trevor Burnard and Emma Hart, "Kingston, Jamaica, and Charleston, South Carolina: A New Look at Comparative Urbanization in Plantation Colonial British America," *Journal of Urban History* 39 (2012): 214–34. Kingston's status was contentious in midcentury Jamaica; see George Metcalf, *Royal Government and Political Conflict in Jamaica, 1729–1783* (London: Longmans, 1965), 122–41. Williamsburg and Annapolis did, of course, have urban slave populations that formed communities and resisted white authority, but they were not as large (either in total or as a proportion of the population) as in Charleston; see Philip Morgan, *Slave Counterpoint: Black Culture in the Eighteenth-Century Chesapeake and Lowcountry* (Chapel Hill: University of North Carolina Press, 1998), 663–64; see also Thad W. Tate, *The Negro in Eighteenth-Century Williamsburg* (Williamsburg, VA: Colonial Williamsburg, 1965); Leone, *Archaeology of Liberty*, chap. 7.

86. TNA CO 5/1314, f.315–18 (quote, 318v).

87. *EJC* 3:111; "Robert Carter to Thomas Corbin, July 6 1705," in *Robert Carter Papers Online*, http://carter.lib.virginia.edu/.

88. TNA CO 391/2, f.257, 283–85; CO 5/717, f.39; CO 5/727, f.126–32. For Bradford, see Papenfuse et al., *Biographical Dictionary*, 158.

89. TNA CO 5/1362, f.438–42.

90. *JHB* 4:321, 324; 5:19–42; *HS* 4:32–36.

91. Thomas, "Settlement, Community, and Economy," 142–56, 185–98; Lucas, "Negotiating Public Landscapes"; Shomette, *Lost Towns*, chap. 2; Riley, "Founding and Development," 69–192; Rutman and Rutman, *A Place in Time*, 225–33; Wertenbaker, *Norfolk*, chap. 1; Reps, *Tidewater Towns*, 67–70.

92. Jones, *Present State of Virginia*, chap. 2 (quotes, 31, 32).

CHAPTER SEVEN

1. *Maryland Gazette*, March 18, 1729.

2. Marion Tinling, ed., *The Correspondence of the Three William Byrds of Westover, Virginia, 1684–1776*, 2 vols. (Charlottesville: University of Virginia Press, 1977), 1:355, 419. For planter hegemony, see Isaac, *Transformation of Virginia*; Charles Sydnor, *American Revolutionaries in the Making: Political Practices in Washington's Virginia* (New

York: Free Press, 1965). For country thought, see Caroline Robbins, *The Eighteenth-Century Commonwealthman* (Cambridge, MA: Harvard University Press, 1959); Pocock, *Machiavellian Moment*, chaps. 13–14; J. G. A. Pocock, *Virtue, Commerce, and History: Essays on Political Thought and History, Chiefly in the Eighteenth Century* (Cambridge: Cambridge University Press, 1985), 230–53. In Britain, country thought was also connected with urban radicalism; see Nicholas Rogers, *Whigs and Cities: Popular Politics in the Age of Walpole and Pitt* (Oxford: Oxford University Press, 1989). For "country" ideology and the American Revolution, see Bernard Bailyn, *The Ideological Origins of the American Revolution* (Cambridge, MA: Harvard University Press, 1967); Bernard Bailyn, *The Origins of American Politics* (New York: Knopf, 1968); for the republican synthesis, see Robert E. Shalhope, "Toward a Republican Synthesis: The Emergence of an Understanding of Republicanism in American Historiography," *WMQ*, 3rd ser., 29 (1972): 49–80. Previous efforts to trace its particular appeal to Chesapeake planters include Jack P. Greene, "'Virtus et Libertus': Political Culture, Social Change, and the Origins of the American Revolution in Virginia," in *Understanding the American Revolution: Issues and Actors*, ed. Jack. P. Greene (Charlottesville: University of Virginia Press, 1995); A. G. Roeber, *Faithful Magistrates and Republican Lawyers: Creators of Virginia Legal Culture, 1680–1810* (Chapel Hill: University of North Carolina Press, 1981); Breen, *Tobacco Culture*. For agricultural reform, see Chaplin, *Anxious Pursuit*; Caroline Winterer, *American Enlightenments: Pursuing Happiness in the Age of Reason* (New Haven, CT: Yale University Press, 2016), chap. 7.

3. For urban growth, see Reps, *Tidewater Towns*, chaps. 9–10; see also Kulikoff, *Tobacco and Slaves*, 122–27.

4. This legislation has been reduced into two useful tables in Mitchell, "Metropolitan Chesapeake," 121–22.

5. "Robert Anderson to Micajah and Richard Perry, 1715," quoted in Hemphill, *Virginia and the English Commercial System*, 45. For the boom, see ibid., 43–51; for the focus on agriculture among the planter elite, see Trevor Burnard, *Creole Gentlemen: The Maryland Elite, 1691–1776* (New York: Routledge, 2002), chap. 2. For planter lobbying, see Williams, "Political Alignments," chap. 5.

6. Statistics for slave imports derived from the Transatlantic Slave-Trade Database, http://www.slavevoyages.org. For the expansion of the slave trade and Virginia's economic cycles, see Parent, *Foul Means*, chap. 2.

7. Parent, *Foul Means*, chap. 4; Hemphill, *Virginia and the English Commercial System*, 59; Williams, "Political Alignments," 203–6; Kulikoff, *Tobacco and Slaves*, 97–99; Rice, *Nature and History*, chaps. 11–12.

8. Hemphill, *Virginia and the English Commercial System*, chap. 2; St. George L. Sioussant, *Economics and Politics in Maryland 1720–1750, and the Public Services of Daniel Dulany the Elder* (Baltimore: Johns Hopkins University Press, 1903).

9. "Robert Carter to Anonymous, July 2, 1723," and "Robert Carter to Micajah and Richard Perry, July 14, 1720," in *Robert Carter Papers Online*, http://carter.lib.virginia.edu; Hemphill, *Virginia and the English Commercial System*, 69–72.

10. "Benedict Leonard Calvert to Charles, Lord Baltimore, 26 Oct. 1729," in *Calvert Papers*, no. 2 (Baltimore: Maryland Historical Society, 1894), 68–81 (quote, 70); "Stephen Bordley to Samuel White, 25 Sept. 1733," quoted in Jacob M. Price, "The Excise Affair

Revisited: The Administrative and Colonial Dimensions of a Parliamentary Crisis," in *England's Rise to Greatness, 1660–1763*, ed. Stephen Baxter (Berkeley: University of California Press, 1983), 301; Hemphill, *Virginia and the English Commercial System*, chaps. 4–7; Paul Langford, *The Excise Crisis: Society and Politics in the Age of Walpole* (Oxford: Oxford University Press, 1975). For Perry, see Jacob M. Price, *Perry of London: A Family and a Firm on the Seaborne Frontier, 1615–1753* (Cambridge, MA: Harvard University Press, 1992), chap. 6.

11. Jacob M. Price, "The Rise of Glasgow in the Chesapeake Tobacco Trade, 1707–1775," *WMQ*, 3rd ser. 11 (1954): 179–99; T. M. Devine, *The Tobacco Lords: A Study of the Tobacco Merchants of Glasgow and Their Trading Activities, c. 1740–90* (Edinburgh: John Donald, 1975); "Robert Carter to Robert Burridge, June 27, 1718," in *Robert Carter Papers Online*.

12. *Maryland Gazette*, April 8, 1729. For Glaswegian competition, see Jacob M. Price, "Glasgow, the Tobacco Trade, and the Scottish Customs, 1707–1730: Some Commercial, Administrative and Political Implications of the Union," *Scottish Historical Review* 63 (1984): 1–36.

13. Henry Darnall, *A Just and Impartial Account of the Transactions of the Merchants in London for the Advancement of the Price of Tobacco . . .* (Annapolis, MD: William Parks, 1729) 9, 35; *Maryland Gazette*, March 11, 1729. For this price-fixing scheme from the London perspective, see Jacob M. Price, *France and the Chesapeake: A History of the French Tobacco Monopoly, 1674–1791*, 2 vols. (Ann Arbor: University of Michigan Press, 1973), 651–54.

14. *Maryland Gazette*, March 11, 1729 (quotes, "Enemy"); March 18, 1729; April 1, 1729. The language here is strikingly similar to that which Breen asserts as an innovation of the 1760s; see Breen, *Tobacco Culture*, chap. 4.

15. *Maryland Gazette*, April 15, 1729; April 29, 1729; May 6, 1729. Darnall, *Just and Impartial Account*, 12–13. For the importance of printing in the planter civic vision, see Jennifer J. Baker, *Securing the Commonwealth: Debt, Speculation, and Writing in the Making of Early America* (Baltimore: Johns Hopkins University Press, 2005), chap. 2; Capper Nichols, "Tobacco and the Rise of Writing in Colonial Maryland," *Mississippi Quarterly* 50 (1996/7): 5–17.

16. Bernard C. Steiner, ed., *Early Maryland Poetry* (Baltimore: Maryland Historical Society, 1900), 33–52 (quotes, 33, 39, 45, 46).

17. J. A. Leo Lemay, *Men of Letters in Colonial Maryland* (Knoxville: University of Tennessee Press, 1972) 166–72 (quote, 171). For the pastoral trope, see Marx, *Machine in the Garden*, chap. 3. For the evolution of the pastoral in eighteenth-century England, see Williams, *The Country and the City*.

18. Jones, *Present State of Virginia*, iii, 32, 35, 36, 45, 48.

19. Burnard, *Creole Gentlemen*, 192–200.

20. Diary of Landon Carter, quoted in Walsh, *Motives of Honor*, 538. For agricultural innovation as a form of gentry leadership, see ibid., 518–38 (Walsh does note that this innovation built upon a tradition of increasing efficiency on individual plantations through the seventeenth century); Rhys Isaac, *Landon Carter's Uneasy Kingdom: Revolution and Rebellion on a Virginia Plantation* (Oxford: Oxford University Press, 2004), chap. 4; Bruce A. Ragsdale, *A Planters' Republic: The Search for Economic Indepen-*

dence in Revolutionary Virginia (Madison, WI: Madison House, 1996), chap. 2. For debates about scientific agriculture in Carolina, see Chaplin, *Anxious Pursuit*, chaps. 3–6.

21. For the expansion of credit, see Jacob M. Price, *Capital and Credit in British Overseas Trade: The View from the Chesapeake, 1700–1760* (Cambridge, MA: Harvard University Press, 1980). For the planter elites' ethics of debt, see Breen, *Tobacco Culture*, chap. 3. For the extent and nature of elite debt, see Burnard, *Creole Gentlemen*, chap. 3. For debt and class relations, see Kulikoff, *Tobacco and Slaves*, 118–31; poor planters became indebted to Scottish merchants, which discouraged elites from extending them credit and fractured community bonds; see Burnard, *Creole Gentlemen*, 76. For merchant complaints about county debt collection, see *JHB* 10:233–35; see also Roeber, *Faithful Magistrates*, chap. 4. For the attitude of planters in other parts of British America, see Trevor Burnard, "Towns in Plantation Societies," 852–54; for changing attitudes in British America more generally, see Serena Zabin, *Dangerous Economies: Status and Commerce in Imperial New York* (Philadelphia: University of Pennsylvania Press, 2009), chap. 1. For English credit culture, see Craig Muldrew, *The Economy of Obligation: The Culture of Credit and Social Relations in Early Modern England* (London: Palgrave, 1998); Wennerlind, *Casualties of Credit*.

22. *HS* 4:247–71. For Gooch's role, see Stacy L. Lorenz, "'To Do Justice to His Majesty, the Merchant and the Planter': Governor William Gooch and the Virginia Tobacco Inspection Act of 1730," *VMHB* 108 (2000): 345–92.

23. *CSPC* 36, no. 796. Hemphill, *Virginia and the English Commercial System*, 150–73; Price, "The Excise Affair," 273. The plan that Darnall negotiated with the London merchants in 1728 had involved sorting and disposing of the worst tobacco; see Darnall, *Just and Impartial Account*, 28–30.

24. Inspectors were not recruited from the elite planter class, but they were dependent upon local county justices for their appointment. Inspectors were respected within their communities but sometimes failed to live up to the elites' polite standards; see Isaac, *Transformation of Virginia*, 77.

25. R. A. Brock, ed., *The Official Letters of Alexander Spotswood, Lieutenant-Governor of the Colony of Virginia, 1710–1722*, 2 vols. (New York: AMS Press, 1973), 2:49; Williams, "Political Alignments," chaps. 4–5. The differences between the two schemes are best articulated in Lorenz, "'To Do Justice,'" 351–64. Fears of corruption and private interest also explain why Maryland failed to institute a similar inspection scheme until 1747. Maryland planters had a tense relationship with Lord Baltimore, whose proprietary authority had been restored in 1715, and were therefore even more acutely sensitive to the potential for patronage. See Mary McKinney Schweitzer, "Economic Regulation and the Colonial Economy: The Maryland Tobacco Inspection Act of 1747," *Journal of Economic History* 40 (1980): 551–69 (esp. 555); Burnard, *Creole Gentlemen*, 194–95.

26. [William Gooch], *A Dialogue Between Thomas Sweet-Scented, William Oronoco, Planters, both Men of good Understanding, and Justice Love-Country, who can speak for himself, Recommended To the Reading of the Planters* (Williamsburg, VA: William Parks, 1732), 9, 11, 16. See also Alexander Haskell, "'The Affections of the People': Ideology and the Politics of State Building in Colonial Virginia, 1607–1754" (PhD diss., Johns Hopkins University, 2004), 395–400.

27. Gooch, *A Dialogue*, 10, 13, 14; *HS* 4:390; Williams, "Political Alignments," 245–46.

28. For the planter-merchant division in Maryland, see Schweitzer, "Economic Regulation," 557. For the inspection system's role in consolidating the elite, see Kulikoff, *Tobacco and Slaves*, 104–16; Isaac, *Transformation of Virginia*, 30, 93.

29. For the store system, see Bergstrom, *Markets and Merchants*, chap. 6; James H. Soltow, *The Economic Role of Williamsburg* (Charlottesville: University of Virginia Press, 1965) 48–63. Allan Kulikoff has traced the increasing social importance of the small towns in Prince George's County; see Kulikoff, *Tobacco and Slaves*, 217–31.

30. "Robert Bogle to John Bogle, 1 April, 1760," Bogle Papers Bundle 15 #17, Mitchell Library, Glasgow. For the Scottish role in perfecting the store system, see Price, "Rise of Glasgow." For the pattern of store placement, see Price, *France and the Chesapeake*, 662; Alan L. Karras, *Sojourners in the Sun: Scottish Migrants in Jamaica and the Chesapeake, 1740–1800* (Ithaca, NY: Cornell University Press, 1992), chaps. 3–4 (statistics about residence derived from pp. 134–35).

31. Charles J. Farmer, *In the Absence of Towns: Settlement and Country Trade in Southside Virginia, 1730–1800* (Lanham, MD: Rowman and Littlefield, 1993).

32. For inspection warehouse locations in Virginia, see *HS* 4:266–68; for Maryland, see *Archives* 44:608–9.

33. Paul G. E. Clemens, *The Atlantic Economy and Colonial Maryland's Eastern Shore: From Tobacco to Grain* (Ithaca, NY: Cornell University Press, 1980); Walsh, *Motives of Honor*, chap. 7; Bergstrom, *Markets and Merchants*, chap. 5; Robert Mitchell, *Commercialism and Frontier: Perspectives on the Early Shenandoah Valley* (Charlottesville: University of Virginia Press, 1977); Warren R. Hofstra, *The Planting of New Virginia: Settlement and Landscape in the Shenandoah Valley* (Baltimore: Johns Hopkins University Press, 2004) chap. 3; Rice, *Nature and History*, chap. 13.

34. Some scholars have argued that the transition to wheat single-handedly explains urban development in the region. However, tobacco still remained the region's largest export, and numerous towns were established in areas where it still dominated. See Earle and Hoffman, "Staple Crops." For wheat agriculture and particular towns, see Gould, "Economic Causes"; Thomas M. Preisser, "Alexandria and the Evolution of the Northern Virginia Economy, 1749–1776," *VMHB* 89 (1981): 282–93; Wertenbaker, *Norfolk*, chap. 2.

35. Dantas, *Black Townsmen*; Charles G. Steffen, *The Mechanics of Baltimore: Workers and Politics in the Age of Revolution, 1763–1812* (Urbana: University of Illinois Press, 1984); Wertenbaker, *Norfolk*. For an overview of towns, see Reps, *Tidewater Towns*, chaps. 9–10 (for Suffolk, see p. 213); for Yorktown, see Riley, "Founding and Development," esp. 212–20; for Winchester and backcountry towns in general, see Warren R. Hofstra and Robert D. Mitchell, "Town and Country in Backcountry Virginia: Winchester and the Shenandoah Valley, 1730–1800," *Journal of Southern History* 59 (1993): 619–46; Christopher E. Hendricks, *The Backcountry Towns of Colonial Virginia* (Knoxville: University of Tennessee Press, 2006).

36. Wright, *Prose Works*, 52, 173–74.

37. For an example of restrictions, see Bridgetown (*Archives* 37:546–47). For the relaxing of such restrictions, see Alexandria (*HS* 8:49); Bladensburg (*Archives* 42:604–6).

38. Ronald Hoffman and Sally D. Mason, *Princes of Ireland, Planters of Maryland: A Carroll Saga, 1500–1782* (Chapel Hill: University of North Carolina Press, 2000), 120–22; Charles G. Steffen, *From Gentlemen to Townsmen: The Gentry of Baltimore County, Maryland, 1660–1776* (Lexington: University of Kentucky Press, 1993), 139–41. For Williamsburg, see *JHB* 10:34, 35, 38, 42, 43, 45, 87, 119, 124, 128; for Norfolk, see Brent Tarter, ed., *The Order Book and Related Papers of the Common Hall of the Borough of Norfolk, Virginia, 1736–1798* (Richmond: Virginia State Library, 1979), 73–74.

39. For Byrd's Richmond lottery, see *Virginia Gazette* (Purdie & Dixon) July 23, 1767; for other lotteries, see *Virginia Gazette* (Purdie & Dixon) July 9, 1767; *Virginia Gazette* (Purdie & Dixon) March 19, 1767. For the popularity of lotteries, see John Ezell, "The Lottery in Colonial America," *WMQ*, 3rd ser. 5 (1948): 185–200. For Byrd's development of Richmond, see Marianne Patricia Buroff Sheldon, "Richmond, Virginia: The Town and Henrico County to 1820" (PhD diss., University of Michigan, 1975), 10–12; for Richmond and Carrollsburg, see Reps, *Tidewater Towns*, 247, 267–69. For town development and land speculation in the west, see Hendricks, *Backcountry Towns*.

40. In Virginia there were a few omnibus acts, but this was for convenience rather than part of a broader vision; see for example *HS* 7:234–36, 305–7.

41. *JHB* 6:11–12, 33–37; *HS* 4:234–39 (quotes, 234); "Governor William Gooch to the Board of Trade, 8 June 1728," *CSPC* 36, no. 241.

42. For Suffolk, see *JHB* 7:47, 61, 63; *HS* 5:199–202 (quote, 199). For Alexandria, see *JHB* 7:265, 355–56, 368; 8:34, 64, 70, 72, 73; Gay Montague Moore, *Seaport in Virginia: George Washington's Alexandria* (Richmond, VA: Garrett and Massie, 1949), 5–9. For Salisbury, see *Archives* 37:537–40. In most cases, particularly in Maryland, the assembly insisted that accommodation with the current landowner be reached before they would pass any legislation.

43. "Gooch to the Board of Trade, 8 June 1728," *CSPC* 36, no. 241; "Augustine Washington to Lawrence Washington, Mount Vernon, July 19th 1749," quoted in Moore, *Seaport in Virginia*, 8.

44. For George Town in Kent County, see *Archives* 39:324, 493–96; for the competitor town (Frederick Town), see *Archives* 39:490–93. On other occasions, landowners were looking for other advantages; in 1744, Robert Smith specified in his will that part of his estate in Caroline County, Virginia, ought to be laid out as a town in order to pay off a mortgage (*JHB* 7:99, 106; *HS* 5:287–92).

45. "William Byrd II to Micajah Perry, 27 May 1729," in Tinling, *Correspondence*, 1:398; Wright, *Prose Works*, 172–74, 388; *HS* 5:191–93; Marie Tyler-McGraw, *At the Falls: Richmond, Virginia, and Its People* (Chapel Hill: University of North Carolina Press, 1994), 44–45. For the limits on self-government in Richmond, see Sheldon, "Richmond, Virginia," chap. 1. See also Newcastle, laid out by William Meriwether in 1744 (*HS* 5:257–59), and Portsmouth, laid out by William Craford in 1752 (Reps, *Tidewater Towns*, 217–18).

46. For Bladensburgh, see *Archives* 42:284–85, 290, 306, 326, 347, 358, 413–16. For Port Royal, see *JHB* 7:99, 106. For Aylett, see *JHB* 7:176, 218. For Cocke's Town, see *JHB* 8:118, 120, 122, 125; *LJC* 2:1102. Legislation for Upper Marlborough was stalled in 1731, 1732, and 1733, before finally being approved in 1744 with an act that explicitly referenced the claims of Daniel Carroll (*Archives* 42:630–35).

47. Fairfax Harrison, *Landmarks of Old Prince William: A Study of Origins in Northern Virginia* (Richmond, VA: Old Dominion Press, 1924), 385–90. For the planter gentry's increasingly tense relationship with the Scots, see Ragsdale, *Planters' Republic*, 36–41.

48. For the court-country divide, see Land, *Colonial Maryland*, chaps. 7 and 9. For quitrent disputes, see, for example, Ceciltown (*Archives* 37:24); Salisbury (*Archives* 37:403). For Janssen Town, see *Archives* 39:3, 15–16, 28, 125–27.

49. For Frederick, see Aubrey C. Land, *The Dulanys of Maryland* (Baltimore: Maryland Historical Society, 1955), 179–84, 327. For Carrollsburg and Hamburg, see Reps, *Tidewater Towns*, 247–51. Planters' fears of proprietary influence were well founded; Baltimore did seek to reassert authority over urban land in the 1760s; see "Cecil Calvert to Governor Horatio Sharpe, 29 Feb. 1764," *Archives* 14:133–42.

50. *HS* 7:236; the quoted text comes from the commission to the trustees of Winchester, but identical phrasing was used in multiple acts from the 1750s onward. For Maryland provisions for storing records with the county clerk, see for example Bridgetown (*Archives* 37:544–47) and Benedict Leonard Town (*Archives* 37:549–52). Only a quarter of the trustees appointed to oversee Virginia towns can be identified as merchants rather than planters. Peter Bergstrom has argued that, when compared to the proportion of merchants in Virginia society, they played a disproportionate role in urban leadership. However, when compared to leadership of towns elsewhere, the Chesapeake towns appear overwhelmingly dominated by planter gentry. See Bergstrom, *Markets and Merchants*, 217–19.

51. A small number of additional powers were granted to select locations in the 1750s and 1760s. For example, Alexandria and Georgetown gained the power to collect wharfage fees; *HS* 8:615; *Archives* 46:630–35.

52. *JHB* 7:9–10, 262; 8:19–20, 82; 9:13, 42, 49, 58, 67–68, 70–71. For Queen Anne Town, see *Archives* 46:470. For urban petitions in England, see Julian Hoppit, "Patterns of Parliamentary Legislation, 1660–1800," *Historical Journal* 39 (1996): 109–31.

53. For acts establishing fairs, see for example, *HS* 5:82–83. For Suffolk, see *JHB* 7: 185. The General Assembly also rejected a similar request from Fredericksburg; see *JHB* 8:22, 30, 31, 98. For Baltimore, see *Archives* 44:655.

54. *LJC* 2:1084.

55. For Williamsburg, see *JHB* 6:270, 293. For Baltimore, see *Archives* 42:278, 333, 466. For Yorktown, see *JHB* 6:367–68, 385. For Tappahannock, see *JHB* 7:353–54, 369–70. For Chestertown, see *Archives* 37:172–77. One exception was William Byrd II's plan for Richmond, which did feature a common; see Reps, *Tidewater Towns*, 266–69.

56. *Virginia Gazette*, September 14, 1739 (thanks to Josh Beatty, who first brought this document to my attention). Some courthouses and churches were moved to new towns, particularly in Maryland; however, by 1745, the Virginia burgesses began receiving requests to move courthouses out of towns (*JHB* 7:183). For the location of courthouses in eighteenth-century Virginia, see Carl R. Lounsbury, *The Courthouses of Early Virginia: An Architectural History* (Charlottesville: University of Virginia Press, 2005), chap. 3.

57. *Archives* 42:434–40, 616–24; 46:464–67. For Charlestown's elaborate street plan, see Reps, *Tidewater Towns*, 233–36. For the boundary dispute, see Land, *Colonial*

Maryland, 169–73. Charlestown did enjoy a short-lived boom in the 1750s, but it was soon eclipsed by Baltimore; see George Johnston, *History of Cecil County, Maryland . . .* (Elkton, MD: self-published, 1881), 265–74.

58. Tarter, *Order Book*, 35–41 (charter), 50–55 (supervision of the poor); *JHB* 6:255, 293, 305–16. For Norfolk's growth, see Wertenbaker, *Norfolk*, chaps. 1–2. For the 1730 rebellion, see Parent, *Foul Means*, 159–62. For a list of Norfolk County justices, noting those who were also corporate officers, see Barrow, "Williamsburg and Norfolk," 112–13.

59. Tarter, *Order Book*, 43–44.

60. Tarter, *Order Book*, 57, 92, 112 (quote, 92). For Dinwiddie's battle with Virginia's provincial council, see Louis Knott Koontz, *Robert Dinwiddie: His Career in American Colonial Government and Westward Expansion* (Glendale, CA: Arthur H. Clark, 1941), 37–50. Early signs of the customs office rivalry came in 1737, when Norfolk petitioned to have the office moved in light of a smallpox epidemic in Hampton; see Tarter, *Order Book*, 49. For relations with Botetourt, see ibid., 156.

61. Tarter, *Order Book*, 59, 61, 68, 72–73, 87, 134, 167; *JHB* 7:364–87; 8:67, 70, 76, 82, 87, 88, 98; *HS* 6:261–65; *LJC* 2:1053. For more detail on the struggle between Norfolk and the General Assembly, see Paul Musselwhite, "'This infant Borough': The Corporate Political Identity of Eighteenth-Century Norfolk," *Early American Studies* 15 (2017): 801–34.

62. *Archives* 42:621.

63. Price, *Capital and Credit*, chap. 2 (statistic drawn from p. 13); Ragsdale, *Planters' Republic*, chap. 1. For the distinct effects in Maryland, see Ronald Hoffman, *A Spirit of Dissension: Economics, Politics and the Revolution in Maryland* (Baltimore: Johns Hopkins University Press, 1975), chap. 2.

64. "Robert Beverley to Unknown, 18 Aug. 1765," quoted in Ragsdale, *Planters' Republic*, 25. For the second wave of Scottish storekeepers, see Karras, *Sojourners in the Sun*, 85–86. For Baltimore and the wheat trade, see Steffen, *From Gentlemen to Townsmen*, chap. 7 (esp. 152–53); Paul Kent Walker, "The Baltimore Community and the American Revolution: A Study in Urban Development, 1763–1783" (PhD diss., University of North Carolina, 1973), chap. 2; Gould, "Economic Causes."

65. *Virginia Gazette* (Rind), October 31, 1771. See also Breen, *Tobacco Culture*, chap. 4.

66. Ragsdale, *Planters' Republic*, 47–51 (quote, "Robert Beverley to John Bland, 5 May 1763," 48); Joseph M. Ernst, *Money and Politics in America, 1755–1775: A Study in the Currency Act of 1764 and the Political Economy of Revolution* (Chapel Hill: University of North Carolina Press, 1973), chap. 3.

67. *Virginia Gazette* (Purdie & Dixon), March 22, 1770. Ernst, "The Robinson Scandal Redivivus: Money, Debts, and Politics in Revolutionary Virginia," *VMHB* 77 (1969): 146–73; Ragsdale, *Planters' Republic*, chap. 2.

68. *Virginia Gazette* (Rind), October 31, 1771; *Virginia Gazette* (Purdie & Dixon), March 22, 1770; *Virginia Gazette* (Purdie & Dixon), August 5, 1773. Statistics on town foundations drawn from Mitchell, "Metropolitan Chesapeake," 121–22. For agricultural societies, see Manuela Albertone, *National Identity and the Agrarian Republic: The*

Transatlantic Commerce of Ideas between America and France (1750–1830) (Burlington, VT: Ashgate, 2014), chap. 6.

69. Ragsdale, *Planters' Republic*, chap. 3 (esp. 86).

70. *Virginia Gazette* (Rind), July 18, 1771; "Charles Carroll of Annapolis to Charles Carroll of Carrolton, 12 Aug. 1770," in Ronald Hoffman, ed., *Dear Papa, Dear Charley*, 3 vols. (Chapel Hill: University of North Carolina Press, 2001), 2:521–22.

71. *Archives* 63:261–71 (quote, 261); Thomas W. Griffith, *Annals of Baltimore* (Baltimore: W. Wooddy, 1824), 47, 68–73; J. Thomas Scharf, *Chronicles of Baltimore* (Baltimore: Turnbull Brothers, 1874), 59–60, 153. For the alliance between Annapolis and Baltimore, see Hoffman, *Spirit of Dissension*.

72. Soltow, *Economic Role of Williamsburg*, 143; Ragsdale, *Planters' Republic*, 28–29; *HS* 8:401–2; for Norfolk's effort to gain broader jurisdiction, see Tarter, *Order Book*, 75.

73. Peter Force, ed., *American Archives, Fourth Series*, 1:370–71; 3:1137–38; "Virginia Legislative Papers," *VMHB* 14 (1906), 51–52 (quote, 52). For Norfolk's early protests, see *Virginia Gazette* (Purdie & Dixon), October 1, 1767; *Virginia Gazette* (Purdie & Dixon), June 6, 1766. For the siege of Norfolk, see Wertenbaker, *Norfolk*, 61–70. See also, Michael A. McDonnell, *The Politics of War: Race, Class, and Conflict in Revolutionary Virginia* (Chapel Hill: University of North Carolina Press, 2007) 152–72.

74. Jefferson, *Notes on the State of Virginia*, 152–53.

75. Burnard and Hart, "Kingston, Jamaica"; Emma Hart, "City Government and the State in Eighteenth-Century South Carolina," *Eighteenth-Century Studies* 50 (2017): 195–211; see also Hart, *Building Charleston*. However, Natalie Zacek has suggested that British Caribbean planters self-consciously embraced their rural identity in ways similar to those described here; see Natalie Zacek, "Rituals of Rulership: The Material Culture of West Indian Politics," in *Material Culture in Anglo-America*, ed. David S. Shields (Columbia: University of South Carolina Press, 2009), 115–26.

EPILOGUE

1. Ragsdale, *Planters' Republic*, chap. 8; for the broader debate, see Cathy D. Matson and Peter S. Onuf, *A Union of Interests: Political and Economic Thought in Revolutionary America* (Lawrence: University of Kansas Press, 1990); J. E. Crowley, *Privileges of Independence: Neomercantilism and the American Revolution* (Baltimore: Johns Hopkins University Press, 1993). For the debate about political economy in the lower South, see Chaplin, *Anxious Pursuit*, chaps. 5–7. For municipal reform, see Jon C. Teaford, *The Municipal Revolution in America: Origins of Modern Urban Government 1650–1825* (Chicago: University of Chicago Press, 1975).

2. The extent to which political economists in the new nation embraced free trade is disputed; see Merrill D. Peterson, "Thomas Jefferson and Commercial Policy, 1783–1793," *WMQ*, 3rd. ser., 22 (1965): 584–610; McCoy, *Elusive Republic*, chap. 3; Crowley, *Privileges of Independence*, chaps. 4–5. For the regional vision of the Chesapeake as the gateway to the west, see Drew R. McCoy, "James Madison and Visions of American Nationality in the Confederation Period: A Regional Perspective," in *Beyond Confedera-*

tion: Origins of the Constitution and American National Identity, ed. Richard Beeman, Stephen Botein, and Edward C. Carter II (Chapel Hill: University of North Carolina Press, 1987), 226–60. For the way in which this project was intended to reestablish the wealth and power of the Chesapeake's planter elite, see Tom Cutterham, *Gentlemen Revolutionaries: Power and Justice in the New American Republic* (Princeton, NJ: Princeton University Press, 2017), chap. 4.

3. Richard Adams to Thomas Adams, June 1, 1778, quoted in Ragsdale, *Planters' Republic*, 254. For social unrest, see McDonnell, *Politics of War*; Hoffman, *Spirit of Dissension*. For court reform, see Roeber, *Faithful Magistrates*, chap. 5. For the decline in planter self-confidence, see Jack P. Greene, "The Intellectual Reconstruction of Virginia in the Age of Jefferson," in *Understanding the American Revolution: Issues and Actors*, ed. Jack. P. Greene (Charlottesville: University of Virginia Press, 1995), 329–58.

4. Statistics for Virginia town legislation from *HS* vols. 9–12. Although few new towns were established in tidewater Maryland, there was a resurgence in town legislation regulating urban public spaces—thirteen towns were the subject of state legislation between 1777 and 1784; see Hanson's *Laws of Maryland 1763–1784*, in *Archives of Maryland Online*, vol. 203 (http://aomol.msa.maryland.gov/000001/000203/html/index.html). As one of the only ports in the mid-Atlantic region to remain open throughout the war, Baltimore flourished; see Gould, "Economic Causes"; Walker, "Baltimore Community"; Steffen, *Mechanics of Baltimore*, chap. 1.

5. George Washington to Robert Morris, February 1, 1785, in *The Papers of George Washington Digital Edition* (Charlottesville: University of Virginia Press, Rotunda, 2008). For Washington's interest in commercial development, see Ragsdale, *Planters' Republic*, 272–74; A. Glenn Crothers, "Banks and Economic Development in Post-Revolutionary Northern Virginia, 1790–1812," *Business History Review* 73 (1999) 1–39. For Washington, DC, see Kenneth R. Bowling, *The Creation of Washington, D.C.: The Idea and Location of The American Capital* (Fairfax, VA: George Mason University Press, 1991); Carl Abbott, *Political Terrain: Washington, D.C. from Tidewater Town to Global Metropolis* (Chapel Hill: University of North Carolina Press, 1999), chap 2; C. M. Harris, "Washington's Gamble, L'Enfant's Dream: Politics, Design, and the Founding of the National Capital," *WMQ*, 3rd ser., 56 (1999): 527–64.

6. *HS* 10:172–76 (quotes, 173).

7. *HS* 10:439–43; 11:45–51, 382–87. For incorporation in postrevolutionary Massachusetts, see Pauline Maier, "The Revolutionary Origins of the American Corporation," *WMQ*, 3rd ser., 50 (1993): 51–84; Pauline Maier, "The Debate over Incorporations: Massachusetts in the Early Republic," in *Massachusetts and the New Nation*, ed. Conrad Edick Wright (Boston: Massachusetts Historical Society, 1992), 73–117. For incorporation elsewhere, see Teaford, *Municipal Revolution*, chaps. 5–6. The city of Charleston was also incorporated in this period; see Hart, "City Government."

8. Petition of the Mayor and Commonalty of Fredericksburg, May 30, 1782, available online through *Legislative Petitions, Virginia Memory Digital Collection*, http://www.virginiamemory.com/collections/petitions.

9. For efforts to reinvigorate corporate governance in Annapolis, see Neil Strawser, "Samuel Chase and the Annapolis Paper War," *MHM* 57 (1962): 177–94. For Annapo-

lis in the 1780s, see Papenfuse, *In Pursuit of Profit*, 153–56; McWilliams, *Annapolis*, 110–12.

10. Thomas W. Griffith, *Annals of Baltimore* (Baltimore: W. Wooddy, 1824), 68, 72–73, 114 (quote); Steffens, *Mechanics of Baltimore*, chap. 6. The Maryland Assembly also incorporated Georgetown in 1789.

11. Edmund Randolph to Thomas Jefferson, May 15, 1784, in *The Papers of Thomas Jefferson Digital Edition*, ed. James P. McClure and J. Jefferson Looney (Charlottesville: University of Virginia Press, Rotunda, 2008–2017). See also James Madison to Jefferson, July 3, 1784, in *The Papers of James Madison Digital Edition*, ed. J. C. A. Stagg (Charlottesville: University of Virginia Press, Rotunda, 2010); "On the Port of Norfolk, May 1784," in *Papers of Thomas Jefferson*; Drew R. McCoy, "The Virginia Port Bill of 1784," *VMHB* 83 (1975): 288–303. For the recovery of Norfolk and the continuity of the corporate government, see Tarter, *Order Book*, 14–20.

12. James Madison to James Monroe, June 21, 1785 ("utility"), in *Papers of James Madison*; Madison to Thomas Jefferson, August 20, 1784 ("trade"); Madison to Jefferson, August 20, 1785, in *Papers of Thomas Jefferson*; for Madison's concern about commercial regulation, see also Madison to Jefferson, May 13, 1783; Madison to Edmund Randolph, May 20, 1783, in *Papers of James Madison*. For previous efforts to explain Madison's thinking in terms of republican or liberal political economy, see McCoy, "Virginia Port Bill"; Norman K. Risjord, *Chesapeake Politics, 1781–1800* (New York: Columbia University Press, 1978), 136–38; Crowley, *Privileges of Independence*, 99–103.

13. James Madison to Thomas Jefferson, August 20, 1784, in *Papers of Thomas Jefferson*; HS 11:402–4; *Journal of the House of Delegates of the Commonwealth of Virginia, May 1784* (Richmond, VA: Thomas W. White, 1828), 60–61; McCoy, "Virginia Port Bill."

14. Petition to the Pennsylvania Assembly, *Freeman's Journal* (Philadelphia), September 10, 1783. Civis "Baltimore Corporation" in *Maryland Gazette* (Baltimore), October 29; debate over a corporation for the city continued in *Maryland Gazette* (Baltimore), November 5, 1784. On the anticharter movement in general, see Maier, "Debate over Incorporations," 81–90.

15. Jefferson to Madison, December 8, 1784, in *Papers of James Madison*; McCoy, "Virginia Port Bill," 291; For Jefferson's plans for the French tobacco trade, see Peterson, "Thomas Jefferson and Commercial Policy," 596–98. For the influence of the physiocrats, see Albertone, *National Identity*; Jeffersonian agrarianism is obviously a heavily contested topic. For the anticommercial agrarian republican tradition, see McCoy, *Elusive Republic*, chap. 3; Robert E. Shalhope, *John Taylor of Carolina: Pastoral Republican* (Columbia: University of South Carolina Press, 1980). For the rejection of these ideas and a focus on liberal capitalism, see Joyce Appleby, "Commercial Farming and the 'Agrarian Myth' in the Early Republic," *Journal of American History* 68 (1982) 833–49; Joyce Appleby, "What Is Still American in the Political Philosophy of Thomas Jefferson?" *WMQ*, 3rd ser., 39 (1982): 287–309; Sarsons, *The Tobacco-Plantation South*, chaps. 1–2. For a nuanced view of agrarianism and commerce in Jeffersonian thinking, see Peter S. Onuf, *Jefferson's Empire: The Language of American Nationhood* (Charlottesville: University of Virginia Press, 2000), 65–73.

16. Robert A. Rutland, ed., *The Papers of George Mason, 1725-1792*, 3 vols. (Chapel Hill: University of North Carolina Press, 1970), 733-37, 859-64, 1014 (quotes, 733, 1014). For Mason's outlook on Virginia's postrevolutionary challenges, see Jeff Broadwater, *George Mason: Forgotten Founder* (Chapel Hill: University of North Carolina Press, 2009) chap. 6; Brent Tarter, "George Mason and the Conservation of Liberty," *VMHB* 99 (1991): 279-304. The only analysis of Mason's opposition to urban constitutional structures is E. Lee Shepard, "Courts in Conflict: Town-County Relations in Post-Revolutionary Virginia," *VMHB* 85 (1977): 184-99; see also a brief discussion in Roeber, *Faithful Magistrates*, 188-89.

17. Rutland, *Papers of George Mason*, 861. For the physiocratic emphasis on the "natural" advantages of planters' estates, see Albertone, *National Identity*, chaps. 2-3.

18. Rutland, *Papers of George Mason*, 1013-16 (quotes, 1013, 1014). Mason's attitude to slavery is hotly contested. He was unequivocally opposed to the slave trade, but he did not emancipate any of his own slaves. He clearly saw slave ownership as a marker of local authority within the new republican society. For the debate and definitive evidence of Mason's support for slavery, see Peter Wallenstein, "Flawed Keepers of the Flame: The Interpreters of George Mason," *VMHB* 102 (1994): 229-60.

19. Rutland, *Papers of George Mason*, 1182-85 (quotes, 1183), 1208-16 (quotes, 1210); Shepard, "Courts in Conflict."

20. Rutland, *Papers of George Mason*, 736-37 (quotes, 736-37), 859-64 (quote, 861), 1014, 1208-11. Ironically, Mason himself often refused to serve in local political offices; see Tarter, "George Mason," 280-85.

21. Rutland, *Papers of George Mason*, 859-64 (quote, 861); for Mason's role in court reform, see Roeber, *Faithful Magistrates*, 176-80.

22. *HS* 12:642-43; Norfolk County Citizens Petition, October 20, 1789, in *Legislative Petitions*; Tarter, *Order Book*, 19-22; Shepard, "Courts in Conflict," 194-99. Other towns sought to defend themselves against assaults on their privileges; see "Fredericksburg Petition, November 16, 1778," "Winchester Petition, October 21, 1791," "Petersburg Petitions, October 24, 1787," in *Legislative Petitions*. For the broader partisan shift in the Virginia Assembly of 1787, which was related to issues of British debts and paper money, see Risjord, *Chesapeake Politics*, 148-56. Steve Sarsons has noted the continuing influence of the planter elite in the early republic despite economic decline; see Sarsons, *The Tobacco-Plantation South in the Early American Atlantic World* (New York: Palgrave, 2013), esp. 11-19; see also an older scholarly tradition emphasizing this continued leadership: Harry Ammon, "The Richmond Junto," *VMHB* 61 (1953) 395-418; Joseph H. Harrison, "Oligarchs and Democrats: The Richmond Junto," *VMHB* 78 (1970): 184-98; Richard R. Beeman, *The Old Dominion and the New Nation: 1788-1801* (Lexington: University of Kentucky Press, 1972); Whitman H. Ridgway, *Community Leadership in Maryland, 1790-1840: A Comparative Analysis of Power in Society* (Chapel Hill: University of North Carolina Press, 1979), chap. 2.

23. *HS* 12:642-43. For city-county separation, see Chester W. Bain, *"A Body Incorporate": The Evolution of City-County Separation in Virginia* (Charlottesville: University of Virginia Press, 1967).

24. For corporations in nineteenth-century Virginia, see Harrison, "Oligarchs and Democrats," 194-98. (Harrison emphasizes that the Junto's control of corporations

was not naked corruption, but rather about the principle of state-level control.) For the conservative faction, see Norman K. Risjord, *The Old Republicans: Southern Conservatism in the Age of Jefferson* (New York: Columbia University Press, 1965); Shalhope, *John Taylor*. For the broader context of Virginia conservatism in the early nineteenth century, see Susan Dunn, *Dominion of Memories: Jefferson, Madison, and the Decline of Virginia* (New York: Basic Books, 2007).

25. David R. Goldfield, *Urban Growth in the Age of Sectionalism: Virginia, 1847–1861* (Baton Rouge: Louisiana State University Press, 1977), 2–3; Sheldon, "Richmond, Virginia," chap. 2. For Baltimore, see Steffens, *Mechanics of Baltimore*, chap. 6. For Washington, DC, see Abbott, *Political Terrain*, 45–52. For the argument that wheat drove urbanization, see Earle and Hoffman, "Staple Crops."

26. For political-economic debate in the antebellum South, see James Oakes, "From Republicanism to Liberalism: Ideological Change and the Crisis of the Old South," *American Quarterly* 37 (1985): 551–71.

27. For Jefferson's focus on the riverine landscape, see Jefferson, *Notes on the State of Virginia*, 152. Scholarship on this issue is outlined in the introduction, n. 4.

28. For the Chesapeake, this interpretation has been advanced by Rainbolt, *From Prescription to Persuasion*. The theory that mercantilism necessarily stunted urban development in plantation societies emerged from dependency theory and was emphasized by Caribbean sociology; see Malcolm Cross, *Urbanization and Urban Growth in the Caribbean* (Cambridge: Cambridge University Press, 1979), chap. 2; Colin G. Clarke, "A Caribbean Creole Capital: Kingston, Jamaica (1692–1938)," in *Colonial Cities: Essays on Urbanism in a Colonial Context*, ed. Robert J. Ross and Gerard J. Telkamp (Dordrecht, Neth.: L Martinus Nijhoff Press, 1985), 153–70; Colin Clarke, "Urbanisation, Planning, and Development in the Caribbean," in *Caribbean Sociology: Introductory Readings*, ed. Christine Barrow and Rhoda Reddock (Kingston, Jamaica: Ian Randle, 2001), 954–72.

29. This interpretation builds upon Braddick, *State Formation*; Benton, *Search for Sovereignty*; Stern, "'Bundles of Hyphens.'"

30. For the inventiveness of local political discourses, see Peter Thompson, "Inventive Localism in the Seventeenth Century," *WMQ*, 3rd ser., 64 (2007): 523–48.

31. For an overview of these divergences and their significance, see Burnard, "Towns in Plantation Societies."

32. The relationship between antebellum planters and urban institutions is contested by historians. See Eugene D. Genovese, *The Political Economy of Slavery: Studies in the Economy and Society of the Slave South*, 2nd ed. (Middletown, CT: Wesleyan University Press, 1989), pt. 3; Douglas R. Egerton, "Markets without a Market Revolution: Southern Planters and Capitalism," *Journal of the Early Republic* 16 (1996): 207–21; Frank Towers, "The Southern Path to Modern Cities: Urbanization in Slave States," in *The Old South's Modern Worlds: Slavery, Region, and Nation in the Age of Progress*, ed. L. Diane Barnes, Brian Schoen, and Frank Towers (Oxford: Oxford University Press, 2011), 145–65; Marc Egnal, "Counterpoint: What If Genovese Is Right? The Premodern Outlook of Southern Planters," in Barnes, Schoen, and Towers, *The Old South's Modern Worlds*, 269–87. For the Virginia elites' resistance to urban institutions in particular, see Dunn, *Dominion of Memories*, chaps. 4–5.

33. Goldfield, *Urban Growth*, chap. 1 (Richmond *Daily Dispatch* quote, 16); Wright, *Prose Works*, 388. For the "direct trade" movement, see Walter Johnson, *River of Dark Dreams: Slavery and Empire in the Cotton Kingdom* (Cambridge, MA: Harvard University Press, 2013), chap. 10 (esp. 289); for the way this was still viewed through the lens of republican and liberal ideologies, see Oakes, "From Republicanism to Liberalism."

INDEX

Page numbers in italics refer to figures.

"Academicus," 247
Accomack County, VA, 159, 201
Act of Union (1707), 223
Adams, Richard, 254
agrarian republicanism, 220, 247; and urban development, 21–22, 247, 254, 259, 262. *See also* rural civic vision
Alexander, Philip, 235–36. *See also* Alexandria
Alexandria, 230, 231, 236; after incorporation, 253, 255, 256, 258, 261–62
Allen, Thomas, 174
Andros, Edmund, 154, 162, 193, 209, 211, 215
Anglican Church (VA), 89, 124, 185, 186, 199, 202; conformity with, 92, 99
Anglo-Dutch wars: First, 104; Second, 127
Anglo-Powhatan wars. *See* Powhatan Empire
Annapolis, MD, 2, 6, 182, 183, 214–15, 231, 257; founding of, 189–90, *191*, 192, 197, 200, 205
Anne, Queen, 197, 213
Anne Arundel County, MD, 92, 170, 189, 200, 238
antipopery, 144, 173–74, 176, 178, 199
Anys, William, 66, 68, 85
archaeological evidence: of structures, 62, 77, 98, 126, 127; of town sites, 5, 36, 49, 106, 110, 131
architecture, 61; elite, 119, 124, 150
Argall, Samuel, 33–38, 52
Argall Town, 35–36, 54
Armitage, David, 112

artisan labor: in Chesapeake, 43, 61, 65, 69; connection of, with towns, 140, 147; encouragement of, 74, 97, 194, 203, 205
Atlantic commercial empire: and colonial Chesapeake, 86, 108–9, 113, 117, 152, 179–80, 182, 216, 266; and economic theory, 87, 92, 153–54, 247, 259; financial crisis of, 245; and postrevolutionary Chesapeake, 253, 256, 260

Bacon, Francis, 49
Bacon, Nathaniel, Jr. *See* Bacon's Rebellion
Bacon's Rebellion, 118, 141, 142–45, 147, 155, 178, 306n71; eyewitness accounts of, 145, 148
Baltimore (city), 6, 220, 231, 233, 239, 240, 246, 248–49, 253; as Chesapeake metropolis, 255, 258; proposed incorporation of, 257, 259
Baltimore, Lord. *See* Calvert, Benedict Leonard (4th Baron Baltimore); Calvert, Cecil (2nd Baron Baltimore); Calvert, Charles (3rd Baron Baltimore); Calvert, George (1st Baron Baltimore)
Barbados, 92, 122, 140, 154
Barbon, Nicholas, 153, 154, 158
Bargrave, John, 51–52, 53
Battle of the Severn, 108
Bennett, Richard, 100, 101, 102–3, 105, 106, 109, 110
Benton, Lauren, 20
Berkeley, borough of, 44–45

333

Berkeley, William, 78, 84, 86, 88–91, 124–27, 139; career of, 100, 102, 103, 110–11, 121, 155; *Discourse and View of Virginia*, 123; and Green Spring Plantation, 110, 128–29; opposition to, 92–93, 96, 97, 98, 99, 105, 140 (*see also* Bacon's Rebellion)
Bermuda City, VA, 29, 30–34, 37–38, 48, 54, 258
Beverley, Robert, 159–61, 164
Beverley, Robert, Jr., 200–201, 202–3; *History and Present State of Virginia*, 201; local civic vision of, 203–4, 207, 215, 217
Bladen, William, 190
Blair, James, 193, 194, 211–14
Blathwayt, William, 151, 194, 209, 211, 212
Blenerhasset, Thomas, *A Direction for the Plantation in Ulster*, 32
Board of Trade, 207, 209–11, 216, 222, 249; influence of, on urban development, 192–93, 205, 211. *See also* Blathwayt, William; Locke, John
Bogle, Robert, 230, 237
boroughs, corporate: English, 42, 43, 46, 114, 117, 119; in Maryland, 49–50, 67, 78–79, 87, 137, 152; in Virginia, 31–32, 36–44, 46, 50–51, 190, 256–57, 258. *See also* urban charters; urban corporate communities
Botero, Giovanni, *A Treatise, Concerning the Causes of the Magnificencie and Greatnes of Cities*, 13, 17, 19, 27, 28
Boulton, Edmund, *The Cities Advocate*, 15, 17
Bradburn, Douglas, 209
Bradford, John, 216
Brady, Robert, 18, 153
Brooke, Robert, 84, 91, 106
Bullock, William, 91, 93; *Virginia Impartially Examined*, 96–97
Burnard, Trevor, 226
Butler, Nathaniel, "The Unmasked Face of our Colony in Virginia," 51, 53
Byrd, William, II, 2, 6, 210, 221, 232, 236–37; rural pastoralism of, 219
Byrd, William, III, 233

Calvert, Benedict Leonard (4th Baron Baltimore), 222
Calvert, Cecil (2nd Baron Baltimore), 5, 57, 67, 73, 91, 105, 106, 109; struggle with puritan communities, 88, 98, 106–8, 111
Calvert, Charles (3rd Baron Baltimore), 116, 117, 129–30, 160, 178, 242; opposition to, 136–39, 144, 150, 176–77; report of, to Crown, 146, 154; and St. Mary's City, 130–32; urban plans of, 132–36, 166–78
Calvert, George (1st Baron Baltimore), 53, 56, 78
Calvert, Leonard, 79–83, 105
Calvert, Philip, 130–32, 134, 136–38
Calvert County, MD, 106, 171, 179. *See also* Charles County, MD
capitalism, 3, 7, 265, 267
Caribbean trade, 128, 155, 202
Carolina, colony of, 4, 120, 140, 141
Carroll, Charles, 233, 237, 248
Carrollsburg, MD, 233, 238
Carson, Cary, 128
Carter, Landon, 226
Carter, Robert "King," 216, 222, 223
Carvile, Robert, 144
Catholicism: and colonization, 73, 78; as source of conflict in Maryland, 81, 82, 129, 137–38, 144, 173–74; in St. Mary's City, 131, 137. *See also* antipopery
Cecil County, MD, 241
Cecilton, MD, 132, 135
ceremonies: of empire, 162, 192, 197; of planter hierarchy, 208; royalist, 17, 124
Charles I, 56, 57, 59, 86, 118; and royal absolutism in Virginia, 62–67, 77–78
Charles II, 116, 118–21, 150–54, 161, 175. *See also* Howard, Francis (5th Baron Howard of Effingham)
Charles County, MD, 91, 92, 106, 173–74, 177. *See also* Calvert County, MD
Charleston, 7, 215, 251
Charlestown, MD, 241–42, 244
charters. *See* proprietary charters; urban charters
Chase, Samuel, 257
Chicheley, Henry, 160
Chilton, Edward, 193, 211, 212
cities. *See* urban spaces
civic humanism: shared assumptions of, 24, 28, 94, 267; and urban spaces, 13, 23, 30, 54, 258, 266
civic virtue. *See* rural civic vision; urban civic virtue
civility, and urban spaces, 99, 100, 104, 112, 123, 202
Claiborne, William: as Commonwealth commissioner, 100, 101, 102–3, 105–7; and Kent Island, MD, 61–62, 69, 72–73, 79, 80, 81, 83–84

Clarke, Richard, 200, 207
College of William and Mary, 193, 194, 212
commerce, regulation of: through urban hubs, 33, 58, 85 (see also Jamestown; port towns; St. Mary's City, MD); under planter control, 223–24, 226–28, 240. See also urban corporate communities
Committee for Trade and Plantations, 151, 154
common good, 39, 44, 266; against private interests, 3, 8, 180, 220, 246, 251, 261; of Realm, 86, 120, 140; security of, in rurality, 111, 228, 229, 235, 261; security of, in urbanity, 13, 16, 23, 85, 94, 140, 256
common land, 39, 141, 144, 190, 240, 241. See also under Virginia Company of London
common law, in Virginia, 42, 110, 249
Commonwealth of England: and Chesapeake urban plans, 86–88, 93–96; commercial empire of, 93, 99, 101, 113–15, 188, 192, 210. See also Council of Trade; Worsley, Benjamin
Company of Royal Adventurers Trading to Africa, 128, 134. See also Royal African Company
Complaint from Heaven with a Huy and crye and a petition out of Virginia and Maryland, A, 144, 167
consignment system, 128, 156, 237
consumerism, 153; and polite culture, 212, 215, 218
Cook, Ebenezer: *The Sotweed Factor*, 2; *Sotweed Redivivus, Or the Planters Looking-Glass*, 224–25
Coombs, John, 9–10, 110
Cornwaleys, Thomas, 80
corporate towns. See urban corporate communities
corruption, sources of, 33, 42, 220, 221, 235, 245, 246. See also "country" ideology; rural civic vision
Cotton, Ann, 145
Council of Trade, 100, 101–2, 113 (see also Worsley, Benjamin); commissioners of, 102–3, 105–6, 107, 108–9
Councils for Trade and Foreign Plantations, 118, 121, 122, 151
"country" ideology: British, 219–21, 245, 252; Chesapeake, 320n2 (see also rural civic vision)

county courts. See Virginia county courts; and also under Maryland county system
county system. See Maryland county system; Virginia county system
crops, alternative, 184, 230–31, 247. See also wheat
Culpeper, Thomas, 148, 151, 153, 155–56, 161, 167
Currency Act (1764), 246
customs: collection, of, 17, 152, 186; duties, 60, 68, 118, 134, 138, 164, 223; officers, 152, 161, 164, 174, 188

Daily Dispatch (Richmond), 269
Dalton, James, 12, 16–17
Darnall, Henry, *A Just and Impartial Account of the Transactions of the Merchants in London*, 224, 227
debt: ethics of, 223, 224, 226, 245, 246, 249; relief for, 190, 263
De Vries, David, 90
Dinwiddie, Robert, 243
District of Columbia, 233, 255, 265
Donne, George, "Virginia Reviewed," 76
Dorchester County, MD, 205, 207, 217
Drummond, William, 141–42, 145
Dublin. See Ireland
Dulany, Daniel, 238
Dunmore, 4th Earl of, 250
Dutton, Richard, 154

Eastern Shore, MD, 10, 145, 188, 198, 230
economic diversification: promotion of, 43, 60–61, 64–65, 69, 72, 125, 265, 290n26; in puritan communities, 97, 99–100; pursuit of, by planters, 123, 224–26, 248; and urban spaces, 76, 134, 230–31. See also tobacco agriculture
Effingham, Lord. See Howard, Francis (5th Baron Howard of Effingham)
English Civil Wars, 17–18, 81, 85, 86, 91
Evelyn, John, 124
Exclusion Crisis, 152–53

Fairfax County, VA, 235–36, 260, 261–62
farmers, 71, 182, 185, 193, 195, 259, 262. See also planters, ordinary; yeomanry
Fauquier County, VA, 248
Ferrar, John, 61, 72, 93, 98
Ferrar, Nicholas, 37–38
Fleet, Henry, 69
France, 182, 184, 185, 259

Frederick County, VA, 222, 235
Fredericksburg, 6, 230, 234, 236, 237, 239, 248; as corporate borough, 253, 256, 257, 258, 262
free trade, 4, 46, 101, 114; debate over, 253, 257, 259, 260, 261; fear of, 42, 95–96
frontiers, 141, 155, 166, 173, 176, 185, 235
fur trade, 61, 79, 80, 85, 289n18

garrison towns. *See* Virginia Company of London
Gates, Thomas, 29, 52
gentry. *See* Maryland planters; Virginia planters
Glorious Revolution, 176, 180, 181, 182, 184
Gooch, William, 227–28, 235, 236, 243
Gray, Robert, *A Good Speed to Virginia*, 28–29, 43–44
"greate Charter," 37, 51. *See also* Sandys, Edwin; Yeardley, George
Green, Roger, *Virginia's Cure*, 123–24

Hale, Matthew, 120
Hamilton, Dr. Alexander, *History of the Ancient and Honorable Tuesday Club*, 215
Hammond, John, 107; *Leah and Rachel*, 111–12
Hamor, Ralph, 30, 31
Hanover County, VA, 240
Harrington, James, *The Commonwealth of Oceana*, 112
Harrison, Benjamin, III, presumed author of *An Essay upon the Government of the English Plantations on the Continent of America*, 210
Hartlib, Samuel, 87, 92, 95–96, 103, 118, 140
Hartwell, Henry, 193, 211, 212
Harvey, John, 2, 67–78, 83, 85, 99; ideas of, adapted, 88, 89–90, 114, 122
Harwood, William, 49
headright system, 5, 193, 195
Henricus. *See* Bermuda City, VA
Herrman, Augustine, 130, 132, 135, 146
Hobbes, Thomas, 117
House of Burgesses. *See* Virginia General Assembly
Howard, Francis (5th Baron Howard of Effingham), 161–65, 166, 175, 183, 186
hundreds, 79, 83, 97. *See also* Maryland county system
Hustings Court, 249
Hyde, Samuel, 224

incorporation, urban. *See* urban charters
indentured servitude, 3, 5, 25, 54, 72, 88, 127–28. *See also* servants
industry, 111–12, 153, 167; and urban spaces, 87, 94, 99, 100, 101, 102, 108
Ingle, Richard, 92; and Ingle's rebellion, 81–82, 84, 88, 91, 98
Interregnum. *See* Commonwealth of England
Ireland: Dublin, 120–21; lessons of, 18–19, 24, 28; Ulster, 32, 35, 53
Iroquois, 166
Isle of Wight County, VA, 143

James I, 17, 25, 49–50, 53, 56, 59, 65
James II, 18, 154, 165, 176; as duke of York, 152
James City County, VA, 75, 143
James River, 5, 23, 195, 233; as geographic divider, 10, 30, 97, 230, 236
Jamestown, 57–58, 127–28, 142–43, 162, 201, 241; as archetype for urban failure, 5; declining fortunes of, 110, 145, 151, 155, 194; as focus of conflict, 75–77, 129, 140–46; New Towne section of, 62, 69, 72; under Berkeley, 88–89, 103, 121–22, 124–28; under Harvey, 68–70, 72; under Virginia Company of London, 24, 27–28
James-York peninsula, 30, 71, 194, 197
Jefferson, Thomas, 251, 254, 264; *Notes on the State of Virginia*, 2, 6, 251, 259
Jenings, Edmund, 215
Johnson, Robert, *Nova Britannia*, 23, 24, 28, 54
Jones, Hugh, *The Present State of Virginia*, 225
Joseph, William, 175–76

Kemp, Richard, 75–76, 77, 91
Kent County, MD, 236
Kent Island, MD, 82–83, 105; conflict over, 61–62, 69, 72–73, 80, 81, 83–84
King and Queen County, VA, 208
King George's County, VA, 230
Kingston, Jamaica, 6, 7, 215, 251
King William County, VA, 237
King William's School (Annapolis), 190

labor, 110, 127–28, 222. *See also* artisan labor; servants; slave labor, African; slave labor, indigenous

land grants, 5, 38, 184, 193, 195, 211, 213, 222. *See also* common land; manors
land speculation. *See under* speculation
Langford, John, *Refutation of Babylon's Fall*, 107
Langston, Anthony, 139–40
Lawrence, Richard, 141–43, 145–46
Lawrence, Thomas, 188, 192, 193
Lee, Richard Henry, 250
Leighton, Ellis, 121
Levy, Barry, 94
Lewis, Richard, *Carmen Seculare*, 225
lobbying. *See* merchant-planter alliance
Locke, John, 193–94, 211–12
London, 95, 119–20, 152–53, 154; as model for Chesapeake, 79, 124, 125, 126, 131
Lower Norfolk County, VA, 159, 186
Ludwell, Thomas, 126–27, 129

Madison, James, 257–59, 263
Magazine (joint-stock company), 33, 35, 36, 42, 50, 60
Makemie, Francis, 1–2, 4, 205, 215–16; *A Plain and Friendly Perswasive to the Inhabitants of Virginia and Maryland for Promoting Towns and Cohabitation*, 201–3
manors, 7, 34, 73, 78–80, 82, 83, 84. *See also* Maryland county system
manufacturing, colonial, 69, 99, 102, 114, 139, 141, 302n27
maps, and urban spaces, 106, 135–36
marketplace courts, 42, 239–40
markets and fairs, 203, 212, 236, 239
Martin, John, 34, 52
Mary II and William III, 176, 180
Maryland, governors of. *See individual listings*
Maryland Assembly, 79, 136–37, 138, 171, 189, 205, 249; Protestant composition of, 146, 166, 170, 177, 178, 188, 207, 208; and town sites, 237–38
Maryland county system, 109, 189; county courts in, 137–38, 190; and proprietary authority, 79, 83–84, 86, 91, 106, 132; struggles over, 108, 170, 205, 207
Maryland Gazette, 224
Maryland planters: response of, to Charles Calvert's urban plans, 166–78; response of, to Nicholson's urban plans, 198–201; response of, to port town plan, 137–39
Mason, George, 260–63, 264

Mayflower, 46
Menefie, George, 62, 72
mercantilism, 69, 102, 113, 116, 147, 179 (*see also* Navigation Act [1651]; Navigation Act [1660]); interpretations of, 4, 20–21, 265–66. *See also* neomercantilism
merchant-planter alliance, 188, 208–10, 215–16, 221; fraying of, 219, 222, 223, 224; and planter class divisions, 199, 201, 205, 207–8 (*see* planters, ordinary)
merchants, metropolitan, 100, 123, 158–59, 162, 174; influence of, on imperial policies, 180, 181–82, 184, 227; influence of, on urban development, 153, 161, 208–9
Meriwether, William, 240–41
Middle Plantation, 110, 194. *See also* Williamsburg
Middlesex County, VA, 159–60, 179, 186, 200, 203, 208, 217
Miller, Henry, 131
Milner, George, 140, 141
monopoly: as commercial regulation, 50, 60, 63, 68, 119; controversies around, 33, 42, 50; slave trade, 120, 128, 210. *See also* Magazine (joint-stock company)
Morecroft, John, 136
Moryson, Francis, 140

Nansemond County, 235, 238
native peoples, 39, 79, 144–45, 222; enslavement of, 128, 147; French alliances with, 166, 173, 176, 178; and towns, 26, 35. *See also* Iroquois; Powhatan Empire; Susquehannocks
Navigation Act (1651), 87, 101–2, 113–14, 122, 267; lax enforcement of, 105, 110
Navigation Act (1660), 118, 124, 134, 184
neomercantilism, 253, 258
Netherlands: economic success of, 92, 95, 96; trade with, 89–93, 122, 126, 130, 296n18. *See also* Anglo-Dutch wars
Newcastle, Marquess of, 119, 121
New England, 134; town model of, 16, 94, 96, 97–98, 108, 144
New Netherland, 130, 134
New Towne. *See* Jamestown
New York City, 154, 162
Nicholson, Francis, 181, 182–85, 202, 218, 312n14; opposition to, 183, 188, 198–202, 207–9, 211–14, 217; urban plans of, for Maryland, 188–93, 205; urban plans of, for Virginia, 182, 186–87, 194–97

Nine Years' War, 184, 185
Noell, Martin, 122, 123, 124, 126
nonimportation associations, 247–48, 250
Norfolk, VA, 6, 7, 186, 220, 231, 232, 233, 263; as corporate borough, 241, 242–44, 256; destruction of, 249–50, 252; Madison's plan for, 257–58
Norfolk County, VA, 242
Northampton County, VA, 110
North East River, 241
Northern Neck peninsula, 98, 110
Notes on the State of Virginia (Jefferson), 2, 6, 251, 259
Nott, Edward, 202, 215–16

oaths, of allegiance, 91, 92, 105, 106
Ogilby, John, *America*, 135–36, 137
Opechancanough, 48

Pagan, John, 110
pastoralism, 219, 220, 225. See also rural civic vision
patriarchy, 21, 183, 212, 213, 218
patronage: critique of, 100, 107; gubernatorial, 88, 91, 93, 113, 208, 213; proprietary, 53, 98, 131, 132, 199; royal, 17, 63, 85, 117
Patuxent. See Providence and Patuxent
Patuxent River, 84, 106, 107, 166, 216, 293n85
Peace of Paris (1783), 254
Peace of Utrecht (1713), 221
Pearce, Gideon, 236
Perry, Micajah, 126, 210, 223
Petersburg, VA, 220, 230, 231, 251, 253, 262
petitions, 19, 28, 116, 173, 199, 210, 261–62; and planter authority, 173, 179, 234–39, 241, 242, 256–57, 258
Pettigrew, William, 210
Petty, William, *Political Arithmetick*, 153–54, 158
Philadelphia, 6, 190, 242, 254, 255, 259
physiocrats, 259, 260, 261, 262, 264
piepowder, court of, 42, 239–40
Piersey, Abraham, 62, 63–64
Plantation Duty Act (1673), 152, 155, 166
plantations, as private commonwealths, 61, 128–29, 225–26
plantation system, 7, 8; postrevolutionary, 254, 262; refinement of, 91, 109, 128, 129, 180, 184, 198 (see also indentured servitude; slave labor, African; slave labor, indigenous); and urban development debates, 11, 21, 54, 165–66, 198,

251, 265–69 (see also Maryland planters; Virginia planters)
Plant-Cutter Riots, 160–61, 308n28
planters, elite. See Maryland planters; Virginia planters
planters, ordinary, 184, 254, 312n5; appeal to, in Maryland, 160, 165–66, 167–68, 170–71; appeal to, in Virginia, 190, 195, 197, 214; elite guardianship over, 225–28. See also Bacon's Rebellion; farmers
Plattes, Gabriel, 95
Pocomoke River, 171
Pope, Nathaniel, 82
Port Royal (Jamaica), 120
Port Royal, VA, 120, 230, 237, 239
port towns: as distinguished from market town, 186, 208, 317n66; importance of, to commercial empire, 120, 121, 122, 152, 154; opposition to, in Maryland, 137–39, 174, 178; opposition to, in Virginia, 211, 258–60; proposed for Maryland, 132–36, 175, 188, 189; proposed for Virginia, 156, 163–65, 231, 257–58
Potomac River, 230, 235, 238, 254, 255
Powell, Thomas, 64
Powhatan Empire, 27, 52; First Anglo-Powhatan War, 30, 33; Second Anglo-Powhatan War, 40, 47, 48, 59, 71; Third Anglo-Powhatan War, 89, 98, 105, 110
Prince George's County, MD, 222
Princess Anne County, VA, 255
Privy Council, 63–66, 67–68, 77
proprietary charters, 53; for colonial Maryland, 73, 78, 79, 83, 106, 137, 178; for Frederick, MD, 234. See also St. Mary's City, MD
Protectorate, Cromwellian, 106, 109, 112, 115, 117
Protestant Association, 176–77, 313n24
Protestantism: and Catholic conflicts (see under Catholicism); and commercial empire, 93, 99, 188, 192, 210. See also Anglican Church (VA); puritans
Providence and Patuxent, 99, 101, 105–8, 111, 129, 130, 144
provincial council. See Virginia General Assembly
puritans: Atlantic network of, 88, 97, 98, 100, 104, 108, 110; communities of, in Maryland, 84, 98–99, 101, 105–8, 111 (see also Providence and Patuxent); communities of, in Virginia, 84, 88, 97, 98, 99, 100;

urban corporate model of, 16, 45–46, 94, 96, 99

race: distinctions of, 11, 141–42, 149, 181, 203; ideologies of, 3, 12
Raleigh, Walter, 19, 25
Randolph, Edward, 184, 188, 201, 208
Randolph, Peyton, 248
Rappahannock County, VA, 144
Rappahannock River, 98, 209, 230, 235
religion: and colonization, 45–46, 73, 78; fostered in towns, 123–24, 202 (see also puritans). See also Anglican Church (VA); Catholicism; Protestantism
Restoration, Stuart. See Charles II
Richmond, VA, 230, 233, 236–37; postrevolutionary, 253, 256, 263, 264
rivers, and town development, 6, 71, 122, 124, 146, 151, 230
Rolfe, John, 32, 33, 37
Rousby, Christopher, 166, 174–75
Royal African Company, 155, 210. See also Company of Royal Adventurers Trading to Africa
rural civic vision, 78, 88; articulation of, 21, 111–12, 129, 248, 251; characteristics of, 166, 216, 224–28, 235, 246, 325n30; and "country" ideology, 220–21. See also Mason, George
rurality, Chesapeake, 1–3, 5–6, 8, 111–12, 146, 251, 259

Sandys, Edwin, 99, 121, 190, 217, 251, 258; urban vision of, for Virginia, 36–38, 42–44, 46–52, 54
scientific agriculture, 220, 227
Scott, William, *An Essay of Drapery*, 15
Scottish merchants, trade with, 201, 223, 242, 245–46; in towns, 230, 237, 250
servants: African, 61; control over, 43, 47–48, 90, 110, 242; migration of, under Virginia Company of London, 9, 32, 35, 39; in uprisings, 141–42, 200, 214. See also indentured servitude
Severn River, 84, 99, 106, 107, 189
Seymour, John, 192, 200, 202, 205, 214, 215, 217
Sharpe, Kevin, 63
Sherwood, William, *Virginia's Deplored Condition*, 148, 150
shires. See individual counties
slave codes, 181, 210, 217

slave labor, African: and headright system, 193–94; increase in, 91, 110, 148, 155, 210, 211, 221–22; role of, in plantation system, 91, 128, 134, 138, 218, 246, 261. See also slave trade
slave labor, indigenous, 128, 147
slave trade, 220. See also Company of Royal Adventurers Trading to Africa; Royal African Company
Slye, Gerard, 199–200, 207
Smith, John, 19, 27–28
Smith, Thomas, *De Republica Anglorum*, 15, 36, 51
smuggling, 184, 188
Somerset County, MD, 170, 171, 177
South Sea Bubble, 222
Spanish colonization, 13–14, 26, 62
speculation: in improvements, 159; in land, 184, 185, 205, 207, 232–33, 236
Spencer, Nicholas, 156
Spenser, Edmund, *View of the Present State of Ireland*, 18
Spotswood, Alexander, 214, 221, 222, 227
Spotsylvania County, VA, 234
Stafford County, VA, 143
Stamp Act, 248, 249, 250
St. Mary's City, MD, 5, 57–58, 79–80, 91, 131, 146, 189; as Catholic center, 131, 137; conflicts over, 81–83, 106–8, 136–38, 144, 199; revitalization of, 130–32
St. Mary's County, MD, 136, 199
Stone, William, 105–8, 111
store system, 229–30, 237, 245
Strong, Leonard, *Babylon's Fall*, 107
subregions, Chesapeake, 10, 11, 159, 210, 230–32
Surry County, VA, 143, 237
Susquehannocks, 61, 83

Talbot County, MD, 134, 177, 189, 199
taverns, 5–6, 229, 232; as alternative culture, 141–42
tenancy: in Maryland, 79; in Virginia, 24, 35, 44, 47–48
Thompson, Peter, 145
tobacco agriculture, 80, 148, 155, 229; and absence of towns, 7, 252, 265; expanding production of, 90, 128, 182, 184, 210; improvements in, 33, 90; limiting production of, 134, 222; planter anxieties about, 60–61, 224–25, 246–47; quality control over, 227–28; regional differences in, 34,

tobacco agriculture (continued) 166, 198; weakness of, in commercial commonwealth, 9, 64–65, 92–93, 99, 113. See also economic diversification

tobacco inspection system: in Maryland, 228–29, 322n25; and urbanization, 227–31

tobacco lobby. See merchant-planter alliance

town building: layouts for, 29–30, 125, 131, *191*, *192*, 194–95, *196*, 240; preference for brick in, 5, 125, 141; process of, 159, 165; site selection for, 159–60, 168, 170–74, 208, 234–39, 313n24. See also towns, establishment of

towns, establishment of: in eighteenth century, 220, 230–39, *234*; by Maryland Assembly (1683–88), *169*; by Maryland Assembly (1706–8), 206; postrevolutionary, 253, 255; by proprietary proclamation (1668–71), *133*; by Virginia Act for Cohabitation and Encouragement of Trade and Manufacture (1680), 156, *157*, 158–65; by Virginia General Assembly (1691), *187*; by Virginia General Assembly (1706), 204. See also port towns; towns, Maryland; towns, Virginia

towns, Maryland: Arundelton, 189; Bladensburg, 237; Calverton, 171, *172*, *173*; Cambridge, 217; Chestertown, 231, 232, 240; Frederick, 220, 238; Londontown, 217; Mount Calvert, 217; Oxford, 177, 189, 231; Queen Anne Town, 239; Salisbury, 236; Upper Marlborough, 220, 237; Vienna, 217; York, 177. See also Baltimore (city); Charlestown, MD; Providence and Patuxent; St. Mary's City, MD; Williamstadt, MD

towns, small, 198, 201–2, 254, 255

towns, Virginia: Argall Town, 35–36, 54; Dumfries, 220, 230, 237, 248; Falmouth, 230, 232, 234, 248; Georgetown, 251; Hampton, 217; Kempsville, 255; Kinsale, 255; Leeds, 230; Newcastle, 240; Onancock, 201; Port Royal, 230, 237, 239, 248; Suffolk, 230, 232, 238, 239; Tappahannock, 217, 239, 240, 258; Urbanna, 217, 231; West Point, 208; Winchester, 220, 232, 253, 256, 262. See also Alexandria; Bermuda City, VA; Fredericksburg; Jamestown; Norfolk, VA; Petersburg, VA; Richmond, VA; Yorktown, VA

Townshend duties, 247–48, 249
Turner, Henry, 26

Ulster. See Ireland
urban charters: in Chesapeake, 131–32, 242–43, 249, 253, 256–57; English, 14–18, 67, 117, 119, 152–53

urban civic virtue, 15, 23, 44, 99, 140, 224; and common good, 46, 266–67; as polite sociability, 181, 183, 198, 207, 212–13, 215, 218. See also civic humanism; rural civic vision

urban corporate communities: commerce in, mediated, 57–58, 124, 129, 182–83; Commonwealth goals for, 87–88, 103–4, 109 (see also puritans); English background of, 15–17; independence curtailed, 117, 119, 137; local control over, 201–2, 205; as nodes of commerce, 139–40, 149, 152, 216, 238–40, 258; postrevolutionary, 256–57, 258, 260–61. See also boroughs, corporate; Charlestown, MD; Norfolk, VA

urban improvement, 149, 179–80; and planter authority, 158–59; and proprietary authority, 167–68, 176, 178

urban infrastructure: assembly control over, 238–39; lack of, 176, 209, 216, 235, 240; responsibility for, 39, 44, 122, 165, 185, 186, 242

urban spaces: opportunity in, 101, 140, 147, 154, 190; populations in, 97, 139, 203, 230, 242, 246, 319n85; purpose of, 1–2, 12–14, 46, 70, 94–95, 153–54, 212–13 (see also civility, and urban spaces; industry); and rurality, 108, 250–51, 263; terminology of, 20, 149, 316n60. See also urban corporate communities

Usher, Robin, 120
utopias, urban, 95

vestries, parish, 89, 199
Virginia, governors of. See individual listings
Virginia and Maryland; or, The Lord Baltimore's printed case, uncased and answered, 107
Virginia Company of London: commercial monopoly in, 27, 31, 33, 34, 35, 42, 50; common land in, 24, 29, 32, 35, 38–39, 41, 47; factors in decline of, 47–50; mili-

tary plan for, 28–30, 32, 48–49, 54; organization of, 26, 28, 56; private patronage in, 33–38, 52, 54; urban corporate plan for, 31–32, 36–44, 46, 50–51 (*see also* Sandys, Edwin)

Virginia county courts, 59, 85, 126, 325n56; challenges to, 104, 129; commercial regulation by, 128, 240, 246, 298n44; impartiality of, 261–62; strengthening of, 74, 89, 109–10

Virginia county system, 123–24, 128, 155, 159, 203; establishment of, 74–75, 78, 292n57; opposition to, 92, 97–98, 148; and planter authority, 58, 78, 262–63 (*see also* rural civic vision); and prerevolutionary resistance, 247, 248; strengthening of, 86, 88–91. See also Virginia county courts

Virginia Gazette, 233, 240, 246, 247

Virginia General Assembly: first, 37, 41, 42; House of Burgesses, 142, 161, 212, 234, 243; provincial council of, 164, 207–9, 213–14, 215–17, 234–35; and urban development plans, 62, 162–64, 203, 205, 242–43

Virginia planters, 59–62, 156, 158; after American Revolution, 253–54, 263, 268 (*see also* Mason, George); and eighteenth-century urban growth, 232–33, 236–37, 238; growing divisions among, 110, 142, 156, 161, 183, 254 (*see also* merchant-planter alliance); and prerevolutionary financial crisis, 245–48; response of, to Commonwealth urban plans, 104, 112–14; response of, to Harvey's urban plans, 72–74, 77, 78; response of, to Jamestown redevelopment plans, 124–28; response of, to Nicholson's urban plans, 207–10, 216, 217; response of, to Sandys's corporate boroughs, 51–52. See also rural civic vision; Virginia county system

Walpole, Robert, 220
warehouses, and urbanization, 125, 126, 148, 168, 220, 229–30, 236–37
Warwick, Earl of, 34, 51, 52
Washington, George, 255, 264
Westmoreland County, VA, 255
Wharton, Thomas, 160, 161
wheat, 10, 230, 246, 247, 248, 265, 323n34
Whig party, 182
William III and Mary II, 176, 180
Williamsburg, 6, 231, 233, 240, 248, 249; polite society in, 183, 212, 215, 218, 225; tensions over, 200, 211, 213–14; under Nicholson, 182, 194–97
Williamstadt, MD, 182, 189, 190, 192, 197, 199
Winthrop, John, Jr., 96
Withington, Phil, 15, 32, 41
Wolstenholme Towne, 45
women, 44, 207
workhouses, 94, 261
Wormeley, Ralph, 159–60, 161, 207, 208, 209, 211
Worsley, Benjamin, 87, 92, 96–102, 104–5, 107–8, 111–14

Yarranton, Andrew, *England's Improvement by Sea and Land*, 158
Yeardley, George, 32, 48, 59; and "greate Charter," 36–38, 41–43, 52, 66, 91. See also Sandys, Edwin
yeomanry, 145, 254, 259, 260
Yong, Thomas, 70
York River, 195
Yorktown, VA, 217, 231, 240, 253, 258